CRIMES
AGAINST
LIBERTY

CRIMES AGAINST LIBERTY

AN INDICTMENT OF PRESIDENT BARACK OBAMA

BY DAVID LIMBAUGH

Since 1947
REGNERY
PUBLISHING, INC.
An Eagle Publishing Company

First paperback edition © 2011

ISBN: 978-1-59698-275-8

The Library of Congress has cataloged the hardcover edition as follows:
    Limbaugh, David.
    Crimes against liberty : an indictment of President Barack Obama / by David Limbaugh.
        p. cm.
    Includes bibliographical references and index.
    ISBN 978-1-59698-624-4 (alk. paper)
    1. Obama, Barack. 2. Political crimes and offenses—United States. 3. United States—Politics and government—2009- I. Title.
    E908.L56 2010
    973.932092—dc22

                                                        2010030283

Published in the United States by
Regnery Publishing, Inc.
One Massachusetts Avenue, NW
Washington, DC 20001
www.regnery.com

Manufactured in the United States of America

10 9 8 7 6 5 4 3 2

Books are available in quantity for promotional or premium use. Write to Director of Special Sales, Regnery Publishing, Inc., One Massachusetts Avenue NW, Washington, DC 20001, for information on discounts and terms or call (202) 216-0600.

Distributed to the trade by:
Perseus Distribution
387 Park Avenue South
New York, NY 10016

To Rush and Kathryn

TABLE OF CONTENTS

SINCE WE LAST SPOKE...

I n the introduction to the hardcover edition of this book, I noted that Barack Obama's presidency has been the most destructive in American history. In the year that has transpired since the book went to print, his destructive patterns have accelerated to the point that our nation is headed toward national bankruptcy. If we don't immediately take steps to reverse course, we will face a national financial catastrophe that could far exceed the Great Depression.

Obama is a virtuoso at avoiding responsibility for his actions, incessantly scapegoating his predecessor George W. Bush for all the nation's problems, even two and a half years into his presidency. If America's comedic community were not in the tank for Obama and his discredited leftist agenda, his blame-Bush mantra would have long since become a regular punch line. Though senior Obama advisor David Plouffe did confess, in an unscripted moment, that

Obama now owns this economy, Obama himself obviously disagrees. For him to publicly concede that his policies have failed would require him to consider changing course—and if there's anything we've learned about the man, a willingness to change course is not in his DNA.

This penchant for blaming Bush wrongly assumes that Bush bequeathed to Obama a predicament so dire that no policies could alleviate it. This grossly understates the culpability of the Democrats in general and of Obama personally in advancing the lion's share of the policies that led to the financial meltdown of 2008. We don't need to revisit, in detail, those policies now; suffice it to say, that all but the most fervent ideologues now recognize that the leftist feel-good quest for "affordable housing" was the primary contributor to the subprime mortgage epidemic. While some GOP members went along in the early stages of this ill-begotten venture, President Bush and other Republicans began to recognize the dangers and tried to rein in Fannie Mae, Freddie Mac, and the other culprits. Meanwhile, Democrats, led by the likes of Barney Frank, stubbornly resisted reform and even denied there was a looming problem. Barack Obama sang in that choir.

Despite the obvious causal relationship between their policies and the financial crash, Democrats never owned up to their dominant role in it; as a foreshadowing of the Obama presidency, they simply blamed it on the usual targets: "fat cat" Wall Street firms and other special interests colluding with Republicans. Obama's habit of blaming the entire crisis on Bush is particularly disingenuous considering the quasi-leadership role then-Senator Obama played in engineering the TARP bailout. Obama's fingerprints were all over TARP, and he lobbied Bush during Bush's final weeks as president to release $350 billion in additional TARP funds. As *ABC News* reported, "Obama and Bush have teamed up to get the money released."[1] These efforts reveal as a farcical fraud Obama's later attempt to wash his hands of the entire era preceding his presidency.

Recall that during much of Bush's second term as president, the unemployment rate was below 5 percent. Following the housing meltdown, it climbed to 7.8 percent by the time he left office in January 2009, which seemed bad at the time—until Obama took charge. Notwithstanding the Obama administration's vows that its near-trillion dollar "stimulus" would keep unemployment under 8 percent, joblessness under Obama skyrocketed above 9 percent and, for a time, even surpassed 10 percent, a near-thirty-year high.

So when Obama glibly and endlessly reminds us that he didn't "create this mess," informed Americans know better—as to the housing crisis, the debt crisis, unemployment, and the overall disastrous state of the economy. Obama and his Democrats maligned the Bush economy for eight years, yet that period saw fifty-two straight months of job growth and the fulfillment of Bush's commitment to halve the deficit in five years. Indeed, as late in Bush's term as 2007, the deficit was just $161 billion, less than 10 percent of Obama's FY 2010 deficit of some $1.65 trillion.

Today, more than halfway into Obama's term, the economy continues on its miserable path while the president masquerades as though he were a mere bystander. Research consistently shows that extending unemployment benefits exacerbates and prolongs unemployment, yet he will not budge from his insistence on that damaging policy. He perversely continues to grow the public sector, sucking all the oxygen out of the private sector and preventing its rebound.

Just before this paperback went to print, Obama held a press conference on the economy. Instead of acknowledging his instrumental role in this ongoing nightmare, he lashed out at Republicans and at Congress for not coming together to agree on a budget. He intoned that while he had been in Washington working hard on bin Laden, Afghanistan, and other issues, Republicans weren't doing their job.

It's as if Obama inhabits his own world, unaware that the public knows it is *he* who has been gallivanting about, playing golf, attending fund-raisers, and lavishly entertaining at the White House instead of exercising leadership on our economic problems. The Republican-controlled Congress did pass a budget, no thanks to Democrats, and it incorporates the Ryan Plan, which seriously and credibly deals with our short-term and long-term budget issues. It's Obama's Democrat-controlled Senate that has failed to pass a budget for 800 days—and Obama has done nothing to cajole them into doing so.

What Obama has offered on budget reform has been nothing but generalities, smoke and mirrors, and deceptive numbers. Under pressure in 2009 to do something—anything—besides engage in more and more spending, Obama assembled the Bipartisan Budget Commission to study the budget crisis and make recommendations. Despite stacking the group with liberals and moderate Republicans, he still ignored its suggestions and once again kicked the can down the road.

After his party was trounced in the November 2010 elections, which were mostly a referendum on his first two years in office, Obama stalled some more. It wasn't until Paul Ryan was about to formally unveil his Path to Prosperity that Obama finally presented a long-term budget. A purely political scheme designed to preempt the Ryan plan and discredit its author, Obama's program offered no real specifics beyond raising taxes on the "wealthy" and bolstering his plans for rationing healthcare by strengthening a 15-member planning board created by the ObamaCare legislation.

Obama is, of course, acutely aware that this nation faces almost $90 trillion in unfunded entitlements, mainly consisting of Medicare and Social Security liabilities. With more and more Baby Boomers reaching retirement age, these liabilities are growing at an alarming rate—by some $10 trillion last year alone. These programs, as presently constituted, are inarguably unsustainable.

The Ryan Plan directly addresses these problems by proposing a restructuring of Medicare and Medicaid and calling for a trigger to initiate Social Security reform in the near future. Hardly the "draconian" plan the Democrats claim, it leaves untouched the benefits of those now fifty-five years and older while restructuring the system for younger Americans. The plan contemplates major tax reform to stimulate a growing economy; the repeal of ObamaCare; and caps on non-defense discretionary spending. It is about as gradual and painless a plan as possible under the circumstances, not even projecting a balanced budget until around 2040.

After misrepresenting Ryan's plan as an attempt to steal Medicare from seniors, Obama finally purported to tell us his plan for balancing the budget—except there actually was no plan to do that, since his ten-year budget didn't even aspire to balance the budget in the long term. In a statement whose mendacity was audacious even for Obama, he claimed his budget would not add one dollar to the national debt. In fact, the plan would add some $8 trillion dollars. Perhaps Obama intended to say he would not add to the existing amount of annual deficits—but one would think the president is sophisticated enough to understand the difference between debt and deficits.

Adding insult to injury, Obama turned again to class warfare, accusing Ryan and other Republicans essentially of being un-American and of seeking to eliminate insurance for autistic children. On Mark Levin's radio show, Ryan responded that he'd never heard a presidential speech stoop to that level of partisanship, demagoguery, and distortion.

Denying the incontrovertible fact that our problems are caused by excess spending, Obama repeatedly lectured us that the wealthy were not paying enough. He is apparently unaware that the top 1 percent of income earners already pay about 38 percent of income tax revenues and the top 10 percent pay almost 70 percent. Increasing their taxes for the sake of satisfying the envy-lust he constantly peddles would reduce—not increase—revenues, especially during a recession.

Obama sought to dodge the spending issue by proposing to convene yet another commission whose findings, we are supposed to believe, he would take more seriously than those of his last commission. Beyond that Obama promised to save $500 billion from Medicaid and Medicare by 2023 and another $1 trillion the following decade, but offered no specifics about how he would accomplish that feat apart from enhancing his super-bureaucratic board, euphemistically dubbed the Independent Payment Advisory Board. These all-knowing bureaucratic presidential appointees would have final, unreviewable authority to impose a one-size-fits-all rate scheme. Only Congress could override the IPAB's authority, and then only with a two-thirds vote. Good luck with that.

This constituted a tacit admission that Obama had no idea how to, or had no intention to, cut Medicare costs except by implementing top down cost controls imposed by impersonal autocrats far removed from patients and their concerns. Obama's bogus projections also included sleights of hand, such as double counting dollars from the Medicare fund in order to create the illusion he would be using those funds for ObamaCare without raiding the Medicare system.

By contrast, the Ryan Plan would reduce the deficit by $5.8 trillion in ten years, primarily with spending cuts and revenue-neutral, growth-oriented tax reforms. Obama claimed his plan would cut $4 trillion in twelve years, but his revenue-killing tax increases might well offset any spending cuts he could achieve through his thinly-veiled plans for Medicare rationing.

If all this weren't appalling enough, revised figures kept pouring in revealing that our financial picture was even bleaker than our most pessimistic outlook from mere months earlier. In May 2011, Medicare and Social Security trustees issued their report showing that Medicare's fiscal hole had deepened by an additional $2 trillion and that its projected insolvency has been moved up by five years to 2024. The projected insolvency of Social Security, which was already $49 billion in the red last year, was advanced to 2036.

The bad news didn't stop there. S&P lowered its outlook on America's long-term credit rating from "stable" to "negative," with CNN Money warning that the move indicated there was a one-in-three likelihood that S&P would downgrade our AAA credit rating within two years. PIMCO, the world's largest bond fund, had already sold off all of its U.S. government holdings.

Through all of this Obama presents an image of a man wholly unfazed by the debt crisis. This leaves conservatives, and a growing number of independents, scratching their heads wondering how any president could so zealously obstruct the reforms necessary to save the nation. More and more Americans are wondering whether Obama is merely incompetent, or if he's following some kind of Machiavellian scheme to deliberately damage the nation's financial future.

In foreign policy, we face the same question as to whether Obama is intentionally sabotaging America or simply displaying rank incompetence. A central focus of Obama's diplomatic efforts—improving America's standing in the Arab world—has already failed completely, as demonstrated most recently by an Arab American Institute poll showing the Arab world views the United States less favorably now than it did during the last year of the George W. Bush administration.[2] Throughout that year, you might recall, the Obama campaign insisted ad nauseam that America's unpopularity stemmed from Bush's "unilateral" policies and his "shredding" of the Constitution. As it turns out, more than two years of Obama's serial apologies, political correctness, and his conversion of the War on Terror into a law enforcement exercise have garnered international contempt rather than respect. Who could have predicted that? Ahem.

In reaction to the turmoil now engulfing the Middle East, Obama has taken a hands-off approach to popular rebellions against our enemies (Ahmadinejad in Iran and Assad in Syria) while commanding that U.S. allies like Egypt's Hosni Mubarak step aside. As the corrupt Palestinian Authority and the Islamic terrorists of Hamas continue to inculcate their people with dreams of exterminating Israel, Obama pressures the Jewish state, our democratic ally, to make ever-increasing concessions for the sake of "peace." Perhaps most notably, in order to prove America's "engagement with"—one might more accurately say "subservience to"—the so-called international community, he has ordered our armed forces to undertake a half-hearted "kinetic military action" against Libya. Without defining any pressing American interest in Libya, his administration trumpeted support for the operation from the Arab League and the United Nations, though Obama saw no need to elicit the support of the U.S. Congress.

To assume Obama has the best interests of this nation at heart offers little comfort. For regardless of his ultimate motives, one thing is clear: he is pursuing an agenda that, unless reversed, will destroy the nation. The inescapable fact is that Obama is an incorrigible leftist ideologue who is unable to comprehend the glaring signs that his policies don't work. With respect to the economy, he believes as an article of faith that Keynesian policies of forced government spending will stimulate growth. Even wasteful government, according to this calculus, will create a salutary multiplier effect, causing dollars to ripple through the economy and generating demand.

This narrow mindset doesn't permit consideration of the empirically verifiable fact that the government's command-control spending of borrowed money necessarily zaps the private-sector dollar for dollar and then some, negating any stimulus it might have otherwise provided. It also fails to acknowledge that such forced spending, arbitrarily decreed by government officials, is less efficient than the invisible hand of the market because it is not, by definition, generated in response to the public's spending desires or preferences. When you factor in the waste inherent in government spending—as we saw with the stimulus bill in spades—such proposals are almost guaranteed to fail. Time and again history has vindicated opponents of Keynesian economics, from the New Deal forward, but liberals won't accept that their supposedly good intentions don't achieve the results they promise.

Thus, when Obama's stimulus egregiously failed to keep unemployment below the projected 8 percent, he offered no mea culpa. Instead, he told us he had under-estimated the severity of Bush's baleful economic legacy. No longer was he saying he'd get us out of this pronto; he changed his tack to, "We didn't get in this mess overnight, and we won't get out of it overnight."

For liberals like Obama, the subject of economic prosperity is a complex and nuanced matter. They are forever preoccupied with how resources are allocated, not just among Americans but between Americans and other peoples of the world. Having no real understanding how the free market works, they can't grasp why socialistic systems cannot produce prosperity on par with capitalistic ones. Even if they do sometimes grudgingly acknowledge it, their obsession with the class struggle compels them, at least subconsciously, to seek out a more even distribution of income and wealth even at the expense of overall prosperity.

How else do you make sense of Obama's answer to Charlie Gibson about raising capital gains rates? As discussed in chapter two of this book, Gibson asked Obama point-blank why he favored such increases when history has shown that they consistently yield less revenue, thus defeating their purpose. Tacitly conceding Gibson's premise, Obama insisted, "It's a matter of fairness, Charlie." Clearly, Obama would prefer that everyone receive less money so long as the policy disproportionately hurts the "wealthy."

I infer from this answer, from Obama's stated commitment to "spreading the wealth around," and from his refusal to change course on taxes and spending despite the damage his policies are wreaking on the country, that something in his political DNA prevents him from adopting the policies we so obviously need to set this country right: shrinking the government, empowering the private sector, reducing government spending, and reforming entitlements.

So in the end, it really doesn't matter whether Obama's specific intention is to harm the country. What matters is that he's hell-bent on implementing policies that will do it.

David Limbaugh
July 2011

INTRODUCTION

This book is about a young presidency—young, but already the most destructive in American history.

Everything about Barack Obama's radical background signals his visceral contempt for America—its culture, its values, and its political and economic systems. His unmistakable goal is to bring America down to size—an America that has been, in his view, too big for its britches, selfish, exploitive, unfairly wealthy, arrogant, and dismissive.

Throughout the 2008 presidential campaign, Barack Obama repeatedly promised to bring "fundamental change." The week before the election, he ominously declared, "We are five days away from fundamentally transforming the United States of America." That same week, I expressed these concerns in my syndicated column:

I am sincerely worried that if Obama wins, the checks and balances incorporated into our Constitution may not be enough to prevent a radical and irreversible diminution of our individual liberties because a confluence of factors has emerged to create a climate conducive to fundamental change. These factors are: a shockingly unknown candidate, whose mysterious past and numerous shady alliances are deliberately left unexplored by a corrupt, supportive media; the candidate's charismatic qualities that inspire a cultish loyalty; his intellectual trappings that create a fascination and allure among the intellectual elite, including some hypnotized conservatives; a major financial crisis that exacerbates the people's fears and uncertainties; a largely manufactured cloud of negativity placed over America by the media and a grossly partisan Democratic Party that places its self-interest above the national interest; and an apparently discredited Republican Party and conservative movement that have been blamed for our actual and perceived problems.

... All of these factors could coalesce to give Obama a mandate to fundamentally move our economy toward socialism in the name of economic fairness and emasculate our war on terrorists in the name of our international image.

I wish I had been wrong, but it turns out my fears were hardly exaggerated. Though Obama denied his extreme liberalism during the campaign, he couldn't conceal it entirely. Since his first day in office he has been trying to uproot our national moorings and "transform" the country into a land consistent with his socialist, secular, multicultural vision for America—an America that in his view has squandered its power and potential for good by: a) failing sufficiently to atone for its racial sins; b) subscribing to an antiquated and discriminatory system of values; c) having an economic system that fosters an "inequitable" distribution of wealth; d) selfishly consuming a disproportionate share of the world's resources; and e) imperialistically projecting its power in the world.

But Obama does have some ambivalence about America. On the one hand he deeply dislikes this country; on the other, he sees in it great potential—a potential he believes, immodestly, he can personally unleash as president. He admires America's wealth and power, even if undeserved in his view, but he is passionate about redirecting them and remaking us into a truly great nation—a part of the global community that shares rather than exploits its resources. In 2007 he told a *Rolling Stone* reporter he has faith in America's capacity for acts of outstanding virtue, but as a black man, he "feels very deeply that this country's exercise of its great inherited wealth and power has been grossly unjust." Obama added, "I'm somebody who believes in this country and its institutions, but I often think they're broken."[1]

Tragically, Obama's ideological blindness precludes him from recognizing America's unparalleled record of benevolence as the world's greatest superpower. It numbs him to the wonders of America's free-market system, which has produced unprecedented prosperity for Americans and contributed to the advancement of civilization throughout the world. It obscures a realistic assessment of global politics that comprehends the existence of rogue nations, evil empires, and Islamic terrorists who intend us harm and who cannot be mollified through pandering and "engagement," but must be approached from a position of strength.

His abundantly documented radical background soured his taste on America, compelling him to believe America's wealth and power were "inherited," rather than *inspired* by America's god-fearing founders, who crafted a government designed to establish and maximize individual liberties—a government that has been preserved with the blood, sweat, and tears of generations of Americans.

Ironically, Obama's domestic policy, foreign policy, and national security prescriptions are the opposite of what America needs. In transforming America to "spread the wealth around," he is actually spreading the misery around, burying us in debt, and potentially enslaving us to our foreign creditors. In the name of improving our image in the world, he is compromising our national security.

He is reaping destruction in America's culture, its Constitution, and in every sector of the American economy (save the public sector), administering one kick in the gut after another and inflicting damage from which it will be difficult to recover.

While holding himself out as a post-partisan, post-racial president, he has exacerbated racial tensions, inflamed partisan divisiveness, engaged in acrimonious class warfare, and demonized anyone to the political right of the late Ted Kennedy.

For someone who inspired so much "hope" and had so much goodwill upon taking office, even among certain commentators and media professionals who consider themselves conservatives, it is striking how far he has fallen so fast. His approval ratings have cratered more rapidly than those of any modern president. He has squandered more political capital than most presidents ever possessed. And he has done it all himself; his popularity freefall hasn't occurred as a result of circumstances beyond his control. But that hasn't prevented him from milking the economic crisis excuse ad nauseam and endlessly scapegoating his predecessor for the "multitude of problems" Obama allegedly inherited. He owns our current set of problems, which if he did inherit, he greatly exacerbated through a series of deplorable policies and actions.

He promised to lead a transparent, ethical administration, free of corruption and sanitized of conflicts of interest generated by the revolving door between lawmakers and lobbyists. But he appointed a host of tax cheats, lobbyists, and leftist radicals, and has cloaked many of his policy actions in secrecy. He has reportedly used his appointment power to offer high-ranking government jobs and other benefits in exchange for votes supporting his agenda. He has brought Chicago-style politics and Saul Alinsky street organizing tactics to Washington, diverting federal funds to the now-defunct ACORN as his political and re-election arm, using the Justice Department as an advocacy bureau and his campaign organization as an ongoing war room. He fired Inspector General Gerald Walpin after Walpin filed two reports implicating one of Obama's prominent supporters in the misappropriation of federal AmeriCorps funds, and then used the power of his office to wrongfully discredit Walpin and whitewash his allegations.

He presented himself as an exemplar of honesty—a new kind of politician with unique character and integrity. But he has been one of the most fundamentally dishonest chief executives in our history. He has broken promises on a broad range of important issues, from his pledge not to raise taxes in any form on those making less than $250,000 a year to his expedient promise to end the practice of extraordinary rendition. Nowhere has his pattern for dishonesty been more apparent than in his obsessive drive for socialized medicine, from his slandering of the nonpareil quality of American healthcare, to his promise to televise the healthcare debates on C-SPAN, to his pledge not to force the uninsured to buy insurance, to his varying claims about the numbers of uninsured, to denying his support for a single-payer plan, to dismissing allegations that the public option was a Trojan horse for a single-payer plan, to his dissembling about whether abortion would be federally funded, to misrepresenting whether "his plan" would cover illegal immigrants, to his promise that he would not interfere with the doctor-patient relationship and would expand healthcare choices, to his pooh-poohing the legitimate charge that his plan would lead to rationing.

He promised to be a uniter, but has proven more divisive than any president in the modern era, including George W. Bush. Pew Research Center reported after only his first few months in office that "for all his hopes about bipartisanship, Barack Obama has the most polarized early job approval of any president in the past four decades."[2] His situation did not improve as the year continued. Gallup reported on January 25, 2010, that Obama has been the most polarizing first-year president in the pollster's history. "The 65 percentage-point gap between Democrats' (88%) and Republicans' (23 percent) average job approval ratings for Barack Obama is easily the largest for any president in his first year in office, greatly exceeding the prior high of 52 points for Bill Clinton."[3] Polls aside, he has behaved as a rabid partisan with little patience for opposing viewpoints. He has routinely mischaracterized Republican positions and demeaned those who dared to oppose him as liars, insisting they shut up, get out of the way, and let him go about handling this mess he "inherited."

He promised to deliver us from racial disharmony, or at least to help ameliorate racial tensions, yet he has appointed race-oriented "czars," has issued reckless statements with racial implications, often reminds us of our "racist" heritage, and unpresidentially injected himself into a local police dispute involving his personal friend, erroneously prejudging the situation from the Oval Office with incendiary language guaranteed to heighten racial discord.

He promised his stimulus bill would "jump-start the economy," create jobs, and grow us out of the recession. He promised to "save or create" three million jobs (or was it two million, or two and a half million?), yet presided over the net loss of millions. He promised these would mainly be private sector jobs, but the only sector that has grown has been the public sector—no surprise, given Obama's big-government orientation. Even after the facts are in, he still clings to his original claims and says he fulfilled them. As they say, if you tell a lie often enough . . .

Obama said he would rigorously ensure the proper expenditure of the stimulus funds. Instead, a great portion of the stimulus money was never intended to be spent in time to do any stimulating, much of it has been sent to phantom addresses with phantom zip codes, and millions upon millions of dollars have been wasted on projects that the American people would never approve if they knew of them. Much of the money has also been used as a political slush fund, going to Obama-friendly groups that will work for his re-election.

He promised no political favoritism but has greased the skids for his union friends, stacking the deck for them against secured creditors in the GM and Chrysler negotiations, carving out exemptions for them in various healthcare proposals, adopting policies to give unionized companies preferences on federal contract bidding, pushing "card-check" legislation to intimidate workers into joining unions, and enlisting union thugs to disrupt conservative grassroots tea party protests.

He promised the Justice Department would be free of politics, but instead has presided over the most politicized DOJ since Janet Reno. Without explanation, Justice dismissed a cinch-lock voter intimidation case against the New Black Panther Party whose members, one armed with a billy club, were videotaped patrolling in front of a Philadelphia voting precinct during the 2008 presidential election. When asked to provide its reasons, DOJ stonewalled.

Moreover, Obama appointed Dawn Johnsen to head the Department's Office of Legal Counsel, which provides authoritative legal advice to the president and all the executive branch agencies. This office should be staffed by professionals who will render their legal opinions free of political influences or bias. It is, according to former federal prosecutor Andy McCarthy, "the last place in government where we would want a hard-edged ideologue—and while that would be true at any time, it is especially true with the current Justice Department, which is political to a fare thee well."[4] Yet Johnsen is a radical's radical. She wrote that one of Obama's first orders of business as president was to "order an immediate review to determine which [Gitmo] detainees should be released and which transferred to secure facilities in the United States" for civilian trials.[5]

Obama promised us he was a "fierce advocate for the free market," but proceeded to demonstrate just how hostile to it he actually is. On behalf of the federal government, he took over GM and Chrysler and unilaterally extended mortgage bailouts to those who had little prospect of repaying, thus magnifying the existing problem. He tried to handcuff the entire private sector with his onerous cap and trade bill, bribed and coerced Congress into assaulting private healthcare, and used every conceivable opportunity to redistribute wealth and increase the dependency classes to the point of covertly reversing the immensely successful welfare reform of the 1990s.

Along the way he demonized corporations, private sector executives, the Chamber of Commerce, oil companies, "fat-cat" banks, pharmaceutical companies, and others who had the audacity to engage in private business.[6]

He promised he was a true "democrat"—a man of the people who would govern according to the popular will. But he has governed like an autocrat, issuing a plethora of executive orders, flagrantly ignoring the manifest will of the American people on such crucial issues as healthcare reform, and implementing guidelines that would force taxpayers to fund embryonic stem cell research. He has proven himself wholly disinterested in the true wishes of the American people, doggedly fixated on his own ideological agenda and his monomaniacal ambition to change the country. Writer Quin Hillyer suggests "there is something way off balance in the character of Barack Obama.... All presidents...think at some level that they know best about policy choices. But almost none of them (Woodrow Wilson perhaps excepted) were so willing to disdain, in pursuit of such radical policy upheavals, such intense and overwhelming public opinion as has been evident in the current health takeover attempt."[7]

Liberal journalist Jonathan Alter gives us an inside view of the extent of Obama's ideological arrogance in his book *The Promise: President Obama, Year One*. Alter wrote that Rahm Emanuel spent almost a week during summer 2009 trying to dissuade Obama from pressing forward with ObamaCare. "I begged him not to do this," said Emanuel. But Obama reportedly ignored his advice, arguing he had not been sent to the White House to do "school uniforms."[8]

Obama has chosen to misinterpret the obvious rejection of his agenda through such objective benchmarks as the Republican takeover of Ted Kennedy's Massachusetts Senate seat. He insisted the public hadn't rejected his policies; merely that he hadn't explained them enough—after giving speech after self-indulgent speech (including at least fifty-four healthcare speeches as of March 19, 2010)[9] to browbeat the American people into climbing on board.

He said, "I think the assumption was if I just focus on policy, if I just focus on this provision or that law or if we're making a good rational decision here, then people will get it." Impervious to the widespread rejection of his agenda, he also blamed the Massachusetts election results on the public's general frustration with incumbents. He told George Stephanopoulos, "The same thing that swept Scott Brown into office swept me into office. People are angry and they're frustrated, not just because of what's happened in the last year or two years but what's happened over the last eight years."[10]

We were told we were getting a cool, calm, steady leader who could rise above emotional impulses to deliver classic statesmanship and prudent governance. But all too often we witness in him a petulant and vindictive bully who doesn't seem to understand why anyone would challenge his omniscience. On more than one occasion when challenged, Obama has cavalierly shot back, "I won, I'm the president."

He pretended he was a moderate on social issues, including abortion and homosexuality, but has been an ardent supporter of the homosexual agenda and is militantly pro-abortion, which is not unexpected considering his record on the issues. In fact, he was almost willing to jeopardize his sacred ObamaCare over his extreme pro-abortion views.

His handlers held him out as a brilliant, eloquent wordsmith who would restore class and elegance to the Oval Office, following President Bush's allegedly countrified demeanor and awkwardness with words. Instead, when the teleprompter is stripped away, we often find someone given to incoherent ramblings and verbal blunders that dwarf those of his predecessor. The best example was his unscripted answer to an unanticipated question at a meeting in Charlotte, North Carolina. A lady named Doris asked whether it was wise to add more taxes onto the public with his healthcare package. "We are over-taxed as it is," she said. Obama's answer was 2,600 words and took more than seventeen minutes, with no one ending up the wiser. It was a rambling, incoherent mish-mash of barely related talking points from a man the elites assured us possessed a "first rate" intellect.[11] During another public address, our Commander in Chief mispronounced "Navy corpsman" as "Navy corpse man," an embarrassing gaffe the mainstream media would have endlessly ridiculed had it been uttered by a Republican president.[12]

Obama has been an unmitigated disaster on national security, downplaying the terrorist threat and politicizing security policy, including his publication of national secrets—such as disclosing details on our nuclear arsenal and our highly sensitive, enhanced interrogation techniques for the purpose of embarrassing, and perhaps incriminating, Bush administration officials. He has gutted essential weapons programs and threatens to unilaterally reduce our nuclear stockpiles, saying the United States is the only nation ever to have used a nuclear weapon—meaning we need to atone for it.

He told us America had lost favor in the international community because of our arrogance and military imperialism, and that he would restore our good reputation with a fresh, conciliatory approach. He proceeded to bow and grovel to our enemies and gratuitously snub our allies. He has castigated America on foreign soil and pandered to the Islamic world, implying Islamic terrorism is our fault. Meanwhile, oppressed dissidents struggling in Iran and other autocratic nations have received the cold shoulder from Obama, who seems to view them as a nettlesome obstacle to his attempts to curry favor with their repressive governments.

He insisted that our policies in the war on terror were serving as a recruiting tool for terrorism. He would close Gitmo and outlaw "torture"—as if we were engaging in it in the first place. He even began to talk about the war as if it weren't a war, invented new euphemisms to describe acts of terrorism, and reverted to our pre-9/11 law enforcement approach to terrorism. But our own intelligence services report that terrorism is on the rise globally and domestically. All his liberal theories have failed utterly in practice.

Obama turns a blind eye to aggression around the world, from Russia to North Korea to Iran, opposes truly democratic movements, and supports the world's dictators and thugs. In exchange for appeasing and coddling tyrants, he has endured consistent ridicule from these very despots. After vowing to employ "bold and aggressive diplomacy" and to "do everything in my power to prevent Iran from obtaining a nuclear weapon," he ultimately reverted to the policy of sanctions for which he harshly criticized Bush.[13] In the process, he set a deadline for Iran to discontinue its nuclear program, let the deadline pass, and then denied ever having set it.

While cozying up to terrorists, he has shunned our ally Israel, strong-arming it to prevent Jews from living in the West Bank and even in parts of Israel's own capital city of Jerusalem, while painting Israel's justifiable acts of defending its people and sovereignty as morally equivalent to Palestinian terrorism.

While criticizing the Iraq war from the beginning, he has claimed full credit for the major gains we have achieved in Iraq thanks to the surge, a policy Obama had vehemently opposed.

He has held himself out as a believing Christian, but has rarely attended church since his inauguration, has snubbed Christianity and Christian symbols at every turn, and has consistently championed values inconsistent with the Biblical ethic. By contrast, he has glorified Islam, including falsely crediting it for major contributions to American society, overstating the Muslim presence and influence in America, and even describing Islam—in his Cairo speech—as a "revealed" religion, a curious thing, indeed, for one professing authentic Christianity.

On the campaign trail, Obama projected his own image as messianic—from the way he conceitedly thrust his chin out during his speeches, to the deliberately choreographed echo effect with his microphone, to his patently absurd, delusional boasts that "generations from now, we will be able to look back and tell our children that this was the moment when the rise of the oceans began to slow and our planet began to heal," and that "we are the ones we've been waiting for."

Based on his behavior as president, it is clear he truly believes his own hype, for we have discovered that instead of messianic, Obama is acutely, perhaps clinically, narcissistic. He behaves and governs as though he has been sheltered all his life, or at least since he was a young adult, living in a bizarre bubble, hearing only positive reinforcement and made to believe in his own supernatural powers. This is a major reason he cannot bear opposition; this is a major reason he is not, in the end, a man of the people and deferential to their will, but a top-down autocrat determined to permanently change America and its place in the world despite intense resistance from the American people themselves.

This book chronicles the words and policies of President Barack Obama and his Democratic Party and their devastating effect on America and its founding principles. Unless stopped—and reversed—the casualties of Obama's systematic assault on this nation will be our prosperity, our security, and ultimately, our liberty.

PART I

OFFENSES AGAINST AMERICANS

Chapter One

THE NARCISSIST

CRIMES AGAINST STATESMANSHIP

ME, MYSELF, AND I

Who is Barack Obama? To say that he has an enormous ego is an understatement. Many commentators, including psychological analysts and foreign leaders, have described him as a narcissist. Columnist Charles Krauthammer, a psychiatrist by training, marveled at Obama's conceit in arranging a speech at Germany's Brandenburg Gate during his presidential campaign, asking, "What exactly has he done in his lifetime to merit appropriating the Brandenburg Gate as a campaign prop? What was his role in the fight against communism, the liberation of Europe, the creation of what George Bush the elder...called 'a Europe whole and free'?...Americans are beginning to notice Obama's elevated opinion of himself....[H]as there ever been a presidential nominee with a wider gap between his estimation of himself and the sum total of his lifetime achievements?"[1] Jack Kelly of the *Pittsburgh Post-Gazette* told FOX News' Greta Van Susteren that his sources close to French president Nicolas Sarkozy said Sarkozy thinks President Obama is "incredibly naïve" and "grossly egotistical"—"so egotistical than no one can dent his naivete."[2]

Obama's patent self-confidence is not just posturing. It's evident he truly believes he is special. He did, after all, pen *two* largely autobiographical books before he had accomplished much of anything. He once told campaign aide Patrick Gaspard, "I think that I'm a better speechwriter than my speechwriters. I know more about policies on any particular issue than my policy directors. And I'll tell you right now that . . . I'm a better political director than my political director." Gaspard related that after Obama's first debate with McCain, Gaspard sent Obama an e-mail saying, "You are more clutch than Michael Jordan," and Obama replied, "Just give me the ball."[3] According to the paperback version of Senate majority leader Harry Reid's book *The Good Fight,* after Reid once complimented Obama for delivering a "phenomenal" speech, Obama simply replied, "I have a gift, Harry." Amazingly, Reid is so entrenched in Obama's personality cult that he interpreted the boast as a sign of "deep humility."[4]

Obama's belief that he is a gift to the world is a theme he would carry forward into his presidency. He truly believes he alone has the power to reverse the mess America has allegedly made of world affairs, and that only he can restore America's supposedly tattered reputation. In his speech to the UN General Assembly in September 2009, he declared, "I am well aware of the expectations that accompany my presidency around the world."[5] When asked on the campaign trail whether he ever had any doubts, he retorted, "Never." As columnist Jeff Jacoby pointed out, when Obama's presidency began he used the royal "we" in describing his preferred policies, but by the time he addressed Congress around a month later, he was already using "the naked 'I.'" Jacoby noted Obama used "I" thirty-four times in his speech on the federal takeover of General Motors alone.[6]

Indeed, it often seems that for our president, American policy, and even American history, is not about the United States, but about *him* personally. At the Summit of the Americas, Obama sat through a 50-minute harangue against the United States by Nicaraguan president Daniel Ortega, who eviscerated the United States for a century of "terroristic" aggression in Central America. When it was Obama's turn, he did not defend the United States, but made himself the issue: "I'm grateful that President Ortega did not blame me for things that happened when I was three months old."[7]

During the contentious debate over Obama's unrelenting push for socialized medicine, many Democratic congressmen were running scared, fearing a 1994-style electoral thrashing. The White House, however, saw it much differently. Democratic congressman Marion Berry noted incredulously, "They just don't seem to give it any credibility at all. They just keep telling us how good it was going to be. The president himself, when that was brought up in one group said, 'Well, the big difference here and in '94 was you've got me.'"[8]

Obama's numerous self-references soon became legendary. According to Kevin Hall of the *Des Moines Conservative Examiner*, Obama referred to himself 114 times in his first State of the Union. He said "I" ninety-six times, and used "my" or "me" eighteen times.[9] By September 23, 2009, FOX News reported Obama had given forty-one speeches so far that year, referring to himself 1,198 times.[10] At his West Point speech in December 2009 (where soldiers were asked before he spoke to show enthusiasm), he referred to himself forty-four times.[11] In a speech in Ohio on jobs on January 22, 2010, Obama referred to himself no fewer than 132 times and, in the same speech, had the unwittingly humorous audacity to proclaim, "This is not about me."[12]

"IT'S NOT ABOUT ME"

That phrase, "This is not about me," cropped up in many of Obama's speeches, signaling that whatever "this" is, it's precisely about him—his ego, his ideology, his agenda, his legacy, or his unbending ambition to have his way. In his mind, it seems, everything is always about him, no matter how much he protests otherwise. The rhetorical device, "It's not about me," is a long established pattern in which he self-servingly pretends to project an air of humility to leave the impression that he is modest about accomplishing great things—thereby shamelessly seeking credit both for his modesty and his greatness. He used a variation of this theme at a February 2010 meeting with Senate Democrats, telling them, "It is constantly important to remind myself why I got into this business in the first place; why I'm willing to be away from my family for big stretches at a time.... You don't get in this for the fame. You don't get in it for the title."[13] Yes, Obama is always about a cause bigger than himself—so big that it's worth his enormous sacrifices.

Likewise, on February 15, 1990, after becoming the first black president of the *Harvard Law Review*, Obama proclaimed, "I realized my election was not about me, but it was about us, about what we could do and what we could accomplish."[14] On November 2, 2004, when he visited the campus of the University of Illinois during his U.S. Senate campaign, he declared, "Ultimately, this election is not about me.... It's about the willingness of our citizens to get engaged and get involved."[15] On December 11, 2006, in New Hampshire, he again insisted, "It's not about me." (But an NPR reporter covering the event remarked, "It really is all about him.")[16] On December 10, 2007, Obama argued, "This campaign is not about me; it is about the hundreds of volunteers...in Rhode Island...and the millions of people across the country who want change we can believe in."[17]

On December 13, 2007, he said during a Democratic presidential debate, "I want to remind myself constantly that this is not about me, what I'm doing today."[18] (Apparently, he feels the need to keep reminding *us* as well.) And in his acceptance speech in August 2008, he said, "This election has never been about me; it's about you."[19] President-elect Obama issued a pre-inauguration video statement in which he said, "This election is not about me. It's about all of us."[20] On a visit to the Children's National Medical Center in Washington, D.C. in July 2009, responding to Senator Jim DeMint's comment that ObamaCare could be his "Waterloo," Obama pleaded, "This isn't about me. This isn't about politics. This is about a health care system that is breaking America's families, breaking America's businesses, and breaking America's economy."[21]

But Obama's obsessive drive to nationalize healthcare has really been all about him, and the American people have issued a clear referendum on his healthcare scheme and his entire agenda through their consistent rejection of Democratic candidates. This trend culminated in the takeover of Senator Kennedy's Massachusetts Senate seat by Republican Scott Brown, whose opposition to ObamaCare was a core part of his campaign. Yet Obama continues to tell us— either as a brazen practitioner of Orwellian deception or as a poster-child for political tone-deafness (the latter being quite unlikely)—"I won't stop fighting for you."[22]

If he were truly fighting for the people, however, he wouldn't have mocked the tea partiers or closed his own counterfeit public forums on healthcare to all but union and other special interest supporters of ObamaCare. Then-White House press secretary Robert Gibbs confessed that Obama is "quite comfortable" with being a one-term president if that's the consequence of passing his agenda.[23] As journalist Kyle-Anne Shiver noted, "What we have here in America today is a real-life jump-the-shark drama, starring a super-narcissistic president so desperate to create his own vainglorious legacy that he is willing to destroy his own political party and do enduring damage to his country in pursuit of his selfish ends."[24]

And while Obama is a leftist ideologue of the first order whose determination to socialize medicine knows no bounds, there is abundant proof his ego is motivating him just as strongly as his ideology. Alabama congressman Parker Griffith, who switched from Democrat to Republican, spoke to Obama's personal investment in

ObamaCare. "You have personalities who have bet the farm, bet their reputations, on shoving a health care bill through the Congress. It's no longer about health care reform. It's all about ego now. The president's ego. Nancy Pelosi's ego. This is about saving face, and it has very little to do with what's good for the American people."[25] Griffith is convinced the Democratic leadership is so driven with this issue that they would accept losing Democratic control of the House. "This is a trophy for the speaker, it's a trophy for the several committee chairs, and it's a trophy for the president."[26]

"THE BURDEN OF BEING SO BRIGHT"

Candidate Obama overtly cultivated a messianic image, from the grandiose pomp accompanying his campaign speech in Berlin to the Greek columns that adorned his acceptance speech at Denver's Invesco Field. His advisers fully bought into the facade, especially to the idea that Obama possessed a superior intellect—so far above the masses that it was difficult to convey his ideas in terms simple enough for the people to understand. At a forum at the Kennedy School of Government, one participant suggested to Obama's adviser and long-time confidant, Valerie Jarrett, that Obama's ideas were so complex that the administration should consider writing simple booklets to explain them to ordinary people (including tea partiers), just like the computer industry originally wrote *DOS For Dummies*. Jarrett said it was an excellent idea. "Everyone understood hope and change" because "they were simple ... part of our challenge is to find a very simple way of communicating. ... When I first got here people kept talking about 'cloture' and 'reconciliation' and 'people don't know what that's talking about.'" Then it really got thick as Jarrett proclaimed, "There's nobody more self-critical than President Obama. Part of the burden of being so bright is that he sees his error immediately."[27]

Similarly, during the healthcare debates, Obama's chief adviser David Axelrod reinforced the administration's low estimation of its hapless subjects. On NBC's *Meet The Press*, Axelrod said, "The one thing I am sure of is that the American people don't know or care much about the sequencing of parliamentary procedures."[28] Clearly, Axelrod believes Americans don't have the sophistication to understand constitutional or legislative principles or the consequences to their liberty when those principles are violated.

The liberal media enthusiastically encouraged Obama's narcissistic sense of superiority over the American people. HBO's Bill Maher complained Americans "are not bright enough to really understand the issues. But like an animal they can sort of sense strength and weakness. They can smell it on you."[29] *Slate's* Jacob Weisberg lamented, "The biggest culprit in our current predicament" is "the childishness, ignorance and growing incoherence of the public at large."[30] *Time's* Joe Klein, in his blog post "Too Dumb to Thrive," made this observation about America's opposition to Obama's stimulus package: "This is yet further evidence that Americans are flagrantly ill-informed...and, for those watching FOX News, misinformed. It is very difficult to have a democracy without citizens. It is impossible to be a citizen if you don't make an effort to understand the most basic activities of your government. It is very difficult to thrive in an increasingly competitive world if you're a nation of dodos."[31] Blogger Matthew Yglesias, after saying Klein's comments were "way too harsh," essentially conceded his point, claiming, "Most people don't know a lot of macroeconomic theory.... The fact of the matter, however, is that most people don't know much about most things."[32]

"HE'S SORT OF GOD"

Media coverage of Obama's presidential campaign was so fawning that Obama's opponent, John McCain, put together an ad mocking the media's "Obama Love"—which was quite a statement coming from a previous darling of the press who was unceremoniously dumped once he challenged the media's Chosen One.

In addition to showing various media sycophants drooling over Obama, the video included a short video clip of a female journalist, acting like a school girl with a crush, urging a Secret Service agent to sit down in a seat on the airplane so the press could ogle Obama as he spoke on the phone.[33] In fact, Obama's sexiness became a popular topic among the press. *Washingtonian* magazine graced the cover of its May 2009 issue with a "pec-tacular" shirtless picture of Obama strutting on the beach. Garrett Graff, editor-at-large of the magazine, told *ABC News* that with the Obamas came a "celebrity aspect that has brought energy to the city and the attention of the paparazzi. The Obamas are the center of attention here and the whole world is looking to Washington now in a way we haven't seen in years." He cooed, "It's a real golden age of Washington."[34]

Indeed, the media's servile coverage of Obama sometimes crossed the line into outright reverence. HBO producer Ed Norton told *Good Morning America* co-host Diane Sawyer that he was impressed with the tranquil "no-drama Obama.... And in a weird way, when you look behind the curtain with that team, they are really zen. It's amazing how zen they are."[35] *Newsweek* editor Evan Thomas infamously told MSNBC's Chris Matthews, "Reagan was all about America ... Obama is—we are above that now. We're not just parochial, we're not just chauvinistic, we're not just provincial. We stand for something. I mean in a way Obama's standing above the country, above the world, he's sort of God."[36]

Thomas was preaching to the choir, as Matthews became well known for proclaiming that an Obama speech sent a "thrill" up his leg. It's less well known that he followed up that statement with an even greater expression of devotion: "The Biblical term for it," gushed Matthews, "since we're in a Biblical era, is deliverance. We're being picked up and moved to where we have to be." On another occasion Matthews declared Obama is "sort of a gift from the world to us in so many ways." *NBC News'* Lee Cowan said it was "almost hard to remain objective, because it's infectious.... It's not cool if you haven't seen Barack Obama in person." The *New*

Republic saw fit to print a cover with Obama's picture reading, "Why You Love Him."

Obama didn't exactly discourage this quasi-deification. In noting Obama's "pathological self-regard," former George W. Bush aide Pete Wehner reported that Obama surrounded himself by aides who referred to him as a "Black Jesus." Wehner noted, "Obama didn't appear to object."[37] Fouad Ajami, a professor of International Studies at Johns Hopkins, wrote, "Americans don't deify their leaders or hang on their utterances, but Mr. Obama succumbed to what the devotees said of him: He was the Awaited One. A measure of reticence could have served him. But the flight had been heady, and in the manner of Icarus, Mr. Obama flew too close to the sun." Even JFK, argued Ajami, didn't fall for his own mystique. "And then there was the hubris of the man at the helm: He was everywhere, and pronounced on matters large and small. This was political death by teleprompter. . . . Mr. Obama was smitten with his own specialness."[38] Even leftist radio host Ed Schultz reported the West Wing of the White House had been turned into a "shrine" to President Obama. "There are pictures all over . . . of President Obama. . . . It was just one picture after another."[39]

OVEREXPOSED

Obama didn't seem averse to all the flattery. To the contrary, the November 25, 2009 *Drudge Report* featured a photo of him leaving the White House holding an issue of *GQ* magazine with his own picture on the cover.[40] Observant bloggers also noticed that when Obama removed his suit jacket before delivering one of his many healthcare speeches, his name was stitched inside.[41]

Obama certainly wasn't above engaging in shameless self-promotion. In his first year as president he gave 158 interviews and 411 speeches—way more than any other president. He held twenty-three townhall meetings, made forty-six out-of-town trips to fifty-eight cities and thirty states, made ten foreign trips (more than any other first year president) to twenty-one nations, held twenty-eight political fundraisers (compared to six for George W. Bush in his first year), and attended seven campaign rallies for three Democratic candidates (all of whom lost, further illustrating the counterproductive effect of his tired rhetoric).[42]

Obama's overexposure began before he was president or even a presidential candidate, leading him to quip in a 2004 speech when he was a senator-elect, "I'm so overexposed I'm making Paris Hilton look like a recluse." But the coverage back then was small potatoes compared to the media infatuation with him as a presidential candidate and then as president. His name or face appeared on half of *Time* magazine's covers in 2008. As of the August 2009 edition, he had appeared on seven *Time* covers since his election in November 2008. One of those covers celebrated him as "Person of the Year," and another as the reincarnation of FDR.[43] *Newsweek* featured Obama on twelve of its 2008 covers'.[44]

The *Washington Post's* Howard Kurtz reported that during Obama's first few months as president, the networks gave him more coverage than George W. Bush and Bill Clinton combined in their first months—and more positive assessments as well.[45] "Obama marked his first 100 days in office with three hundred photos . . . all of him."[46] The broadcast networks were so in awe of our president they were willing to suffer big monetary losses to accommodate his self-indulgence. As Obama approached his 100th day in office, the networks granted his request to air a news conference the following week, which was the important ratings "sweeps" week, to talk about his banking and auto bailouts. It was the fourth such episode, with the first three having cost ABC, CBS, NBC, and FOX about $30 million total.[47] Accuracy in Media reported that Obama appeared to be breaking every record kept on U.S. presidential press coverage. In the first six months of 2009, his name was cited in 1.1 million stories across the mainstream and social media and the Internet, constituting an average of 6,100 references a day. That was more than three times the coverage for George W. Bush or Bill

Clinton during their comparable periods. Obama was also tagged on 216,000 YouTube videos and mentioned in some 15,000 blog posts a week.[48]

Writing about "Obama the Omnipresent," the *New York Times*' Mark Leibovich commented, "As President Obama prepares for his speed date with the Sunday morning talk shows, a familiar question dogs his aides: 'How much Obama is too much Obama?'" Leibovich then answered his own question: "Even by the norms of his ubiquity, Mr. Obama has been on an especially prodigious media binge lately, pitching his health care plan seemingly everywhere but the Food Channel and FOX News."[49] All of this, wrote Leibovich, "sparked another debate over the O word—'overexposure'—which has become a principal topic around the White House in recent days." But that didn't deter Obama, who even accepted an invitation to appear on *America's Most Wanted* to commemorate its 1,000[th] episode.[50]

Obama's countless, redundant personal media appearances speak volumes about his priorities—and self-infatuation. His appearances on five Sunday programs to promote ObamaCare prompted Karl Rove to remark, "His time might be better spent praying for public support."[51]

The *Washington Post's* Howard Kurtz concluded Obama's overexposure was a deliberate ploy by the White House. "Clearly, the White House has made its choice. Obama will hit the airwaves whenever he can, as often as he can, in as many formats as he can, any time he's got something to sell. Which is pretty much all the time."[52] Kurtz pointed out that Obama had already done ESPN, Leno, the network anchors, *60 Minutes*, and a slew of other programs. "Then there was NBC's day in the life, ABC's townhall forum, the four prime-time news conferences, the comedy bits for Conan and Colbert, and on and on." And Obama was preparing for sitdowns with Steve Kroft and CNBC's John Harwood, interviews on *Meet the Press*, *Face the Nation*, *This Week*, *State of the Union*, and a Univision show. "And in case that doesn't provide

enough pop," wrote Kurtz, "he'll do Letterman on Monday."[53]
Time's James Poniewozik, in his article, "Obama to Appear on
Everything, Everywhere, Except Fox," asked, "Should he just put
a 24-hour webcam in the White House and be done with it?"[54]

Obama was oblivious to the diminishing returns his media satu-
ration and endless speechifying were yielding. At one point he said,
"Everything there is to say about health care has been said"—and
then he promptly gave another healthcare speech. Amazingly,
Obama regarded one of his cardinal problems to be his ostensible
lack of communication with the public. He told ABC's George
Stephanopoulos, "If there's one thing that I regret this year, [it] is
that we were so busy just getting stuff done and dealing with the
immediate crises that were in front of us, that I think we lost some
of that sense of speaking directly to the American people about
what their core values are and why we have to make sure those
institutions are matching up with those values."[55]

Baltimore Sun TV critic David Zurawik skewered Obama for
insinuating himself into virtually every square foot of the public
arena, writing, "He's baaack: TV Obama is everywhere—again."
Speaking of Scott Brown's victory in the Massachusetts Senate race,
Zurawik argued,

> Yes, the president did indeed get the message from Massachu-
> setts, but it might not be the one angry and frightened Ameri-
> cans meant to send. The message he appears to have received:
> Get back on TV like it's 2008 and you are running for president.
> Because while this governing thing has not been working out too
> well during the first year, the one thing you can do is perform in
> front of the camera like no other politician since Ronald Rea-
> gan. Work it, baby, work it. As I have written before, when the
> going gets tough, President Obama gets on television.
>
> ...Last year at this time, as a media and TV critic, I was
> delighted at the thought of having the most savvy TV president
> since Ronald Reagan to write about for the next four years.

Today, as a citizen, I am utterly dismayed by the way those TV skills have been used to paper over what appears to be a lack of vision and sustained effort from the man behind the video image.[56]

With kudos to Zurawick for correctly pinpointing Obama's overemphasis on media and under-emphasis on governance, it's not Obama's lack of vision but the nature of his vision that is most troubling, as we will discuss in later chapters.

Well into his second year in office, Obama still couldn't get enough of himself on television—no matter the occasion. Obama agreed to appear on CBS's *Early Show* with co-anchor Harry Smith in a court-side interview for the Final Four basketball games. As part of the telecast, Smith and the network's NCAA analyst, Clark Kellogg, shot hoops with Obama on the White House basketball court. The interview and the "game" aired during CBS's coverage of the Final Four.

With so much invested in Obama, it was unsurprising that some of his biggest media supporters tried to hide the unpopularity of his policies. For example, during the healthcare debate in July 2009, a *New York Times*/CBS poll showed that Obama's healthcare plan was deeply unpopular: 69 percent of respondents believed it would hurt the quality of their own healthcare; 73 percent believed it would limit their access to tests and treatment; 62 percent believed it would require them to change doctors; 76 percent believed it would lead to them paying higher taxes; and 77 percent believed it would cause their healthcare costs to increase. How did the *New York Times* cover the results of its own poll? It buried the story on page A-17.[57]

Obama, of course, knew where his bread was being buttered. In October 2009 he invited a number of his favorite liberal media mouthpieces, such as MSNBC's Keith Olbermann and Rachel Maddow, the *New York Times*' Maureen Dowd, Gwen Ifill of PBS, Gloria Borger of CNN, and Eugene Robinson of the *Washington Post*, to a two and a half hour off-the-record briefing. As some commentators noted, Obama only gave General Stanley McChrystal, then-commander of U.S. troops in Afghanistan, a mere twenty-five minutes after the general flew from London to discuss national security with the president in Copenhagen.[58]

Obama's self-infatuation didn't falter with the public's declining support. Toward the end of 2009, his approval ratings had plummeted to their lowest point to date, with 18 percent more Americans strongly disapproving of his performance (42 percent) than strongly approving (24 percent).[59] Unfazed, he told Oprah Winfrey he would give himself "a good solid B+ for his first year in office," stressing again that he had *inherited* "the biggest set of challenges of any president since Franklin Delano Roosevelt." And the only reason he humbled himself to a mere B+ was because "of the things that are undone. . . . If I get health care passed we tip into A minus."[60]

SEEDS OF MSM DISENCHANTMENT

As enamored of Obama as the media were, it was not a relationship without some snags. As sure as familiarity breeds contempt, some reporters began to notice Obama's unflappably high opinion of himself and that in some cases he was acting like a prima donna. The *New Republic's* Gabriel Sherman wrote in August 2008 that the press's flame for Obama "seems to have dwindled." Reporters had begun to complain Obama was not transparent as he claimed, with one exclaiming Obama's handlers were "total tightwads with information." Another asserted the Obama campaign approached the press with a sense of entitlement. "They're an arrogant operation. Young and arrogant. They don't believe in transparency with their own campaign."

Obama's team was most defensive when reporters looked into Obama's sketchy biography. "They're terrified of people poking around Obama's life," said one reporter. "The whole Obama narrative is built around this narrative that Obama and David Axelrod built, and, like all stories, it's not entirely true. So they have to be protective of the crown jewels." The campaign reportedly went so far as to request Obama's old friends and Harvard classmates not to talk to the press without permission.[61]

New York Times chief political correspondent Adam Nagourney received a terse e-mail from Obama's press office complaining about a *Times* poll and about Nagourney and Megan Thee's corresponding front-page article interpreting it, "Poll Finds Obama Isn't Closing Divide on Race." Nagourney responded and thought the matter was resolved, but discovered the next day the Obama campaign had issued a statement slamming his article. Nagourney said, "I've never had an experience like this, with this campaign or others. I thought they crossed the line. If you have a problem with a story I write, call me first. I'm a big boy. I can handle it. But they never called. They attacked me like I'm a political opponent."[62]

Nagourney was not the only reporter gratuitously offended by Obama. In April, *New York Times* reporter Helene Cooper complained that in a joint presser with British prime minister Gordon Brown, Obama tried to cut off the press after only six questions. "Is President Obama trying to muzzle his press corps?" she asked.[63]

In June 2008 Obama "ditched" the press on his plane for a secret meeting with Hillary Clinton at Senator Dianne Feinstein's Washington home, leaving reporters "trapped" on the flight to Chicago. This provoked a number of D.C. bureau chiefs for major news organizations to send an irate letter to Obama aides Robert Gibbs and David Plouffe, threatening not to reimburse the Obama campaign for the flight. "The decision to mislead reporters is a troubling one," said the letter. "We hope this does not presage a relationship with the Obama campaign that is not based on a mutual respect for the truth."[64]

The *Washington Post*'s Dana Milbank also commented on Obama's "presumptuousness" in the summer of 2008 for virtually assuming the role of president before he won the election. "Barack Obama has long been his party's presumptive nominee," wrote Milbank. "Now he's becoming its presumptuous nominee." Milbank cited Obama's "presidential-style world tour," where world leaders and American military brass lined up to show him respect; his teleconference with the actual president's Treasury secretary; his meeting with the Pakistani prime minister; his meeting with the Federal Reserve chairman for a briefing; and his appearance at a House Democrat "presidential-style pep rally" on Capitol Hill. On his way to that meeting, according to Milbank, his motorcade was more insulating than the actual president's. Traffic was routinely shut down for his cars, even to facilitate his appearance at high money fundraisers. He reportedly told congressional Democrats, "This is the moment...that the world is waiting for....I have become a symbol of the possibility of America returning to our best traditions."[65]

As president, Obama has been quick to lecture others, but just as fast to exempt himself from his own advice. When he signed his "stimulus" bill into law, he lectured that everyone must sacrifice for the greater good—that everyone must have "some skin in the game." But Obama reportedly threw a party at the White House every three days during his first year in office. As Republican congressman Bob Latta sardonically remarked, "Let the good times roll."[66]

GET BACK IN TOUCH

It wasn't just the press that began to notice that Obama, the man, didn't quite live up to Obama, the mirage. Among the first to withdraw support were conservative elites who'd given him the benefit of the doubt. Independents followed suit, and by the end of his first year in office, even many Democrats and much of the hard Left had begun to turn against him for various reasons. The same held true for some mainstream Democrats.

In March 2010, Dee Dee Myers, White House press secretary under President Clinton, wrote an open memo to Obama urging him to "Get Back in Touch." Clinton "never tired" of happily mixing with the people and demonstrating his empathy for their plight, she argued. Clinton might have been faulted for his "neediness," but at least that caused him to interact with the people. Obama, on the other hand, projects "self-reliance: he's calm, he's cool; he's self-possessed. . . . But while eschewing emotion—and its companion, vulnerability—Obama should be careful not to sacrifice empathy, the 'I feel your pain' connection that sustained Clinton. . . . If people believe you're on their side, they will trust your decisions." But too often, said Myers, Obama sends the signal "that he stands alone—and likes it that way."[67]

According to Myers, Obama needs to emulate Clinton's habit of reminding "people that he was like them." People, though, still personally approve of Obama even if they don't approve of his policies, she said. They like him; they "want to have a beer with him. They're just not sure he wants to have a beer with them."[68]

On these points Myers is right, except her advice is wishful thinking. Obama sends the signal that he likes standing alone because he does. He is aloof and arrogant. He most certainly *doesn't* want to have beers with the people, except where he can exploit that image to extricate himself from a political jam—as with the "beer summit," designed to contain the political damage he sustained after accusing a Cambridge police officer of "acting stupidly" and implying the officer was racist for arresting his friend, Harvard professor Henry Louis Gates Jr., even though Obama admitted he didn't know all the facts of the incident.

It's not just that Obama doesn't want to have a beer with "ordinary folks," as he refers to us; he also didn't seem too anxious to pay his respects to the victims of the Fort Hood terrorist attack, in which Islamic fanatic Nidal Malik Hasan killed twelve U.S. soldiers and a civilian and wounded dozens more. Apparently, Obama feared a high-profile reaction to the attack might call more attention to this horrific act of Islamic terrorism, undermining his dogmatic denial of any connection between Islam and terrorism. So he casually waited a few days after the massacre to travel to Fort Hood, showing a "strange disconnectedness," according to British reporter Toby Harnden. Harnden wrote, "A year into his presidency. . . Mr. Obama seems a curiously bloodless president. If he experiences passion, he seldom shows it."

Obama's first comments on the attack were certainly "disconnected" and "bloodless." As Americans across the nation tuned in to live TV for the president's reaction to the massacre of American troops on U.S. soil, they encountered a strange scene. Speaking at the conclusion of a conference on Native American issues, Obama opened his speech by good-naturedly praising the "extraordinary" conference, giving a bizarre "shout out" to "Dr. Joe Medicine Crow," and declaring that continuing the conference's business was a "top priority" for his administration. Then, he paid a few minutes of eerily dispassionate lip service to the victims of the "horrible incident" at Fort Hood before finishing his remarks by once again praising the results of the conference.

Writer Robert A. George was horrified at the inappropriateness of Obama's performance. He wrote, "Instead of a somber chief executive offering reassuring words and expressions of sympathy and compassion, viewers saw a wildly disconnected and inappropriately light president making introductory remarks. . . . *Anyone* at home aware of the major news story of the previous hours had to have been stunned. An incident like this requires a scrapping of the early light banter."[69]

In his next press conference on the event Obama offered "an update on the tragedy that took place," which, as Toby Harnden noted, was like treating Hasan's killing spree "as if it was an earthquake and not a terrorist attack from an enemy within. . . . Completely missing was the eloquence that Mr. Obama employs when talking about himself. Absent too was any sense that the President empathized with the families and comrades of those murdered."[70]

Contrast Obama's reaction to that of former President George W. Bush, who upon hearing about the massacre, drove thirty miles with his wife Laura to Fort Hood and spent "considerable time" visiting the victims' families in private, having instructed the base commander they wanted no press coverage of their visit.[71]

Obama similarly turned heads at his signing of the Daniel Pearl Freedom of the Press Act, with his ludicrous comments on the Islamic terrorists' beheading of Pearl. Obama told reporters, "Obviously, the loss of Daniel Pearl was one of those moments that captured the world's imagination because it reminded us of how valuable a free press is." As blogger Jim Hoft aptly noted, "No, Barack. It was horrifying.... It had nothing to do with freedom of the press. They beheaded Daniel Pearl because he was an American and a Jew. They beheaded Daniel Pearl because they were Islamic radicals. Something you have not yet figured out."[72]

OBAMA MOSTLY HEARS OBAMA

While many Obama supporters laud his supposed willingness to listen, he is actually better at pretending to listen. His mind is generally set in stone on his big agenda items. As Sarah Palin wrote following the Massachusetts Senate election, "Instead of sensibly telling the American people, 'I'm listening,' the president is saying, 'Listen up, people!'"[73] Similarly, former congressman Ernest Istook wrote, "I've attended at least 15 State of the Union speeches, and this one will stand out mostly for the fact that Obama could have said he listened to America and learned from us—but he didn't."[74]

Obama's disinclination to genuine listening was starkly evident during his televised healthcare summit. In his promos for the event and in his opening remarks, he promised to listen to all ideas. But as the *Washington Times* noted, "Turns out he meant he'd be listening to his own voice." He spoke 119 minutes, more than all Republicans combined (110 minutes), and more than all other Democrats combined (114 minutes), resulting in 233 total minutes for Democrats and 119 minutes for Republicans—illustrating his idea of partisan balance. When Senate Republican leader Mitch McConnell complained early in the proceedings that Democrats had controlled more than twice the amount of time as Republicans, Obama first denied it, then shot back, "You're right. There was an

imbalance on the opening statements because—I'm the president.... I didn't count my time in terms of dividing it evenly."[75] Just
in case Obama wasn't clear, he reminded Senator John McCain during the summit, after McCain suggested that the American people
overwhelmingly rejected ObamaCare and opposed special deals for
certain states: "Let me make this point, John, because we're not
campaigning anymore, the election is over."[76]

Of all the stories illustrating Obama's unwillingness to listen, the
granddaddy had to be his statement following the partisan passage
of ObamaCare that fateful Sunday night, March 21, 2010. He
announced, "We proved that this government—a government of the
people and by the people—still works for the people.... To every
unsung American who took the time to sit down and write a letter
or type out an e-mail hoping your voice would be heard—it has
been heard tonight.... Tonight's vote ... is a victory for the American people."[77] All this, in the face of the people's overwhelming
opposition to ObamaCare as shown in poll after poll. And all this,
despite the fact that the bill, notwithstanding overwhelming Democratic majorities in both chambers, could only be passed through
legislative trickery, executive deception, political bribes, arm-twisting, and a meaningless executive order to supposedly negate the
bill's abortion funding provisions.

It was easy for Obama to appear congenial, even-tempered, and
empathetic when everything was going his way and he was being
treated as supernatural and infallible. But when reality finally set in,
some of his seemingly positive attributes (coolness) were recognized
for what they were (detachment). As *Commentary's* Jennifer Rubin
noted, "It's hard to change who you are. And who Obama is, though
an asset in the campaign, has now become a liability for him."[78]

SOBBING KINDERGARTENERS

As shown in his statements on the Fort Hood massacre and the
Daniel Pearl tribute, Obama seems to lack ordinary human emo-
tions. This isn't just a lack of empathy, but a marked insensitivity

to things big and small, and a tendency to convert any situation into being about himself—no matter how inappropriate. While stumping for his healthcare bill at a Democratic National Committee fundraiser in Washington, he drew upon the usual anecdotal sob story to prove that yet another ill person had been mistreated by an insurance company. But with this one there was a particular twist. He injected into the dying woman's sad story the bizarre tidbit that "she insisted she's going to be buried in an Obama t-shirt." The crowd laughed uncomfortably at his odd statement. But his determined expression showed he wasn't joking, and that he believed the story was more poignant with the inclusion of the lady's Obama-adoring request.[79]

In another incident, more than 100 kindergarteners from Stafford County, Virginia, got up early for a field trip to the White House. When they arrived just ten minutes late because of heavy traffic, they were locked out. "We were going to the White House," said 5-year-old Cameron Stine, "but we couldn't get in so I felt sad." Obama staffers claimed the kids' entry into the White House would have interfered with the president's scheduled event with the Super Bowl champion Pittsburgh Steelers. Cameron's mother Paty Stine said, "I was angry cause they were disappointed.... Here we have President Obama and his administration saying, 'we are for the common, middle class people,' and here he is not letting 150 5- and 6-year olds into the White House because he's throwing a lunch for a bunch of grown millionaires." The White House later released a statement claiming the kids were really an hour late and expressing hope the tour could be rescheduled.[80]

Though Obama frequently denounced President Bush for tarnishing America's image abroad, he didn't hesitate to snub Europeans when they interfered with his personal agenda. The day before he was scheduled to receive his Nobel Peace Prize in Oslo, Norway, Obama made news across Scandinavia for declining lunch with Norway's King Harald V and even deciding not to visit his own Nobel exhibit—a tradition among prize recipients. "Everybody wants to visit the Peace Center except Obama," reported the Norwegian daily

Aftenposten. "A bit arrogant—a bit bad," read the headline. "It's very sad," said Bente Erichsen, the Nobel Peace Center Director. "I totally understand why the Norwegian public is upset."

Obama also skipped a concert in Oslo that had been arranged in his honor, as well as a meeting with Norwegian children who had planned to greet him in front of City Hall. "The American president is acting like an elephant in a porcelain shop," observed Norwegian public relations expert Rune Morck-Wergeland. "In Norwegian culture, it's very important to keep an agreement. We're religious about that, and Obama's actions have been clumsy. You just don't say no to an invitation from a European king. Maybe Obama's advisers are not very educated about European culture, but he is coming off as rude, even if he doesn't mean to."[81]

CAN'T BE BOTHERED

Obama's impatience for dealing with the day to day details of his office has been widely noted. He has a big vision and doesn't enjoy getting his hands dirty in policy details, even legislation essential to his agenda. He had a grand vision for socialized medicine that pundits routinely called "Obama's plan," or "ObamaCare," but he didn't even have his own plan when the Senate passed its controversial healthcare bill on Christmas Eve 2009. He later announced the basic points of his plan, but it was all smoke and mirrors, because the only bill that had been passed, and stood a chance of being signed into law, was the Senate bill. And that bill contained provisions Obama claimed he didn't approve, and omitted essentials he promised his bill would contain. How else could he get away with lying about the fact that "his plan" would not include federal funding for abortion, for example, when the Senate bill clearly did?

By issuing his demands while standing outside the legislative process, Obama could deny accountability for controversial provisions of the healthcare bill. He was so far removed at times that

Republican senator Charles Grassley jabbed him for his "nerve" in going "sightseeing in Paris" while exhorting lawmakers back home to ramrod the bill through Congress.[82] He reluctantly learned his lesson when he was pressured into postponing a family trip to Indonesia to stay in Washington until the House voted on the Senate bill. By then, he realized he would have to personally twist arms of recalcitrant Democratic congressmen, some of whom, according to *Politico*, were "ducking" his calls.[83]

Obama also showed his aloofness in taking a Gulfstream Air Force jet with his wife for an expensive, taxpayer-supported date-night in New York City. So absorbed was this White House with photo-op-itis that it made the enormous blunder of dispatching a backup aircraft for Air Force One for a low-altitude flight over New York City, costing more than $300,000 and panicking some local residents who thought they were witnessing another 9/11-style attack.[84]

CLINICAL NARCISSISM?

The *Encyclopedia Britannica* defines narcissism as a "mental disorder characterized by extreme self-absorption, an exaggerated sense of self-importance, and a need for attention and admiration from others." If the condition is acute it can rise to the level of a disorder marked by "deeply ingrained and lasting patterns of inflexible, maladaptive, or antisocial behavior."[85] Narcissism is described in one physician-reviewed online health journal as featuring an "excessive preoccupation with self and lack of empathy for others; an exaggerated sense of the person's own importance and abilities. People with this trait believe themselves to be uniquely gifted."

They are "arrogant" and "egotistical" and are "often snobs." "They expect special treatment and concessions from others . . . and find it difficult to cope with criticism." They have "a powerful need to be admired" and are consumed with their own feelings, having an "inflated sense of their own importance and of the significance

of their achievements. . . . They feel entitled to great praise, attention, and deferential treatment by others, and have difficulty understanding or acknowledging the needs of others."[86]

The *Diagnostic and Statistical Manual of Mental Disorders (DSM
IV-TR)*, a diagnostic manual used by mental health professionals,
lists nine traits of a narcissist, at least five of which must be present
and continue for a substantial period of time for a diagnosis to be
made.[87] More than five of these traits easily apply to Obama.

1) Grandiose sense of self-importance.
2) Preoccupation with fantasies of unlimited success,
   power, beauty, or ideal love.
3) Sense of specialness, belief he can only be understood
   by or should associate only with other special or high-
   status individuals or institutions.
4) Need for excessive admiration.
5) Heightened sense of entitlement, leading to unreasonable expectations that others should treat him especially favorably or comply automatically with his
   expectations.
6) Tendency to be interpersonally exploitive. A person
   with NPD does not hesitate in taking advantage of others to meet his own ends.
7) Lack of empathy, an inability or unwillingness to recognize or identify with the feelings or needs of others.
8) An envy of other people, or conversely, a belief that
   other people envy him.
9) A tendency toward arrogant behavior or attitude.

A psychotherapist called "Robin of Berkeley" wrote a fascinating
and insightful profile of Obama on the *American Thinker* website,
analyzing whether Obama is a narcissist. She says that most highly
successful people have some degree of narcissism, and she acknowledges that the identifying attributes of a narcissist aren't always

clear-cut. She surmises that when people ask whether Obama is a narcissist, they aren't talking about the "garden variety narcissist," but more likely what M. Scott Peck called the "malignant narcissist" in his book *People of the Lie*. These types, she said, are "very dangerous creature[s] capable of great evil—the Hitler's of the world, as well as the SS guards." Peck's malignant narcissist is "a witch's brew of psychopathology: a narcissist, sociopath, and paranoid, with a generous dollop of delusional disorder thrown in."[88]

Robin admits she can't offer a definitive diagnosis of Obama, but believes there are reasons to be concerned about his character and his ability to "look reality squarely in the face." She explains that for people to become well-functioning adults they need to become attached to people in order to develop a capacity for empathy, and they must form a firm and solid identity through healthy role models. She traces Obama's background, detailing how unlikely it is that he acquired the essential personal relationships necessary to become a well-functioning adult. Without definitely stating whether Obama fits Peck's description of a malignant narcissist, Robin paints a picture that makes the possibility quite plausible.

Whether or not Obama ultimately fits the definition, his background is instructive for anyone trying to understand his personality and his attitudes, especially toward America and its system of government, its economic system, its record on race and foreign policy, and the overall character of its people. There is simply no way to understand Obama and his grandiose plans for America without examining relevant facts about his upbringing and mentorship.

Robin summarizes pertinent information about Obama's history that is on the public record. He was raised, she says, "with an odd assortment of characters who seemed to have no clue about the emotional needs of a child," and "dragged like a rag doll all over the place, and subjected to conditions that had to be disturbing and alienating." He was abandoned by both parents, "schlepped" from country to country, treated to an alcoholic stepfather and alcoholic father, and eventually left with his grandparents with whom he'd "arrived at an unspoken pact: . . . I could live with them and they'd leave me alone so long as I kept my troubles out of sight." His grandfather had been abandoned by his own father when he was eight, and he found the body of his mother after she had committed suicide. As an adult the grandfather was so disappointed he didn't have a son that he gave his daughter—Obama's mother—the male name "Stanley." Then he entrusted Obama's mentorship to Frank Marshall Davis, who was not only a Communist but also "a pedophile . . . an alcoholic, a racist, and a misogynist."[89]

According to Robin and others, Davis, who blamed racism and capitalism for most of society's ills and injustices, strongly influenced Obama. Obama's search for his own identity was answered when he concluded, under Davis's tutelage, that he "could wrap his mind around—rage at the system. Obama apparently became filled with resentment and anger even though he lived a privileged life in Hawaii." As Obama became an adult he surrounded himself with people of a similar worldview who "reinforced and hardened" his own beliefs, people such as the Reverend Jeremiah Wright, Bill Ayers, and even his wife Michelle, whose animus toward this country prior to Obama's ascension are quite well known. Robin concludes that dealing with the hardships he had encountered in life, "he made the personal political," transferring culpability from his parents and grandparents to racism and the system.

She says she hopes Obama is not, in the end, a malignant narcissist, but closes with a chilling description of such people from *People of the Lie*: "The evil are 'people of the lie,' deceiving others as they build layer upon layer of self-deception. . . . Evil may be recognized by its very disguise. . . . We see the smile that hides the hatred, the smooth and oily manner that masks the fury, the velvet glove that covers the fist. . . . The evil hate the light—the light of goodness that shows them up, the light of scrutiny that exposes them, the light of truth that penetrates their deception."[90]

James Lewis, also writing for *American Thinker*, further examines the question of Obama's narcissism. Lewis acknowledges many people talk like narcissists, such as when teenagers "get grandiose," but Obama has "turned all his grandiose talk into irrevocable action." He observes Obama might well be the most radical president in American history. "We don't have a national crisis today," writes Lewis. "Obama *is* a national crisis." Not only is he trying to cram his agenda down America's throat almost without regard for whether it will damage his chances for re-election, but he has exhibited consistently odd behavior over the last two years, from giving Hillary the finger in the campaign, to "thrilling to the sound of his own voice" in Berlin, to presuming to speak to the whole Muslim world in Cairo at the Al Azhar Mosque, to personally trying "to rescue a scientifically phony climate treaty in Copenhagen," to reacting with rage when Congressman Paul Ryan dismantled the fiscal credibility of ObamaCare straight to Obama's face during the healthcare summit.[91]

This final incident, by the way, seems eerily similar to M. Scott Peck's description of those hating "the light of truth that penetrates their deception." Even CNN aired a montage of Obama's peeved facial expressions at the healthcare summit. Host Candy Crowley observed, "All we're saying is this is not the face a man who ought to play poker anytime soon. Whether you heard it or saw it, the message was pretty clear, patience and the days of debating health care are growing short."

As Noel Sheppard of *NewsBusters* noted, this was a mild way of putting it. What Crowley would have said, had this been a Republican president, was, "The president acted like a spoiled child not only in front of America's leaders but also on national television. The President demonstrated a surprising lack of leadership and diplomacy with his behavior, and not at all what we expected from the most powerful man on the planet whose greatest skill was supposed to be communicating and being able to bring people together."[92]

This arrogance was evident in the sheer pretension of the ObamaCare legislation itself. Senator Lamar Alexander described ObamaCare as "the most brazen act of political arrogance since Watergate . . . in terms of thumbing your nose at the American people and saying 'We know you don't want it, but we're going to give it to you anyway.'"[93]

James Lewis could have cited many other examples of Obama's narcissistic behavior beyond the healthcare issue, from saying small town Americans "get bitter and they cling to guns or religion or antipathy toward people who aren't like them," to Obama's alarmingly pedestrian, unpresidential, $3 million, taxpayer-funded jaunt to Copenhagen, with his wife flying on a separate plane, to lobby for the Olympics to be held in his hometown of Chicago.[94] It was remarkable both in terms of Obama's audacity in believing he could personally deliver the prize, and his egotism in placing himself center stage in such an endeavor and in demeaning his office by reducing himself to a glorified sports agent.

But in Copenhagen it was evident he truly believed his very presence would make a difference. Additionally, it was a chance to demonstrate how the world already viewed this nation more favorably simply because he was now president. When his bid for the Olympics failed, his team blamed it on some nefarious activities among those making the decision. Aide David Axelrod said Obama is held in "very high esteem by leaders around the world," but "there are internal politics at the IOC [International Olympic Committee] that were at play," and the president's appearance didn't overcome them.[95] Clearly, it couldn't just be that the IOC believed the Olympics should be held elsewhere or, Heaven forbid, that Obama's presumptuous personal intervention backfired.

Lewis goes on to explore, without rendering a definitive opinion, whether Obama fits the description of a malignant narcissist by citing a partial checklist of attributes of such a person. The list includes a person's rage in reaction to criticism or resistance to accomplishing his grandiose goals; his grandiose sense of self-worth; his attempt to pull down the self-worth of others when he senses his own self-worth is under attack; and his two-faced personality where the creation of a "false-self" is linked to the narcissist's fear of being inadequate and results in his projecting a sense of superiority at all times.

Whether or not Obama can be fairly considered clinically narcissistic, it is hardly in doubt that he has a larger-than-life view of himself and his role in history ("when the rise of the oceans began to slow and our planet began to heal"); that he has grandiose plans ("transformational change"); that he expects to get his way simply by virtue of his self-perceived importance ("I won the election"); that he often reacts adversely to criticism ("I don't want them to do a lot of talking"); that he tries to bring others down who resist him and thus challenge his self-esteem (reminding John McCain "the election is over"); and that he attacks the honesty of those who challenge him (Senator McConnell's claims are "just plain false").

Surrounding himself with sycophants and egged on by an adoring media, Obama assumed the presidency with the arrogant ambition of transforming America. He believed he was The One—a visionary whose great deeds would be remembered generations from now. But while his charisma was a great asset on the campaign trail, as president he quickly found that his trademark oratory could not convince a skeptical nation of the wisdom of his extravagant plans. Moreover, his personal magnetism proved ineffective on foreign leaders—including those of our enemies, whose fists remain stubbornly clenched against us.

But rather than adjusting his policies to these unpleasant realities, he persisted—and still persists—in his maximalist course, convinced that his growing legion of critics simply doesn't comprehend the beneficence of his actions. The notion that his detractors, and the American people overall, *do* understand what he's doing, and that's precisely why they are increasingly hostile to his agenda, is an unacceptable concept to our budding autocrat.

Chapter Two

FRAUD AGAINST THE ELECTORATE

CRIMES AGAINST THE PUBLIC TRUST

President Obama came to office with a strong wind at his back. He established high expectations for himself, and the public took him at his word. He set himself up as having extraordinary gifts that could unite people around a new consensus to solve America's problems. Though distinctly ideological—the nonpartisan *National Journal* ranked him as the most liberal U.S. Senator in 2007[1]—he managed to convince many Americans he was above ideology and partisanship and was committed to implementing the best ideas, no matter on what side of the ideological spectrum they originated.

Even a disappointing number of conservative intellectuals came to believe he transcended ideology and possessed a refreshing mental acuity. Pete Wehner, former deputy assistant to President George W. Bush, admitted Obama was "an appealing figure to many Republicans" who "would find it hard to generate much enthusiasm in opposing him." Why? Because of his "eloquence," his "personal grace and dignity," and because he appeared to be a "well-grounded, decent, thoughtful man" who came across as "nonpartisan" and seemed to "transcend politics." "Even when he disagrees with people, he doesn't seem disagreeable," marveled Wehner. Beyond Obama's personal attributes, Wehner credited part of Obama's appeal to his message, which "at its core, is about unity and hope rather than division and resentment."[2]

Wehner's praise for Obama was no isolated incident. As conservative philosopher and columnist Thomas Sowell observed, many Republicans were planning to vote for Obama, Republicans whom fellow columnist Robert Novak labeled "Obamacons."[3] Pollster John Zogby said he had "polling showing one-fifth of conservatives supporting Obama."[4]

Christopher Buckley, the son of the godfather of modern conservatism, William F. Buckley Jr., endorsed Obama, citing his "first-class temperament" and "first-class intellect." Buckley acknowledged Obama is a "lefty" while insisting, "I am not. I am a small-government conservative who clings tenaciously and old-fashionedly to the idea that one ought to have balanced budgets." But, said Buckley, "I've read Obama's books, and they are first-rate." Oddly, Buckley persuaded himself that through the sheer power of his presumed intellect, Obama would "surely understand that traditional left-politics aren't going to get us out of this pit we've dug for ourselves."[5]

Similarly, Doug Kmiec, head of the Office of Legal Counsel under President Reagan and George H. W. Bush, endorsed Obama, believing "him to be a person of integrity, intelligence, and genuine good will." Like Buckley, Kmiec was impressed with Obama's books and what they supposedly revealed about his intelligence and bipartisanship. "I am convinced, based upon his public pronouncements and his personal writing, that on each of these questions [abortion, traditional marriage, constitutional interpretation, and religious freedom] he is not closed to understanding opposing points of view and, as best as it is humanly possible, he will respect and accommodate them."[6]

David Brooks, the *New York Times*' reputedly conservative columnist, gushed that he was "dazzled" by Obama's intellect, based on an interview with him where Obama effortlessly expostulated the "very subtle thought process" of Reinhold Neibuhr, which is "based on the idea that you have to use power while it corrupts you." Brooks was also impressed with Obama's "tremendous powers of social perception," in part, at least, because Obama noticed that Brooks, in a column he had written attacking the Republican Congress's excessive spending, had thrown in a few sentences attacking Democrats to make himself feel better.[7]

Francis Fukuyama, author and Professor of International Political Economy at Johns Hopkins University, a neo-conservative who had become disillusioned with the war in Iraq, endorsed Obama. Like Obama's other center-right supporters, Fukuyama expressed optimism in Obama's potential for "delivering a different kind of politics."[8] Scott McClellan, a former spokesman for President George W. Bush, jumped on the Obama bandwagon for similar reasons: in his view, Obama had "the best chance of changing the way Washington works." Ken Adelman, described by the *Wall Street Journal* as "a prominent conservative on foreign policy matters,"[9] told the *New Yorker* he was supporting Obama "primarily for two reasons, those of temperament and judgment."[10] Former Massachusetts governor William Weld, while by no means a staunch conservative, endorsed Obama as a "once-in-a-lifetime candidate who will transform our politics and restore America's standing in the world."[11]

Shortly before the election, former Reagan chief of staff Ken Duberstein announced his support for Obama.[12] Around the same time, a group of five former appointees of Republican president Dwight Eisenhower released a statement endorsing Obama, saying he "has the judgment, the intellect, the character, the vision, the values, the empathy, the natural leadership ability and the capacity to attract the most qualified people to his administration—all the qualities that would make him a great President."[13] Even the *Economist* magazine, whose editorial board is considered fiscally conservative, backed Obama, citing his "style, intelligence and discipline."[14]

THE EXPLOITATION OF A GIFT

Alas, Obama's self-portrait as a uniter was at best an exercise in self-delusion, at worst an example of old-fashioned deceit. As *Newsweek* revealed in its behind-the-scenes retrospective of the campaign, Obama knew he had a gift, "a way of making very smart, very accomplished people feel virtuous just by wanting to help Barack Obama." He exploited this talent in his successful run for president of the *Harvard Law Review* in the mid-1980s. Though his politics were "conventionally liberal," he garnered the support of conservatives because he "was a good listener, attentive, and empathetic, and his powerful mind could turn disjointed screeds into reasoned consensus." But there was something more—something deeper. As a black man, he appeared to have moved beyond racial politics and narrowly defined interest groups, seeming indifferent to "the politics of identity and grievance" and showing "no sense of entitlement or resentment."[15]

But, the article continued, "Obama had a way of transcending ambition, though he himself was ambitious as hell." *Newsweek* might as well have simply said Obama was not—at least as regards personal ambition—as he appeared. It could have made the same point regarding his seeming indifference to the politics of identity and grievance or his showing "no sense of entitlement or resentment."[16]

For in fact, while Obama talked a good game about having risen above race issues, eschewing any sense of entitlement, rejecting identity politics, and demonstrating a willingness to listen to all sides and bring them together into a magical consensus, the reality was starkly different. Obama's unifying facade only appeared when dealing in the generalities and routine doubletalk of a campaign. Once in office, when he began encountering resistance to his extreme liberal policy agenda, the congeniality and counterfeit bipartisanship withered away, to be replaced by the strident, arrogant, patronizing narcissism that brooked neither criticism nor opposition. His trademark "cool" also gave way, at times, to impulses of haughty impatience and intolerance to ideas outside his ideological comfort zone.

He proved to be anything but post-racial, as we saw in his Justice Department's summary dismissal of the slam-dunk case against New Black Panther Party members for voter intimidation. He was anything but post-partisan, as we saw in his repeated "calling out" of Republicans for their alleged dishonesty when they dared oppose his agenda on its merits. He was anything but post-grievance when he repeatedly denounced America's blemished history, for which it clearly had to atone.

And resentment? It permeated his every speech and policy proposal: resentment at America's history on race, resentment at capitalism for allowing disparities of income, resentment at America for consuming too many natural resources, resentment at America for its "arrogance" and "dismissiveness" and "imperialism" in dealing with other nations, and resentment at banks, corporations, insurance companies, pharmaceuticals, conservatives, and small-town Americans for all their supposed sins.

None of this should have surprised conservatives, especially self-described intellectual ones, who should have seen through his feigned centrism and bipartisanship to his uncompromising liberalism. Signs of his radicalism were everywhere, from his parents, mentors, and college and post-college associations, to his autobiographies, to his street organizing and other political activism in Chicago, to his record in the state senate and U.S. Senate, to his church and its illustrious, America-hating, racially obsessed, Marxist-leaning pastor, to his spontaneous statements on the presidential campaign trail.

Despite the gaping biographical holes and general mysteriousness of Obama's background, there was abundant information in the public domain to show, beyond doubt, that both of his natural parents, his stepfather, and his primary mentor Frank Marshall Davis were all radicals; that the pastor and church he chose were steeped in the Marxism and racialism of Black Liberation Theology; and that he associated and worked with leftist street activists in Chicago. Everything about his past pointed to radicalism.

In fact, during some unscripted moments on the campaign trail he couldn't conceal his redistributionist mindset, such as when he told Joe the Plumber he wanted to spread the wealth around, or confessed to Charlie Gibson during the primary presidential debate that he supported capital gains tax increases as "a matter of fairness," even knowing they would reduce tax revenue. Those who didn't see the unmistakable signs of Obama's radicalism were trying not to see them, for many of us were sounding the alarm bells. As Ben Domenech wrote in the *Washington Times* in June 2008, "Barack Obama has been ranked as the most liberal member of the United States Senate. He favors socialized health care, significant tax increases, abortion on demand. He is supported enthusiastically by George Soros, Walter Mondale, and Jimmy Carter. So why would any thinking conservative support Sen. Obama for president in 2008?"[17]

Why indeed? Well, as columnist Robert Novak wrote, "The Obamacon syndrome is based on hostility to Bush and his administration, and revulsion over today's Republican Party."[18] Conservatives were up in arms over the Republicans' dismal record on spending—a record that now seems relatively austere. Additionally, conservative elites felt revulsion at Bush's alleged anti-intellectualism and were growing disenchanted with the Iraq war—not to mention John McCain was hardly the conservatives' ideal candidate.

The "intellectual" conservatives were embarrassed by Bush and anxious to identify with one of their own. To some extent, it was no more complicated than a revenge of the nerds. They identified with Obama and their hubris drove them to get behind him as a form of self-approbation, elevating trappings of intellectualism above experience and certainly above ideology. For all their intelligence, they were either pathetically naïve or had engaged in self-deception about his "conservative values." They were willing to look the other way on his liberalism because they placed a higher emphasis on his supposed intelligence than on how he would use it. Former *National Review* editor Wick Allison, explaining his support for Obama,[19] pointed one reporter to an op-ed his conservative wife had penned for the *Dallas Morning News*. Hailing Obama as "prudent, thoughtful, and courageous," Christine Allison exclaimed that Obama's "life story embodies the conservative values that go to the core of my beliefs."[20]

Despite all their accolades for Obama, some Obamacons still seemed anxious he would end up governing like a liberal. Christopher Buckley declared, "If [Obama] raises taxes and throws up tariff walls and opens up the coffers of the DNB to bribe-money from the special interest groups ... then he will almost certainly reap a whirlwind that will make Katrina look like a balmy summer zephyr."[21] Likewise, Ken Adelman confessed, "I sure hope Obama is more open, centrist, sensible—dare I say, Clintonesque—than his liberal record indicates, than his cooperation with Nancy Pelosi and Harry Reid portends. If not I will be even more startled by my vote than I am now."[22]

But in fairness to the center-right intellectuals, Obama is a poseur who masked his liberalism to buttress his image as an exemplar of a new kind of politics. During his first Illinois state senate run in 1996, he sat for an interview and then filled out a questionnaire issued by a liberal Chicago non-profit group, revealing very liberal positions on key issues. He expressed opposition to parental notification on abortions, though later amended it to say he might support it for 12- or 13-year-olds, but no older. He flatly opposed the death penalty, and he supported bans on the sale, possession, and manufacture of guns.

During his presidential campaign, Obama's staff unconvincingly claimed the responses were filled out by a campaign aide who "unintentionally mischaracterize(d) his position," but they never explained the similarity of the respondent's handwriting to his own, nor did they refute *Politico's* finding that Obama himself actually sat for the interview and submitted the amended questionnaire.[23] Despite this evidence, Obama's campaign presented a fact sheet denying he ever held those views, insisting he "consistently supported the death penalty for certain crimes but backed a moratorium until problems were fixed," and "has consistently supported common-sense gun control, as well as the rights of law-abiding gun owners."[24]

Obama wouldn't own up to his liberalism throughout the entire presidential campaign. He took umbrage at anyone calling him a liberal. In one campaign speech he mocked his critics, saying,

> "Oh, he's liberal, he's liberal." Let me tell you something. There's nothing liberal about wanting to reduce money in politics. That is common sense. There's nothing liberal about wanting to make sure [our soldiers] are treated properly when they come home. . . . There's nothing liberal about wanting to make sure that everybody has healthcare. We are spending more on healthcare in this country than any other advanced country, but we've still got more uninsured. There's nothing liberal about saying that doesn't make sense, and we should do something smarter with our healthcare system.[25]

Some of those assertions may be correct, but there *is* something liberal—very liberal—about spending America into oblivion, resurrecting failed welfare schemes, kowtowing to big labor, nationalizing healthcare and automakers, and seeking to foist crushing energy and other taxes on the American people—all of which Obama has done or is trying to do as president.

COMMUNITY ORGANIZING WRAPPED IN A BIPARTISAN PACKAGE

Even if some conservative intellectuals were slow on the uptake, Obama's fellow liberals knew he was one of them. Mark Schmitt, executive editor of the *American Prospect* (subtitled "Liberal

Intelligence"), wrote about Obama's duplicity as early as late 2007—though Schmitt hardly used the pejorative "duplicity." He argued Obama was not so ideologically different from Hillary Clinton; rather, he was employing tactics designed to make him appear less ideological in order to advance his agenda. The two Democratic candidates, wrote Schmitt, though having similar ideologies, have different "assumptions about the current circumstance and how the levers of power can be used to get the country back on track."[26]

Schmitt rejected the claim of some leftists that Obama was naïve about "power and partisanship." He was playing the electorate, saying what it wanted to hear as a "tactic," a method of "subverting and breaking the unified conservative power structure." Political commentators, Schmitt argued, have a duty to "describe the [political] situation exactly." But if you're a presidential candidate, looking to impose "progressive governance," you have a duty to "subvert it. . . . Claiming the mantle of bipartisanship and national unity, and defining the problem to be solved (e.g., universal health care) puts one in a position of strength, and Republicans would defect from that position at their own risk."

In other words, seduce the people to vote for you with promises of hope and change and, once elected, enact transformational change the voters actually oppose. "The public, and younger voters in particular," wrote Schmitt, "seem to want an end to partisanship and conflictual politics, and an administration that came in with that premise (an option not available to Hillary Clinton), would have a tremendous advantage, at least for a moment."

"For a moment"—how prescient!

Obama's "bipartisan" approach, according to Schmitt, was "better positioned to take advantage" of the "math": persuading sufficient numbers of Republican senators to cross the aisle on issues such as healthcare in order to reach the filibuster-proof number of sixty votes, which Schmitt wrongly assumed Democrats would not achieve in the 2008 elections. Schmitt also maintained that Obama could use his skills as a "community organizer" to leverage his self-made reputation as a bipartisan against the Republicans' image as a "bad-faith opposition" party. You "draw the person in, treat them as if they were operating in good faith, and draw them into a conversation about how they actually would solve the problem. If they have nothing, it shows. And that's not a tactic of bipartisan Washington idealists—it's a hard-nosed tactic of community organizers, who are acutely aware of power and conflict. It's how you deal with intractable demands—put 'em on a committee. Then define the committee's mission your own way."[27]

Schmitt couldn't have been more accurate in analyzing Obama's strategy, which he employed, for example, in his bogus healthcare summit. Unhappily for Obama, Republicans didn't "have nothing." Obama did—and it showed. Congressional Republicans like Paul Ryan and Eric Cantor deftly challenged his dubious assertions, frustrating Obama and robbing him of his trademark eloquence. Obama tried to stigmatize his Republican challengers during and after the summit, but his plan backfired, as he revealed his own pettiness, partisanship, and dogmatism.

The *New Republic's* Jonathan Chait, who once penned a hysterical screed against George W. Bush saying he hated almost everything about him,[28] recently wrote about the difference between Obama's inclusive rhetoric and actual practice, all but admitting Obama's deceit—and apparently approving it. "I still find it strange," wrote Chait, "how little understood President Obama's political method is. The first person I know who identified it is Mark Schmitt, over two years ago. At the time, many liberals viewed Obama's inclusive rhetoric as a sign that he intended to capitulate the liberal agenda for the sake of winning Republican agreement. Schmitt disagreed. Obama's language is highly conciliatory, he wrote, but the method isn't."[29]

In a previous piece, Chait had likened Obama's approach to Republicans to his approach to "foreign enemies like the Iranian regime: take them up on their claim to some shared goal (nuclear disarmament, health care reform), elide their preferred red herrings, engage them seriously, and then expose their disingenuousness." Chait wrote, "This apparent paradox is one reason Obama's political identity has eluded easy definition. On the one hand, you have a disciple of the radical community organizer Saul Alinsky turned ruthless politician. On the other hand, there is the conciliatory post-partisan idealist. The mistake here is in thinking of these two notions as opposing poles. In reality it's all the same thing. Obama's defining political trait is the belief that conciliatory rhetoric *is* a ruthless strategy." Bingo, but it gets even better:

> Obama's health care summit is a classic example of the Obama method. Once again, skeptics are viewing it as a plot that depends on securing Republican cooperation.... That's not the point. Obama knows perfectly well that the Republicans have no serious proposals to address the main problems of the health care system and have no interest (or political room, given their crazy base) in handing him a victory of any substance. Obama is bringing them in to discuss health care so he can expose this reality. [30]

Chait understands Obama's method. Why don't conservative "intellectuals?"

OBAMA'S NO RONALD REAGAN

But Obama's deception about his liberalism was not as simple a ruse to pull off as his charade as a bipartisan, nor has he employed it as deftly as Bill Clinton executed his strategy to sell himself as a New Democrat and Third Way politician. Clinton was a card-carrying member of the reputedly centrist Democratic Leadership Council and far more willing to compromise his agenda and deviate from his true ideology if it would increase his popularity or divert attention from his myriad scandals. In a speech to the DLC in 1993 he hailed its approach of infusing "new ideas and new energy, a new direction and reinvigoration into the party that most of us belong to by heritage, instinct, and conviction." He went on to express his fealty to the DLC's commitment to bringing the Democratic Party closer to the center on fiscal and national security policies.[31]

Obama's task was more complex, both because he had greater ambitions than Clinton and because he was less inclined to compromise, being far more of a leftist ideologue than Clinton. Obama said he saw himself as a transformative figure like Ronald Reagan; he truly intended to "fundamentally change" America. Of course, ideologically, Obama was the anti-Reagan, who intended to undo what remained of the Reagan agenda as well as that of the 1994 Republican Contract with America. But he couldn't afford to let Americans know that (any more than he already had through his previous activism, his liberal voting record, and his unscripted comments), because America is still a center-right nation, even if many Americans were disenchanted with Republicans at the time Obama was running.

Obama held himself out as transformative all right, but also above ideology. It's difficult to be transformative from the center, however, or even to make that case. In the end, that's a major reason Obama's campaign was so filled with platitudes and vague, emotional catch phrases such as "hope" and "change." By luck he came onto the presidential scene when we were beset by financial crises and the public had grown weary of the Iraq war. Obama seized on the public's mood, played their fears like a virtuoso musician, and depicted America as being in dire straights from which only he could deliver us. By playing up the crisis mentality, and with unprecedented support and cover from the press, he was able to get away with his vacuous slogans without ever defining them.

It didn't take long for Obama to reveal his true colors once in office. He had sold himself as post-racial, bipartisan, sagacious and mature beyond his years, effortlessly fluent and articulate, moderate, transparent, honest, non-ideological, and open to opposing views. But inside a few months, he showed himself to be deeply racial, aggressively partisan, grossly incompetent, often verbally awkward apart from his teleprompter, an inflexible liberal ideologue, secretive, dishonest, undemocratic, dogmatic and dictatorial, and intolerant and dismissive of his opposition.

His signature "charismatic charm" and "congeniality" soon degenerated into what *Washington Examiner* White House correspondent Julie Mason described as his "irritation, imperiousness and dissatisfaction." "More than a year later" wrote Mason, "a different picture of Obama is emerging. Impatient with gainsayers and frustrated with political process, the president seems increasingly disenchanted as progress on his own agenda remains elusive." She quoted Republican strategist Kevin Madden saying, "The entire 2008 Obama campaign was built around a cult of personality. He is totally lacking the kind of leadership skills you forge after a long time on Capitol Hill."[32] In fact, at this point Obama's incompetent leadership had only begun to emerge, as we later realized with his disastrous mismanagement of the Gulf oil spill.

We'll take a closer look in the next several chapters at how Obama's true nature and personal attributes emerged during his first year-plus in office, and revealed that he was nothing like the messianic figure he had presented himself to be, in attitude or substance.

Chapter Three

THE LIAR

CRIMES AGAINST GOOD GOVERNANCE
AND THE OFFICE OF THE PRESIDENCY

O bama was certainly duplicitous on the campaign trail, but he's been even more deceitful in office. As an *Investors Business Daily* op-ed noted, "Barack Obama has an elastic (capable of being stretched) approach to reality. Facts that do not suit him are set aside and replaced with fabrications. . . . He is a master practitioner of sophistry. . . . In Washington, nearly everything said or done is calculated to deceive. Many of its residents are of the fabulist persuasion, but none compares to Obama."[1]

While the typically cynical view is that all presidents break campaign promises, the truth is that some—like Obama—are worse than others. Not only has he already broken an astounding number of core campaign promises, but he's done so with brazen dishonesty; when he breaks a promise, he simply changes it—retrospectively. Everything about him reeks of Alinskyite, end-justifies-the-means politics. It's as if he's saying he owes the electorate no moral obligation to live up to his promises, so long as he fundamentally transforms America—not in the ways he led us to believe he would, but toward a socialist utopia he *knows* will be better for us even though we disagree. What are a few hundred broken promises en route to nirvana? Let's review a smattering of Obama's broken promises and other deceits.

TRANSPARENCY

Obama promised to be the most transparent president in history and make himself readily available to the press—but at one point went over 300 days without a press conference. He has also been strongly critical of "foot high" budgets being "rushed through without any deliberation or debate." The official White House website says, "Transparency—President Obama has committed to making his administration the most open and transparent in history, and WhiteHouse.gov will play a major role in delivering on that promise." It further vows, "One significant addition to WhiteHouse.gov reflects a campaign promise from the President: we will publish all non-emergency legislation to the website for five days. And allow the public to review and comment before the President signs it."[2] Obama made the same promise during the campaign: "When there is a bill that ends up on my desk as a president, you the public will have five days to look online and find out what's in it before I sign it, so that you know what your government is doing."[3]

Obama grossly and repeatedly breached this promise. He signed the Lilly Ledbetter Fair Pay Restoration Act on January 20, 2009—two days after it passed Congress. He signed the State Children's Health Insurance Program three hours after Congress passed it. He waited one business day to sign the enormous, far-reaching, $800 billion stimulus bill.[4] The Cato Institute's Jim Harper reported that as of April 13, 2009, Obama had broken this five-day posting pledge ten—arguably eleven—times out of the eleven bills he had signed. He only bothered to post six of the eleven bills on the website, and none were posted for a full five days. Only the DTV Delay Act came close.

Harper discounted the occasional White House efforts to satisfy the pledge by posting a bill while it was still pending in Congress, because they didn't give the public ample time to review the *final* legislation. Most of the bills Obama signed, as those mentioned above, were signed within a day or two from their presentment from Congress. Other bills he signed without posting for five days include an appropriations bill and the omnibus spending bill.[5] On the transformative ObamaCare legislation, the House passed the bill Sunday night, March 21, 2010, and Obama signed it two days later.

During the Democratic presidential primary campaign, Obama promised (the promise being captured on videotape no fewer than eight separate times)[6] he would televise the healthcare debates on C-SPAN, in contrast to the Clintons' attempt in the 1990s to broker HillaryCare behind closed doors. At a debate in Los Angeles on January 31, 2008, he declared, "That's what I will do in bringing all parties together, not negotiating behind closed doors, but bringing all parties together, and broadcasting those negotiations on C-SPAN so that the American people can see what the choices are, because part of what we have to do is enlist the American people in this process."

But until the final few weeks of the process, he wouldn't even allow Republicans to participate, much less open the process to the cameras. When asked about it in an interview, he dissembled, saying, "Now, keep in mind, most of the action was in Congress, so every committee hearing that was taking place, both in the House and the Senate, those were all widely televised. The only ones that were not were meetings that I had with some of the legislative leadership trying to get a sense from them in terms of what it was that they were trying to do." Only after that qualifier did he grudgingly concede it was a "fair criticism."[7] *PolitiFact* agreed, declaring his promise "broken."[8]

In a townhall meeting a few days later, Obama rationalized his broken pledge again, saying it was "tricky" because if the proceedings were televised, some participants would just "posture" instead of debating honestly.[9] He later admitted in an interview with ABC's Diane Sawyer that he would "own up" to his broken promise, but even here, he characterized it as a "legitimate mistake" as if it had been unintentional. He also employed another Clintonesque personal accountability dodge in pretending he had played a passive role, assuring us he'd be addressing the fact that "the process didn't run the way I ideally would like it to."[10]

Pushing bills through Congress without the promised transparency was part of the Obama administration's overall strategy to weaken the impact of any organized opposition. Another component of that strategy was to overwhelm the opposition with the sheer volume of programs the White House pushed at any one time, thus impeding Republicans' ability to coordinate effective opposition.

But Obama doesn't just owe the public answers about being AWOL on White House press conferences, his conducting of healthcare meetings in secret, or his failure to post bills in a timely manner on his website. We also deserve answers on his broken promises concerning lobbyists and, more consequential, his surreptitious packaging of unpopular provisions in larger pieces of legislation to avoid public scrutiny. These include his reversal of the highly successful welfare reform of the 1990s and his establishment of a super medical bureaucratic board (which some call a "death panel"), both of which were contained in his "stimulus" bill,[11] as well as the government takeover of student loans buried within the ObamaCare bill.

He should come clean about myriad other deceptions as well: his townhall meetings where he took questions only from planted supporters; his phony assertions of executive privilege; his punitive firing of AmeriCorps watchdog Gerald Walpin for investigating his friend; his administration's lack of accessibility on stimulus fund data; and his Justice Department's dismissal of the already-won voter intimidation case against New Black Panther Party members, along with DOJ's subsequent stonewalling of both the Civil Rights Commission and a Freedom of Information Act request by the *Washington Times* seeking reasons for the arbitrary dismissal.

He should explain his frequent denials of other FOIA requests; his FCC's shielding of diversity czar Mark Lloyd from media questions about his past advocacy of using federal regulations to squelch conservative talk radio; his withholding of documents requested by Republicans from private meetings between the White House and medical providers; his withholding of data from the Cash for Clunkers program;[12] his hiding of information on the expenditure of union dues; his failed effort to exclude FOX News from access to his pay czar, Kenneth Feinberg; and his "secret slush fund . . . for taxes and spending on climate change hidden inside the administration's 2011 budget," as reported by FOX News.[13]

BIPARTISANSHIP

Bipartisanship was unquestionably a central theme of Obama's campaign. When he introduced Joe Biden as his vice presidential running mate, he proclaimed Biden would "help me turn the page on the ugly partisanship in Washington, so we can bring Democrats and Republicans together to pass an agenda that works for the American people." In *USA Today* Obama wrote, "The only way to end the petty partisanship that has consumed Washington for so long and make a difference in the lives of ordinary Americans is by bringing Democrats and Republicans together to pass an agenda that works for the American people."[14]

But as president, Obama deliberately and consistently cordoned Republicans off from the political process. He didn't pass an agenda that "works for the American people," but one that contradicted their express will. Only three Republican senators and no House Republicans supported his "stimulus" bill, while no GOP senators and no GOP House members voted for ObamaCare. In fact, the only evident bipartisanship was the opposition to ObamaCare in the House, where thirty-four Democrats joined all the Republicans in voting nay.[15]

"HE'S BEGINNING TO NOT BE BELIEVABLE TO ME"

Don't confuse actual bipartisanship with Obama's feints toward bipartisanship in order to advance his agenda. We saw this opportunism in his offer to drop the $50 billion fund in the financial reform bill, which sounds major but would not constitute any substantive change. We saw it in his false assertion that he'd adopted numerous Republican ideas in his healthcare bill. We saw it in his belated push for offshore oil drilling, his promise to jump start nuclear energy production, and his duplicitous overtures to the coal industry after he had promised to bankrupt it. Addressing Obama's stated commitment to coal, Senator Jay Rockefeller complained Obama "says it in his speeches, but he doesn't say it in [his 2011 budget proposal]. He doesn't say it in the actions of [EPA Administrator] Lisa Jackson. And he doesn't say it in the minds of my own people. And he's beginning to not be believable to me."[16]

We saw the same counterfeit bipartisanship in Obama's pretend promise to look into tort reform as a means to curb some "defensive medicine [that] may be contributing to unnecessary costs"—while his Health and Human Services Department stated in a congressional staff report that medical malpractice reform was "not a priority" of the administration.[17] A comically weak provision eventually made its way into the final healthcare bill, involving a negligible $50 million grant to states to launch "demonstration projects" to test tort reform. Lisa Rickard, president of the U.S. Chamber of Commerce's Institute for Legal Reform, commented, "I don't know anybody who thinks this is actual medical-liability reform, or finds this meaningful at all.... The bill is a demonstration of the interests of the trial bar over the views of the American people."[18]

CAMPAIGN CONTRIBUTIONS
PolitiFact called Obama out on his boast that "the vast majority of the money I got was from small donors all across the country." It reported that the nonpartisan Campaign Finance Institute found that though Obama raised more than his opponents from small donors, that money did not constitute the majority of the funds he raised. In the primary, he received 30 percent of his money from those who gave $200 or less, 28 percent from those giving between $201 and $999, and 43 percent from those contributing at least $1,000. In the general election, 34 percent of his funds came from small donors ($200 or less), 23 percent from those giving between $201 and $999, and 42 percent gave $1,000 or more. While Obama claims he won the presidency without much money from large donors, the evidence shows otherwise. Overall, said *PolitiFact*, Obama's statement was "false."[19]

CONVOKING COMMISSIONS
During the campaign, Obama attacked Senator McCain for proposing a commission to study the economic crisis, calling it an effort to "pass the buck." "We know how we got into this mess," Obama declared, asserting he could provide the "leadership" we need to get out of it. Obama had a point—except in 2010, President Obama formed, among other bodies, the National Commission on Fiscal Responsibility and Reform—the exact kind of board he'd blasted McCain for advocating.[20]

ENDING NO-BID CONTRACTS
Candidate Obama said in Grand Rapids on October 2, 2008, "I will finally end the abuse of no-bid contracts once and for all. The days of sweetheart deals for Halliburton and the like will be over when I'm in the White House." Early in his first term he signed a memo pledging to "dramatically reform the way we do business

on contracts across the entire government." He promised to "end unnecessary no-bid and cost-plus contracts.... In some cases, contracts are awarded without competition.... And that's unacceptable."

But less than a year later, his administration awarded a $25 million no-bid federal contract for work in Afghanistan to Checchi & Company, a firm owned by a major donor to Democratic campaigns. Unlike some of the no-bid scenarios for which Obama and other demagogic leftists condemned President Bush, Checchi & Company, according to FOX News' sources, was "but one of a number of private firms capable of performing the work in Afghanistan for which USAID retained it."[21] In fact, Assistant Secretary of State P. J. Crowley, when questioned by FOX News about this no-bid award in light of Obama's campaign pledge, admitted, "You make a valid point. If you want to say this violates the basis on which this administration came into office and campaigned, fair enough." Amidst public criticism, the contract was eventually terminated.[22]

EARMARKS

In Green Bay, Wisconsin, candidate Obama declared, "The truth is our earmark system...is fraught with abuse. It badly needs reform—which is why I didn't request a single earmark last year, why I've released all my previous requests for the public to see, why I've pledged to slash earmarks by more than half when I am president of the United States." He said he would return earmarks to "less than $7.8 billion a year, the level they were before 1994." Yet once in office, he quickly broke this promise—apart from his $800 billion "stimulus" bill, which could be said to be one gigantic package of earmarks.

Although the $410 billion omnibus spending bill had more than 8,500 earmarks, Obama didn't blink before signing it. When questioned about his hypocrisy, Obama and his administration were typically disingenuous and dismissive. OMB Director Peter Orszag said, "We want to just move on. Let's get this bill done. Get it into law and move forward." In other words, *We have more important things to focus on than keeping our silly campaign promises. There's nothing to see here; move on.* Obama's chief of staff, Rahm Emanuel, passed it off as a kept promise because Obama had already passed the "major economic recovery act" and the "children's healthcare bill," which he said were both "earmark free." Both Emanuel and Orszag declared, "This is last year's business."[23] That is, it's Bush's fault.

Taxpayers for Common Sense reported that for the fiscal year 2010, appropriations bills contained 9,499 congressional earmarks worth $15.9 billion, up from $15.6 billion the previous year. Thus, Obama has not only failed to slash earmarks in half or to the 1994 level of $7.8 billion, but on his watch they've actually increased.[24]

LOBBYISTS

President Obama said in January 2010, "We must take action on both ends of Pennsylvania Avenue to end the outsized influence of lobbyists; to do our work openly; and to give our people the government they deserve. That's what I came to Washington to do. That's why—for the first time in history—my Administration posts our White House visitors online. And that's why we've excluded lobbyists from policy-making jobs or seats on federal boards and commissions."

Yet his words had a remarkably short shelf life. Upon taking office, Obama signed the Executive Order on Ethics Commitments, which prohibited lobbyists from working in his administration for two years on issues for which they had lobbied. But he repeatedly exempted people from the rule. He granted a waiver for Defense Secretary Bill Lynn just two days after he signed the Executive Order, and later exempted Jocelyn Frye and Cecelia Muñoz as well. *PolitiFact* reported that in all, as of January 27, 2010, the White House had issued seven waivers to its ethics rules, which apply to lobbyists and to people who served as officers and directors of a company or organization, while executive branch agencies have issued an additional fifteen waivers.[25] Always ready with an excuse, the administration claimed Frye and Muñoz were appointed "because of the importance of their respective positions and because of each woman's unequaled qualifications for her job."[26] Of course, that could be said of nearly every lobbyist-appointee; by definition they have expertise in the area in which they lobbied.

Obama's broken pledge to curtail the influence of lobbyists is perhaps best exposed through a mere partial list of former lobbyists serving in his administration. The list includes: Deputy Defense Secretary William Lynn (lobbyist for Defense Contractor Raytheon); Attorney General Eric Holder (clients included Global Crossing); Agriculture Secretary Tom Vilsack (lobbied for the National Education Association); Deputy Health and Human Services Secretary William Corr (lobbied for Campaign for Tobacco-Free Kids); Deputy Interior Secretary David Hayes (clients included San Diego Gas & Electric); Mark Patterson, Timothy Geithner's chief of staff (lobbied for Goldman Sachs); Vice President Joe Biden's chief of staff Ron Klain (clients included the Coalition for Asbestos Resolution, U.S. Airways, and Airborne Express); Mona Sutphen, deputy White House chief of staff (clients included Angliss International in 2003); Melody Barnes, domestic policy council director (lobbied for liberal advocacy groups); Cecilia Muñoz, White House director of intergovernmental affairs (lobbied for Hispanic advocacy organization the National Council of La Raza); and Patrick Gaspard, White House political affairs director (lobbyist for the Service Employees International Union).[27]

BUDGET ACCOUNTING GIMMICKS

Obama promised to end budgetary accounting gimmicks used by his whipping boy predecessor, George W. Bush, yet ObamaCare was defined by egregious budgetary gimmicks. As Pete Wehner, a senior fellow at the Ethics and Public Policy Center, noted, in

Obama's speech to a joint session of Congress he claimed to have identified $2 trillion in "savings," but $1.6 trillion of those were based on the Iraq surge continuing for ten more years, even though Obama had promised to promptly discontinue the surge.[28] Even *New York Times* Obamacon David Brooks acknowledged ObamaCare was "stuffed. . . . with gimmicks and dodges designed to get a good score from the Congressional Budget Office but don't genuinely control runaway spending."[29]

THE FREE MARKET

In an interview with *Bloomberg Business Week*, Obama called himself a "fierce advocate" of the free market. "You would be hard pressed," he said, "to identify a piece of legislation that we have proposed out there that, net, is not good for businesses."[30] In a speech in New York City on April 22, 2010, while stumping for his financial reform bill, Obama averred, "As I said two years ago on this stage, I believe in the power of the free market."

It's noteworthy that no other president has felt the need to repeatedly make that point. Does he protest too much? Well, in New York, he couldn't even wait a full paragraph to qualify his statement. He added, "But a free market was never meant to be a free license to take whatever you can get, however you can get it."[31] Whoever said it was? And what system of laws ever permitted such a thing by the private sector? One wonders why we don't hear Obama apply the same qualifier to the power of the federal government; could he bring himself to say, "But the federal government was never supposed to have a license to take whatever it can get, however it can get it"?

In fact, as Obama continually protested that he loved capitalism, he was doing everything in his power to permanently dismantle much of it in the United States, from his auto takeover, to ObamaCare, to cap and trade, to the financial overhaul bill.

Along the same lines, Obama said he wanted to "disabuse people of this notion that somehow we enjoy meddling in the private sector." In that case, perhaps he regrets having taken over GM and Chrysler, firing its CEOs and its board of directors, intervening by force in the mortgage business, interfering with existing private contracts, subsuming one-sixth of the economy with ObamaCare, trying to saddle businesses with stifling cap and trade laws, preventing TARP companies from paying their loans back, setting executive compensation, demonizing the insurance industry and Big Pharma, and paving the way for the abolition of private health insurers.

FISCAL HAWK

With a straight face, Obama characterizes himself as a fiscal hawk, vowing to usher in a "new era of responsibility," to rise above petty politics, and to cut the deficit in half by the end of his term—all while submitting bankrupting ten-year budgets. He says he wants to steer America "from an era of borrow and spend" to one of "save and invest." The CBO, meanwhile, reported that the national debt would double in six years under Obama and triple in ten years.

READ MY LIPS—SORT OF

During the campaign, Obama said, "I can make a firm pledge. Under my plan, no family making less than $250,000 a year will see any form of tax increase. Not your income tax, not your payroll tax, not your capital gains taxes, not any of your taxes."[32] But just weeks into his presidency, Obama violated his pledge by signing a law to triple the federal excise tax on cigarettes, from 39 cents to $1.01 per pack—a tax that would fall hardest on individuals and families making far less than $250,000 per year.[33] When questioned about this, White House press secretary Robert Gibbs flippantly responded, "People make a decision to smoke."

Later, when asked whether Obama's tax pledge applied to his healthcare plan, Gibbs replied, "The statement didn't come with caveats." But smoking was precisely such a caveat, and healthcare quickly became another one. Obama brazenly denied an excise tax on the uninsured—which was part of a healthcare reform proposal drafted by his Democratic ally, Montana senator Max Baucus— would violate his pledge. In fact, he was visibly irritated when ABC's George Stephanopoulos invoked a dictionary definition of "tax" to contradict him, shooting back, "I absolutely reject that notion." At many other times, Obama's various spokespersons refused to answer the question, employing evasions like, "We're going to do what's necessary," "It is never a good idea to absolutely rule things out, no matter what," and "We're going to let the process work its way through."[34]

Obama himself has tried to weasel out of his "firm pledge," saying on February 9, 2010, in an interview in the Oval Office, that he was "agnostic" on whether his budget commission should consider raising taxes as a deficit-fighting measure. "The whole point of it is to make sure that all ideas are on the table. So what I want to do is to be completely agnostic, in terms of solutions."[35] Continuing to meander all over the board, he said on April 10, 2010, that his pledge, which he made in the campaign and vacillated into agnosticism in February, now only applied to income taxes. "And one thing we have not done is raise income taxes on families making less than $250,000. That's another promise we've kept."[36] In fact, he did not keep that promise because that was not the promise he made. His new focus solely on income taxes was an implicit acknowledgement that his tax hike on cigarettes had already broken his actual promise not to raise "any of your taxes."

And we're in store for even more tax increases via ObamaCare. Americans for Tax Reform broke down the policy "by the numbers" revealing a startling expansion in the federal government. Among their findings, the healthcare bill will include nineteen new tax increases, seven of which "unquestionably violate" Obama's "firm pledge" not to raise "any form" of taxes on families making less than $250,000. Furthermore, the bill will have $497 billion worth of tax increases over the first decade it is effective; increase the top federal tax rate on wages and self-employment earnings to 43.4 percent; increase the annual tax for every man, woman, and child in America by $165; increase the top federal tax rate on early distributions from Health Savings Accounts to 59.6 percent (how's that for promoting thrift?); and limit the "currently unlimited" amount parents of special-needs children can save tax-free for tuition in Flexible Spending Accounts to $2,500.[37]

Republicans on the House Ways and Means Committee cite fourteen tax hikes on middle class families in ObamaCare totaling more than $316 billion, including a new tax on individuals who do not purchase government-approved health insurance; a new tax on employers who fail to fully comply with government health insurance mandates; a new 40 percent excise tax on certain high-cost health plans; a new ban on the purchase of over-the-counter drugs using funds from FSAs, HSAs, and HRAs; an increase, from 7.5 percent to 10 percent of income, on the threshold after which individuals can deduct out of pocket medical expenses; a new $2,500 annual cap on FSA contributions; a new annual tax on health insurance; a new annual tax on brand name pharmaceuticals; a new 2.3 percent excise tax on certain medical devices; a doubling of the penalty for non-qualified HSA distributions; a further increase in the tobacco tax with expanded enforcement authority; and an extension of federal unemployment surtaxes through June 2011.[38]

CAP AND TAX

Obama also attempted to violate his tax pledge with the Waxman-Markey cap-and-trade bill. In testimony before the Senate Republican Conference, Heritage Foundation expert Ben Lieberman described the bill as "nothing more than an energy tax in disguise," and "the most convoluted attempt at economic central planning this nation has ever attempted." The way the bill works, Lieberman explained, is by "raising the cost of energy high enough so that individuals and businesses are forced to use less of it." It's about "inflicting economic pain" to ensure the "emissions targets will be met."

Cap and trade is a tax in all but name—and a massive one at that. Heritage estimates for a household of four, energy costs will increase by $436 the first year it's in effect, reach $1,241 by 2035, and average $829 per year in increased costs over that period. Electricity costs are projected to increase 90 percent by 2035, gasoline by 58 percent, and natural gas by 55 percent. The cumulative direct costs for a family of four by 2035 will be an astounding $20,000. But since these higher energy costs will cause prices on many other items to increase, Heritage projects the average annual cost for a family of four between 2012 and 2035 will be even higher—$2,979.

Lieberman also estimates manufacturing net job losses averaging 1.14 million at any given time from 2012 through 2035. The hardest hit sector will be farming, whose profits are expected to drop by a staggering average of 57 percent between 2012 and 2035. This would put American farmers at a "global disadvantage" if, as is expected, competing food exporting nations are saddled with no such burdens.

The bill's stunning overall impact is projected to be an average reduction of gross domestic product by $393 billion annually between 2012 and 2035 for a cumulative loss of $9.4 trillion. Lieberman concludes, "In other words, the nation will be $9.4 trillion poorer with Waxman-Markey than without it."[39]

Highlighting the profound disingenuousness and hypocrisy of the Obama Democrats, this horrendous piece of legislation hurts low-income households the most, because they spend a disproportionate share of their incomes on energy. And it is extremely doubtful the bill's proposed rebates to low-income families will offset the enormous net losses they will sustain.

VAT

On April 21, 2010, Obama suggested a new value-added tax on Americans is still on the table. This was just two days after White House spokesman Robert Gibbs insisted a VAT "is not something the President has proposed nor is it under consideration."[40]

Of course, adopting a VAT would flagrantly breach his promise not to raise taxes. Yet on April 27, 2010, as he was discussing the first meeting of his National Commission on Fiscal Responsibility, Obama attacked the media for even asking whether he would still honor his no-new-taxes pledge:

> Our friends in the media, will ask me and others once a week or once a day about what we're willing to rule out or rule in. That's an old Washington game and it's one that has made it all but impossible in the past for people to sit down and have an honest discussion about putting our country on a more secure fiscal footing. So I want to deliver this message today: We're not playing that game. I'm not going to say what's in. I'm not going to say what's out. I want this commission to be free to do its work.[41]

Clearly, Obama can't allow pesky questions about old promises to obstruct his quest to transform America.

ELIMINATION OF CAPITAL GAINS TAX

In his so-called comprehensive tax plan, Obama promised on the campaign trail to end capital gains taxes for small businesses. His advisers Austan Goolsbee and Jason Furman affirmed the promise a few weeks prior to the election. Although his stimulus bill raised the 50 percent gain exemption to 75 percent, it did not eliminate it.[42] Moreover, it is no secret that Obama plans on increasing the capital gains tax rate from 15 percent to 20 percent.[43] His new 3.8 percent Medicare tax also constitutes a capital gains tax increase, as well as a tax on dividends.

JOBS: "THE MOST IMPORTANT DOMESTIC PRIORITY"

In his first State of the Union address, Obama said, "That is why jobs must be our number one focus in 2010 and that is why I am calling for a new jobs bill tonight." After canceling his trip to Asia a few months later to lobby for final passage of ObamaCare, Obama told an Indonesian TV reporter that healthcare is the "most important domestic priority here in the United States."[44]

UNEMPLOYMENT

Obama insisted unemployment would spiral out of control unless Congress passed his stimulus bill, which he said would boost the economy and keep the unemployment rate below 8 percent. Yet more than a year after the bill passed, unemployment continued to hover between 9 and 10 percent. Long before that, in July 2009, *Time* magazine declared that the "$787-billion stimulus plan is turning out to be far less stimulating than its architects expected" and was "failing by its own measure."[45]

That obvious conclusion didn't keep Obama's advisers from blithely bragging about the bill's supposed benefits. But for the bill, we are told, we would have faced financial collapse—something very likely false, but in any event, impossible to disprove. Other Democrats offered different excuses for Obama's failed promise, claiming the stimulus had not failed (to say otherwise would be a breach of faith in liberal orthodoxy), but that Obama's advisers had simply underestimated the magnitude of Bush's economic crisis. That excuse barely passes the laugh test when you consider the degree of urgency Obama brought to the discussion, as when he stated as president-elect that the nation needed to address the "great and growing" economic crisis.[46]

STATE OF THE UNION SPEECH

Amazingly, the Associated Press followed Obama's 2010 State of the Union speech with a damning fact check.[47] The AP and many others savaged Obama's credibility, as the following examples amply illustrate:

- Obama said that starting in 2011 he would "freeze government spending for three years" except for national
  security, Medicare, Medicaid, and Social Security. Yet
  during the campaign, he ridiculed Senator McCain for
  a similar proposal, saying it was "using a hatchet where
  you need a scalpel." Tellingly, his proposed freeze
  wouldn't quite even make it to the scalpel level. The
  Cato Institute reported the freeze only covers 13 percent
  of the total federal budget, and doesn't cover the enormous spending mandated under the stimulus bill.[48]

  Heritage Foundation scholars report Obama did
  not even propose a real freeze because it would not be
  imposed across the board, but would simply adjust priorities within categories. Without controls on the
  fastest growing budgetary items, i.e., entitlements, any
  attempt to bring the budget under control is a farce.
  Nor was it clear whether the freeze would begin at pre-
  stimulus levels or at the artificially higher levels following Obama-budgeting. As Heritage put it, "The simple
  fact is this: no matter how they spin it, the President
  must hold spending level with last year—minus all the
  temporary stimulus, TARP and other bailout spending—otherwise this freeze is a fakeroo."[49]
- Obama said ObamaCare "would preserve the right of
  Americans who have insurance to keep their doctor and
  their plan."[50] But he knew his plan had no such guarantee, and he also knew the plan would likely crowd out
  private insurers. The chief actuary of the Medicare program estimates 14 million people will lose their
  employer coverage under ObamaCare, even though
  many will want to keep it.[51] In fact, many companies are
  now evaluating whether they can save money by paying
  the penalty in lieu of providing their employees healthcare coverage. AT&T, Caterpillar, John Deere, and Ver-

izon have all made their internal calculations, and those results don't portend well for their employees.[52]

Additionally, *Investors Business Daily* reported that internal White House documents show ObamaCare may result in 51 percent of employers (and 66 percent of small business employers) relinquishing their current healthcare coverage by 2013.[53] Another ObamaCare rule is that if an employer switches its healthcare provider to a more cost effective plan it will lose its federal health plan exemptions, which will cause even more employees to lose their current coverage. Of course, just as he exempted unions from the Cadillac tax on high-cost insurance coverage, he reportedly has exempted organized labor from this new rule as well.[54]

Furthermore, Obama has publicly supported the elimination of private employer-provided insurance, as discussed below. It's bad enough his plan would destroy private insurers or turn them into public utilities, but it's especially offensive that he demonstratively claims otherwise. A few months after ObamaCare was signed into law, Dr. Scott Gottlieb, a former official at the Centers for Medicare and Medicaid Services, wrote that it was already clear that Obama's promise that Americans could keep their insurance plans and their doctors under ObamaCare "cannot be kept. Insurers and physicians are already reshaping their businesses as a result of Mr. Obama's plan."

The bill imposes caps on insurance company spending and profits. One of the only ways to manage expenses is to reduce the actual cost of products, which means "pushing providers to accept lower fees and reduce their use of costly services like radiology and other diagnostic testing." To accomplish this, insurers will have to exert more control over doctors—so they

"are trying to buy up medical clinics and doctor practices." In the meantime, says Gottlieb, in anticipation of
ObamaCare's stifling effects, doctors "are selling their
practices to local hospitals." He spells out the bottom
line: "Defensive business arrangements designed to
blunt Obamacare's economic impacts will mean less
patient choice."[55] The *Washington Examiner's* editors
agree, noting a *Fortune* magazine article reporting that
"companies across the country are looking at dropping
health coverage for their employees because ObamaCare makes it profitable to do so."[56]

- Obama said the White House and Congress should
  "do our work openly, and . . . give our people the government they deserve." But as the AP noted, instead of
  working with Republicans, Democrats and the White
  House had made their private multi-million dollar
  deals behind closed doors with hospitals, pharmaceuticals, and other stakeholders.

- Obama claimed his administration had "excluded lobbyists from policymaking jobs." As discussed earlier,
  with his numerous exemptions to his own ethics rules,
  this is hardly the case.

- Obama claimed he had saved two million jobs through
  his "stimulus" bill and was "on track to add another
  one and a half million jobs to this total by the end of
  the year." The Heritage Foundation's Brian Riedl suggests we keep in mind an "important number" relevant
  to this discussion: 6.3 million, which represents the
  "Obama jobs gap—the difference between 3.3 million
  net jobs President Obama said would be created (not
  just saved) and the nearly 3 million additional net jobs
  that have since been lost."

  The administration's argument that "it would have
  been worse" without the stimulus is, says Riedl, "com-

pletely unprovable"—it is "faith-based economics." He notes the president's SOTU claim that millions of jobs had been saved is not based on any actual numbers, but on Obama's "unshakable belief that deficit spending must create jobs and growth"—in other words, Obama has blind faith that the stimulus must have created jobs, because an economic theory predicted it would.

Indeed, there is further proof that Obama has an "unshakable belief" that government money will stimulate the economy, even if that money has been taken from the private sector: his refusal to allow firms to pay back TARP money because he believed the money needed to keep circulating in the economy. As Riedl explains, "The idea that government spending creates jobs makes sense only if you never ask where the government got the money. It didn't fall from the sky. The only way Congress can inject spending into the economy is by first taxing or borrowing it out of the economy. No new demand is created; it's a zero-sum transfer of existing demand.... Yet the White House continues to wave the magic wand of 'stimulus.' All evidence that it failed be damned."[57]

Investors Business Daily is equally dismissive of the administration's bogus claim to have saved or created millions of jobs, saying it has "moved the yard markers" to distort the data. *IBD* editors recall the administration's warning that without the stimulus there would be 133.9 million U.S. jobs in the fourth quarter of 2010 ("that's the baseline"), and with the stimulus we would have almost 3.7 million more that that: 137.6 million. Instead, they wrote, we have 129.7 million jobs—8 million less than the administration predicted—and yet the administration claims it saved or created 2.8 million jobs. This means they "had to lower the baseline by 7 million jobs to only 126.9 million."[58] The administration's counting gimmicks make your head spin, and they're hoping the confusion helps prevent their accountability.

- Obama claims he inherited overwhelming deficits from his predecessor. But as we detail in the next chapter, Congressman Jeb Hensarling refuted this claim to Obama's face at the Republican congressional retreat in Baltimore, showing that average deficits during the twelve years when Republicans controlled the House were $104 billion, contrasted with average deficits under the three years of Democratic control of $1.1 trillion.

- Obama announced, "Let me repeat: we cut taxes. We cut taxes for 95 percent of working families. We cut taxes for small businesses. We cut taxes for first-time homebuyers. We cut taxes for parents trying to care for their children. We cut taxes for 8 million Americans paying for college. As a result, millions of Americans had more to spend on gas, and food, and other necessities, all of which helped businesses keep more workers." The Cato Institute rejoined that Obama could hardly cut taxes for 95 percent of Americans, since more than 40 percent of Americans pay no federal income taxes in the first place—the administration has simply counted increased subsidy checks to members of these groups as tax cuts. But refundable tax credits are unearned subsidies, not tax cuts.[59] Put another way, he dishonestly reclassified spending increases as tax cuts.

HEALTHCARE LIES

When Obama spoke to a joint session of Congress on healthcare on September 9, 2009, he said, "Under our plan no federal dollars will be used to fund abortions." This was one of the assertions prompting Congressman Joe Wilson to yell, "You lie." It turns out Wilson was right. Congressman Bart Stupak, who was then at least posturing as an uncompromising advocate for life, claimed Obama told Stupak he was not talking about the actual bill then under consideration in the House, but about "his" plan, which hadn't yet been written.[60] The bill that finally went through obviously allowed funding for abortion because Stupak only agreed to vote for it after Obama pledged to sign a meaningless executive order to prohibit such funding.

During that same speech Obama also asserted, "There are now more than 30 million American citizens who cannot get coverage," which was a curious number because he had previously been citing a figure of 46 million. Clearly, he was forced into reducing the number by conscientious conservative critics who had pointed out various inaccuracies in the statistic, including the fact that millions of those uninsured were not U.S. citizens. But his revised claim was still outrageously wrong because millions included in that number could afford insurance but *chose* not to purchase it for their own reasons, and millions more were already eligible for government benefits but did not avail themselves of them. Additionally, the Census Bureau figures underreport insurance coverage because they count many people as uninsured even though they are only without coverage for part of the year.[61]

Once ObamaCare passed, it proved so unpopular that Health and Human Services secretary Kathleen Sebelius, according a May 30, 2010 *Washington Examiner* editorial, "resorted to sending millions of senior Americans a sales brochure that is packed with blatantly false claims about Obamacare." Among its falsehoods, the report, published by the HHS's Centers for Medicare and Medicaid Services (CMS), guaranteed Medicare benefits would remain unchanged, even though CMS experts have testified ObamaCare's Medicare cuts could "jeopardize access" for millions of seniors. Eight GOP senators sent a letter to Sebelius asking her to explain the report's misstatements. According to the *Examiner*, they're still waiting for a reply.

SINGLE-PAYER PLAN AND THE PUBLIC OPTION

Throughout his presidential campaign and into his presidency, Obama has routinely misrepresented his position on healthcare reform. He repeatedly denied he supported a single-payer health-care system, for example telling a New Hampshire townhall meeting on August 11, 2009, that he never said he supported such a system. This came in sharp contrast to his videotaped 2003 assertion that "I happen to be a proponent of a single payer universal health care plan."[62]

Obama also obfuscated his position on the so-called public option. On December 22, 2009, he declared, "I didn't campaign on the public option."[63] But on March 24, 2007, he had told an SEIU healthcare forum, "The public option is your friend." In fact, his address to the SEIU revealed his true goal was not only to introduce a public option, but eventually to kill off private health insurance altogether: "My commitment is to make sure that we have universal health care for all Americans by the end of my first term as president.... But I don't think we'll be able to eliminate employer coverage immediately. There's going to be potentially some transition process. I can envision a decade out or 15 years out or 20 years out."

Although in other venues, Obama vehemently rejected speculation that the public option would be a Trojan horse for single payer, his Democratic allies were quite open about it. Congressman Barney Frank admitted, "If we get a good public option it could lead to single-payer and that's the best way to reach single-payer." Democratic congresswoman Jan Schakowsky similarly confessed, "The public option would put the private insurance industry out of business."[64]

Throughout most of the healthcare debate, Obama pressed hard for the public option on his website and in media appearances. He said in his weekly radio address on July 17, 2009, "any plan" he signs "must include...a public option." Three days later he told leftist bloggers he still believed "a robust public option would be the best way to go." On September 20, 2009, he told NBC's David

Gregory a public option "should be a part of this [health] care bill" and denied it was "dead."[65] The head spins.

Although Obama ultimately failed to get a public option included in ObamaCare, he probably achieved the equivalent of it with all the provisions enabling him to destroy private insurance or turn it into a public utility. The *Washington Examiner's* editors agree that the "public option is alive and well, but hidden"—"residing in Section 1334, pages 97-100, of the new healthcare law. That section gives the U.S. Office of Personnel Management— which presently manages the federal civil service—new responsibilities: establishing and running two entirely new government health insurance programs to compete directly with private insurance companies in every state with coverage for people outside of government."[66]

ALLOWING IMPORTED PRESCRIPTION DRUGS

Obama campaigned on a promise to "allow Americans to buy their medicines from other developed countries if the drugs are safe and prices are lower outside the U.S."[67] Thankfully, he caved on this one as part of his bribe to get Big Pharma to support ObamaCare.

GOP HEALTHCARE PROPOSALS

Decrying the GOP as the "Party of No," Obama denied for months that Republicans had any healthcare solutions. But he quickly changed his tune when he invited them to the televised "healthcare summit" to discuss *their* ideas. He also said his proposal contained many Republican ideas, which is odd, since he'd insisted those ideas didn't exist. Of course, Republicans in fact put forth many healthcare proposals, including market-based solutions in proposals such as Congressman Paul Ryan's Roadmap for America's Future, that were shot dead in their tracks—proposals Obama was aware of and wouldn't even acknowledge, much less consider.

IRAN AND ISRAEL

During his presidential campaign, Obama denied rumors he was unfriendly to Israel and to Jewish interests. While this whopper is big enough to get its own chapter in this book, we'll touch on just a few issues here.

While campaigning, candidate Obama told the American Israel Public Affairs Committee his goal would be to eliminate the nuclear threat to Israel from Iran. "I'll do everything in my power to prevent Iran from obtaining a nuclear weapon. Everything.... I will always leave the threat of military action on the table to defend our security, and that of our ally Israel." As president, however, Obama has shown more passion for denouncing Israeli settlements than for stopping Iran from getting the bomb. In fact, he supported a resolution by members of the Nuclear Non-proliferation Treaty that singled out Israel for criticism while *not even mentioning* Iran, which has repeatedly vowed to annihilate the Jewish state.

Furthermore, Obama proclaimed the city of "Jerusalem will remain the capital of Israel and must remain undivided."[68] Almost as quickly as he uttered the commitment, he backtracked under heavy Palestinian criticism and later clarified that the status of Jerusalem would need to be negotiated in future peace talks. The Associated Press reported on March 20, 2010, that Secretary of State Hillary Clinton told Israeli prime minister Benjamin Netanyahu all issues between Israel and the Palestinians, including the possibility of a divided Jerusalem, must remain part of the negotiations.[69] Moreover, if Obama were strictly committed to an undivided Jerusalem, why did he demand that the Israeli government halt any new settlement construction or expansion in Eastern Jerusalem?

WITHDRAWING TROOPS FROM IRAQ

Candidate Obama was adamant that he would "remove one to two combat brigades each month and have all of our combat brigades out of Iraq within 16 months"—even against the advice of the generals on the ground. The promise delighted many of his supporters and boosted his profile among the antiwar Left at the expense of his Democratic primary rival, Hillary Clinton, who wouldn't make such a promise. But he didn't come close to meeting this schedule and even abandoned his insistence on complete withdrawal, saying he would leave behind a residual force of 35,000 to 50,000 until the end of 2011.[70] However, Obama obviously derived some satisfaction from formally changing the name of our Iraqi effort from "Operation Iraqi Freedom" to "Operation New Dawn," perhaps to punctuate his disapproval of the effort from the outset as a "war of choice."

NATIONAL SECURITY

When campaigning for president, Obama lashed out at President George W. Bush for employing legal justifications to support enhanced interrogation techniques. He piously pledged to "abide by the Geneva Conventions. We will uphold our highest ideals." Yet his own Justice Department used those very same legal arguments when trying to convince the U.S. Supreme Court to dismiss *Rasul v. Rumsfeld*, saying the plaintiffs didn't clearly establish that their constitutional rights had been violated.[71] Candidate Obama had also vowed to stop "extraordinary rendition," but as president, his Justice Department adopted the Bush Justice Department's supposedly unacceptable arguments in defending against five men who claimed they had been subjected to the practice in the case of *Mohamed et al. v. Jeppesen Dataplan Inc.*[72]

Indeed, one columnist correctly argued, "On state secrets, indefinite detention, warrantless surveillance, the Patriot Act and signing statements, President Obama has used the language of transparency to give the appearance of change. In practice, however he has asserted virtually the same executive authority he reviled as abuses by his predecessor."[73] The same holds true for his targeting of suspected al Qaeda members in Afghanistan and Pakistan.

ARMENIAN GENOCIDE

Obama boasted of having "criticized the Secretary of State for the firing of U.S. Ambassador to Armenia, John Evans, after he properly used the term 'genocide' to describe Turkey's slaughter of thousands of Armenians starting in 1914.... As President I will recognize the Armenian Genocide." He so far has not honored that pledge despite making statements on memorials for the event, and reportedly tried to scuttle a House Foreign Affairs Committee resolution officially recognizing the genocide.[74]

THE BORN ALIVE INFANT PROTECTION ACT

Critics who accuse Obama of having supported infanticide are not engaging in hyperbole. While in the Illinois Senate, Obama opposed the Illinois Born-Alive Infants Protection bill—a measure almost identical to the federal Born Alive Infant Protection Act. These bills were designed to provide immediate protection to a child born as a result of a failed abortion. In 2001, Obama voted against the Illinois bill in committee and gave a floor speech opposing it, but voted "present" on the bill. After passing the Illinois Senate, the bill failed in the House. In 2002 the bill was proposed again, and Obama voted "no" in committee, spoke against it on the Senate floor, and voted "no" on the floor. The bill failed again. In 2003, the bill was reintroduced, and after certain amendments were added, became virtually identical to the federal bill. Obama then led committee Democrats in voting to kill the amended bill.[75]

During the presidential campaign, Obama repeatedly lied about his record on this while audaciously accusing his critics of lying. In an interview with CBN's David Brody, Obama said the National Right to Life had lied in asserting he had voted against a state bill that was virtually identical to the federal Born-Alive Infants Protection Act. After being repeatedly challenged—though not by Brody—Obama issued a statement acknowledging he had misstated his position in the CBN interview and that in fact he had voted against an identical bill in the state senate.[76]

The video, however, makes it clear this wasn't a mere misstatement. Obama clearly understood what he was saying, and he was adamant in calling his accusers "liars," knowing that it was *he* who lied. On the floor of the Illinois Senate, Obama coldly expressed more concern for the doctors who would risk liability than for the live babies. He argued there was already an Illinois bill that would protect infants born as a result of a failed abortion. But in fact, Illinois state senator Patrick O'Malley said he had drafted that legislation only after the state attorney general's office told him that existing Illinois law *would not* protect such babies.[77] Obama also claimed doctors would take care of infants who were born alive and therefore no new law was needed. But in fact, as many as one in five babies were left to die, which is why the bill was offered in the first place. And Obama knew it.

VAN JONES, COMMUNIST

Obama brought on himself a firestorm of criticism when he named Van Jones as "Green Jobs Czar." Appointed in March 2009, Van Jones resigned under pressure in September 2009 because of revelations about his radical past (including ties to Communist groups and his self-identification as a Communist at one point), his vulgar, incendiary statements against Republicans, and his signing of a "Truther" petition suggesting the Bush administration may have facilitated the 9/11 attacks.

Or did he actually resign? White House adviser David Axelrod said Jones made the decision himself, but Accuracy in Media reported he was forced out of his position, and that documents obtained through a FOIA request indicate the administration even wrote his resignation letter for him.[78] The Obama administration was also untruthful in claiming they had not properly vetted Jones before appointing him. Not only did their appointment of many other radicals discredit the claim, but Jones was the specific choice of Obama confidant and close adviser Valerie Jarrett, who bragged that she had recruited him for the position.[79] The insufficient vetting

excuse was also suspect considering that the White House specifically created this position for Van Jones because of his unique background. They knew what they were getting. They just didn't want
us to know.

BLOCKING FOX NEWS

CBS News exposed false denials by the Obama administration that
they had blocked FOX interviews with pay czar Ken Feinberg.
Treasury said "there was no plot to exclude FOX News and they
had the same interview that their competitors did. Much ado about
absolutely nothing." But the other four networks who were granted
interviews knew better. The only reason the interview was granted
is that the other four networks of the press pool, including CBS,
refused to participate without FOX. CBS reporter Chip Reid said
the administration "crossed the line."[80]

LOCKERBIE BOMBER RELEASE

Obama and Secretary of State Hillary Clinton, as well as other U.S.
officials including Attorney General Eric Holder, sharply criticized
Scottish authorities for releasing from prison Abdelbaset Al
Megrahi, a Libyan convicted for the 1988 bombing of a Pan Am
flight over Lockerbie, Scotland, killing 270 people. But Downing
Street denounced the criticism as "disingenuous." According to
British officials, Obama and Clinton had been kept informed at all
stages of the discussions and spoke out only because of the public
backlash against the release, not because they were unaware of
what was about to happen. "We would never do anything about
Lockerbie without discussing it with the US," said a Whitehall aide.
"It is disingenuous of them to act as though Megrahi's return was
out of the blue." Prime Minister Gordon Brown and Foreign Secretary David Miliband were "disappointed" by the force of Washington's reaction.[81]

As shown in this chapter, Obama's disingenuousness is not just a matter of stretching the truth once in a while or engaging in a little old-fashioned hyperbole. His outright, habitual lies are a fundamental aspect of his governance. Past campaign promises are changed retroactively or brazenly denied, while he dissimulates and deceives about the true scope of healthcare reform, cap and trade, and his other signature policy goals. This is, perhaps, unsurprising, since he is pursuing an extremist agenda that he hid from the American people on the campaign trail and continues to mask today.

Chapter Four

DIVISIVE AND HYPER-PARTISAN

CRIMES AGAINST THE UNION

While Obama prayed at the National Prayer breakfast for a "spirit of civility" in Washington, he didn't seem to consider himself a contributor to the incivility. "You can question my policies without questioning my faith," he said. "Or, for that matter, my citizenship."[1]

Indeed, as a presidential candidate, Obama turned his ostensible bipartisanship into a central plank of his campaign. His camp featured a 60-second national TV ad emphasizing Obama's cooperation with Republicans in the Illinois legislature and the U.S. Senate, including a clip from Obama's 2004 Democratic National Convention speech in which he rejected the red state–blue state dichotomy. Obama said in March 2008, "I'm a big believer in working with the other side of the aisle. Even if we've got a majority of Democrats, I think it's very important to listen to Republicans, to respect them . . . I want to have a weekly meeting with

Republican and Democratic leaders to talk about the economy, to talk about foreign policy, so that we're actually trying to solve problems away from the TV cameras, not trying to score political points."[2] Likewise, Senator Claire McCaskill announced, "He understands that we've gotta move forward with a different kind of politics."[3]

But Obama's idea of bipartisanship is to consider each and every idea Republicans offer, except those he refuses to consider. In May 2009, he made overtures toward reaching across the aisle on the abortion issue, claiming he was seeking common ground between pro-lifers and pro-abortionists. He brought together the two factions in a series of meetings and immediately "took off the table any discussion of whether abortion should be legal."[4] That's bipartisanship, Obama style.

If Obama truly sought to establish an atmosphere of civility and bipartisanship, he could lead by example. Former adviser to President George W. Bush, Karl Rove, told FOX News's Chris Wallace that Obama holds himself out "as some bipartisan, post-partisan kind of politician, but in reality he is a very—you know, a hyper-partisan who's failed to reach across party lines when he had a terrific opportunity to do so in the aftermath of his victory."[5]

Obama's notion of a bipartisan Super Bowl party was to invite one Republican congressman along with about forty Democrats.[6] He told Republicans they "seem to be almost rooting against [economic] recovery."[7] He said at a Philadelphia fundraiser during the campaign, "If they bring a knife to the fight, we bring a gun."[8] He encouraged his supporters to "argue with (your neighbors); get in their face.... you are my ambassadors."[9] He refused Senator McCain's call for a series of joint bipartisan townhall meetings. As a U.S. senator, he politicized the plight of injured soldiers by falsely accusing President Bush of doing the same, declaring, "The problems plaguing our military hospital system will not be solved with a photo-op. Our military hospital system is in a state of crisis. Delays and rhetorical band-aids will not move us closer to a solution."[10] His administration even issued documents character-izing pro-life activists as racist extremists and likely terrorists.[11]

Obama's the guy who had issued a "declaration of war" in one of his healthcare speeches, according to conservative columnist, economist, and TV host Larry Kudlow. Kudlow wrote, "He's more than willing to use a 51-vote reconciliation majority to jam through a roughly $2 trillion healthcare plan that amounts to a government takeover of nearly one-fifth of the economy."[12] Obama's the guy whose administration intends to purge Republicans from the civil service, according to a memo from the Office of Personnel Manage-ment.[13] And Obama's the guy who nominated Larry Persily—a for-mer aide to former Alaska governor Sarah Palin who wrote scathing pieces against her on the *Huffington Post* website—for an Alaska pipeline job, an appointment described by blogger Pamela Geller as "transparent, petty and small."[14]

Most notably, Obama's the guy whose attorney general pushed for criminalizing the previous administration based on a difference in legal and political opinions—pejoratively dubbed "torture memos"—concerning enhanced interrogation techniques. It was not enough to slander his predecessor and CIA operatives; Obama was determined to use the force of criminal law to punish them. This, despite the fact that congressional Democrats had been briefed about interrogation techniques more than thirty times since 2002, and had approved funding for the program.[15]

Obama's partisanship is not confined to the national level—he habitually injects himself into state-level politics as well. The *Wash-ington Post* reported that the White House played a critical, behind-the-scenes role in convincing Dede Scozzafava, Republican candidate from New York's 23rd Congressional District, to endorse Democrat Bill Owens after she suspended her campaign. The administration later downplayed their role in the Scozzafava episode, which they hoped to exploit in order to convey the impres-sion there was a major splintering in the Republican Party and that it had become a narrow home for extremist conservatives. This kind of local interference by the Obama team even upset some Democrats. After the White House reportedly attempted to dissuade New York governor David Paterson, a Democrat, from seeking reelection in 2010, the *New York Times* noted that "some Democrats expressed anger at what they saw as heavy-handed tactics by the president's political team."[16]

SHUTTING REPUBLICANS OUT OF THE PROCESS

From the beginning of Obama's relentless drive to impose his agenda of "fundamental change" on America, he talked bipartisan and acted partisan. Had a Republican president behaved in such a flagrantly partisan way, the mainstream media would have gone ballistic. House Republican whip Eric Cantor grumbled, "In 2009, on the rare occasion when we were invited to the White House, the President paid Republican proposals lip service while cameras were on, only to completely rebuff those ideas afterward."[17]

Obama's agenda was so radical he rarely secured any Republican congressional support for his initiatives, and when he did it was only the very liberal ones from the blue states. His $800 billion stimulus bill was supported by just three Senate Republicans—if you can call them that—on the cloture vote. Susan Collins, Olympia Snowe, and Arlen Specter (who later switched parties) voted with fifty-six Democrats and two independents to thwart a filibuster.

As they rammed the stimulus through Congress, Obama and his congressional Democrats were determined to shut Republicans out of the process. The president met with congressional Republicans on the stimulus just one day before Democrats completed drafting the 1,073-page bill. As Karl Rove pointed out, there was no effort to consult and exchange ideas; it was merely a photo-op.[18]

Republican Conference chairman Mike Pence told *Human Events*, "I think the American people deserve to know that legislation that would comprise an amount equal to the entire discretionary budget of the United States of America is being crafted without a single

House Republican in the room."[19] Senator Charles E. Grassley protested that he and his fellow Republicans had been prevented from offering amendments. "I'm not convinced the majority wanted to have open debate and take votes on many of these amendments including mine," said Grassley. "It's too bad because this bill still can be made a bipartisan bill." Senator James Inhofe noted, "This is the largest spending in the history of mankind, the largest spending in the history of the world. It's something that we should not let happen, but it is going to happen right down party lines."

Similarly, Senator Mitch McConnell complained, "This package, had it been developed in genuine consultation, could have had a different result." McConnell criticized the White House for excluding Republicans from the process, remarking, "At the end of the day, it was—the administration decided—let the package be developed in Congress by the majority, and old habits die hard. You know, there was no meaningful consultation in the early part of the process. So if you don't have that on the takeoff, you don't end up having it on the landing."[20]

The Obama adminstration engaged in similar partisan opportunism on the "jobs bill" in February 2010. They initially praised a bipartisan bill by senators Baucus and Grassley, but they defended Senate majority leader Harry Reid when he moved to scuttle the bill and replace it with a solely Democrat-written measure. Even Democratic senator Blanche Lincoln decried her party's rank partisanship, exclaiming, "Most Americans don't honestly believe that a single political party has all the good ideas. We're not going to accomplish anything until we start governing from the center." To deflect criticism of Obama's partisanship, White House press secretary Robert Gibbs assured Republicans they could "trust the president."[21]

Toward the end of 2009, when it was increasingly clear Obama's stimulus plan was a bust, he convened a bogus "jobs summit" to create the impression he was seeking ideas from all quarters to get the economy back on track. But predictably, it was all show. Obama denied invitations to free-market advocates, critics of

ObamaCare, and opponents of his demonstrably failed stimulus package, including members of the U.S. Chamber of Commerce and the National Federation of Independent Business. Peter Morici, a professor at the University of Maryland's Robert H. Smith School of Business, observed, "He's going to get lots of recommendations to spend more money. These [jobs summit attendees] are the very same people who gave us the stimulus package. My feeling is we're not going to get what we need, and that's a complete change in direction on economic policy." Economics professor John Coleman of Duke University's Fuqua School of Business added, "My chief concern is that the list features no serious and prominent labor economist, which seems essential to offering a sound, long-run policy to put us on a path of lower unemployment."[22]

Whenever his political interests demanded it, Obama portrayed Republicans as pure obstructionists bereft of their own ideas. But when his propaganda began to lose its appeal, especially on healthcare, he needed to pretend to adopt a bipartisan approach. Just as he called the meaningless jobs summit to create the impression he was focusing on unemployment (which his stimulus bill only exacerbated), he convened a healthcare summit "inviting all ideas." But he didn't invite obvious essential participants such as Senator Judd Gregg, a ranking Budget Committee member who had recently extended an olive branch to Obama to work on a bipartisan solution to healthcare. Obama also excluded the Budget Committee chairman, Senator Kent Conrad, a Democrat who had shown genuine willingness to cooperate with Republicans.[23]

As noted, Obama had previously insisted "obstructionist" Republicans had no ideas—forget expanding health savings accounts, tort reform, tax law reform on employer provided insurance, legalizing the purchase of insurance across state lines, eliminating unnecessary but costly mandated coverage, supporting retail health clinics, and providing vouchers for the working poor and chronically uninsured. But now that he needed Republicans as props for his "bipartisan" summit charade, he intimated they actually did have some ideas. He even bragged he was willing to adopt some of them, such as tort reform.

Leading up to the summit, Obama really played up his "bipartisan" shtick. "Despite the political posturing that often paralyzes this town," he intoned, "there are many issues upon which we can and should agree. . . . The people who sent us here expect a seriousness of purpose that transcends petty politics. That's why I'm going to continue to seek the best ideas from either party as we work to tackle the pressing challenges ahead."[24] Obama then proceeded to engage in petty, one-sided politics, rejecting Republican proposals and steamrolling his bill through Congress along party lines.

He orchestrated the entire healthcare summit as an Alinsky-type community organizing tactic to stigmatize Republicans as the "Party of No." Thankfully, this time the Republicans didn't take it sitting down. They stated publicly that Obama had been mischaracterizing them as partisans when he had closed them out of the process from the beginning. House minority whip Eric Cantor told the *Washington Times* in October 2009 that after offering their ideas on healthcare to Obama in May, they heard nothing from him. "No matter what the cry is from the White House, no matter what the president claims, they have not engaged with us," said Cantor. "The White House at this point has shut down, as far as any kind of engagement. I think that the last time that we as a Republican leadership were at the White House was in May, and that's when they called us in at the beginning of the health care discussion so that they could get our ideas. . . . Boehner and I sent a letter to the White House in response to that request. Nothing."[25] Then-House minority leader John Boehner revealed that in response to their message, the administration sent a terse letter indicating they had healthcare reform under control.[26]

Republican congressman Tom Price commented,

You'll have to excuse us for questioning the sincerity of the President's newfound desire to work together. As Chairman of the

Republican Study Committee, virtually every week in 2009, we requested to meet with the President to discuss health care and other central issues. Each time, a polite "thank you" email from the White House was the extent of our bipartisan discussions. It's interesting that only now—once his big-government dream is on political life support—does the President see a use for Republicans. And it appears that use may be more political than rooted in policy goals.[27]

As Price went on to say, it's a pretty tough sell for the president to paint Republicans as the roadblock to this bill when he enjoyed a 77-seat majority in the House and fifty-nine Democratic senators, and he still had to resort to political bribery and ruthless threats in order to get the bill approved.

Obama's partisan approach to healthcare simply reflected the governing style he adopted as soon as he took office. With his first major legislative initiative, the $800 billion stimulus package, his idea of bipartisanship was essentially to say he'd considered all Republican proposals before rejecting them. It was clear from the beginning he would not consider any ideas to reduce the grand scale of his plan. He might show some movement on "the crumbs," but not "the pie," as his National Economic Council director Lawrence Summers said. Yet upon making that very statement, Summers added that the president "has been prepared to walk a long mile for bipartisan support,"[28] apparently confident the public wouldn't notice the contradiction.

Overall, for Obama, "bipartisanship" means Republicans supporting his agenda and refraining from engaging in activities he condemns as partisan—even though as a U.S. senator he had engaged in those activities himself. For example, as president he blasted Republicans for using "holds" to delay consideration of his nominees, when he had done precisely the same to President George W. Bush's selections.[29] In his weekly radio address, he said Republicans should "avoid the political posturing and ideological brinksmanship that has bogged down this (nomination) process, and Congress in the past." Yet, he played a "unique role in history as the first U.S. president to have ever voted to filibuster a Supreme Court nominee"—now-Justice Samuel Alito.[30]

But for a guy who worked so hard to depict himself as bipartisan, indeed post-partisan, he didn't cover his tracks very well. Often he couldn't contain his true combative nature—as when he imperiously warned the nation's mayors that although they have a friend in the White House, he would use the "full power" of his presidency to "call them out" if they misused any of their stimulus funds.[31] He issued the same admonitions to congressional Republicans.

In his remarks to a Joint Session of Congress on healthcare in September 2009, he warned, "But know this: I will not waste time with those who have made the calculation that it's better politics to kill this plan than to improve it. I won't stand by while the special interests use the same old tactics to keep things exactly the way they are. If you misrepresent what's in the plan, we will call you out. And I will not . . . accept the status quo as a solution. Not this time. Not now."[32] It was during that speech that Joe Wilson shouted, "You lie" and "Not true" when Obama claimed ObamaCare would not cover illegal immigrants or fund abortion.[33] While Democrats widely condemned Wilson for his supposedly unprecedented display of disrespect, many of these critics were part of the group that displayed far worse disrespect for President Bush in the same setting, booing and heckling him during his 2005 State of the Union speech.[34]

Just as important, Wilson was correct on the underlying issue of abortion funding, for which Obama has never been held accountable. Wilson was substantively correct on immigration as well, because even though the then-active healthcare bill prohibited illegal immigrants from participating in the "exchange," the bill contained no practical method for verifying the applicants' citizenship. The administration implicitly admitted as much when it later backed a provision to require proof of citizenship as a condition to enroll in a plan on the exchange.[35]

It's also worth noting that during that speech Obama hardly had clean hands. He was accusing Republicans of opportunistic partisanship and misrepresentations while he was opportunistically misrepresenting their positions and their actions. Obama wearily announced, "What we have also seen in these last months is the same partisan spectacle that only hardens the disdain many Americans have toward their own government. Instead of honest debate, we have seen scare tactics.... Too many have used this as an opportunity to score short-term political points, even if it robs the country of our opportunity to solve a long-term challenge."[36] Yet in the same address, Obama accused his Republican opponents of being "cynical and irresponsible," peddling "misinformation," and asserting "bogus," "wild," or "false" claims through "demagoguery and distortion."[37]

THE STATE OF THE UNION IS PARTISAN

Obama's partisanship was in overdrive in his 2010 State of the Union speech, in which he invoked the self-serving whopper, "Our union is strong." Most commentators believed that having just been spanked in the Massachusetts Senate election—which was every bit about him—Obama would show some contrition, some indication that he received the voters' resounding message and would embark on a course change. Instead, he launched into full-scale attack mode. He wasn't about to acknowledge that the voters thoughtfully considered his ideas and rejected them. Rather, it was that he had not explained them "more clearly to the American people." He did not offer to consider the people's ideas or those of the Republican Party. He said, "I want everyone to take another look at the plan we've proposed." Then he taunted Republicans to "let [him] know" if any of them had "a better approach that will bring down premiums, bring down the deficit, cover the uninsured, strengthen Medicare for seniors, and stop insurance company abuses."

Of course, Republicans did have a better approach to address most of those problems, and they *had* let him know, but he turned a deaf ear and later denied they'd offered any plans. The hard reality was that Obama was ideologically opposed to the only approach that could lower healthcare costs without rationing or decreasing the quality of care—which is to reduce the role of government. Had Obama been honest he would have said, "If any of you can offer constructive ideas that will fit within my framework of expanding government control over healthcare, I'll consider them."

On spending, Obama once again blamed George W. Bush instead of taking ownership of his own bankrupting policies. He said he would freeze discretionary spending, but his proposed freeze would apply only to a small fraction of the total federal budget, which the *Wall Street Journal* noted would have but a "small impact on the deficit." It was a trivial concession designed to mislead people into thinking he was getting serious about spending. In another display of his "bipartisanship," he broke protocol by castigating the non-political branch, the Supreme Court, for its recent decision on campaign finance reform. Obama's warning that the ruling would open the door to campaign contributions from foreign corporations was so erroneous that Justice Samuel Alito was seen shaking his head and saying, "Not true."

Then, in a surreal move, Obama blamed Washington for the nation's problems, as if he weren't the biggest player in that city. Even worse was his brazen complaint about the atmosphere of partisanship—as if he weren't its most egregious contributor. He declared, "Washington may think that saying anything about the other side, no matter how false, no matter how malicious, is just part of the game. But it's precisely such politics that has stopped either party from helping the American people. Worse yet, it's sowing further division among our citizens, further distrust in our government. So no, I will not give up on trying to change the tone of our politics."[38]

THE BALTIMORE CAUCUS

A few days after his State of the Union speech, Obama met with House Republicans at their caucus in Baltimore. His aim was to convince the public he was reaching out to the GOP in a gracious, bipartisan gesture, but his real purpose—as usual—was to paint Republicans as partisan obstructionists. While his scheme produced superficial dividends in temporarily boosting his approval ratings, he further alienated Republicans by his many misrepresentations at the meeting.

Wearing his innocent face, Obama said, "I don't understand . . . why we got opposition [to the stimulus package] . . . before we had a chance to actually meet and exchange ideas." But as previously noted, Obama gave Republicans no opportunity to meet with him on the stimulus until its drafting—by congressional Democrats alone—was all but complete. Obama also denied his budget would triple the national debt—which it would—and denied he had demonized Republicans for offering no ideas and no solutions, when he had made that claim repeatedly, branding the GOP from the earliest stages of his presidency as the "Party of No."[39]

At the retreat, Obama didn't take kindly to Congressman Jeb Hensarling's observation that the Democrats' monthly deficits were nearly as high as the annual ones when Republicans controlled the House. Obama, with dripping condescension, told Hensarling, whom he mistakenly called "Jim" three times, that he disagreed with "half of his assertions" and that he didn't like having to sit there and listen to them. He complained he wasn't being allowed to answer. Obama further lectured Hensarling that he made "bipartisanship" very difficult with that kind of question, which "was structured as a talking point for running a campaign." Then Obama insisted Hensarling's assertions about the deficit were "factually just not true."

Standing his ground, Hensarling issued a statement at the end of the retreat that cited CBO statistics showing the average annual deficit of $104 billion during the twelve years when Republicans controlled the House, contrasted with the average $1.1 trillion deficit under the three years of Democratic control.[40] Hensarling noted Obama "didn't answer my specific question on whether he would continue us on a path to tripling the national debt and increasing government spending to 24.5 percent of the economy."[41]

"I WANT THEM TO GET OUT OF THE WAY"

Obama adopted the same divisive, accusatory tone a few days later when he became frustrated with his inability to shepherd his health-care bill through Congress, despite his large majorities. In a tough-talking press conference, he accused Republicans of trying to sabotage his entire agenda for political gain. He proclaimed, "We can't afford grandstanding at the expense of getting something done. . . . I won't hesitate to embrace a good idea from my friends in the minority party, but I also won't hesitate to condemn . . . what I consider to be obstinacy rooted in substantive disagreements."[42] Note the subjective standard he invoked—what *he* considered to be obstinacy, which is anything falling short of fully embracing his agenda. He was lecturing Republicans about grandstanding on job creation policy, when his own stimulus bill—a year later—had netted millions of lost jobs.

This was a regular partisan routine for Obama. Months before, at a campaign rally for Virginia governor hopeful Creigh Deeds, he declared, "I expect to be held responsible for these issues because I'm the president. But I don't want the folks who created the mess to do a lot of talking. I want them to get out of the way so we can clean up the mess. I don't mind cleaning up after them, but don't do a lot of talking."[43]

On another occasion Obama said, "I told my Republican friends I want to work together with them where I can—and I meant it. And I told them I will also call them out if they say they want to work on something then when I offer a hand, I get nothing in return." Eventually even Reuters recognized Obama's ruthless strategy to "appeal to Republicans to make compromises and if they do not, accuse them of obstruction."[44]

Obama typically speaks more candidly when addressing Democratic audiences. For example, at a New York City Democratic fundraiser, Obama told the attendees that "Republicans—they're another story altogether. They just kind of do what they're told." You know, sort of simpleton robots. But Democrats were different. "Ya'll thinkin' for yourselves. I like that in you, but it's time for us to make sure that we finish the job here, we are this close and we've got to be unified."[45]

Showing the same partisan belligerence, Obama told Senate Democrats in a question-and-answer session in early February 2010 that Republicans had been obstructionist throughout. "I'm reminded that when it came to the health insurance reform in particular, I sought out and supported Republican ideas from the start. So did you. . . . And I told them I want to work together when we can, and I meant it. And I believe that's the best way to get things done for the American people." Then the other—and now familiar shoe dropped. "I also made it clear that we'll call them out when—when they say they want to work with us and we extend a hand and get a fist in return."[46] As conservative Gary Bauer commented, "This is nearly the same rhetoric Obama used last year in describing his outreach to the Islamofascists in Iran when he said, '. . . if countries like Iran are willing to unclench their fist, they will find an extended hand from us.'"[47]

VILIFICATION THROUGH SURROGATES

Obama's surrogates got into the act as well. His adviser David Axelrod was always quick to demonize Republicans as obstructionist partisans or special interest tools while simultaneously calling for bipartisanship, as when he said, "One thing for sure that people want is for us to have honest, open debate. The question is whether we can overcome the obstacles of hyperpartisanship and the excessive influence of special interests here. We are going to communicate that."[48]

Organizing for America, a group run by the Democratic National Committee to advance Obama's legislative agenda, routinely sends group e-mails to supporters. One such e-mail, signed by Obama's handpicked political strategist, David Plouffe, called opponents of ObamaCare "swiftboaters" who were flooding the airwaves with "distortions."[49] The group later sent an e-mail to Obama "supporters" in congressional districts represented by Republican congressmen who voted "no" on the healthcare bill. "Unfortunately, your representative caved to intense pressure from insurance industry lobbyists and voted against health reform," the e-mail read. A Democratic official, according to *ABC News* senior White House correspondent Jake Tapper, admitted the e-mail was not sent to constituents of the thirty-nine Democratic congressmen who also voted against the bill. "It's our belief that all Democrats want reform and we believe some if not many Democrats will support a final bill," said DNC spokesman Brad Woodhouse. "We believe that Republican opposition is political—intended to curry favor with the insurance industry and to break the president politically."[50]

Following Obama's lead, his partisan lieutenants in Congress were every bit as polarizing as he was. Just before the final House vote on ObamaCare, Democrats announced they planned to inflict "pain" on Republicans who tried to slow down or block the bill's passage. Democratic senator Sherrod Brown warned, "If they're going to try to filibuster in the traditional sense or the more modern sense that they do, they're going to have pain, too."[51] No, you don't dare get in their way—that's partisanship, as they define it. But rolling over for them—that's bipartisanship.

Obama's choice of advisers also proves his partisanship. His first chief of staff, Rahm Emanuel, is Exhibit A. The profanity-spewing Emanuel, a.k.a. "Rahmbo," is known for being "ruthless" and "a relentless partisan warrior."[52] Steve Clemmons of the *Washington Note* commented, "The Rahm Emanuel I know is tenaciously focused on results and will do nearly anything to win."[53] Early in Obama's presidency, writer Camille Paglia referred to Emanuel as "the arrogant Chicago scrapper," saying he "already seems like an albatross who should be thrown overboard as soon as possible. Nobody wants a dawning presidency addicted so soon to stonewalling, casuistry and the Nixonian dark arts of the modified limited hangout."[54] Congressman Darrell Issa of California said Emanuel would "smile at the same time he flips you the bird. The best way to describe Rahm is that he's a brass-knuckle Chicago politician."[55]

While some said Emanuel had settled down since he notoriously sent a dead fish to an uncooperative pollster twenty years before he joined the White House, he was still coarse, to say the least. During a weekly strategy session with liberal groups and White House aides, Emanuel got miffed when some attendees said they were going to air ads attacking conservative Democrats who were balking at ObamaCare. He called them "F—ing retarded" and warned them not to alienate any Democratic congressmen. He later apologized for the epithet to the head of the Special Olympics.[56]

Emanuel is also famous for uttering the remark, "You don't ever want a crisis to go to waste; it's an opportunity to do important things that you would otherwise avoid." This cynical statement was an early indication of Obama's intention to exploit the economic and financial crises that existed when he came to office in order to advance the most extreme leftist agenda of any president in history.

"SO AM I"

Some have noted a pattern in how this administration deals with unexpected problems—they immediately shift into CYA mode and downplay any suggestion they did anything wrong. Only after a few days have passed and the intensity of the initial moment has subsided will the administration admit their involvement in some way. When, for instance, a pair of party crashers gained access to the

White House and President Obama due to a security breach, the administration denied any error on their part, only to quietly concede the truth later.[57]

The Obama White House must always have the last word over any slight to the president or any criticism of his policies. Based on Obama's behavior at the healthcare summit—tediously responding personally to each and every Republican speaker—it's fair to assume this attitude comes from the top. Whereas President George W. Bush rarely spoke up to defend himself against outrageously spurious attacks from leftist Democrats, Obama compulsively lashes out when criticized, putting the lie to his reputation as a gentlemanly stoic. When Republican senator Judd Gregg withdrew his nomination to be commerce secretary citing "irresolvable conflicts" with Obama's domestic agenda, the White House immediately attacked Gregg, insisting he had volunteered for the position and had expressed support for Obama's agenda.[58]

The administration exhibited the same pugnacious attitude toward critics of its national security policy. In an op-ed titled, "We need no lectures...," John Brennan, Obama's national security aide, wrote, "Politically motivated criticism and unfounded fear-mongering only serve the goals of al-Qaeda." Brennan accused critics of the administration of "misrepresenting the facts to score political points, instead of coming together to keep us safe." Brennan also employed the perennial Obama strategy of blaming Bush, saying the Obama administration was doing a better job than Bush in taking the fight to al Qaeda. "We need no lectures about the fact that this nation is at war," wrote Brennan. *USA Today*'s editorial writers saw it quite differently, observing that although "the Obama administration's national security officials have struggled to assure the public that they know exactly what they're doing," they are "achieving the opposite, and they're needlessly adding some jitters in the process."[59]

Obama's pugnacity was not spontaneous. He was spoiling for a fight with Republicans from the get-go. In an early speech stumping for his $3.6 trillion budget, he made clear he would paint all opponents of his ambitious domestic agenda as being in the pockets of the "special interests" and lobbyists. "I know," said Obama, "these steps won't sit well with the special interests and lobbyists who are invested in the old way of doing business, and I know they're gearing up for a fight as we speak. My message to them is: So am I." As *Politico's* Jonathan Martin wrote, "Obama was "making his case for the budget" in an "unmistakable us-versus-them tone." He quoted Obama saying, "The system we have now might work for the powerful and well-connected interests that have run Washington for far too long, but I don't. I work for the American people."[60]

"A SUPERJUMBO DEMOCRAT"

For a while Obama successfully passed himself off as a bipartisan gentleman who, in the words of Camille Paglia, "projected a cordial dignity and thoughtful reserve that seem to have impressed and reassured observers across the political spectrum."[61] But some, like liberal writer Peter Beinart, at least noticed an "ambiguity" in Obama's bipartisan overtures. Obama, said Beinart, struck some "as a polished Howard Dean," and others as a "Joe Lieberman," who "wanted to be loved on the other side of the aisle." And, according to Beinart, Obama didn't resolve this ambiguity in his first year. (Others, as mentioned in chapter two, recognized this as a tactical ploy on Obama's part.)

But after Obama's healthcare drive, even Beinart admitted the doubt "is over." The Massachusetts Senate election, said Beinart, had forced Obama to choose either to moderate his position, like President Clinton did following his Democratic congressional thrashing in 1994, or to go all out with an unabashed liberal agenda—and Obama pursued the latter course. He pushed unrelentingly for approval of ObamaCare despite overwhelming public opposition. "And," added Beinart, "in acting the way he did, Obama has turned himself into a superjumbo Democrat. For the foreseeable future, he has forfeited any chance of bridging the red-blue divide."

Of course, that conclusion should have been evident well before Obama took office, but many denied the obvious. However slow Beinart and other liberals were in arriving at this conclusion, they now understand the truth; any hope that Obama would appeal to the centrist wing of his party and "nurture a new generation of centrist candidates," said Beinart, is "now gone. From top to bottom, Democrats have decided to bet the party's future on the belief that Americans prefer bold liberals to cautious ones."[62] Either that, or their ideology is more important to them than winning—provided that before they're thrown out of office they impose permanent foundational change on America's institutions and founding principles.

TRANSCENDENTLY POLARIZING

Obama's divisiveness transcends party politics and far exceeds that of President George W. Bush, who liberals still falsely insist was the most polarizing president in history. In delivering the commencement address for the University of Notre Dame, Obama made the subject of abortion a principal part of his speech, apparently believing his boundless capacity for reconciling the irreconcilable would enable him to articulate a unique position that, once delivered, would cause a contagious "a-ha" moment to engulf the university, indeed, the entire Western world. Everyone would instantly realize, to their relief, that there actually is a common ground and everyone on both sides of this life and death issue would better appreciate their opponents' arguments.

News of Obama's upcoming speech at Catholic Notre Dame provoked strong opposition, including the Cardinal Newman Society's gathering of 255,000 signatures protesting Obama's appearance. It also led former Vatican ambassador Mary Ann Glendon, a pro-life advocate and Harvard law professor, to announce she would not speak at the university on the same day as Obama, when she was slated to receive the Laetare Medal—an annual award given in recognition for outstanding service to the Roman Catholic Church and to society. Glendon submitted a letter to university president John Jenkins saying, "The task that once seemed so delightful has been complicated. I could not help but be dismayed by the news that Notre Dame also planned to award the president an honorary degree...in disregard of the U.S. bishops' express request" that Catholic colleges should not give abortion advocates a platform to speak to students or be honored with special awards and degrees.[63]

As a result of Obama's (and the university's) stubborn insistence on proceeding with his speech, Notre Dame allegedly lost some $8.2 million in donations.[64]

Similarly, Obama could not restrain his self-indulgence and hyper-partisanship long enough to omit the subjects of politics and—his favorite—himself, from a commencement address at the University of Michigan. Instead of imparting advice about career choices and the future, Obama turned the speech into another platform to whine about the bitter grind of Washington politics—again, as if he were an outsider.

While continuing to portray himself as a nonpartisan pragmatist, Obama is governing as the most committed ideologue in American history. Contemptuous of the will of the people as expressed in every possible medium—public opinion polls, House and Senate elections, the birth and rapid expansion of the tea party movement—the president obsessively pursues his transformative vision like Captain Ahab hunting his great white whale. He does not view those who oppose this vision as potential partners or people worth consulting. No, they are his political enemies—people who, by virtue of their failure to understand Obama's moral superiority and enlightened vision, must be ridiculed, discredited, and marginalized to make room for his reconstituted America.

Chapter Five

THE BULLY

CRIMES AGAINST THE PEOPLE

Obama is the quintessential partisan, for sure, but he doesn't reserve his vitriol for Republican politicians. He'll turn on anyone who stands in his way, and he'll make it personal through bullying, ridicule, and demonizing. Obama believes he can use his presidential bully pulpit to say whatever he wants about anyone or any group, whether foreign leaders, bankers, or tea party protestors.

Then-House minority leader John Boehner commented on team Obama's bellicosity, "If you look at these attacks on people who question the administration, you begin to wonder what the real plan is. And it really does, to me, look like Chicago-style politics, like they're trying to demonize their opponents, and do everything they can to make them distasteful."[1] At one point even moderate Republican senator Lamar Alexander appeared surprised at the administration's belligerence, remarking, "Street fighting and

111

brawling belongs outside the White House. . . . I think calling people out, taking their names, threatening to take away their anti-
trust exemption . . . I think it's unpresidential to bring them in the
White House."[2]

Politico reported in October 2009 that Obama was working
"systematically to marginalize the most powerful forces behind the
Republican Party," unleashing "top White House officials to undermine conservatives in the media, business and lobbying worlds."
Through public taunts, reported *Politico*, Obama went after the
U.S. Chamber of Commerce, Rush Limbaugh, Wall Street executives, and FOX News. White House press secretary Robert Gibbs
had "mocked Limbaugh from the White House press room
podium," adviser Valerie Jarrett had "disparaged" the Chamber,
and Rahm Emanuel and Anita Dunn had "piled on FOX News."[3]
Political commentator Michael Barone observed, "Having encountered un-Chicago-like dissent and disagreement, he has responded
with classic Chicago brass knuckles. We'll see how far this kind of
thuggery gets him."[4]

REPUBLICANS

Consistent with his narcissistic proclivities, Obama is angrily intolerant of his critics. He dismissed President Bush's rare criticism by
snapping, "We won." Likewise, he lashed out at Senator John
McCain for objecting to his stance on Iran, declaring, "Only I'm
the president of the United States . . . and I'll carry out my responsibilities the way I think is appropriate"—completely ignoring the
substance of McCain's criticism.[5]

While much has been written about Obama's arm-twisting in trying to shove ObamaCare through Congress, he had done the same
thing with his cap and trade proposal some nine months earlier. This
is a hallmark of Obama's governing style: he takes things personally
and keeps score. Jane Hamsher wrote in *Politico*, "The White
House is smoking mad at Rep. Lloyd Doggett (D-Texas), who says

he's voting against the climate bill—despite the lobbying of the entire First Family in the Oval Office last night. If the bill goes down, Obama won't forget Doggett's role, Democrats say. It's 'stunning that he would ignore the wishes not just of his president, but of his constituents and the country,' said an administration official."

Obama exudes a sense of entitlement about his agenda, expecting legislators to vote as he commands, as opposed to, say, their consciences or the wishes of their constituents. *Salon's* Glenn Greenwald wrote, "This has become an emerging theme among both the White House and House leadership: that progressive members of Congress have an obligation to carry out 'the wishes of the President' even when they disagree." Greenwald lamented the "subservient mentality" of Congress and the "bullying tactics" of the president. "The duty of Congress," he noted, "is not to obey the wishes of the President."[6]

For Obama, it's more than just a matter of political power. There's also his egotistical sense that he is absolutely right about everything, that everyone else is wrong, and that if given enough time, he can persuade the rest of the rubes of the superiority of his positions. We've seen how he attributed the public's repudiation of his agenda via the Massachusetts Senate election to his failure to sufficiently explain his healthcare position—though he had talked ad nauseam on the issue. But it was true of other issues as well—even strong moral issues for which there would never be a consensus, as with his attempt to confront pro-life forces at Notre Dame.

He took the same tack with the issue of homosexuality. At a White House celebration of Gay Pride Month—a controversial act in itself—Obama said he aspired to persuade all Americans to accept homosexuality—as if the issue were simply about "accepting homosexuals," and that anyone opposing special legal classifications for homosexuality was prejudiced, discriminatory, and as Obama claimed, possessed of "worn arguments and old attitudes." He added, "There are good and decent people in this country who don't yet fully embrace their gay brothers and sisters—not yet.

That's why I've spoken about these issues—not just in front of you—but in front of unlikely audiences, in front of African-American church members."[7]

CONSERVATIVES

In a celebratory speech following passage of ObamaCare, the president proved he is also an ungracious winner. "I heard one of the Republican leaders say this was gonna be Armageddon! Well, two months from now, six months from now, you can check it out, we'll look around. And we'll see. You don't have to take my word for it."[8]

Believe me, we won't. But Obama must have quickly forgotten that he acknowledged it would take some time to assess the critics' predictions. Just a week later he implied that if Republicans were correct, then Armageddon should have already arrived. In a speech at a healthcare rally in Portland, Maine, on April 1, he complained about the "misinformation," "fear-mongering," and "overheated rhetoric" about ObamaCare. He said that if you turned on the news you'd hear people "shouting about how the world will end because we passed this bill."

He wasn't exaggerating, he assured his audience. "Leaders of the Republican Party have actually been calling the passage of this bill 'Armageddon.' They say it's the end of freedom as we know it." So, he taunted, "after I signed the bill, I looked up to see if there were any asteroids headed our way. I checked to see if any cracks had opened up in the ground. But you know what? It turned out to be a pretty nice day. Birds were chirping. Folks were strolling down the street. Nobody lost their doctor, or was forced into some government plan."

It's inconceivable Obama was unaware that the provisions of his bill have yet to go into effect, rendering his entire rant irrelevant. In fact, he revealed that very thing in his next statement, when he attacked his critics. "Every day since I signed the reform into law, there's another poll or headline that says 'Nation still divided on health reform. No great surge in public support.' Well, yea, it's only been a week! Before we find out if people like health care reform maybe we should wait until it actually happens. Just a thought."[9] Yes, and where was that thought in his previous, incoherent sentence?

At a fundraiser for Senator Barbara Boxer in April 2010, Obama, on the warpath to bullying the nation into passing yet another transformative package of regulations—his financial overhaul legislation—unleashed his venom on Senate minority leader Mitch McConnell. He told the group that McConnell "paid a visit to Wall Street a week or two ago and met with some of the movers and shakers up there. I don't know exactly what was discussed. All I can tell you is when he came back, he promptly announced he would oppose the financial regulatory reform."

In his Alinskyite outburst, Obama once again accused anyone who stood in his way of dishonesty. He said McConnell's objections to the bill were "just plain false" and "cynical." Taken together, he was clearly suggesting McConnell was lying about the financial bill because he had been bought off by Wall Street. That's Obama, the paragon of civility and bipartisanship.[10]

"DOMESTIC TERRORISTS"

Obama's intolerance of criticism filters down through the bureaucracy, finding expression in unexpected, disturbing places. For example, a Department of Defense manual identified "protests" as a form of low-level terrorism.[11] Likewise, Obama's Department of Homeland Security released a report to the nation's law enforcement officials titled, "Rightwing Extremism: Current Economic and Political Climate Fueling Resurgence in Radicalization and Recruitment." According to the *Washington Times*, the report warned the "economic recession, the election of America's first black president, and the return of a few disgruntled war veterans could swell the ranks of white-power militias."[12]

The characterization of war vets as potential racist terrorists was bad enough, but the report cast suspicion on other conservative-leaning groups as well. In a footnote, the department defined "rightwing extremism in the United States" as including not just racist or hate groups, but also advocates of states' rights, and possibly "groups and individuals that are dedicated to a single-issue, such as opposition to abortion or immigration." Americans for Limited Government (ALG) filed a FOIA request demanding to know how DHS had arrived at that conclusion. In the administration's response, officials admitted they had relied mostly on websites and didn't do any statistical analysis or interview any of those it defined as terrorists. As ALG noted, they "did not conduct even the most rudimentary research or investigation." They just "cruised the Internet" and cherry-picked information from "disreputable sites" to stage their "attack" on "rightwing targets."[13]

The administration's report vilifying veterans and ordinary Americans outraged the American Legion. "I think it is important for all of us to remember that Americans are not the enemy. The terrorists are," said David K. Rehbein, the Legion's national commander.[14] Due to the public outcry, the report was recalled within hours from state and local law enforcement officials.[15]

On the heels of that controversial report, the Obama administration compiled a terrorism dictionary that tied "antiabortion extremists" to racism. It defined them as "a movement of groups or individuals who are virulently antiabortion and advocate violence against providers of abortion-related services, their employees, and their facilities. Some cite various racist and anti-Semitic beliefs to justify their criminal activities." Republican congressman Peter King, the ranking member on the House Homeland Security Committee, was infuriated by the dictionary, which he said "causes further concern that Congress needs to get to the bottom of exactly how DHS determines what intelligence products to distribute to law enforcement officials around the country."[16]

The administration denied any political motivation behind the DHS documents, protesting that they had drafted reports on the dangers of leftwing extremism as well. But that's not quite accurate. Michelle Malkin pointed out that past DHS reports had "always been very specific in identifying exact groups, causes, and targets of domestic terrorists." By contrast, wrote Malkin, the DHS report on rightwing extremism constituted "a sweeping indictment of conservatives." The "intent," she said, "is clear. . . . It is no coincidence that this report echoes Tea Party-bashing left-wing blogs . . . and demonizes the very Americans who will be protesting in the thousands on Wednesday for the nationwide Tax Day Tea Party."[17]

Perhaps even more damning, however, was that it was Obama's own political action group, "Organizing for America," that dubbed opponents of ObamaCare "Right Wing Domestic Terrorists."[18] The administration and its leftist enablers sought to distance themselves from this sordid event, but they are the ones who for years have been trying to connect conservative speech—especially talk radio—with violence, in order to lay the groundwork for chilling and censoring such speech. Former president Bill Clinton's attack on conservative talkers and so-called hate speech at his 1995 commencement speech at Michigan State University, his speech at the Center for American Progress in April 2009, and his April 2010 interview with the *New York Times*, in which he connected tea party-type anti-government rhetoric with violence like the Oklahoma City bombing, were not mere spontaneous utterances.

Indeed, from its very inception, the tea party movement was a prime target of team Obama's demonization campaign, with its members accused of being lawless extremists. In a private pep talk to Democratic congressmen, Obama, according to Congressman Earl Blumenauer, posed this question: "Does anybody think that the teabag, anti-government people are going to support them if they bring down health care? All it will do is confuse and dispirit" Democratic voters, "and it will encourage the extremists."[19] (For the uninitiated, the term "teabag" or "teabagger," used by liberals to slander the peaceful protestors of Obama's radical agenda, is a vulgar epithet involving a sexual act.) On another occasion White House press secretary Robert Gibbs demeaned tea party protestors as an irrelevant fringe group, telling *CBS News*'s Harry Smith, "I gotta tell you, Harry, I think most of what you're seeing on TV, no offense, is good TV and that's about it."[20]

Senator Chuck Schumer joined the White House's campaign against dissenters, calling then-Massachusetts Senate candidate Scott Brown a "far-right tea bagger" in an e-mail.[21] Obama himself couldn't resist taking unpresidential jabs at Brown, repeatedly ridiculing his pickup truck (which, as it turns out, was a GM). "Anybody can own a truck," Obama snidely remarked. Brown shot back, "Mr. President, unfortunately in this economy, not everybody can buy a truck. My goal is to change that by cutting spending, lowering taxes and letting people keep more of their money."[22]

Aside from deriding tea partiers as unruly rabble, the administration constantly portrayed them as vaguely threatening. Addressing the movement on CBS's *Face the Nation*, presidential adviser David Axelrod said, "I think any time you have severe economic conditions, there is always an element of disaffection that can mutate into something that's unhealthy." Demonstrating the administration's obliviousness to the public's concern about its explosive acceleration of our national debt, Axelrod expressed bewilderment that protestors would even be concerned by such issues, since "this president just cut taxes for 95 percent of the American people. So I think the tea bags should be directed elsewhere because he certainly understands the burden that people face."[23] On his 100th day in office, Obama personally ridiculed the tea party protestors, admonishing, "Let's not play games" and pretend out of control federal spending is just a matter of "the Recovery Act, because that's just a fraction of the overall problem we got."[24]

Tea party rallies only intensified the following year, with protestors meeting nationwide to denounce the administration's runaway spending, excessive taxation, expansion of government control, and other irresponsible policies. Obama continued to show both his aloofness (characterizing the protests as only about taxes) and his thin-skinned arrogance. He mocked tea partiers at a Democratic

Party fundraiser, saying he was "amused over the last couple of days where people have been having these rallies about taxes. You would think they would be saying 'thank you'" because "in all, we passed 25 different tax cuts last year. And one thing we haven't done is raise income taxes on families making less than $250,000 a year—another promise that we kept." His original promise, as previously noted, was that he wouldn't raise *any form* of taxes for that income group, on which he has now increased or imposed at least fourteen separate taxes.[25]

THE WAR ON FOX

It's hard to remember a president being treated so deferentially by the media, but the press can never be loyal enough for Obama. If you aren't with him 100 percent of the time, you are against him. *Time* political analyst Mark Halperin admitted to television host Charlie Rose that Obama was the first president to avoid media scrutiny, saying he had a "charmed" Senate race and a "charmed" presidential campaign. And yet, Halperin said, Obama is nevertheless "thin-skinned" about the press and "increasingly says that 'the press is against me.'"[26]

When FOX News wouldn't kowtow to his demands to air his third prime-time presser, Obama began to snub the network by refusing to call on its reporters at press conferences. FOX News White House correspondent Major Garrett called the snubbing "retribution" for FOX's decision not to air the press conference. He added, "I was warned that it might be considered as part of the overall consideration as to whether or not I'd get called on. I wasn't. I can add one and one to make two."[27] Obama's treatment of FOX wasn't a "one-off" event, but was part of a larger strategy to marginalize the only television network scrutinizing his policies.

The administration waged war against FOX not only for its direct criticism of Obama, but for the rippling effect of its critique into mainstream media outlets, including even the *New York Times*.

White House press secretary Robert Gibbs just couldn't stand for the *Times*, which had invariably supported Obama, to air the slightest criticism of his boss. When the *Times* ran a front-page story about parental outrage at Obama's address to school children—a story that had been closely covered on FOX—Gibbs became unglued. "This thing," he said, "has become a three-ring circus." The White House was also miffed when the *Washington Post* ran, without questioning it, an op-ed from a Republican politician that decried Obama's thirty-two policy czars.

According to *Time* magazine, in response to these stories "the White House decided it would become a player, issuing biting attacks on those pundits, politicians and outlets that make what the White House believes to be misleading or simply false claims. . . . Obama, fresh from his vacation on Martha's Vineyard, cheered on the effort, telling his aides he wanted to "call 'em out."[28] The White House blog was central to the effort, regularly denouncing the administration's critics, especially FOX. White House online programs director Jesse Lee railed against FOX's coverage of Obama's attempt to secure the 2016 Olympics for Chicago, accusing the network of continuing "its disregard for the facts in an attempt to smear the Administration's efforts to win the Olympics for the United States. . . . For even more FOX lies, check out the latest 'Truth-O-Meter' that debunks a false claim about a White House staffer."[29]

The pugnacious White House defiantly defended its behavior. Gibbs declared, "The only way to get somebody to stop crowding the plate is to throw a fastball at them. They move." So much for the new, post-partisan politics.

Then-White House communications director Anita Dunn, in lockstep with Gibbs, recommended a "rapid response" to counteract "FOX's blows" against the administration. Dunn described FOX as "part of the Republican Party" and as "opinion journalism masquerading as news. They are boosting their audience. But that doesn't mean we are going to sit back. . . . Let's not pretend they're a news network the way CNN is."[30] Dunn continued, "FOX News

often operates almost as either a research arm or a communications arm of the Republican Party. . . . When he [Obama] goes on FOX, he understands he's not going on it really as a news network at this point; he's going on to debate the opposition."[31] She claimed White House critics would "say anything. . . . They will take any small thing and distort it. . . . In other words, after eight months at the White House, the days of nonpartisan harmony are long gone—it's us against them. And the Obama Administration is playing to win."[32]

It wasn't as if Dunn was a loose cannon acting independently of the White House. Presidential adviser David Axelrod echoed Dunn's charges, telling ABC's George Stephanopoulos that FOX "is not a real news organization" and that "other news organizations, like yours, ought not to treat them that way." Senior adviser Valerie Jarrett told CNN's Campbell Brown, "Of course they're (FOX) biased." But she would not, when pressed, make the same claim about MSNBC.[33] To the contrary, Kareem Dale, Special Assistant to the President for Arts and Culture, publicly proclaimed, "At the White House, as we always like to say, we love MSNBC."[34]

Dunn's resignation in November 2009 did not end the administration's offensive against FOX. Her successor, Dan Pfeiffer, told the *New York Times*, "[FOX has] a point of view; that point of view pervades the entire network. We don't feel the obligation to treat them like we would treat CNN, or an ABC, or an NBC, or a traditional news organization, but there are times when we believe it makes sense to communicate with them." He vowed to continue Dunn's approach of treating FOX like a "wing of the Republican Party."[35]

Gibbs aggressively attacked FOX for reporting on unsavory stories involving Obama's "safe schools czar," Kevin Jennings. Gibbs was angered by FOX's reporting that Jennings had been praised by Harry Hay, founder of North American Man/Boy Love Association (NAMBLA), and that Jennings failed to report to authorities that a student told him the student was having sex with older men. Gibbs

commented, "It's a shame. I hope people watch what they (FOX News) do."[36]

The White House tried hard to shut FOX out of the news loops. When it scheduled round robin interviews on all the networks for its executive pay czar Kenneth Feinberg, it excluded FOX, which had been part of the White House press pool since 1997. To their credit, the other four TV networks refused to participate unless FOX were allowed to join, after which the White House relented.[37] *Baltimore Sun* TV critic David Zurawik called the administration's attempt to exclude FOX "outrageous." "What it's really about to me is the Executive Branch of the government trying to tell the press how it should behave. I mean, this democracy—we know this—only works with a free and unfettered press to provide information." When asked about his administration's campaign against FOX, a typically arrogant Obama likened the network to "talk radio"—a major insult in the liberal lexicon. He said, "If media is operating, basically, as a talk radio format, then that's one thing. And if it's operating as a news outlet, then that's another. But it's not something I'm losing sleep over."[38]

One Sunday in September 2009 Obama did a marathon of interviews on every network but FOX. He snubbed it *and* took thinly veiled digs at it on the other networks. On his interviews with CNN, ABC, CBS, and NBC, he criticized "television news" for making stars out of "rude" people, and complained that TV producers didn't book more guests who displayed "decency" and "civility." Obama told CNN's John King, "If you're civil and polite and you're sensible, and you don't exaggerate the bad things about your opponent . . . you might get on one of the Sunday shows, but you're not going to be in the loop." He told ABC's George Stephanopoulos the media "encourages some of the outliers in behavior," because being "rude" is the easiest way to get on TV. He complained of the "24-hour news cycle," where controversy and "the extreme statement" is what "gets you on."[39] This type of public whining is not something we've ordinarily seen from a president of the United States,

especially one as media-pampered as Obama, and one who himself engages in the very type of behavior he condemns.

In late 2009, *Politico* reported that executives at National Public Radio, which is partially funded by the federal government, asked Mara Liasson, NPR's top political correspondent, to reconsider her frequent appearances on FOX News because of its "political bias." The executives asked Liasson to watch FOX for thirty days to confirm it had become more partisan. Liasson complied but disagreed with the assessment, so she continued on FOX. *Politico* reported that NPR executives denied there was any connection between their pressuring Liasson and the White House's campaign "to delegitimize the network by painting it as an extension of the Republican Party."

SHOOTING THE MESSENGERS

The administration's attacks extended beyond FOX to other networks' correspondents who were perceived as hostile. They blasted CNBC's Rick Santelli in what *Politico* described as "unusually personal terms" for daring to challenge the administration's mortgage bailout plan.[40] "The government," thundered Santelli, "is promoting bad behavior. This is America! How many of you people want to pay for your neighbor's mortgage that has an extra bathroom and can't pay their bills?"[41] Santelli's rant is widely credited with sparking the tea party movement, thus making him an obvious target for the White House's press war. Gibbs said, "I've watched Mr. Santelli on cable the past twenty-four hours or so. I'm not entirely sure where Mr. Santelli lives or in what house he lives but the American people are struggling every day to meet their mortgages, stay in their jobs, pay their bills, send their kids to school. I think we left a few months ago the adage that if it was good for a derivatives trader that it was good for Main Street. I think the verdict is in on that."

Gibbs further claimed Santelli was misrepresenting the president's plan in saying it rewards people who don't play by the rules.

He insisted, "I'd be more than happy to have him come here to read it. I'd be happy to buy him a cup of coffee—decaf." Santelli was neither amused nor intimidated. He responded, "Pretty much everybody we know's 401k is now a 201k. Why did that happen?...We want our 401k money back. I want my stock money back. The retirement funds of many Americans [are] much larger of a loss than some people on their housing at this point in time."[42]

Next in line for a White House comeuppance was CNBC's *Mad Money* host Jim Cramer, who said he believed "the president's policies, his agenda had contributed to the greatest wealth destruction he's ever seen by a president." Gibbs responded by attacking Cramer's overall credibility: "You can go back and look at any number of statements that he's made in the past about the economy and wonder where some of the backup for those are too." Next, Gibbs turned on Cramer's network. "I'm going to get in a lot of trouble if I continue," he said. "The president—again, if you turn on a certain program, it's geared to a very small audience—no offense to my good friends, or friend at CNBC. But the president has to look out for the broader economy and for the broader population—many of whom are investors, but not exclusively investors."[43] Interestingly, Cramer is a long-time liberal Democrat.

The White House's relentless denunciation of Obama's critics provoked Rowan Scarborough to comment, "The White House is using the daily press briefing to launch personal attacks on President Obama's critics, signaling the vast liberal media to join in. In just 50 days in office, Press Secretary Robert Gibbs has taken on Rick Santelli and Jim Cramer at CNBC; conservative radio king Rush Limbaugh; and, most recently, former Vice President Dick Cheney." (Scarborough was referring to Gibbs's swipe at Cheney as being part of a "Republican cabal.") "The personal slap downs" of the White House's critics, wrote Scarborough, "stand in contrast to how the Bush White House used the daily briefing."

The arrogant Gibbs was particularly unrepentant about his own thuggish behavior. He bragged, "There are very few days that I've had more fun. I was afraid I was going to have too much more fun."[44] Can you imagine Gibbs's behavior had he faced a truly hostile press instead of a lapdog "state-run" media?

The administration even went after critics of its "Cash for Clunkers" program. The auto website Edmunds.com published an unflattering analysis of Clunkers, saying its actual costs to taxpayers amounted to some $24,000 per car, not the $4,500 per car of government rebates represented by the White House. In its calculations, Edmunds used the number of cars that were sold as a direct result of the program, excluding those vehicles that would have been sold anyway. Edmunds said the administration's economic claims about the program "have been rendered quite weak."[45]

The report incensed the White House which, in the words of the liberal NPR, "responded with snark." The White House Blog featured a responsive post titled, "Busy Covering Car Sales on Mars, Edmunds.com Gets It Wrong (Again) on Cash for Clunkers." Condemning Edmunds' "faulty" analysis for assuming the market for cars outside the Clunkers program was completely unaffected by the program (as if all other cars "were being sold on Mars"), the post claimed the findings "appear designed to grab headlines and get coverage on cable TV. Like many of their previous attempts, this claim doesn't even withstand basic scrutiny. . . . So put on your space suit and compare the two approaches yourself."[46]

NPR was not impressed, noting that Edmunds' response "was, by contrast, snark-free and fairly persuasive." Edmunds calmly dismantled the White House's lame rebuttal, showing how its key points rested on assertions based on anecdotes, not objective data. Edmunds concluded with a suggestion to the White House that, "with all respect" it shouldn't "shoot the messenger."[47]

"NOT THE KIND OF CHANGE YOU CAN BELIEVE IN"

Unsurprisingly, the Democrats' bête noir, my brother Rush Limbaugh, was singled out for especially harsh criticism. The *New York*

Post reported, "President Obama warned Republicans on Capitol Hill today that they need to quit listening to radio king Rush Limbaugh if they want to get along with Democrats and the new administration. 'You can't just listen to Rush Limbaugh and get things done,' he told top GOP leaders, whom he had invited to the White House to discuss his nearly $1 trillion stimulus package."[40]

Obama's activist supporters, such as MoveOn.org and Americans United for Change, launched radio and TV ads expressing false outrage at Limbaugh's condemnation of Obama's profligate spending. In the spirit of street agitator Saul Alinsky, Limbaugh was the target to be frozen and demonized, and then Republican lawmakers as well, by association with Limbaugh.[49] *Politico* took notice, observing that "liberal groups are dispensing with the niceties and seeking to drive a wedge between Republicans and one of the right's most influential leaders." *Politico* reported that Americans United for Change was about to air radio ads in three states asking Republican senators, "Will you side with Obama or Rush Limbaugh?" The ad referred to Limbaugh as an "extreme partisan" who "wants President Obama's Jobs program to fall.... Will our Senator... side with Rush Limbaugh too?"[50]

The administration's campaign against Limbaugh provoked a *Time* magazine story titled, "Team Obama's Petty Limbaugh Strategy." *Time* noted Obama won the presidency "promising to be a different, more substantive, less gimmicky leader" who would not engage in "phony outrage," but would work on solving problems. Instead, the subject of Limbaugh and his influence on the Republican Party was dominating the news. *Time* quoted *Politico's* Jonathan Martin saying the entire Limbaugh "controversy" had "been cooked up and force fed to the American people by Obama's advisers." In other words, said *Time*, "it's not the kind of change you can believe in."[51]

Time discovered the Democrats' anti-Limbaugh campaign was hatched following a poll taken by Bill Clinton's pollster Stanley Greenberg—who just happens to own the house where Obama's then-chief of staff Rahm Emanuel stayed while in Washington. The poll allegedly found "Limbaugh was deeply unpopular among wide swaths of the American electorate." So Greenberg and Clinton henchmen James Carville and Paul Begala devised a strategy to taint the Republican Party by connecting it to Limbaugh.[52]

The White House set the strategy in motion when Limbaugh announced he hoped Obama would fail, by which he meant—as he clearly explained—that he hoped his agenda failed because otherwise the nation would fail. Rooting for the failure of Obama's agenda was tantamount, in Limbaugh's expressly articulated view, to championing the nation's success and well being. Yet Gibbs and other Democratic operatives colluded to paint Limbaugh as an anti-patriot who wished for America's failure for crass partisan purposes.

But the distortion of Limbaugh's statement was too blatant even for some members of the mainstream media. *Time*'s David Von Drehle quoted Teddy Roosevelt saying, "To announce that there must be no criticism of the President, or that we are to stand by the President, right or wrong, is not only unpatriotic and servile but is morally treasonable to the American public."[53] The inherent virtue of even the most outrageous expressions of "dissent," of course, was an ever-present Democratic talking point throughout the entire presidency of George W. Bush. As Hillary Clinton declared back then, "I am sick and tired of people who say that if you debate and you disagree with this administration somehow you're not patriotic. And we should stand up and say we are Americans and we have a right to debate and disagree with any administration."[54] Under Obama, however, critics of the president have suddenly degenerated from brave dissidents into unpatriotic and divisive demagogues.

Despite the protests of some rebels like Von Drehle, much of the mainstream media predictably parroted the White House's allegations against Limbaugh and even attributed to him racist comments and other outlandish statements he'd never made. *National Review*'s editors observed that journalists had incorporated into their reporting, "without substantiation," "a rash of manufactured quotes attributed to Limbaugh," doing "collectively what Dan Rather did individually: allow themselves to be duped by phony documents." It was a part of the "Democratic media's recent campaign to prevent Rush from becoming part-owner of a professional football team, but the lies reached a level that is remarkable even by the standards of the corrupt and incompetent American media."

The attribution of these false quotes to Limbaugh, observed *National Review*, was "to lie—viciously." But, what made the partisan and dishonest assault "disturbing" was "that the White House [was] a participant in it. . . . There may be some precedent for a modern White House's attempting to use the machinery of the presidency to destroy a critic in this fashion, but Barack Obama did not run as the Second Coming of Richard Nixon."[55]

Aside from Limbaugh, Obama attacked other conservative media figures as well, such as Sean Hannity. Obama repeatedly denounced the radio and FOX News host, once implying Hannity promoted hatred against him after Sean got under his skin for connecting the dots between Obama and his radical friends such as his pastor Jeremiah Wright, the unrepentant terrorist William Ayers, and Ayers's wife, the former FBI fugitive Bernardine Dohrn.[56]

Columnist Paul Ibrahim rejected the White House's efforts to distance and sanitize Obama from the administration's war against its opponents. He wrote, "The fact that this systematic operation to intimidate and demonize Obama's opponents was launched so soon after his inauguration is tremendously perturbing. What is even more alarming is that Obama is not only a member of this campaign—he is the driving force behind it." Ibrahim identified why this pattern of behavior, coming from the president of the United States, is inimical to freedom. "Within 100 hours of taking office, the president of the United States proceeded to single out a private citizen for his mere dissent, effectively expelling him from the government's marketplace of ideas, and with him the millions of listeners of the same political stripe. . . . Welcome to the politics of hope 'n' change.

Obama's startling attempt to hang Limbaugh's scalp on the wall is a warning that the new ruler does not want unity—he demands it."[57]

The crusade against Limbaugh was nothing new for Obama; it simply resurrected a strategy he had employed as a presidential candidate in attempting to smear his opponent, John McCain, by tying him to Limbaugh, whom they had slandered with a manufactured racial slur against Mexicans by taking some of his radio comments grossly out of context. Limbaugh himself, in an op-ed in the *Wall Street Journal* a few months before Ibrahim's piece, chastised Obama for stoking the flames of racial antagonism on Limbaugh's back. "What kind of potential president," he asked, "would let his campaign knowingly extract two incomplete, out-of-context lines from two radio parodies and build a framework of hate around them in order to exploit racial tensions? The segregationists of the 1950s and 1960s were famous for such vile fear-mongering."[58] This was the candidate not only claiming to be above dirty politics, but who held himself out as post-racial. "We've made such racial progress in this country. Any candidate who employs the tactic of the old segregationists is unworthy of the presidency."[59]

No one should operate under the misapprehension that Obama's White House didn't have its hands all over the effort to demonize Limbaugh and other political opponents. His relationship with his supporters is symbiotic. *Newsbusters* reported, for example, that Obama confidantes such as his discredited, radical, former green jobs czar Van Jones were tied to StopTheWitchHunt.org—a group specifically formed to "call out" so-called "mischaracterizations and hate speech" of Limbaugh, Glenn Beck, Lou Dobbs, Pat Buchanan, and Paul Brown.[60]

Obama is also intolerant of criticism of his wife, but it wasn't as if the criticism was gratuitous. He had encouraged her to speak out on policy issues, and when she did and called America "downright mean," she earned the righteous indignation of patriots everywhere. Yet Obama lashed out at *National Review* and FOX News (again), as well as the rest of the "conservative press," for going "fairly deliberately at her in a pretty systematic way." He added, "I think that it is an example of the erosion of civility in our political culture that she's been subjected to these attacks."[61]

SARAH PALIN AND CARVILLE'S "LIMBAUGH STRATEGY"

Sarah Palin is a close second to Rush Limbaugh in the Left's roster of most hated conservatives. The attacks on Palin began almost from the moment McCain picked her as his running mate. Obama derided the McCain-Palin reform rhetoric with, "You can't put lipstick on a pig. It's still a pig." Obama also disparagingly referred to Palin as a "moose shooter"[62] and all but called her a liar in portraying herself as an earmark watchdog. "Come on!" said Obama. "I mean, words mean something, you can't just make stuff up."[63]

The demonization of Palin did not abate with Obama's election. The UK *Telegraph's* Toby Harnden pointed out in November 2009 that "Barack Obama's Organizing for America" sent out "pleas for cash" citing Palin's book *Going Rogue* as an incentive to donate "to oppose 'Sarah Palin and her allies.'" The e-mail from these Obama surrogates bitterly denounced Palin for claiming ObamaCare would institute "death panels" and for "opening the flood gates for months of false attacks by special interests and partisan extremists." It suggested Palin is "dangerous" and called her a liar, referring to "whatever lie comes next [from her],"and declaring, "We can't afford more deception and delay."[64] A few months earlier Gibbs had named Palin as one of "the biggest purveyors of disinformation."[65]

Those who believe the Left's negative reaction to Palin is merely visceral fail to see that Obama leftists smeared Palin for the same strategic purpose they vilified Limbaugh: to taint all conservatives and the Republican Party by association. The *Washington Post*'s The Plum Line blog reported that James Carville, the architect of "the Limbaugh strategy," said Democrats would seek to elevate Palin more and more and turn her into the new Rush Limbaugh. "Her name conjures up all kinds of reactions in people's minds," said Carville, who conceded he was attempting to alienate moderates from the GOP by focusing on Palin. "She's an uncomfortable figure for a lot of Republicans. They want to move beyond her. *We* like her." Another Democratic strategist said, "Luckily, she seems to present us with an opportunity every few days. You could say it's a turkey shoot."[66]

The White House was obviously knee-deep in this "Carville strategy" to demonize Limbaugh, Palin, FOX News, and other conservatives. In an off-the-record briefing at the White House with leftist commentators including Rachel Maddow, Keith Olbermann, Frank Rich, and Bob Herbert, Obama "gave vent to sentiments about the network [FOX], according to people briefed on the conversation." Michael Clemente, a FOX News executive, suggested the targeting of FOX "was part of a larger White House strategy to marginalize critics," citing a report in *Politico* about a White House strategy session to "move more aggressively against opponents."[67] Clemente's analysis is certainly consistent with *Time* magazine's citing of *Politico*'s report that the Limbaugh "controversy" had "been cooked up and force fed to the American people by Obama's advisers."[68]

While Palin, Limbaugh, and others were certainly special targets of the White House, anyone who opposed Obama's priorities could find themselves subject to personal attack. For example, Obama's team became incensed when Republican senator Jim Bunning blocked their move to extend unemployment and health benefits. Bunning's opposition was based on a simple, commonsense proposition: "Before we expand a program, let's make sure we can pay for it." Bunning was not even opposed to extending the benefits per se; he just wanted them paid out of unspent "stimulus" funds, which seemed exceedingly reasonable, since the "stimulus" funds that had already been spent had not created the jobs Obama promised they would. Bunning was also intent on forcing Obama and lawmakers to honor their "paygo" legislation, which mandated that new government spending be funded through other spending reductions, funds allocated elsewhere, or from new taxes.

But Gibbs made it personal, stating, "I don't know how you negotiate with the irrational" and even admitted using his position of
influence to "shame" Bunning. "Sometimes," bemoaned Gibbs,
"even using their names doesn't create the shame you would think
it would."[69]

"IN LAS VEGAS, HE'S SURE NOT OUR FRIEND."

As a candidate, Obama usually told voters what he thought they
wanted to hear. He told an audience of 18,000 in Las Vegas he
wanted to help "not just the folks who own casinos but the folks who
are serving in casinos." But after becoming president he wasn't quite
as solicitous. In one of his many anti-capitalist riffs he took a cheap
shot at CEOs at a townhall meeting in Elkhart, Indiana, in February
2009. "You can't take a trip to Las Vegas or down to the Super Bowl
on the taxpayers' dime." Obama's careless statement elicited a strong
reaction from Las Vegas businessmen, many pointing out that if their
business suffers, the first and hardest hit are the front line workers—
the people at the front desk, the bell staff, and the taxi drivers, precisely the people Obama courted during the campaign.[70]

Nevada governor Jim Gibbons wrote to Obama requesting a
meeting with him to discuss the economic damage to the convention and tourism business caused by Obama's statement. The Las
Vegas Convention and Visitors Authority reported that more than
400 conventions and business meetings scheduled in the city had
been canceled, translating into 111,800 guests and more than
250,000 "roomnights," costing the city's economy more than $100
million, apart from lost gaming revenue. Obama, showing his char-
acteristic petulance toward critics, refused to meet with Gibbons,
who responded, "I am disappointed at the hypocrisy shown by this
administration. President Obama is coming to Las Vegas later this
month for a fundraiser, but he will not help the struggling families
in Las Vegas and Nevada who are out of work because of his reckless comments."[71]

During a townhall meeting in New Hampshire a year later, Obama took another gratuitous swipe at Las Vegas, saying, "When times are tough, you tighten your belts"—apparently exempting his own federal leviathan from the admonition. "You don't go buying a boat when you can barely pay your mortgage. You don't blow a bunch of cash in Vegas when you're trying to save for college." Las Vegas mayor Oscar Goodman fired back that Obama is "no friend to Las Vegas" and that "I think he has a psychological hang-up about us. . . . He's not welcome in my city, as far as I'm concerned. He's not our friend. I don't know about people in Nevada, but in Las Vegas, he's sure not our friend."

Goodman said he was "incredulous" that Obama would attack the city again and that a simple apology wouldn't cut it now that the damage had been done. "It has to be a real *mea culpa* and a promise not to do it again," stated Goodman. Governor Gibbons' reaction was equally strong. "How dare he insult any American city?" he asked. "I'm writing a letter to him today telling him to tone down or temper his remarks about Las Vegas. This is another slap in the face of the hard-working families in Nevada." Senator John Ensign noted Obama had become "quite comfortable criticizing Las Vegas" and that he has "failed to grasp the weight that his words carry." He has caused "countless companies and federal agencies" to cancel their conventions at Las Vegas hotels, costing them "and our city millions of dollars."[72]

THE STATE OF ARIZONA

When Arizona enacted a law to deal with its illegal immigration problem in response to continuing immigrant-related crime and violence, Attorney General Holder threatened to sue the state because the law allegedly "has the possibility of leading to racial profiling." He later admitted he hadn't even been briefed on the law much less read it himself.[73] Homeland Security secretary Janet Napolitano admitted under questioning from Senator John McCain that she hadn't read the law either, even though she had vehemently denounced it.

Ironically, Napolitano sang a different tune before she went to work for Obama. According to Arizona governor Jan Brewer, when Napolitano herself served as Arizona governor she wrote letters to Washington insisting, "We need our borders secure. We need our money from the federal government for the incarceration of the illegal immigrants that we have in our jails and in our prisons." Brewer revealed, "She repeated it over and over. She sent a big blown up check of what they owed us. So she knows. She understands. For her to say she hadn't even read the bill that I signed because she already had it on her desk is unconscionable. The bill is the same bill she had before her."[74]

Obama attacked what he called a "misguided" law that threatened "to undermine basic notions of fairness we cherish as Americans." He also blatantly misrepresented the bill and stirred up racial animus by claiming the law would lead to harassment of people who take their kids out to get ice cream, if they don't have their papers on them. In fact, the law expressly prohibited racial profiling and had several layers of safeguards against it: before anyone could be arrested, state authorities would have to verify with federal authorities the suspect was illegal; no U.S. citizens could be prosecuted under the law; and only those with whom law enforcement had made *lawful contact*, as in a traffic stop, could be asked to show identification, and only in cases where officers had a "reasonable suspicion" that an immigration law had been violated.

Yet the administration savaged Arizonans en masse for adopting the bill, portraying them as renegades operating outside federal authority. But in fact Arizona legislators had drafted the bill in close consultation with law professor and immigration law expert Kris Kobach, who carefully crafted the law to adhere to the Constitution, making it a mirror image of existing federal law, and requiring state authorities to defer to their federal counterparts in determining whether the law had been violated. A Pew Poll showed an overwhelming 73 percent of Americans approved of the Arizona law's requirement that people verify their legal status, and two-thirds support police detaining people who can't.[75]

As the Arizona law put the issue of illegal immigration back in the spotlight, Obama began taking heat over the issue. In response, he pledged to put several thousand National Guard troops on the Arizona border. In a meeting with Governor Brewer, he promised to get back to her within two weeks with details on the deployment. When he failed to keep his word, Brewer went on FOX News' *On the Record* to denounce the situation as "unacceptable." She indicated to host Greta Van Susteren that Obama's promise was empty posturing: "I think that the people of Arizona and the people of America put a lot of pressure on this issue and that [the administration] responded to kind of cool it down. And I think they thought maybe they could go away and placate us. Unfortunately, they didn't."[76]

An even bigger snub of Brewer and her state followed shortly thereafter, as Hillary Clinton announced during an interview with an Ecuadorean TV station that the administration would sue Arizona over the law. Brewer was furious. "This is no way to treat the people of Arizona," she exclaimed. "To learn of this lawsuit through an Ecuadorean interview with the Secretary of State is just outrageous. If our own government intends to sue our state to prevent illegal immigration enforcement, the least it can do is inform us before it informs the citizens of another nation."[77]

Brewer thus highlighted the crux of the issue. Arizona only adopted its own law because the federal government refuses to fulfill its constitutional duty to secure the border. And make no mistake, the porous border is not a "failure" in the traditional sense, but rather a calculated policy. Obama admitted as much during a private meeting with Senator Jon Kyl. As Kyl revealed to an Arizona townhall meeting, Obama told him, "The problem is . . . if we secure the border, then you all won't have any reason to support 'comprehensive immigration reform.'" Kyl translated: "In other words, they're holding [border security] hostage. They don't want to secure the border unless and until it is combined with 'comprehensive immigration reform'"—a euphemism for amnesty.

Although the White House denied Kyl's account of the meeting, the lawsuit against Arizona makes Obama's position crystal clear: non-enforcement is the only acceptable policy on border security.[78]

OBAMA'S RED STATE ALLERGY

Obama's disdain for those who refuse to toe his line extends to entire regions of the nation that he perceives to be immune to his Kool Aid. Perhaps he was projecting his own feelings when he suggested on the campaign trail that small town Americans "get bitter and they cling to guns or religion or antipathy toward people who aren't like them." Could it be that he harbors antipathy toward people who aren't like *him*—who don't share his vision to fundamentally turn America 180 degrees from its founding principles?

It seems so. *Hot Air*'s Ed Morrissey noted while Obama visited every state during his presidential campaign, he hasn't been quite as indiscriminate since becoming president. Morrissey cited a study by University of Minnesota professor Dr. Eric Ostermeier revealing that during the first 14-plus months of his term, Obama gave more speeches outside the country (sixty-three) than in America's red states put together. Of the speeches he delivered outside Washington, he made almost ten times as many in states he won (116) than in states won by John McCain (fifteen). Morrissey concludes, "Democrats may argue that they can compete in every state, but it's hard to reconcile that with Obama's reluctance to appear in states that didn't catch Hopenchange Fever the first time around. Indeed, it looks as though Obama would rather go abroad than visit those states."[79]

ATTACKING THE SUPREME COURT

For Obama, ever the Chicago politician, everything is political. When it serves his cause to politicize, everyone and every institution is fair game. When the Supreme Court issued its ruling in *Citizens United v. Federal Election Commission*, which lifted curbs on corporate campaign contributions, Obama publicly condemned the third branch of government, portraying its decision as politically driven and a huge victory for "big oil, Wall Street banks, health insurance companies and the other powerful interests that marshal their power every day in Washington to drown out the voices of everyday Americans."[80] Obama said in his weekly radio address, "This week the United States Supreme Court handed a huge victory to the special interests and their lobbyists—and a powerful blow to our efforts to rein in corporate influence. This ruling strikes at our democracy itself."

In fact, the Court's majority ruling was a triumph for free speech and democracy. But Obama almost immediately threatened to try to nullify the court's ruling with new legislation. His language as chief executive, directed at the judiciary branch, was inflammatory and highly inappropriate. He said he couldn't "think of anything more devastating to the public interest." Pitting the Court against the "American people" and the "special interests," he said it would be his "priority" to "repair the damage that has been done."[81]

Obama's public assault on the court during his State of the Union address, with many of the justices present, drew criticism from the *Los Angeles Times* blog. It might not be unusual in U.S. history for a president to disagree with the Supreme Court, said the blog, but "what is considerably more unusual is for the chief executive of the executive branch (Barack Obama) to look down on members of the said Supreme Court in public at a joint session of Congress and to their faces denounce their independent actions. And then to receive a resounding ovation from fellow Democrats standing to applaud and cheer Obama as the surrounded Justices sat mute, motionless and unable to respond."[82]

The normally low key chief justice, John Roberts, commented on Obama's attack at a speech at the University of Alabama Law School in Tuscaloosa. Roberts lamented that the atmosphere of the State of the Union had "degenerated to a political pep rally." Roberts said he had no problem with anyone criticizing the court, but "there is the issue of the setting, the circumstances and the decorum. The image of having the members of one branch of government standing up, literally surrounding the Supreme Court, cheering and hollering while the court—according to the requirements of protocol—has to sit there expressionless, I think is very troubling."[03]

"WE WILL KEEP. . . OUR BOOT ON THE THROAT OF BP"

Despite British Petroleum's assurances that it was "absolutely" responsible for the disastrous oil spill in the Gulf of Mexico, Obama unleashed on BP a non-stop barrage of verbal abuse. Using language not usually heard from a U.S. president, he told NBC's *Today Show* that he consults experts about the spill to find out "whose ass to kick." (Hint: it's not his own.) Moreover, in keeping with his penchant for prejudging situations and assessing fault without benefit of all the facts, Obama used his office to decree BP's legal liability, declaring, "BP is responsible for this leak, BP will be paying the bill."[84] Though Obama received generous campaign contributions from the oil giant (contrary to the MSM narrative that Republicans alone are "in the pocket of Big Oil"), White House press secretary Robert Gibbs said the administration "will keep our. . . boot on the throat of BP to ensure that they're doing all that is necessary while we do all that is humanly possible to deal with this incident."[85]

Gibbs's gangster imagery was no mere rhetorical flourish, as BP executives discovered when they were summoned to the White House. Flanked by Attorney General Eric Holder, who has threatened criminal action against BP, Obama shook down BP into forking over a $20 billion installment to defer the government's further wrath. Although the company's liability was legally capped at $75 million, its managers had little choice but to submit to Obama's diktat—the U.S. president was relentlessly denouncing them in every public forum, and they had a criminal investigation hanging over their head. While it's difficult to feel sorry for BP, claims against the company are supposed to be handled through the judicial process, not by a grand-standing president extorting cash through threats and bullying.

Even Obama's supporters recognized he was resorting to sheer intimidation. As Democratic strategist James Carville noted, "It looks as if President Obama applied a little old-school Chicago per-suasion to the oil executives." But American presidents, of course, are not supposed to resort to this kind of outright thuggery to get their way. As Conn Carroll remarked on the Heritage Foundation's blog, "Making 'offers you can't refuse' may be a great way to run the mob, but it is no way to run a country."[86]

BP was not Obama's only scapegoat as he desperately sought to deflect the public outcry over his manifestly incompetent response to the oil spill. He also denounced the Minerals Management Serv-ice, the federal agency that oversees oil and gas drilling in the Gulf. "For too long, for a decade or more," said Obama, "there has been a cozy relationship between the oil companies and the federal agency that permits them to drill." He then suggested that the agency just gave out permits like candy, at the simple request of the oil companies with nothing more than their assurances of safety. He also angrily condemned oil industry officials for pointing fingers of blame at each other, imperiously declaring, "I will not tolerate more finger pointing or irresponsibility."[87]

Amidst all the furious accusations and blame shifting, it was clear BP is but another prop Obama has chosen to advance another plank of his statist agenda—this time his plan to shut down our conventional energy industry in favor of new, quixotic alternative energy methods that will succeed only in propelling this nation even faster toward third world status.

IT'S BUSH'S FAULT

No list of Obama's targets would be complete without an account-ing of his perpetual thrashing of George W. Bush. Out of a sense of decorum, most presidents refrain from directly criticizing their

predecessor. For example, President George W. Bush jealously safe-
guarded the dignity of his office and rarely censured Bill Clinton.
And even out of office Bush studiously refrains from criticizing
Obama, saying he "deserves my silence."[88] The one time Bush
made an exception and criticized Obama for his economic policies
and his decision to close Gitmo, Gibbs snarkily responded that
many of those policies were debated during last year's election.
"We kept score last November, and we won."[89]

As Obama began his term in office, one might have assumed his
continued hammering of President Bush was just a short-term
holdover from a contentious campaign, where Obama and the
Democrats ran against Bush perhaps more than they did against
Republican nominee John McCain. (A *New Yorker* profile of Bush
observed, "There was an almost obsessive singularity in the way
that Obama and his chief strategists—Axelrod and David Plouffe,
the campaign's manager—saw the contest. In their tactical view, all
that was wrong with the United States could be summarized in one
word: Bush."[90]) But as his presidency wore on, Obama kept sniping
at Bush at the same feverish pace. As columnist Charles Krauthammer asked, "Is there anything he hasn't blamed George W. Bush
for? The economy, global warming, the credit crisis, Middle East
stalemate, the deficit, anti-Americanism abroad—everything but
swine flu. It's as if Obama's presidency hasn't really started."[91] Consider some examples:

- In March 2009, Obama announced he would be sending 21,000 additional troops to Afghanistan. But in
  October he authorized and dispatched an additional
  13,000 troops there, bringing the total increase he had
  approved to 34,000. When asked about the additional
  troops, which brought the total number of U.S. troops
  deployed in Iraq and Afghanistan even above their
  peak levels during the Iraq "surge," Gibbs said that
  Bush, not Obama, had authorized the additional

13,000 troops. But Pentagon spokesman Bryan Whitman contradicted Gibbs, saying, "The 21,000 are only combat forces, and when the combat forces go in, there are a certain amount of additional forces that are required." Another defense official confirmed this, saying, "Obama authorized the whole thing."[92]

- Also in March 2009, Obama took a shot at the previous administration on a *60 Minutes* interview, attacking former vice president Dick Cheney, who had been criticizing him for jettisoning major components of the Bush administration's approach to the war on terror. "How many terrorists have actually been brought to justice under the philosophy that is being promoted by Vice President Cheney?" asked Obama. Then he implied the Bush administration had endangered the country, insisting Cheney's approach to terrorism "hasn't made us safer. What it has been is a great advertisement for anti-American sentiment."[93]

- On May 11, 2009, White House budget director Peter Orszag wrote in a blog post that increases in the estimated federal budget deficit of $89 billion for 2009 and $87 billion for 2010 were due to "the economic crisis inherited by this administration."[94]

- The Obama administration even blamed Bush for its own bailout of General Motors. Obama's senior economic adviser Austan Goolsbee said Obama's options were sharply limited by Bush's handling of the auto industry because Bush "ran out the clock." This was despite the fact that when the Bush administration allocated $17.4 billion of TARP funds to GM and Chrysler the previous December, Obama praised the move as "a necessary step." Even the *Hill* acknowledged Obama's culpability, saying, "The Obama administration has steered the two troubled companies into bankruptcy."[95]

- In July 2009, when the unemployment rate hit a 26-year high, Obama denied any responsibility, saying, "It took us years to get us into this mess, and it will take more than a few months to get us out." As *National Review Online*'s Jim Geraghty noted, "This ignores the fact that after the stimulus passed, [he] has not 'gotten us out of the mess,' but the mess has gotten worse."[96]

- In a July 2009 press conference, Obama referred to the Bush years nine times, three of which were direct complaints that he inherited a $1.3 trillion debt that had hampered his progress in restoring economic growth. The *Washington Times'* Joseph Curl commented on Obama's Bush-bashing habit in light of his promise to usher in a "new era of responsibility" that would transcend partisan politics, quoting former Bush deputy press secretary Tony Fratto as saying, "For a guy who campaigned on taking responsibility and looking forward, he spends an awful lot of time pointing fingers and looking backward."[97]

- In a townhall meeting in Shaker Heights, Ohio, Obama said, "Folks have a lot of nerve who have helped us get into this fiscal hole and then start going around trying to talk about fiscal responsibility. I'm always a little surprised that people don't have a little more shame about having created a mess and then trying to point fingers."[98]

- At a DNC fundraiser in San Francisco in October 2009, responding to the spate of criticism he'd been receiving over the economy and the sky-rocketing national debt, Obama accused his critics of having "a selective memory" about the fact that he didn't create the current economic crisis, which was "unlike any that we've seen in our times. We were losing 700,000 jobs a month. Our financial system was on the brink of collapse. Economists of every political stripe were saying we might be slipping into the next Great Depression. . . . Another way of putting it is when, you know, I'm busy and Nancy is busy with our mop cleaning up somebody else's mess—we don't want somebody sitting back saying, 'You're not holding the mop the right way.' Why don't *you* grab a mop, why don't you help clean up."[99]

■ At his West Point speech in December 2009, Obama said, "The decision to go into Iraq caused substantial rifts between America and much of the world. . . . Today, after extraordinary costs we are bringing the Iraq war to a responsible end." Did he mean the costs were not worth the result? That it was less important to spend money in Iraq against an evil regime than it was to waste it on quixotic "stimulus" fantasies at home? That even if we were justified in invading Iraq we shouldn't have done it if it resulted in "rifts" with other nations—implying that opposition to the right thing means not doing the right thing?

Obama declared, "I opposed the war in Iraq precisely because I believe that we must exercise restraint in the use of military force, and always consider the long-term consequences of our actions. We have been at war for eight years, at enormous cost in lives and resources. Years of debate over Iraq and terrorism have left our unity on national security issues in tatters, and created a highly polarized and partisan backdrop for this effort." He then turned to his favorite subject, the "worst economic crisis since the Great Depression," which he made clear he "inherited" and personally remedied.[100]

■ On NBC's *Meet the Press*, Vice President Joe Biden said the Iraq war wasn't worth the "horrible price, not only in loss of life, the way the war was mishandled from the outset, but we took our eye off the ball, putting us in a much different and more dangerous position in Afghanistan. We lost support around the world."[101]

- FOX News reported on January 25, 2010, that Obama and his top advisors had "been pinning the blame on the prior administration, directly or obliquely, ever since Obama's inauguration a full year ago." What's more, they did so "at least seven times since last Tuesday's stunning upset in the Massachusetts Senate election." Obama referred to the "economic downturn we inherited," "the year of failing to pay for new policies," and "the trillion dollars in deficits" Bush created. Gibbs claimed "the hole we inherit and the hole that we have to fill is very, very deep."

  Aide David Axelrod said, "When the president walked in the door, he was handed the worst economic downturn since the Great Depression, a financial crisis that held out the prospect of the collapse of the financial system and a fiscal crisis." With unmatched chutzpah, adviser David Plouffe declaimed that Democrats should not "accept any lectures on spending" from Republicans. "Republicans' fiscal irresponsibility," said Plouffe, "has never been matched in our country's history."[102]

- In his first State of the Union address, Obama issued a bitterly strident and partisan harangue, blaming Bush for coming into office with a $200 billion budget surplus and leaving office with a $1.3 trillion deficit, which Obama blamed on "paying for two wars, two tax cuts, and an expensive prescription drug program." "All this," he claimed, "was before I walked in the door."

Sadly, the mainstream media enabled Obama's unbecoming behavior just as it had indulged his messianic mystique. Carrying on in its tradition of demonizing President Bush and deifying President Obama, the MSM reinforced the "it's Bush's fault" theme at every turn. In November 2009, *Time's* cover story was "The End of the 2000s: Goodbye (at Last) to the Decade From Hell." Andy Serwer, who wrote the cover story, expounded on it on MSNBC's *Morning Joe*, "Overall, it was a decade where Americans really suffered. There was, you know, a deferral of responsibility, neglect, and these things all sort of came home to roost this decade. . . . If you lived in China or Brazil, not a bad decade. But here in the United States, it was kind of tough."[103]

Reality doesn't quite match Serwer's rhetoric, considering that the George W. Bush years saw mostly robust economic growth. But so did the Reagan years, which liberals denounced as the "Decade of Greed." Though both periods were prosperous, liberals couldn't abide the tax cuts that strongly contributed to their prosperity. *Time* editor Rick Stengel, appearing with Serwer on *Morning Joe*, predicted the next decade was "going to turn out to be a lot better than we think, in part because we have a lot of these excesses [read: tax cuts] behind us."[104]

Despite the media's rank sycophancy, Obama's scapegoating eventually lost its glimmer. A FOX News poll in April 2010 showed that 66 percent of American voters believed it was time for Obama to take responsibility for his own actions and quit blaming Bush.[105]

PART II

OFFENSES AGAINST AMERICAN INSTITUTIONS

Chapter Six

THE DICTATOR

CRIMES AGAINST THE CONSTITUTION, RULE OF LAW, AND CIVIL SOCIETY, PART 1

In the past year and a half, we've seen Obama cram ObamaCare through Congress against the will of the people. We've seen Health and Human Services secretary Sebelius summon insurance executives to the White House so she and President Obama could lecture them on their greed-born resistance to ObamaCare. We witnessed them browbeat insurance executives over the premiums they charge. And we saw the administration send a threatening letter to Humana and other companies threatening legal action for expressing their opinion that under ObamaCare some seniors would lose coverage.

We've observed how Obama has surrounded himself with numerous radical "czars"—those powerful advisers who are not confirmed by the Senate and thus not accountable to the legislative branch. We saw him appoint leftist activist judges. His most recent Supreme Court nominee, Elena Kagan, in her undergraduate thesis

at Princeton, lamented the decline of socialism in the United States
as "sad" for those who desire to "change America."[1] When clerking
for Justice Thurgood Marshall, Kagan argued the Constitution con-
fers "positive" rights to government aid, as opposed to being solely
an instrument of limitation that protects liberty against governmental interference[2]—an odious position to all who believe the Constitution means what it actually says.

Moreover, many of Obama's appointees were corrupt, ranging
from tax cheats to those involved in shady business dealings—
which didn't seem to matter a whit to Obama, as long as they could
help him advance his agenda. The *Washington Post* acknowledged
the administration's willingness to appoint ethically challenged people "when an appointee's qualifications appeared to trump other
concerns," from auto task force czar Steve Rattner, to Treasury Secretary Tim Geithner, to Health and Human Services nominee Tom
Daschle.[3]

The administration is steeped in an end-justifies-the-means culture, committed to doing whatever it takes to advance their agenda,
details like the Constitution or legislative rules be damned. When
criticized for resorting to secrecy, political bribery, intimidation, and
other legislative shenanigans to enact ObamaCare, Obama advisor
David Axelrod said the American people didn't much care about
the legislative process—they just wanted results. Axelrod had long
subscribed to this cynical view; eight months earlier he said, "Ultimately, this is not about a process, it's about results. If we're going
to get this thing done, obviously time is a-wasting."[4]

In dismissing as mere "process" the kind of transparent, honest
governance he had promised on the campaign trail, President
Obama has exercised significantly greater power than our constitutional framers intended in his quest to transform America from free
enterprise to socialism, from a nation primarily of earners to one
primarily of dependents. Along those lines, Obama's congressional
ally Nancy Pelosi, speaking of ObamaCare, said, "We see it as an
entrepreneurial bill, a bill that says to someone, if you want to be

creative and be a musician or whatever, you can leave your work, focus on your talent, your skill, your passion, your aspirations because you will have health care."[5] In other words, *don't worry about your healthcare bills, someone else will pay them.*

Obama and his team are liberal ideologues who believe their mission is to impose on the rest of us—by whatever means available—their vision of a virtuous society. They view the Constitution, as originally understood, as an impediment, but reinterpreted, as a marvelous vehicle for transforming society in their image, which is the same way they regard the rule of law. But the rule of law is blind to ideology, a concept so foreign to the Obamites as to be unintelligible. As veteran conservative columnist George Will wrote, "Anyone could govern as boldly as their whims decreed, were it not for the skeletal structure that keeps civil society civil—the rule of law. The Obama administration is . . . careless regarding constitutional values and is acquiring a tincture of lawlessness."[6]

"JUST LIKE YOUR TEENAGE KIDS"

A key reason why this administration feels justified in flouting the rule of law is that they see themselves as benevolent tutors who cannot let trivial technicalities like the Constitution impede their mission to enlighten the unwashed American masses. At a seminar on reconstructing America's electrical grid, Secretary of Energy Steven Chu commented, "The American public, just like your teenage kids, aren't acting in a way that they should act. The American public has to really understand in their core how important [energy conservation] is." Chu has incorporated that patronizing attitude into the administration's energy policy. As the *Wall Street Journal*'s Ian Talley observed, "The administration aims to teach [the American public]—literally." Translating this outlook into practice, the Environmental Protection Agency is going to partner with the Parent Teacher Organization on a cross-country tour of 6,000 schools to teach (read: indoctrinate) actual children about climate change and energy efficiency. "We're showing people across the country how energy efficiency can be part of what they do every day. Confronting climate change, saving money on our utility bills, and reducing our use of heavily-polluting energy can be as easy as making a few small changes."[7]

After Chu's patronizing comments were publicized, Energy Department spokesman Dan Leistikow assured us Chu was not comparing the public to teenagers, but merely insisting we need to educate teenagers about ways to save energy.[8] Since they believe the Constitution doesn't mean what it says, it's unsurprising the administration would insist Chu's actual words—that Americans were acting improperly "just like your teenage kids"—are infinitely flexible as well.

GOING WHERE NO MODERN PRESIDENT HAS GONE BEFORE

Obama's lawless tendencies are starkly evident in his dealings with NASA and the space program, which he has subordinated to environmental projects like developing alternative energy—an effort he suggested should be our "next Apollo Program."[9] First, some background: during the Democratic primary, Obama indicated his $18 billion education plan (including his misguided ambition to federalize preschool) would be funded, in part, by delaying for five years NASA's Constellation program, which would return humans to the moon.[10] This plan stoked criticism about the futility of defunding one of the federal government's greatest investments in math and science in the name of renewing its investment in math and science education. There are also national security implications: Obama's plan could leave the United States unable to send people into space for a decade absent the aid of foreign nations, such as Russia and China; we might not be able to service the International Space Station; and we risk falling behind China, which could beat us back to the moon.[11]

After coming under sustained criticism, Obama attempted to "clarify" his plan, vowing to continue developing the next generation of space vehicles and complete the international space station. He said he "endorses the goal of sending human missions to the moon by 2020, as a precursor in an orderly progression to missions to more distant destinations, including Mars."[12] He also declared, naturally, that global warming monitoring would have to be a major part of the space program.[13]

Upon taking office, however, Obama made it clear space exploration was not a high priority. In addition to delaying any return to the moon and abandoning the manned space program, he showed a preference for largely turning over space travel to the private sector. It shouldn't surprise anyone that when Obama finally found a government program he wanted to leave to the private sector, it would be one of the few that is best controlled by the government, because of its national security implications.

It also follows he would abandon a program that has long symbolized American exceptionalism, a concept Obama rejected with his famous comment, "I believe in American exceptionalism, just as I suspect that the Brits believe in British exceptionalism and the Greeks believe in Greek exceptionalism." As one blogger noted, "From now on, whenever we remember with pride the courage and sacrifice of the Mercury astronauts, or Neil Armstrong taking 'One small step for a man, one giant step for mankind,' or Jim Lovell and the crew of Apollo 13 calmly tinkering with the duct tape to repair their capsule, we'll quickly deflate with the afterthought: 'Oh yeah. Now the Russians do that. We don't.'"[14]

Once he was elected, Obama's funeral plans for Constellation quickly became clear, notwithstanding his campaign promises to retain the program. Office of Management and Budget director Peter Orszag announced, "We are proposing canceling the program, not delaying it." The *New York Times* reported Obama had no other space exploration mission planned to replace the moon voyage. "What the administration calls a 'bold new initiative' does not spell out a next destination or timetable for getting there," the *Times* noted, adding Obama's NASA would be "fundamentally different" from today's NASA. It would cease to "operate its own spacecraft, but essentially buy tickets for its astronauts."[15]

All too typically, the Obama administration skirted the law in implementing its new space policy. Obama's proposed 2011 budget envisioned canceling Constellation and its Ares rockets and Orion crew capsule. So NASA notified bidders, including Boeing and United Space Alliance, that it was withdrawing a 2009 bid for work on the Constellation program.[16] This angered Congressman Bill Posey, who argued the "administration's unilateral decision to cancel contracts associated with the Constellation program absent congressional consent is a direct violation of the law and of congressional intent. . . . Congress has not directed the administration to cancel the Constellation program, in fact it has done just the opposite in recent legislation."[17] Posey was referring to "The Consolidated Appropriations for Fiscal Year 2010," which expressly prohibits the "termination or elimination of any program, project or activity of the architecture for the Constellation program."

Posey joined with some thirty congressmen in sending a letter to NASA administrator Charles Bolden accusing the administration of further violating the law by forming five "tiger teams" and setting aside FY2010 Constellation funds to shut down Constellation and "transition to the new program" without congressional approval. NASA administrator Bolden fired a letter back to Congress claiming NASA had not broken the law because it was only *looking into* canceling the program, but had not actually canceled it yet.[18] This was hard to take seriously, since NASA had already canceled Constellation's bidding process.

A month later, six Republican senators began an effort to save Constellation. Citing Congress's rightful authority over the space program, Senator George LeMieux declared the program's cancellation "would reverse nearly 50 years of U.S. space policy and would effectively end the United States' leadership role in space."[19]

It turns out the senators' concerns were not exaggerated. By June, NASA had begun to wind down construction of the rockets and spacecraft that would have transported our astronauts back to the moon, dismantling the program in defiance of the congressional ban on canceling it.[20]

Obama's unilateral decision would "force as many as 30,000 irreplaceable engineers and managers out of the space industry," and the "human exploration program, one of the most inspirational tools to promote science, technology, engineering and math to our young people," would be "reduced to mediocrity," according to an open letter signed by former NASA administrator Michael Griffin, legendary flight director Gene Kranz, and several NASA astronauts.[21] Lockheed Martin issued a statement saying the program's elimination would cause the loss of "significant investment [that] has already been made by the nation and private industry."[22]

The administration gave short shrift to planning how private firms would take over the program, to attendant safety concerns, and to the poor record of commercially oriented NASA programs. Indeed, it is remarkable how casually Obama approached such a crucial decision that could, according to Democratic congresswoman Donna Edwards of Maryland, "essentially decimate America's human space-flight capacity."[23]

Aside from the dubious legality, Obama's restructuring of NASA fit another pattern of his governing style. He made a firm decision early on, then pretended to consider other viewpoints as he systematically built a phony case to support his decision. He employed the same chicanery with ObamaCare, when he pretended to the end he was "open to all ideas," and with his "jobs summit," which was a mere prop to validate his "jobs bill." Likewise with NASA, he convened the "Human Space Flight Plans Committee" to review NASA's plan to return to the moon by 2020.[24] Coincidentally, the panel reached conclusions that bore a striking resemblance to Obama's own preferences, including the evaluation that returning to the moon by 2020 was just too ambitious. Author Mark Whittington aptly observed that Obama's "selective fiscal discipline" with NASA "suggests a president who is not prudent with spending public funds, but rather a president who will shower resources on programs he likes—socialized medicine and a pork laden stimulus bill—and defund programs he does not like—space exploration and national defense."[25]

It also suggests a president who is not at all about "hope" and "inspiration," but about dampening our dreams and expectations and relegating this nation to second tier status—it would appear—by design. His "vision" is to redirect billions of dollars toward the quixotic pursuit of a utopian "green" economy run on windmills and solar panels. As the *Washington Times* wrote, when it comes to space, "'Yes we can,' has become 'mission impossible.'"[26]

Responding to heavy criticism of his NASA policies, Obama, in a speech to NASA employees at the Kennedy Space Center in April 2010, suddenly seemed to reverse course, saying he wanted crew missions beyond the moon and deep into space by 2025 and orbiting Mars by 2030. He also announced the revival of the NASA crew capsule concept he had canceled along with the moon program earlier in the year. Notably, he did not back off his plans to subcontract these missions to commercial industries or to cancel the moon mission. But he at least paid lip service to the program's potential for inspiring "wonder in a new generation—sparking passions and launching careers. . . . If we fail to press forward in the pursuit of discovery, we are ceding our future and we are ceding that essential element of the American character."[27]

The administration's overall confusion and lack of vision in space policy was captured in a May 2010 preliminary report from the Center for Strategic and International Studies, which concluded that U.S. leadership in space is threatened by poor coordination in establishing space policy. CSIS reported there are some twenty-nine "recently completed or ongoing space launch studies within the U.S. government," but no entity has oversight over all of them. Gregory Kiley, a lead analyst on the report, said Defense secretary Robert Gates had stated publicly he was "not adequately" consulted on the policy shift at NASA. "Making a decision in one sector without thinking through the implications and ramifications for the others is not good policy," said Kiley.[28]

The confusion, it seems, comes from the top. According to a July 5, 2010 article on FOXNews.com, Bolden told Arabic-language TV network al Jazeera that when Obama appointed him to head NASA, "Perhaps foremost, he wanted me to find a way to reach out to the Muslim world and engage much more with dominantly Muslim nations to help them feel good about their historic contribution to science...and math and engineering." Making Muslims feel good—a very strange charge for the head of America's space agency.

THE POLITBURO

Believing his administration possesses vast authority over the private sector, Obama colluded with the Democratic Congress to intimidate corporate executives of AT&T, John Deere, and Verizon when those companies disclosed, in required regulatory filings, that ObamaCare will dramatically raise the cost of their employees' health insurance. Democratic congressman Henry Waxman, then-chairman of the House Committee on Energy and Commerce, summoned these CEOs to Capitol Hill and demanded they provide Congress internal company documents detailing their healthcare finances. One Republican on the committee called it "an attempt to intimidate and silence opponents of the Democrats' flawed health care reform legislation."[29] Here we see some of the magnificent "change" Obama has delivered—we are becoming a country in which corporate executives, for fear of offending powerful politicians, are not allowed to state that new laws will cause higher costs.

Then again, there is hope. Waxman's attempt to bully the CEOs fizzled quickly. The Committee on Energy and Commerce majority staff issued a memorandum stating that the companies had properly compiled their estimates, which they were legally required to disclose to their shareholders.[30] Amidst growing criticism of this blatant bullying, Waxman called off the witch-hunt, seeking to avoid a major embarrassment to Obama and his party should the CEOs be given a public forum to detail the "unforeseen" consequences of ObamaCare.

In his memo to committee members canceling the hearing, Waxman tried to save face and candy-coat the facts. The memo stated, "Several companies and their representatives expressed the view that the new law could have beneficial impacts on large employers if implemented properly." But as writer Jed Babbin noted, "There is nothing to support the implication" that the summoned companies "were being less critical of the new healthcare law."[31]

Regardless, it's none of Waxman's business whether the companies were critical or supportive of the law—they have the right to express their views. Waxman's thuggish behavior in service to this thuggish administration was an extraordinary abuse of power. But it was nothing new; Republican congressman Joe Barton had previously denounced similar bullying by Waxman in launching an investigation into the American Farm Bureau's opposition to the cap and trade bill. Barton even suggested it was Waxman himself who should be investigated.[32]

Obama's Democrats were routinely unapologetic about their abuses. When CNS News asked Senate judiciary chairman Patrick Leahy under what authority the Democrats passed ObamaCare, including its mandate forcing nearly all Americans to purchase health insurance, Leahy exclaimed, "We have plenty of authority. Are you saying there is no authority? Why would you say there is no authority? I mean, there's no question there's authority. Nobody questions that." Nobody that matters to congressional liberals, that is—as in the majority of Americans.

Other Democrats answered the question with similar evasions. An incredulous Nancy Pelosi, then-House Speaker, demanded, "Are you serious? Are you serious?" Democratic senator Mark Warner declared, "There is no place in the Constitution that talks about you ought to have the right to get a telephone, but we have made those choices as a country over the years." Senator Roland Burris stammered, "Well that's under certainly the laws of the—protect the health, welfare of the country. That's under the Constitution. We're not even dealing with any constitutionality here. Should we move in that direction?" Senator Bob Casey confessed, "Well, I don't know if there's a specific constitutional provision."[33]

EXECUTIVE ORDERS

The Left, which had railed against "King George" Bush for his supposed abuse of presidential powers, didn't seem to mind when Obama and his veto-proof Congress broke the rules and shredded the Constitution to pass ObamaCare. When the bill's passage seemed questionable due to opposition from Democratic congressman Bart Stupak and other allegedly pro-life Democrats, Obama promised to issue an executive order denying federal funding for abortion in exchange for the "pro-lifers'" vote for the bill. The proper procedure would have been for House Democrats to adopt new abortion language in their bill and then send the bill to the Senate, but Democrats couldn't risk that, having lost their veto-proof majority in the Senate with Republican Scott Brown's election in Massachusetts.

No problem for Obama; he just issued an order purportedly negating the statute's provision authorizing federal funding for abortion. The order was likely void on its face, both because it would function as a line item veto, which the Supreme Court has already declared unconstitutional,[34] and because executive orders cannot alter legislation without congressional action. But it was just another day at the office for a man who behaves as though he's above the law.

Furthermore, Obama intended to unilaterally change the law via executive orders on other issues on which Congress would not deliver the goods for him. When the Senate voted 90 to 6 against bringing Gitmo detainees to U.S. soil, Obama disregarded Congress's objection and announced plans to move them to a prison in Illinois.

The full strategy of using executive orders to circumvent Congress became clear following Scott Brown's victory in Massachusetts. As much of Obama's agenda remained stalled in Congress, the *New York Times* reported Obama was planning on "an array of actions using his executive power to advance energy, environmental, fiscal and other domestic policy priorities." White House chief of staff Rahm Emanuel said, "We are reviewing a list of presidential executive orders and directives to get the job done across a front of issues." Obama's plans to skirt Congress included his scheme to create a bipartisan budget commission under his own authority when Congress wouldn't; his reversal of the military's "Don't Ask, Don't Tell" policy on homosexual soldiers; and the EPA's regulatory end-run around lawmakers to regulate carbon—an unprecedented government power-grab—due to Congress's refusal to pass a cap and trade bill.[35]

ADMINISTRATION TREATING
STIMULUS MONEY AS ITS OWN

Republican senator Jon Kyl learned through experience that you can't criticize the Obama administration's policies with impunity. In July, on *This Week with George Stephanopoulos*, Kyl asserted Obama's beloved stimulus package hadn't helped the economy. Noting that only 6.8 percent of the money had actually been spent, Kyle suggested the government freeze any further expenditures beyond those items already under contract. The next day Arizona governor Jan Brewer received letters from the secretaries of Transportation, Agriculture, Department of Housing and Urban Development, and Interior—all insisting billions of stimulus dollars were en route to Arizona. Transportation secretary Ray LaHood's letter was outright threatening, intimidating, and bullying. He wrote that Kyl "publicly questioned whether the stimulus is working and stated that he wants to cancel projects that aren't presently under-way. I believe the stimulus has been very effective in creating job opportunities throughout the country. However, if you prefer to for-feit the money we are making available to your state, as Senator Kyl suggests, please let me know."

The letter's assertions ranged from doubtful to despicable. First, the stimulus wasn't effective in creating jobs hardly anywhere and certainly not "throughout the country." Second, LaHood and the administration knew Kyl was referring to an across-the-board freeze of stimulus monies, not just those slated for Arizona. And third, it is outrageous these autocrats would suggest this is *their money* to dole out or withdraw as they saw fit, or that they were doing Ari-zona a favor by allocating a share to it. This was taxpayer money.

This was the height of arrogance from an administration with near-dictatorial aspirations. The letters from the other cabinet offi-cials were similarly patronizing and improper. That all four cabinet secretaries fired off these similar letters simultaneously indicates Obama and his henchmen run the executive branch with an iron fist and that his cabinet officials operate with utterly no independence.[36]

Kyl responded, "It's unfortunate that President Obama and his administration seem unwilling to debate the merits of the stimulus bill and acknowledge its shortcomings. Instead, they have resorted to coordinated political attacks with the Democratic National Com-mittee and the politicization of departments of government by using cabinet secretaries to issue thinly veiled threats to the governor and the people of Arizona." Kyl and Senator John McCain, in a joint response, referred to LaHood's threats as "patently offensive," adding they hoped this didn't characterize the administration's deal-ings with Congress in the future.[37] A spokesman for Governor Brewer said he hoped cabinet members weren't threatening to deny Arizona stimulus funds, which he said would be "a tremendous mistake by the administration."[38]

This wasn't the first time the administration abused its power over funding to the states. Six months earlier they objected to a measure by California's Democrat-controlled legislature to trim $74 million from one of its rapidly growing programs for low-income and incapacitated elderly residents. Although the move only cut 1.4 percent of the program's total funding, the Obama administration threatened to withhold from California $6.8 billion in stimulus money unless the cut was reversed. Notably, the administration's swift, powerful reaction was not on behalf of the poor and elderly, but of the Service Employees International Union, which hauls in almost $5 million a month from California's 223,000 healthcare providers who are SEIU members.[39]

INTERFERING WITH THE CBO

As a further indication of Obama's disregard for constitutional restraints, he initiated a meeting with the Congressional Budget Office during the thick of the legislative process on ObamaCare. This was a gross infringement on the independence of the CBO, which is responsible for "scoring" the fiscal soundness of legislative proposals. Having grown accustomed to throwing his weight around Washington, Obama apparently didn't even realize his meeting with the CBO was improper; he revealed to NBC *Today Show* host Meredith Vieira he had "just met with the Congressional Budget Office today" and discussed their scoring of the very health-care proposals he was trying to shove through Congress. The CBO's scoring process, of course, should not involve advocacy, but impartial analysis of the data.

HotAir blogger Ed Morrissey contacted two sources in Washington to inquire whether presidents normally confer with the CBO on budget scoring, and they both told him it was a "highly unusual" move that they didn't remember *ever* having occurred. Obama had actually invited CBO director Doug Elmendorf to the White House to meet with him and his key budget and health advisers and some outside experts, according to a blog entry by Elmendorf, who revealed that in addition to discussing scoring items he "discussed various policy options that could produce budgetary savings in the long run." As Morrissey noted, "CBO doesn't create policy. It's supposed to be a scorekeeper and allow Congress to create policy. This feels like an attempt to either intimidate or co-opt the CBO, neither of which would be a good thing. The entire meeting seems highly inappropriate."[40]

COOKING THE BOOKS ON OBAMACARE

Only three weeks after ObamaCare was shoved through Congress, an amazing 58 percent of American voters supported full repeal of the measure. Just imagine what the numbers would have been had they been fully apprised of the extent to which Obama and his Democratic allies distorted the numbers in order to rig a passing grade from the CBO. With this administration's vintage audacity, White House budget director Peter Orszag not only denied the CBO numbers were skewed in favor of the administration, he argued the CBO numbers actually understated the *savings* from the bill. Citing no specific facts, he based his argument on two generalities: 1) "On major pieces of legislation," the CBO's projections historically have been "too conservative rather than too optimistic"; 2) the CBO's scoring "largely does not take into account this evolution toward paying for quality," which "in this decade will begin to pay off."[41]

On Orszag's first point, we know the government has historically underestimated the cost of health-related legislation by a country mile. In 1965 the government projected Medicare Part A would cost $9 billion by 1990, but its actual costs came to $67 billion. Its 1987 estimates for Medicaid's special hospital subsidy was $100 million, but its actual costs by 1992 were $11 billion—100 times more than projected![42] But if you want to revert to generalities, try this one: most Americans believe government programs almost always cost more than expected, if for no other reason than that government seems to employ a static model in its projections. Pollsters Scott

Rasmussen and Doug Schoen reported that 81 percent of voters believe it's likely ObamaCare will cost more than projected.[43]

Former CBO director Douglas Holtz-Eakin contended the CBO's scoring greatly understated the costs simply due to the incomplete information that the organization received. "The budget office is required to take legislation at face value and not second-guess the plausibility of what it is handed. So fantasy in, fantasy out." He said the CBO reported, based on the information provided to it by Congress, that ObamaCare would reduce federal deficits by $138 billion over the next ten years. But if we remove "the gimmicks and budgetary games" and recalculate, he argued, we'll discover ObamaCare "will raise, not lower, federal deficits, by $562 billion."[44]

Holtz-Eakin cited the gimmick in the bill's front-loading revenues and backloading spending: the taxes and fees begin immediately, but many of the expenditures are deferred "so that the first 10 years of revenue would be used to pay for only 6 years of spending." In addition, he said, some costs are omitted entirely. In order to operate some of the bill's new programs, Congress would have "to vote for $114 billion in additional annual spending." This amount presumably was left out of the calculation because it is technically not required spending, but "discretionary spending." Yet the program can't function without it. By speciously categorizing it as discretionary spending, Democrats distorted the figures.

Within about a month of the bill's passage, Holtz-Eakin was vindicated on this point when the CBO, responding to an inquiry from Congressman Jerry Lewis, confirmed an additional $115 billion in discretionary spending. This trickery can be laid directly at the feet of Barack Obama and his Democrats for forcing this bill through Congress too fast—on purpose and in violation of their pledge for transparency. FOX News reported that CBO simply didn't have enough time to respond to the inquiry before the bill was passed. Risibly, Obama threatened to veto any additional spending in the ObamaCare bill unless this $115 billion was offset elsewhere—as if he didn't know about this huge expense before signing the bill."[45]

This was by no means the only sleight of hand Democrats employed in calculating ObamaCare's costs. There is also the matter of $70 billion in premiums that are expected to be collected during the first ten years for the payment of benefits that will mostly materialize after the first ten years—a complete sham. Another trick was to manipulate revenues by making corporations deposit $8 billion in higher estimated tax payments in 2014, "thereby meeting fiscal targets for the first five years." But because the corporations' actual taxes will remain the same, the money will have to be refunded the following year, so dollars are simply being shifted from 2015 to 2014. This is outright fraud which, if being perpetrated by anyone other than Congress, would be subject to investigation.

Another deceitful item is the estimated $53 billion in higher Social Security taxes resulting from an expected increase in wages as employers "shift from paying for health insurance to pay higher wages." But even if that comes to fruition, notes Holtz-Eakin, the higher wages will result in increased Social Security benefits down the road when they retire, which means the extra estimated Social Security revenues will not help pay for ObamaCare at all without robbing the same amount from future Social Security. Congressional manipulators also rolled into the bill the nationalization of student loans, which has nothing to do with healthcare but is projected to generate $19 billion in deficit reduction, which CBO was obliged to consider.

But "the most amazing bit of unrealistic accounting," says Holtz-Eakin, is the projected savings of $463 billion from Medicare spending, which will be used to finance insurance subsidies. But Medicare has no extra funds at all to donate to the cause: it "is already bleeding red ink." The upshot: "Removing the unrealistic annual Medicare savings ($463 billion) and the stolen annual revenues from Social Security and long-term care insurance ($123 billion), and adding in the annual spending that so far is not accounted for ($114 billion) will generate additional deficits of $562 billion in the first 10 years. And the nation would be on the hook for two more entitlement programs rapidly expanding as far as the eye can see." (Holtz-Eakin's $562 billion figure is derived by subtracting the CBO's calculation of $138 billion in reduced deficits from the $700 billion of increased deficits from Medicare [$463 billion], Social Security and long-term care [$123 billion], and annual spending not accounted for [$114 billion].)

The bottom line: "Congress would spend a lot more; steal funds from education, Social Security and long-term care to cover the gap; and promise that future Congresses will make up for it by taxing more and spending less."[46]

Paul Ryan, then-ranking Republican on the House Budget Committee, asked the CBO to recalculate ObamaCare's impact on the budget based on more realistic assumptions:

- Assume that the House will reduce ObamaCare's scheduled 21 percent cut in Medicare's reimbursements to physicians. This is the so-called "doc fix," which Speaker Pelosi had promised to implement.
- Assume that the so-called Cadillac tax—the proposal to tax individuals' higher-premium health insurance plans—will never be implemented. Under ObamaCare this new tax was delayed until 2018 because of union pressure. If Congress removes it entirely—and if they didn't have the courage to implement it now, why would they in the future?—it will add further to the deficit.
- Assume that Medicare cuts projected to be made by an independent payment advisory board will never actually be made (because that's what history shows).

With these assumptions, Ryan explained ObamaCare would "*increase* Federal deficits by at least $59 billion, but more likely $260 billion over the next 10 years" instead of reducing them by $138 billion, as the CBO's scoring indicates based on the Democrats' unrealistic assumptions.

Ryan also asked the CBO to recalculate the ten years following 2019 based on different assumptions that he submitted. He summarized the CBO's ominous response this way:

> Removing these assumptions reveals a stark reality. If these assumed savings are never realized—as is the likely scenario—CBO projects that rather than reducing the deficit in the years beyond 2019 the deficit would increase over the decade following 2019 "in a broad range around one-quarter percent of GDP." Using the majority's own methodology, this amounts to a second-decade deficit of $600 billion.[47]

EXECUTIVE SALARIES

Obama, ever the consummate class warrior, delighted in demonizing corporate executives and in imposing limits on their salaries, as we've seen. This issue first arose when populist Democrats went ballistic after AIG publicly revealed a small percentage of its bailout money went toward executive bonuses. Senator Charles Schumer intoned, "They should voluntarily return [the money]. If they don't, we plan to tax virtually all of it." The Democrat-controlled House quickly passed a bill to tax 90 percent of the bonuses, a bill critics rightly protested would be a Bill of Attainder, forbidden by the Constitution because it targeted a single group of people and would confiscate their property without due process. As offensive as their disregard for the Constitution was, equally egregious was the Democrats' power-drunk effort to retroactively veto corporate actions that were not only legal at the time, but that had been *expressly authorized* by the stimulus bill passed the previous month.[48] If these bonuses were such an affront to democracy, one wonders why Democrats didn't penalize themselves for authorizing them in the first place?

The Senate threatened to follow suit with the retroactive penalty tax, but ended up shelving the bill after Obama wisely expressed doubts about the bill's constitutionality during an interview on CBS's *60 Minutes*. Senate majority leader Harry Reid warned the Senate could still act on the bill, however. "The issue is not over and that's an understatement. We're going to keep an eye on this [and look for] a window to do something," said Reid.[49]

In March 2010, Democratic senators Jim Webb and Barbara Boxer offered a slightly different proposal through an amendment to a jobs bill, which would impose a one-time, 50 percent tax on 2009 bonuses in excess of $400,000 paid to employees of thirteen companies that received more than $5 billion in TARP monies. That bill was also shelved because Republicans would not consent to a vote on the jobs bill. Webb vowed to reintroduce his bonus tax proposal by amendment to another bill when feasible.[50]

Obama's method is clear, as is his goal: to exert the greatest degree of government control possible over the private sector, thereby reducing CEOs to submissive government clients, dependent on Obama's goodwill for everything, right down to their own salaries. He first imposed government control, by fiat, of executive compensation at taxpayer-owned companies. But it wasn't long before he extended the government's control over compensation to private companies that had received bailout money. Obama's "pay czar" Kenneth R. Feinberg met for weeks in the fall with executives of the country's largest firms, including AIG, Citigroup, Bank of America, General Motors, and Chrysler, to exercise his "sole discretion" to set the compensation for the top twenty-five employees of each of these "bailout" companies. One unaccountable federal bureaucrat was micromanaging this decision, yet he reportedly didn't even provide the executives with a clear sense of how he planned to evaluate their compensation.

The companies were adamant that they needed to pay competitive salaries to acquire talented employees who could produce sufficient profits for shareholders.[51] But their concerns fell on deaf ears as Fienberg announced pay cuts of up to 90 percent for 175 top executives at seven major banks and automakers that received

TARP money, and he tied more compensation to long-term stock awards. Feinberg claimed there was a better way than large cash salaries to ensure long-term corporate growth. He said he hoped this "methodology we developed to determine compensation... might be voluntarily adopted elsewhere."[52]

Federal Reserve chairman Ben Bernanke proposed less severe but broader cuts for all banker salaries—even in banks that didn't receive bailout money—and for U.S. subsidiaries of foreign companies. The Fed, in its beneficence, would allow banks to set their own pay but would reserve veto power over the compensation if it determined the soundness of the bank was threatened. This rule would cover tens of thousands of bank employees. Obama, commenting on the move, said, "I've always believed that our system of free enterprise works best when it rewards hard work. But it does offend our values when executives of big financial firms—firms that are struggling—pay themselves huge bonuses even as they continue to rely on taxpayer assistance to stay afloat."[53]

How convenient for him to be referring only to firms relying on taxpayer assistance. Did anyone actually believe it didn't offend his values when *any* private sector executives (other than his friends) received large bonuses? And how about those whose values are offended by the government dictating salaries for private employees?

The White House had earlier indicated it would seek new powers for the Securities and Exchange Commission to force public companies to allow their shareholders to vote on executive pay. It said it would name a "special master" to monitor compensation plans for firms that receive "exceptional assistance."[54] It appears the Dodd–Frank financial overhaul bill partly achieved Obama's goal. It requires a regular nonbinding vote from shareholders of public companies to approve executive compensation—a so-called "say on pay" vote. The bill also requires companies to disclose the relationship between executive compensation and financial performance.[55]

An amendment was attached to the proposed finance bill in March 2010 that included, among other provisions, "internal pay equity" disclosure rules for publicly traded companies. Now the companies would be required to disclose the median annual total compensation of all employees other than the CEO; the annual total compensation of the CEO, and the ratio of the median employee annual total compensation to that of the CEO.[56] It is no secret that the class-warfare statists intend these provisions to affect actual compensation of employees of these firms.

The administration, apparently hedging its bets in case the finance bill failed, went the regulatory route. In December 2009 the SEC approved rules to require all publicly held companies—not just financial firms—to reveal more information about their executive compensation practices,[57] perhaps to get the government's foot in the door toward ultimately assuming control over public company compensation. SEC chairman Mary L. Schapiro said, "By adopting these rules, we will improve the disclosure around risk, compensation, and corporate governance, thereby increasing accountability and directly benefiting investors." "Accountability," she said, "is impossible without transparency."[58]

The *New York Times'* Floyd Norris hinted that the disclosure rule might actually affect compensation levels. Requiring companies to disclose compensation policies that increase the risk of companies having to take large losses, according to Norris, could cause firms to think twice about the compensation and "being forced to think about it could produce needed changes in policies."[59] The SEC also approved a rule to require companies to disclose whether the company considers diversity in its board nomination process.

Obama also engaged in serious talks about changing compensation practices across the financial services industry, including at companies that did not receive TARP funds. The administration's rationale was that as long as the government is regulating these firms, it should have the right to "regulate" their employees' compensation. After all, they can always argue—and have argued—that financial firms' compensation structure could threaten the "safety and soundness" of the institution.

Of course, the administration denied its statist intentions for the proposal. One official said, "This is not going to be about capping compensation or micro-management. It will be about understanding what is the best way to align compensation with sound risk management and long-term creation."[60] But given an administration that regards profits as immoral, what would stop it from micromanaging and capping compensation once invested with the regulatory power to do so? And the financial overhaul bill did employ the very rationale of "safety and soundness" to include a compensation provision that applies only to financial firms. The bill makes it an unsafe and unsound practice for the holding companies of depository institutions to provide excessive compensation that could lead to material financial loss, and directs bank regulators to prohibit such unsafe and unsound practices. It also gives bank regulators the authority to impose higher capital charges if an institution's practices "pose risk of harm."[61]

The Cato Institute's Daniel J. Mitchell expressed concern that the administration's imposition of limits on executive pay could indeed lead to a slippery slope whereby the government might attempt to assert control over private salaries as well. Mitchell said, "I fear as politicians get a taste for interfering with executive pay for one little subset of companies where you actually could have sympathy for the approach, what's going to stop them from saying, 'Hey, this was popular. Let's do a little demagoguery before the next election and go after all the CEOs.'"[62]

Obama claims to be a constitutional scholar, but his actions as president show a marked indifference toward legal niceties. Once ensconced in the Oval Office, he no longer seemed interested in concepts like separation of powers and checks and balances. Although he campaigned heavily on promises to roll back the alleged expansion of executive power under President Bush, Obama has exploited his position to steamroll over Congress's authority, bully ostensibly independent bodies to bend to his will, and to preside over a massive assault on the private sector. This is definitely "change," but it's not at all the change many Americans anticipated when they cast their ballots for Obama.

Chapter Seven

THE DICTATOR

CRIMES AGAINST THE CONSTITUTION, RULE OF LAW, AND CIVIL SOCIETY, PART 2

I n March 2009, top government representatives from the United States and Europe met at the G-20 summit in London to discuss the global financial crisis. The conference produced a joint commitment to boost International Monetary Fund resources by $750 billion to a total of $1 trillion, with the United States contributing $140 billion.

Not only did Obama summarily agree to this plan without consulting Congress, he flouted the express will of Congress. The IMF was originally established as a lender of last resort to protect nations against balance of trade deficits, but since the world monetary system moved away from the gold standard, the IMF has increasingly focused on redistributing wealth to poorer nations. Along these lines, the London agreement will increase the IMF's foreign aid role and America's participation in it—even though for twelve years Congress had been resisting IMF pressure to do so. As the *Wall Street Journal* editorialized, this additional $140 billion will "amount to a massive expansion in U.S. foreign aid. We can see why the G-20 applauded. But this is the opposite of the 'transparency' this Administration has promised, and someone on Capitol Hill should blow the whistle."[1]

Obama quickly began fulfilling his unauthorized foreign aid commitment via executive signing statements—ironically, a practice for which the Left had fiercely denounced President Bush. However, while Bush used signing statements simply to express objections to bills or parts of bills he was signing, Obama intended his signing statements to have more teeth. In June 2009 Obama declared he didn't intend to comply with provisions in a war spending bill that impose conditions on aid given to the World Bank and IMF. Employing Orwellian logic, Obama argued, in effect, that foreign aid fell under the rubric of foreign policy, over which, he implied, he had near-plenary authority.

He insisted he wasn't "skirting the law," but defending his executive powers, and he wouldn't permit the bill to interfere with his authority to conduct foreign policy and negotiate with other governments—as if he had carte blanche authority and the power of the purse to hand out any amount of U.S. money to any nation.[2] Even four senior House Democrats—David Obey, Barney Frank, Nita Lowey, and Gregory Meeks—wrote a protest letter to Obama stating they were "surprised" and "chagrined" by his action.

Obama also used signing statements to place his administration above the law with frivolous executive privilege claims. After Obama signed a bill designed to curb financial fraud and created an independent panel (the "Pecora Commission") with subpoena power to investigate the "root causes" of the financial collapse, he immediately issued a signing statement reserving the right to assert executive privilege over any subpoenaed documents.[3] That is, his passion for uncovering the truth stopped short of disclosing any information that might embarrass his administration.

A TRANSFORMATIONAL ADMINISTRATION

Obama liberals are intent not just on remaking government, but on reordering many aspects of our society and culture, from the type of transportation and energy we use, to the food we eat and the condiments with which we season it, to how much time we spend outdoors. They almost always use an environmental excuse to justify these power grabs.

Transportation secretary Ray LaHood is a prime example. As the *Daily Telegraph* reported in 2010, "In March, Mr Obama's transportation secretary, Ray LaHood, announced a policy 'sea change' that gives biking and walking projects the same importance as automobiles in transportation planning and the selection of projects for federal money." And LaHood had already put your tax money where his mouth is, more than doubling federal spending on biking and walking initiatives to $1.2 billion.[4] What's more, LaHood, who once bragged that he had joined a "transformational administration," clearly intends to strictly enforce this risible policy, having announced his explicit intention to "coerce people out of their cars."[5]

When asked how he would respond to conservative criticism that this is another example of government intrusion in people's lives, LaHood flippantly replied, "About everything we do around here is government intrusion in people's lives. So have at it."[6] LaHood's unbridled arrogance, including his declaration that "I think we can change people's behavior," caught the attention of columnist George Will, who fittingly dubbed him the "Secretary of Behavior Modification."[7]

LaHood's bizarre jihad against traditional modes of transportation extended beyond cars. The airline industry was outraged that $8 billion of federal stimulus money was allocated for high-speed rail projects while air traffic control modernization got a goose egg. Making matters worse, these rail projects were hardly "shovel ready" and may not be in operation for decades, but the next-generation air-traffic control system could reduce flight delays and increase air-travel capacity almost immediately. When airline industry members asked LaHood about the rail projects at an FAA conference, he responded, "Let me give you a little bit of political advice: Don't be against the high-speed rail. It's coming to America. This is the president's vision, this is the vice president's vision, this is America's vision.... We're going to get into the high-speed rail business. People want alternatives.... So get with the program."[8] The Great and Powerful Oz had spoken.

Obama himself clearly aims to insert government into the most minute areas of our personal lives, having once declared, "We can't drive our SUVs and eat as much as we want and keep our homes on 72 degrees at all times ... and then just expect that other countries are going to say OK.... That's not leadership. That's not going to happen."[9] In line with his own enthusiasm for behavior modification, in April 2010, Obama launched the "America's Great Outdoors" program to conserve land and encourage more Americans to spend time outside. Obama laughably argued the program was an integral part of economic growth because it would allegedly create jobs.[10] But in truth, it was just another one of Obama's intrusive, pie-in-the-sky green schemes. Those tempted to dismiss the initiative as a harmless presidential pet project should consider this question: if it is a proper function of government to put people back in touch with nature, is there anything beyond government's reach?

Well, apparently not. In June 2010, Obama issued an executive order "Establishing the Prevention, Health Promotion, and Public Health Council," which will focus on "lifestyle behavior modification" (including smoking cessation, proper nutrition, appropriate exercise, mental health, behavioral health, substance-use disorder, and domestic violence screenings). It will also recommend federal policy changes to reduce "sedentary behavior." Obama's propensity to overreach his constitutional authority is only exceeded by his obsession with controlling every aspect of our lives in complete disregard for our individual liberties.[11] It seems George Will's description of Secretary LaHood as "Secretary of Behavior Modification" could apply just as fittingly to LaHood's boss, Barack Obama, the President of Behavior Modification.

PUTTING HUMAN BEINGS IN THEIR PLACE: LAST

One of the biggest yet least publicized outrages in recent memory is the Obama administration's assault on California farmers. Environmental regulations purporting to protect endangered species of fish resulted in tens of billions of gallons of water being diverted away from mountains close to Sacramento and into the ocean, greatly exacerbating drought conditions and ruining hundreds of thousands of acres of farmland—a crushing blow to California agriculture.

In August 2009, some fifty mayors in California's San Joaquin Valley sent Obama a letter requesting him to witness the devastation for himself. But Obama didn't seem any more open to their appeal than he did to Governor Arnold Schwarzenegger's request to designate California a disaster area. The administration refused Schwarzenegger's plea, some believed, because to have granted it would have been an implicit admission that the administration itself had helped cause the drought. But with an administration that sees no limits to its power, why should anyone be surprised that it would effectively seize control of a state's water supply in order to place the interests of fish above the health of human beings?[12]

Presidential adviser Rahm Emanuel wasn't kidding when he said the administration would unleash a raft of executive orders across a number of fronts (read: those few areas where Congress won't roll over for Obama's agenda). This became one of Obama's preferred methods of advancing his green policies. On June 12, 2009, Obama created, by memorandum, an Interagency Ocean Policy Task Force, led by the White House Council on Environmental Quality. The task force "is charged with developing a recommendation for a national policy that ensures protection, maintenance, and restoration of oceans, our coasts and the Great Lakes . . . to make [them] healthier—both environmentally and economically."[13] But one of the key purposes of the task force, and of the "National Ocean Council" that the task force created, was to "deal with the effects of climate change."[14] The task force's report recommended the government view all ocean policy with an "ecosystem-based approach," representing a "key philosophical shift" in the nation's approach.[15]

Frank Miniter at *National Review Online* observed that the task force "has decided that the opinions of America's 60 million anglers aren't worthy of its consideration," despite their enormous environmental and tax contributions. Miniter predicted the task force, with its "agenda of federal control and environmentalist ideology," would recommend closing many of the nation's saltwater and freshwater recreational-fishing areas.[16] This policy flowed naturally from a president who is closely connected to extreme environmental groups, and whose policy course "precisely mirrors" what the green groups outlined in their position paper, "Transition Green." Essentially, it would involve the federal government gobbling up wide swaths of land to preserve natural resources, irrespective of the effects on private industry. All these green groups, Miniter observed, share the "conviction that green ideology trumps ordinary human freedoms."[17]

EPA'S CARBON END RUN

Obama's initial failure to push cap and trade legislation through Congress didn't deter him from skinning the cat another way—showing again that he would not allow constitutional checks and balances to hinder his agenda. After cap and tax, as it's often rightly called, stalled in Congress, the EPA issued a decree in late 2009 defining carbon dioxide and other greenhouse gases as toxic air pollutants subject to regulation under the Clean Air Act. EPA administrator Lisa Jackson declared, "The administration will not ignore science or the law any longer, nor will we avoid the responsibility we owe to our children and our grandchildren."[18]

Thus, Obama's EPA claimed unilateral authority to act, such as setting new carbon emission standards for power plants, factories, and cars, *whether or not Congress passes supporting legislation.*

Environmental groups, naturally, were busting their buttons at this usurpation of congressional authority. Sierra Club chief climate counsel David Bookbinder said, "What it says for the rest of the world is that although Congress has not succeeded in passing the big piece of climate legislation, nevertheless the United States is prepared to move forward in dealing with carbon dioxide."

The administration showed no concern over the enormous damage to the economy that carbon taxes would cause. As Republican senator James Inhofe noted, "Today the American public are getting a raw deal. All cost and no benefit. Yet the Obama administration is moving forward anyway." Keith McCoy, with the National Association of Manufacturers, commented, "I've heard from every industry sector, I've heard from utilities, I've heard from large manufacturers, I've heard from small manufacturers. There is significant concern from every single manufacturing sector out there."[19] Coal-fired power plants would likely be hardest hit—not that this would concern Obama, who unapologetically boasted during the presidential campaign that under a cap and trade regime, any company that builds a coal-fired plan would go bankrupt.[20]

Furthermore, seeking to exploit anxiety over the Gulf oil spill, Obama ordered the government in May 2010 to set the first-ever mileage and pollution limits for big trucks and to tighten rules for future cars and SUVs, giving federal agencies until July 2011 to come up with fuel efficiency and greenhouse standards for commercial trucks and buses.[21] Former U.S. senator George Allen and the Competitive Enterprise Institute's Marlo Lewis responded that the EPA "is carrying out one of the biggest power grabs in American history," having "positioned itself to regulate fuel economy, set climate policy for the nation and amend the Clear Air Act—powers never delegated to it by Congress."[22]

"A 2,100-PAGE MONSTROSITY FULL OF SPECIAL DEALS"
ObamaCare was an unmitigated disaster in its own right, but it was also a playground for assorted abuses of power by the Obama

administration, beginning with certain ancillary provisions that were smuggled into the bill. An analysis of the Joint Economic Committee and the House Ways and Means Committee minority staff shows ObamaCare will lead to the largest increase in the IRS since World War II, with as many as 16,500 new IRS personnel required to collect, examine, and audit returns.[23] Dave Camp, the ranking Republican on the Ways and Means Committee, warned the bill involves "a very dangerous expansion of the IRS's power and reach into the lives of virtually every American."[24]

Under the bill, the IRS will have to ensure Americans comply with the mandatory provision that they acquire health insurance. Taxpayers who fail to prove on their annual tax return that they are policyholders would be subject to a fine of $2,250 or 2 percent of their income, whichever is greater. The IRS would have the authority to confiscate tax refunds for this purpose. Some young Americans will probably gamble on their good health and opt to pay the penalty, but that fine will almost certainly lead to outright noncompliance among many young people, as well as among those in cash-oriented businesses who will have greater incentive to work under the radar.[25] So Obama's IRS will doubtlessly prepare itself to chase down these healthcare recalcitrants.

Republicans contend these changes would fundamentally alter the relationship between an already overly powerful and intrusive IRS and the American taxpayers, making the IRS responsible for "tracking the monthly health insurance status of roughly 300 million Americans."[26] (Note that almost half the mandated coverage will be imposed on people making less than $66,150 for a family of four.) The IRS would also collect hundreds of billions of dollars in new fees assessed against employers, drug companies, and device makers. The IRS budget is expected to increase by some $10 billion over the next decade to help administer this new program.[27]

Another IRS-related surprise in the bill, since repealed, is a hidden change in the tax law that would have forced companies to submit IRS 1099 forms for any individual or company from which they purchase more than $600 in goods or services a year. This would have meant the required filing of millions of new forms each year to be sent to vendors and the IRS.[28]

Also folded into ObamaCare was an insidious federal power grab over student loans. The bill gave the government a monopoly on the student loan industry, with an expected profit to the government—literally robbed from the private sector—of $60 billion over the next decade. In keeping with Obama's penchant for growing government, he wouldn't just subsume the student loan business; he would expand it by some $40 billion, which would still leave a profit of around $20 billion that the CBO was required to consider in its scoring of the bill—even though its only relation to healthcare was that it was smuggled into the bill.

Obama snuck this provision into ObamaCare because it probably wouldn't have been able to secure the sixty votes necessary for passage on its own. The student loan section of the bill also contained a hidden payoff to North Dakota senator Kent Conrad, who happens to be Budget Committee chairman. The bill would "establish a new program for lenders who were chartered before July 1, 2009, and are owned by a state under the control of a board including the governor and offered guaranteed loans prior to June 30, 2010." For all that fancy and misleading language, the program will only apply to one lender: the Bank of North Dakota.[29]

The administration presumptuously began transitioning toward the new student loan program half a year before the bill even passed, when Education secretary Arne Duncan sent colleges and universities a letter in October 2009 pressuring them to prepare to transition to the government-run system for the 2010–2011 academic year. At the time, schools generally preferred private lenders to the government-run "public option" available to them, because private firms provided better service. But the administration, possibly as a foreshadowing of what we can expect with ObamaCare, was intent on making the public option the only option.

But not all school administrators were happy with this transition, which was not, as the White House promised, "as simple as throwing a switch." Dewey Knight, a financial aid officer for the University of Mississippi, called the administration's approach "an insult to people who spent years getting delivery systems in place. We didn't just throw a switch to get where we are." Knight, one of the few financial aid administrators willing to criticize Obama's student loan machinations, revealed the White House had pressured aid administrators to support the nationalization of student loans by going above their heads to university presidents.

A Republican staffer on the House Education and Labor Committee confirmed Knight's perspective, noting that financial aid professionals expressed opposition to the plan early in the process, but were pressured to be quiet after the administration refused to satisfy their concerns. The staffer divulged she'd even been told about "specific instances at individual schools where administration officials or members of Congress had contacted school leadership in an effort to tamp down opposition."[30] This strong-arming reflects the same MO Obama has employed with all his significant legislative bills. Shortly after the bill passed, lender Sallie Mae announced it would cut 2,500 jobs due to the government takeover of the student loan program.[31]

ObamaCare also earned notoriety because the administration resorted to the crudest kind of political bribery to pass it, marking a shocking violation of Obama's core campaign promises of transparent government and an end to backroom deals. There was the "Louisiana Purchase," whereby Obama and his Democrats bought Senator Mary Landrieu's vote with a promise to send $300 million in additional Medicaid funding to Louisiana. There was the "Cornhusker Kickback," the administration's disgraceful bribe of Nebraska senator Ben Nelson with a promise to exempt his state from its share of Medicaid expansion, meaning that the other forty-nine states would subsidize Nebraska's new Medicaid recipients to the tune of about $45 million over the first decade. Obama, in an interview with ABC's Diane Sawyer, denied he had been involved in the Nelson deal, which was ultimately dropped from the bill due to public opposition. "Let's hold on a second, Diane.... So let's just clarify. I didn't make a bunch of deals."[32] But his aid Rahm Emanuel, when asked about the Cornhusker Kickback, told a different story to CBS's Katie Couric: "Look, we were involved in the legislation all the way through.... We were helpful in getting the bill off the Senate floor."[33]

Then there was Senator Bernie Sanders, who secured $10 billion in new funding for community health centers for Vermont, though he denied it was a "sweetheart deal." Nebraska's Senator Nelson and Michigan senator Carl Levin also secured an exemption for non-profit insurers in their respective states from a significant excise tax, which will be borne by the other forty-eight states. Pennsylvania, New York, and Florida received special protections for their Medicare Advantage beneficiaries when the program was making nationwide cuts.[34] Senator Chris Dodd received $100 million in funding for a university hospital—not that his vote was ever in doubt. Vermont and Massachusetts will receive federal subsides for their Medicaid expansion costs.[35]

Obama silenced Big Pharma's opposition by agreeing not to further cut Medicare's payments to them and by abandoning his campaign promise to push for importing drugs from Canada. He allegedly won the support of the American Medical Association by agreeing to cancel all or part of the 21 percent cut in physicians' reimbursements (the "doc fix"). He seduced AARP with a promise to eliminate subsidies for Medicare Advantage, which was eating into AARP's side business, the Medi-gap insurance program, which supplements Medicare coverage.[36] In exchange for its support and in keeping with Obama's unsavory alliance with unions, Big Labor earned an exemption from the new Cadillac tax on high-cost insurance coverage.[37]

But one industry wouldn't give in to Obama: the medical device industry, which rejected Obama's Godfather-like offer to cut costs in exchange for his promise not to impose even worse cuts.[38] Now those crucial, life-saving companies are facing a 2.3 percent excise tax on sales of medical devices, which is expected to raise $20 billion over ten years to help fund ObamaCare. Industry experts fear the tax will destroy jobs, innovation, and small companies with thin profit margins.[39] It will also likely increase the cost, and thus reduce the availability, of such devices as automatic external defibrillators (AEDs), whose wide availability, according to research reported by the *New England Journal of Medicine,* could significantly improve the survival rates of cardiac arrest patients.[40]

Perhaps even more disturbing were indications Obama's parade of bribes and threats at times may have descended into illegality. For example, there was widespread speculation that Obama offered judgeships to secure healthcare votes. *The Weekly Standard* reported that in March 2010 Obama hosted ten House Democrats who had voted against the House bill the previous November. One of the ten was Utah's Jim Matheson, whose brother Scott M. Matheson, Jr., was nominated by Obama *that very day* to the U.S. Court of Appeals for the Tenth Circuit.[41]

Along the same lines, *Human Events* reported a "rumor" that two retiring Democratic congressmen from Tennessee, Bart Gordon and John Tanner, were promised positions as NASA administrator and U.S. Ambassador to NATO, respectively, in exchange for their ObamaCare votes.[42] (Gordon ultimately voted for ObamaCare, while Tanner opposed it.) And perhaps most inglorious in this sordid process was Obama's last minute promise to Congressman Bart Stupak and other allegedly pro-life Democrats, as previously mentioned, to issue a counterfeit executive order denying federal funding for abortion in exchange for their "yes" votes.

In addition to all this, Democrats reportedly threatened to strip Connecticut senator Joe Lieberman of his chairmanship of the Homeland Security Committee for opposing Obama's public option.

Taking in the full ugliness and corruption of this process, Senate Republican leader Mitch McConnell said, "This bill is a monstrosity, a 2,100-page monstrosity full of special deals for people who are willing to vote for it. And they're playing these kind of games with the nation's health care. This is an outrage."[43] And indeed it is.

"TARP IS NOT A PIGGY BANK"

Obama has shown a similar disregard for the rule of law in his handling of TARP bailout funds. Obama brags about how much TARP monies have been repaid (notwithstanding his refusal to allow some banks to pay their loans back and his plans to immediately spend recovered funds on yet more quixotic jobs creation programs).[44] But it's hard to take seriously his pledges to safeguard these funds when he frequently treats them as his personal stash.

One particularly egregious example was the administration's effort to transfer $30 billion of repaid TARP money to a new small-business credit program. Senator Judd Gregg upbraided OMB director Peter Orszag over what would have been an illegal act. Holding up a copy of the TARP bill, Gregg declared, "Let me read to you again, because you don't appear to understand the law. The law is very clear. The monies recouped from TARP shall be paid into the general fund of the Treasury for the reduction of the public debt." TARP, said Gregg, is not "a piggy bank." Heritage Foundation senior legal policy analyst Andrew Grossman agreed. "The administration," said Grossman, "lacks legal authority" to use TARP monies for anything it chooses outside the bill's specific intent. "If the authority is as broad as the administration and some lawmakers say, then it is unconstitutional. Congress cannot pass the buck and give unlimited power to the executive."[45]

BIG BROTHER

In light of their intolerance of criticism, their belief in behavior modification, and their cavalier rejection of the rule of law, it's unsurprising this administration sometimes seems like it comes straight out of *1984*. For example, one Big Brother-sounding post on the White House blog read as though the administration had declared a private war on U.S. citizens—the ones who opposed ObamaCare, at any rate—and was recruiting "spies" to snitch on the offenders. The post, by White House "new media director" Macon Phillips, said,

> Scary chain e-mails and videos are starting to percolate on the Internet, breathlessly claiming, for example, to "uncover" the truth about the President's health insurance reform positions. . . . There is a lot of information about health insurance reform out there, spanning from control of personal finances to end of life care. These rumors often travel just below the surface via chain e-mails or through casual conversation. Since we can't keep track of all of them here at the White House, we're asking for your help. If you get an e-mail or something on the web about health insurance reform that seems fishy, send it to flag@whitehouse.gov.[46]

The blog entry brought fire from conservatives. Senator John Barrasso declared, "If you get an e-mail from your neighbor and it doesn't sound right, send it to the White House? People, I think all across America, are going to say, is this 1984? What is happening here? Is big brother watching?" Accusing the White House of compiling an "enemies list," Senator John Cornyn sent a letter to Obama, saying, "I am not aware of any precedent for a president asking American citizens to report their fellow citizens to the White House for pure political speech that is deemed 'fishy' or otherwise inimical to the White House's political interests." Cornyn expressed understandable concern that the White House's speech monitoring effort could chill citizens' political expression.[47]

The more Obama overreached, the more simmering citizen angst boiled into outrage. In response to the snitch program, the Association of American Physicians and Surgeons and the Coalition for

Urban Renewal and Education filed a federal lawsuit to prohibit the Executive Office of the President, the White House Office of Health Care Reform and its director Nancy-Ann DeParle, and Macon Phillips from collecting and maintaining data on citizens' protected speech.[48]

Eventually, the White House reversed its policy of encouraging citizens to report ObamaCare opponents to the White House. But less than a month later, the White House came under criticism for engaging in another form of data mining and archiving. It had implemented a plan to permanently archive citizen comments posted on the White House's Facebook, MySpace, YouTube, and Twitter pages. The White House insisted it was just acting "out of an abundance of caution" to comply with the Presidential Records Act, which requires that information generated by the president and his staff be preserved.

A conservative government watchdog group, the National Legal and Policy Center, didn't buy that excuse. "This is a huge, secretive effort by the White House to capture web material far beyond what is required by the Presidential Records Act, which only requires archiving materials produced by the president and his staff at the Executive Office of the President," said NLPC chairman Ken Boehm. A spokesman for the Competitive Enterprise Institute said he didn't share the NLPC's concern, but believed the government should make extra efforts to inform posters that their contributions will be archived.[49]

Within a day or two Obama himself got into the act, attempting to use his office to directly mobilize his supporters on the health-care effort. He sent out his own e-mail castigating opponents of ObamaCare for "filling the airwaves and the Internet with outrageous falsehoods to scare people into opposing change."[50] He later used the same language in a radio address bashing insurance companies for "filling the airwaves with deceptive and dishonest ads."

During the final push for healthcare reform, Nancy-Ann DeParle, the White House's pointwoman for ObamaCare, began "feverishly" sending out unsolicited e-mail to federal employees proselytizing for ObamaCare. The chief executive's allocation of federal dollars to pressure federal employees into supporting his policies was obviously improper, but what's more, these e-mails were sent to the employees' official government e-mail accounts for weeks without permission or request. Some of the employees felt threatened by "the overt political language," according to *CBS News*. Tellingly, many State Department employees complained privately about the partisan messages but wouldn't publicly object for fear of retribution. Richard Grenell, a former spokesman for four U.S. ambassadors to the UN, noted, "Federal employees are public servants, not partisan foot soldiers for President Obama and shouldn't have to decide whether a partisan White House request can be ignored without consequences."[51]

A similar incident occurred at the Obama–Holder Justice Department, which formed a secret, in-house blogging group to influence public opinion. Set up and operating out of the Justice Department's Office of Public Affairs, the "Blog Squad" used liberal bloggers to scour the Internet for news stories, commentaries, and blog posts critical of the administration and then post comments supporting their agenda. Similarly, the administration and its allies enlisted supporters to call conservative radio talk shows to create the appearance of widespread grassroots support of Obama and dissent from conservative positions. The administration is obviously projecting when it falsely depicts the genuine grassroots tea party protests as an "Astroturf" phenomenon—a manufactured, top-down, artificial publicity campaign—because that is precisely the type of activism the administration was sponsoring.

In fact, Cass Sunstein, who "has long been one of Barack Obama's closest confidants" and is now his head of the Office of Information and Regulatory Affairs, has advocated the government's use of fake websites and outside 501(c)(3) interest groups to front as independent supporters of government policy and to "cognitively infiltrate" opposing websites. This is especially troubling considering Sunstein's new position entails him "overseeing policies relating to privacy, information quality, and statistical programs."

Sunstein had the right background to lead this kind of effort for Obama. While at Harvard Law School in 2008, Sunstein, according to *Salon* magazine's Glenn Greenwald, co-wrote a "truly pernicious paper proposing that the U.S. Government employ teams of covert agents and pseudo-'independent' advocates to 'cognitively infiltrate' online groups and websites—as well as other activist groups—which advocate views that Sunstein deems 'false conspiracy theories.'" The purpose would be to "increase citizens' faith in government officials and undermine the credibility of conspiracists."[52]

Does this not sound familiar? Is this not precisely the strategy the administration has used to depict tea party protestors as fringe, violent, "conspiracist," and downright crazy? Based on these factors, *Red State*'s Eric Erickson speculated the Obama administration could be behind a new anti-tea party website called "The Other 95," which "defends the government from tea party criticisms and attacks the tea party movement as fringe." The designer of the site, reported Erickson, is affiliated with MoveOn.org and other leftwing sites and causes. But "most notable," Erickson said, "the donations page makes donations out to Democracy in Action," which "is *not* for individual activists to use," but for small and medium sized 501(c)(3) organizations and other leftists. Its clients include ACORN and True Majority.[53]

Given the Justice Department's duty to enforce the laws of the land *impartially*, as opposed to campaigning for the administration's agenda, the Blog Squad is an outrage. It is chilling that a government charged with protecting its citizens instead conceals its identity and surreptitiously trolls among those citizens on the Internet, attempting to sway public opinion by stealth. On *National Review Online*, Hans von Spakovsky wrote, "I doubt that the Office of Public Affairs (OPA) has received an ethics opinion from Justice's Professional Responsibility Advisory Office (PRAO) saying that it is acceptable for OPA employees to be harassing critics of the department through postings that deliberately hide their DOJ affiliation (a practice that is not very 'open' or 'transparent'). DOJ lawyers," continued Spakovsky, should be "aware of" ABA ethical rules that specify as professional misconduct, a lawyer's engagement "in conduct involving dishonesty, fraud, deceit, or misrepresentation. If the report [about the Blog Squad] is correct, tax dollars are being used directly for such dishonest, deceitful behavior."[54]

Meanwhile, the White House continued to use its blog as a cudgel against ObamaCare opponents. When Congressman Henry Waxman's heavy-handed tactics failed to intimidate companies from accurately reporting the cost increases associated with ObamaCare, Obama's electronic storm troopers sprung into action. Commerce secretary Gary Locke posted an entry on the White House blog ridiculing the companies and implying they didn't know what they were talking about. He parroted White House disinformation that ObamaCare "will bend the health care cost curve" and "reduce premiums and increase business competitiveness in the U.S."[55]

The *Business Insider* observed, "We listened to the CEO of one of the biggest healthcare companies say unequivocally on NPR that Obamacare would make premiums go up. He made it sound like the height of obviousness—and it was so obvious that the interviewer didn't even follow up on it." So, it was "hardly startling news," said the *Insider*, that companies were warning their shareholders and employees about it. "Could it be that the Democrats are only now discovering that Obamacare *won't* actually provide more healthcare for less? Or is it just that they're angry that everyone else has noticed?"[56] Locke later appeared on CNBC to intensify his attack on dissenters, suggesting they were acting irresponsibly and prematurely.

The *New York Daily News* reported in April 2010 that the White House had also employed "Twitter and other social media outlets" to speak "directly to the people." "Twitter is the rage at the White House," but is "only one weapon in its communications arsenal. It also liberally employs an interactive Web site, Facebook,

YouTube, chat rooms, its own blog, videotaped press releases, Flickr photos and a still growing 13-million-member campaign e-mail list." All on the public dime, no doubt.

The article confirmed the obvious: the White House doesn't just use these outlets to augment its communications, but as tools to carefully control its messages through top-down, organized communiqués. Obama is not about transparency; the *Daily News* noted he hadn't held a wide-ranging press conference in nine months and "rarely talks to the small press pool following him around." His aides even admit that this is because "they don't want to craft 'message events,' only to have the press ask about something else that makes news and steps on their spin."

Obama has gone so far as to bypass conventional media routes and deliver information concerning important events directly through Twitter, such as his decision to forego his trip to Indonesia and Australia to remain in Washington for the final push on ObamaCare. This is some way to show gratitude to the fawning mainstream media! But when some reporters complained, White House press secretary Robert Gibbs arrogantly replied that the whiners should join the 55,000 people who follow Gibbs's tweets.[57]

Conservatives also spoke out against another potential invasion of privacy spawned by Democrats. The ObamaCare bill reportedly created a new office under the FDA's umbrella, the National Medical Device Registry, with authority to engage in "postmarket device surveillance activities on implantable medical devices," including those with radio-frequency identification. The *Washington Times* noted "postmarket surveillance" is a term of art in the medical community and that the monitoring in this case is ostensibly to ensure the medical devices are functioning properly. But privacy concerns are nevertheless justified, said the *Times*, because the White House has publicly supported using innovative techniques to track people. Indeed, the Justice Department argued government agents should be allowed to track citizens by cell phone triangulation without search warrants because citizens have "no reasonable expectation of privacy" when it comes to their "personal communications devices." The *Times* argued it's "not a great leap to believe the same rule would apply to an implanted radio chip," given the administration's "incessant drive to expand government power over Americans' lives."[58]

"OBAMA TURNS HIS BACK ON THE PRESS"

At a presser in May 2010, reporter Les Kinsolving asked Gibbs a question that elicited applause from his fellow reporters: why hadn't Obama held a press conference since July 2009? Instead of answering the question directly, Gibbs made rude, snide, and condescending comments purporting to define what a press conference is.[59] About a week later, CBS's Chip Reid tried to ask the elusive Obama a question immediately following his signing of the Freedom of Press Act. Obama haughtily declared, "I'm not doing a press conference today, but we'll be seeing you guys during the course of the week." Reid said the irony of asking Obama a question just as he signed the Freedom of Press Act was too rich to resist, describing it as a way of "expressing frustration from the press corps because Obama does so little in the way of press conferences and answering questions from us."[60]

Two days later, as Obama held a so-called "news conference" in the Rose Garden with the president of Mexico, Chip Reid assumed Obama might finally field some questions. But he took only one from the U.S. news media. When Reid shouted a question about the recent election loss of Senator Arlen Specter, Obama ignored him. The *New York Times* story reporting the incident was aptly titled, "Obama Turns His Back On the Press."[61]

Obama treated other media representatives with the same disdain, especially when they pressed him on controversial issues such as the lingering allegation by Pennsylvania Democratic congressman Joe Sestak that the administration offered him a job if he would agree not to go after Arlen Specter's Senate seat. ABC's Jake

Tapper asked Gibbs to elaborate on conversations Gibbs said occurred in the White House about the charge. Tapper noted, "You never really explained what the conversation was." Gibbs characteristically snapped back, "Then I don't have anything to add today."

When other media tried to follow up, Gibbs became "noticeably irritated"[62]—even though he was the one being evasive. The Department of Justice, in a letter to Republican congressman Darrell Issa, rejected a Republican request to appoint a special counsel to investigate the allegations, insisting nothing inappropriate had happened. Issa said the DOJ's refusal was highly improper, commenting, "You have a sitting U.S. congressman who has made a very specific allegation numerous times that someone inside the Obama White House offered him what amounts to a bribe in order to manipulate the Pennsylvania Senate primary. The attorney general's refusal to take action in the face of such felonious allegations undermines any claim to transparency and integrity that this administration asserts."[63]

Despite Obama's aggressive use of the new media virtually as a propaganda ministry, he still complains when his plebian subjects dare to avail themselves of the same technology. He is uncomfortable when he isn't in total control of the message. Just as he told congressional Republicans they shouldn't be paying too much attention to Rush Limbaugh or FOX News, he decried the new tools of the information age, apparently because they make it more difficult for him to act covertly. He whined, "Meanwhile, you're coming of age in a 24/7 media environment that bombards us with all kinds of content and exposes us to all kinds of arguments, some of which don't rank all that high on the truth meter. With iPods and iPads; Xboxes and PlayStations, information becomes a distraction, a diversion, a form of entertainment, rather than a tool of empowerment. All of this is not putting new pressures on you; it is putting new pressures on our country and on our democracy."[64] Only a true Alinskyite could talk about a "tool of empowerment" and view the proliferation of information throughout the population as a threat to democracy.

REMAKING THE BROADCAST WORLD

The Obama administration hasn't tried to hide its intention of using all means at its disposal to shut down conservative talk radio, whether through the Fairness Doctrine, local content, or diversity regulations. If they can't muzzle Rush Limbaugh through public ridicule, or wedge FOX News out of the White House press pool, or marginalize tea party protestors, they'll explore other avenues to suppress speech from political opponents, including regulating the Internet through "net neutrality rules," which some have argued constitute a Fairness Doctrine for the Internet.

Net neutrality rules would prohibit Internet operators from treating some online traffic differently than others. Many conservatives and libertarians fear regulators would exploit these rules to get their foot in the door under the seductive pretense that they are protecting all Internet users. Once in, they would seek to impose their content-based regulations.

In 2009, the FCC issued rules to force Internet service providers to conform to net neutrality principles, but when Comcast challenged the rules, a three-judge panel of the Court of Appeals for the D.C. Circuit unanimously decided the FCC didn't have the power to enforce its rules against the firm. But this was just a temporary setback for liberal regulators, whose congressional backers have vowed to look at legislation to further expand FCC regulating powers. Predictably, Gibbs said Obama was still committed to net neutrality, despite the court's ruling.[65]

Obama's FCC also has a "National Broadband Plan," which includes such gems as taxpayer-funded broadband as well as a plan for the FCC to recapture almost half the radio spectrum currently being used by 1,600 TV stations and rededicate it to broadband services. Some speculate the FCC really aims to end all broadcasting and move all news, information, and entertainment to the Internet. From there the government could regulate content beyond that contemplated by the administration's proposed "net neutrality" rules. As Mark Hyman, commentator for Sinclair Broadcast Group, Inc. wrote, "It would be much easier for a president to shut down the Internet than to turn-off 1,600 individual television transmitters and whose content is much more cumbersome to monitor." Hyman's warning seemed eerily prescient in June 2010, when the technology website CNET reported that "a new U.S. Senate bill would grant the president far-reaching emergency powers to seize control of or even shut down portions of the Internet."[66]

The administration's overreaching has not gone unnoticed by major broadband providers. When the FCC voted to continue considering broadband regulations that would grant it greater authority to regulate the Internet and classify it as a telecommunications service, AT&T, Comcast, and Verizon "lashed out" at the administration. AT&T senior executive vice president Jim Cicconi said, "This is impossible to justify on either a policy or legal basis, and we remain confident that if the FCC persists in its course—and we truly hope it does not—the courts will surely overturn their action."[67]

According to Mark Hyman, the administration's plans don't end with the National Broadband Plan and its "net neutrality" initiative. The FCC, says Hyman, "has dived headlong into another topic: manipulating news and information."[68] A major player in administration efforts to manipulate news is Mark Lloyd, the FCC's Chief Diversity Officer, known as the "diversity czar." This Obama appointee has a frightening view of free speech, arguing that "the purpose of free speech is warped to protect global corporations and block rules that would promote democratic governance." Like a good totalitarian, he believes the First Amendment can impede the greater societal goals that only government can bring about. Lloyd greatly admires Venezuelan dictator Hugo Chavez and has written favorably of his two-year war against the private media, in which

Chavez closed most of those outlets down in order to suppress criticism of the government. Obama's appointment of Lloyd is a truly ominous sign, especially from a president who laments the proliferation of information enabled by new technology.

Then there's Obama's new Supreme Court nominee, Elena Kagan, who has also shown the radical's proper approach to free speech, remarking, "If there is an 'overabundance' of an idea in the absence of direct governmental action—which there well might be when compared with some ideal state of public debate—then action disfavoring that idea might 'un-skew', rather than skew, public discourse."[69]

David Martin of the Media Research Center translated Kagan's jargon: "So, if talk radio suffers from an 'overabundance' of conservative voices, government action to 'un-skew' this particular public discourse is acceptable according to Kagan." Martin added that Kagan has also taken the position that "government can restrict speech if it believes that speech might cause harm, either directly or by inciting others to do harm."[70] Hmmmm . . . Tea party, anyone? The Washington Times also sounded the alarm on Kagan, noting her "First Amendment work repeatedly promotes the idea that speech rights are granted by government rather than inherent in the God-given nature of man." Then again, to many liberals, government is a substitute for God.[71]

Under Obama, even the simple calculating of radio listenership has become a politicized issue requiring government involvement. In 2007 Arbitron adopted the Portable People Meter (PPM), a new, more accurate measurement system for radio listenership. But there was a problem, at least for the Left: PPM produced higher conservative talk ratings and lower ratings for urban and minority-owned stations. Unsurprisingly, just as leftists have squealed about the loss of their media monopoly with the advent of conservative talk and FOX News, they cried foul at the new ratings system. At the urging of the National Association of Black Owned Broadcasters, Obama's FCC ordered an inquiry into the PPM data collection process—in the name of "diversity."

The Radio Equalizer's Brian Maloney opined that the Left's goal was to "restore hip-hop's ratings and undo the newly-precise measurement of Rush Limbaugh's statistics. Combined with a White House-led effort to destroy the talk titan, ratings have recently gone through the roof."[72] *Newsbusters'* Seton Motley aptly noted, "If [Obama] is willing to take on this most ridiculous of claims in the name of media 'Diversity,' we are naturally left to think that there is nearly nothing he won't do to ensure that the broadcast world is remade in the manner he thinks it should be."[73]

POLITICIZATION OF THE DEPARTMENT OF JUSTICE

The Department of Justice under Obama and Attorney General Eric Holder has been acutely politicized, from its appeasement approach to the war on terror to its denunciation of Arizona's sovereign immigration law. But perhaps its most inexcusably politicized action was its dismissal of the voter intimidation case against New Black Panther Party members. The case arose when voters complained that nightstick-wielding Black Panthers were guarding the door of a Philadelphia polling station. The Bush Justice Department filed suit against NBPP leader Malik Shabazz and two other NBPP members, none of whom even filed an answer to the lawsuit. Rather than accepting a default judgment against the defendants, Obama's DOJ dismissed the case against two of the three. Justice claimed it dropped the lawsuit "after careful review," but was never forthcoming about its reasons.

A year after the dismissal, Todd Gaziano, a member of the U.S. Commission on Civil Rights, told the *Washington Times* he believes "a racist application of the voting rights laws may have been at play" in the decision to dismiss the case. Gaziano said he "wanted to believe" there were "wrongheaded but not racist reasons" leading to the dismissal, but "there apparently is a culture in the civil rights division" of the Justice Department where section chiefs and other supervising attorneys "don't believe the voting rights laws should ever be enforced against blacks and other minorities." If there were a "good reason for something (dismissal), and the reason has been called into question, a decent law enforcement agency... would want to provide the reasonable explanation—and they still haven't done that." Additionally, the DOJ refuses to allow the commissioners to interview key department employees they have subpoenaed and others.[74]

Chris Coates, the DOJ career voting section chief, reportedly shocked his coworkers at his going-away luncheon by reciting a written defense of his decision to file the case against the NBPP members. In the memo, Coates said he did his best "to enforce all our voting statutes for all Americans, and I leave here with my soul rested that I did the right thing to the best of my ability." Republican congressman Frank Wolf, speaking before the Commission on Civil Rights, said, "Although the Attorney General will not allow the career attorneys to testify before this commission, I believe this anecdote helps to convey the ardent opposition of the department's career attorneys to the dismissal of this voting rights case." Wolf called on the Attorney General to comply with the subpoenas and permit the career attorneys to testify.[75]

Christian Adams, a trial attorney with the DOJ's voting rights section, later resigned over the government's refusal to prosecute the case or to allow him and his colleagues to testify before the commission despite being subpoenaed. In his resignation letter, Adams cited the "explicit federal statute" upon which the subpoena is based. He also invoked the increasing belligerence of the NBPP defendants toward the attorneys who brought the case, and his intimate knowledge of "the criminal character and violent tendencies of the members of the New Black Panther Party."[76]

Adams later made the explosive allegation that the Justice Department had dismissed the case because under Holder, it simply refuses to prosecute voting rights cases when the victims are white. As Adams ominously noted, the dismissal "raises serious questions about the department's enforcement neutrality in upcoming midterm elections and the subsequent 2012 presidential election."[77]

The New Black Panther Party's methods are hardly worse than those of the Obama administration. Though Obama doesn't use a nightstick to intimidate people from voting, his subordinates protect those who do. Though Obama doesn't shove a gag into his opponents' mouths, he presides over agencies that are furiously searching for ways to silence his critics. He talks a good game of transparency while using secretive and corrupt methods to pass legislation; he speaks of openness, while avoiding questions and sometimes mocking the once starry-eyed White House press corps; and he insists on bipartisanship while White House operatives troll the Internet to malign and snitch on everyday citizens who dissent from his agenda. It is no wonder his cynical, ruthless administration has ushered in among Americans a seething discontent with the governing majority in Washington.

Chapter Eight

OBAMA THE IMPERIOUS

CRIMES AGAINST THE PRIVATE SECTOR, PART 1

Obama's assault on the private sector began early in his term. His main tactic was pitting people against people and groups against groups with unprecedented stridency. He couldn't just push for a "fairer" tax system; he first had to vilify lobbyists, "special interests," the wealthy, and corporate America. When he called for an end to tax breaks for U.S. corporations doing business abroad, he blamed "a broken tax system, written by well-connected lobbyists on behalf of well-heeled interests and individuals."

While advocating almost any legislation, Obama identified some nefarious, private-sector villain he claimed needed to be put in line. Introducing his plan to revamp the student loan program, he said, "We have a student loan system that's rigged to reward private lenders without any risk." During his efforts to strong-arm a restructuring of Chrysler, he accused the firm's secured creditors of seeking "an unjustified taxpayer-funded bailout"—when they were just trying to defend their legal rights that the administration was trampling in favor of Chrysler's union. He accused credit card companies of dishonestly imposing "all kinds of harsh penalties and fees," and he lambasted large U.S. companies for diverting some of their profits overseas. Jade West, a lobbyist for the National Association of Wholesale-Distributors commented, "It is traditional class-warfare rhetoric. It's a little bit frightening."[1]

DEMONIZING BIG PHARMA

When ObamaCare was being debated, Obama was determined not to repeat the mistakes of the Clintons, who had been outmaneuvered by opponents of socialized medicine in the early nineties. One thing he would do more effectively was to shore up support, or at least nullify major opposition from, certain sectors such as the American Medical Association and pharmaceutical companies. He was willing to do whatever it took to pass healthcare, including resorting to the bullying and bribery described in previous chapters.

While campaigning, Obama talked tough against the drug companies, saying, "We'll tell the pharmaceutical companies 'thanks, but no, thanks' for the overpriced drugs—drugs that cost twice as much here as they do in Europe and Canada."[2] But in summer 2009, he reached a mutually shameful deal with the drug-makers' main lobbying group, Pharmaceutical Research and Manufacturers of America (PhRMA), whereby drug-makers agreed to cut drug costs by $8 billion a year for ten years in exchange for Obama's commitment not to further cut Medicare's payments to them and not to push for importing drugs from Canada[3]—directly contradicting his campaign promise. "It's got to be a little awkward," said Senator Tom Carper, in reference to Obama's about-face.[4]

An unlikely source, the Left-wing website the *Huffington Post*, exposed the shady deal's details based on an internal memo "prepared by a person directly involved in the negotiations." The White

House agreed to oppose any congressional attempts to push for lower drug prices or to import drugs from Canada. It also pledged "not to pursue Medicare rebates or shift some drugs from Medicare Part B to Medicare Part D, which would cost Big Pharma billions in reduced reimbursements." Both PhRMA and the White House denied the memo's accuracy, but critics nevertheless accused Obama of reneging on his promises both to use government to reduce drug costs to Medicare and to conduct his negotiations in the open.[5]

Other mainstream media sources cast further suspicion on the White House's denial of a backroom deal. The *New York Times'* David Kirkpatrick reported that the White House "assured drug makers that the administration stood by a behind-the-scenes deal to block any congressional effort to extract cost savings from them beyond an agreed-upon $80 billion." Reports that the White House wasn't standing behind the deal led Billy Tauzin, a former congressman and PhRMA's lead lobbyist, to publicly confirm a deal had been struck: "We were assured: 'We need somebody to come in first. If you come in first you will have a rock-solid-deal. . . . Who is ever going to go into a deal with the White House again if they don't keep their word? You are just going to duke it out instead." The *Times* reported that White House deputy chief of staff Jim Messina had confirmed Tauzin's version of the deal.[6]

Tauzin was firm about the White House's involvement in the deal. He said the White House had tracked negotiations from the beginning and had "assented" to the deal's basic components: not negotiating prices or importing drugs from Canada in exchange for the $80 billion—"no more, no less. Adding other stuff changes the deal." Tauzin even said he met twice at the White House on the matter with top Obama operatives Messina, Rahm Emanuel, and Nancy-Ann DeParle. "They blessed the deal," said Tauzin.[7]

But another complication developed. House Democrats were miffed at being cut out of the negotiations, though their counterparts in the Senate Finance Committee (primarily represented by Senator Max Baucus) had been included. Raul M. Grijalva, the

Democratic co-chairman of the House progressive caucus, called the deal "disturbing." "We have all been focused on the debate in Congress, but perhaps the deal has already been cut. That would put us in the untenable position of trying to scuttle it," he said.

Grijalva was concerned Congress was being ignored in favor of lobbyists, and that this might set a precedent for the Obama White House to follow on other issues. "It is a pivotal issue not just about health care," said Grijalva. "Are industry groups going to be the ones at the table who get the first big piece of the pie and we just fight over the crust?" Adding further tension, House Speaker Nancy Pelosi reportedly asserted the House was not bound by any deals between the White House and the Senate.[8]

The White House was forced to distance itself from its own deal amidst public criticism after the terms had been leaked. Communications Director Linda Douglass, for example, confirmed PhRMA's commitment to reduce drug costs by $80 billion but, incredibly, denied PhRMA was promised anything in return—as if the $80 billion were a spontaneous act of altruism. "The issue," claimed Douglass, "was not discussed."[9]

Her denial contradicted Tauzin's account as well as the statements of White House press secretary Robert Gibbs. According to *ABC News'* Political Punch, Gibbs tacitly confirm the deal when he told CNN's Ed Henry, "We feel like $80 billion is—is an appropriate amount." When Henry asked if "there is a deal that you won't squeeze any more?" Gibbs responded, "Well, I hate to blow our cover here, but we announced it publicly." When Henry asked why the White House had privately told Democratic senators there was no such deal, Gibbs replied, "I don't know where that's coming from. I don't know what that's being based on."[10]

Given Obama's reputation for brilliance, it's surprising he failed to foresee the drug companies would raise their prices in anticipation of the promised cost cutting. As the *Boston Globe* reported in November 2009, "Big Pharma has taken savings off the table. A new AARP analysis has found that drug companies raised their prices for prescription drugs by 9.3 percent over the last year, amounting to $10 billion in revenues. That is $2 billion more than the promised annual cost cuts."[11]

One explanation of the drug-makers' apparent double-cross is that perhaps they had never agreed to any cost cutting measures at all. In other words, Obama might have merely been trying to make it appear he had extracted concessions to give him cover for a uni-lateral bribe—promising not to negotiate prices or import drugs from Canada in exchange for PhRMA's support for ObamaCare. Perhaps that explains why drug companies had given up their long-standing support for Republicans to endorse Obama.[12]

Regardless of what PhRMA had ultimately promised, the deal showed the White House to be a hardball player of Chicago-style politics, willing to violate campaign pledges or political deals to accomplish its goals. It was all on display here. Obama promised he would make no deal with pharmaceuticals, and he reneged. He presented Big Pharma's support of the bill as a result of some mag-ical conversion they'd undergone toward his socialized medicine scheme, when in fact they were simply bought off. He said he would operate openly, but this deal was so secretive even his own staff couldn't get their stories straight, and his congressional allies were kept out of the loop. He said he would reduce the influence of lobbyists. Instead, he elevated their influence on a deal involving one-sixth of the U.S. economy, giving unelected people he had pre-viously demonized a bigger seat at the table than the elected mem-bers of the House of Representatives, thereby empowering the "special interests" he routinely decried.

There is also a lesson in this story for drug companies and oth-ers who deal with Obama: as soon as he gets what he wants and doesn't need you anymore, you're expendable. For shortly after the deal was allegedly struck, the drug companies found themselves tar-geted again by the administration—this time over exclusive rights to produce drugs called "follow-on biologicals (FOB)" that treat certain major diseases. Biologicals are not, according to a FOX

News report, drugs like Prozac, which the company patents for a period of years until other companies are allowed to replicate generic forms of the drug. They are among a group of some 600 "cutting-edge, new-wave drugs derived from living plant and animal cells and can cost upwards of $20,000 to $25,000 per year."

So far Congress had supported "data exclusivity" for these biologicals for twelve years, when other companies could not develop similar versions. The administration was pushing to reduce the data exclusivity period to seven years, but the drug companies were resisting, based in part on the enormous cost of bringing a biological to market—an average of $1.2 billion, which doesn't count another $250 to 500 million to build a facility and manufacture the drug.[13]

Eventually, the drug companies threatened to withdraw their support for ObamaCare if the White House persisted. Billy Tauzin said, "We are letting everyone we know hear that we could not support the bill if this happens." PhRMA senior vice president Ken Johnson added, "This well-intentioned effort will ultimately fail if it becomes a roadblock to medical progress in America."[14] The administration must have taken Tauzin's and Johnson's threats seriously, as the final ObamaCare bill did not reduce the twelve year data exclusivity period.[15]

WAR ON INSURANCE COMPANIES

The drug companies were lucky enough to strike a deal with Obama early, thus avoiding his presidential wrath. The insurance companies, in contrast, became the quintessential bogeyman. Even before he realized how unpopular socialized medicine was in this freedom loving country, Obama had demonized health insurers. But after his healthcare scheme encountered heavy resistance, he ratcheted up his assault on them, reframing his entire healthcare reform as "insurance reform." At one point, he implied Americans didn't understand the implications of their own preferences. After acknowledging some polls revealed as many as 80 percent of Americans were satisfied with their health insurance, Obama scoffed, "The only problem is that premiums have been doubling every nine years, going up three times faster than wages."[16]

In addition to deliberately inflating the number of uninsured as described in chapter three, Democrats bludgeoned health insurance companies for their "obscene profits." House Speaker Nancy Pelosi declared, "I'm very pleased that [Democratic leaders] will be talking, too, about the immoral profits being made by the insurance industry and how those profits have increased during the Bush years." Congressman Chris Van Hollen argued, "Keeping the status quo may be what the insurance industry wants. Their premiums have more than doubled in the last decade, and their profits have skyrocketed." The vilification reached something of a crescendo with a MoveOn.org ad claiming, "Health insurance companies are willing to let the bodies pile up as long as their profits are safe."[17]

During the healthcare debate, Obama vehemently denied he favored government-run healthcare. But his right-hand lady, Health and Human Services secretary Kathleen Sebelius, was not so circumspect in May 2009, when she told a House panel that a government-run plan was needed to exert better control over private insurers that often allegedly fail to serve the public interest. She said, "The president is committed to—and I'm committed to—a design that needs to level the playing field, and it's on two fronts."

The two fronts were a more regulated private sector and a *government-run* public option insurance plan, which Obama was selling at the time under the Orwellian argument that it would enhance competition.[18] Obama claimed the public option was "an important tool to discipline insurance companies," which "have been spending more time thinking about how to take premiums and then avoid providing people coverage than they have been thinking about 'how can we make sure that insurance is there, healthcare is there, when families need it.'"

Obama also promoted the myth that Medicare and other government-run plans have lower administrative costs than private healthcare plans, saying if the government-run program "is able to reduce administrative costs significantly...I'd like the insurance companies to take note and say, 'Hey, if the public plan can do that, why can't we?'"[19] In her book *The Top Ten Myths of American Health Care: A Citizen's Guide*, Sally Pipes cites this as the very first myth. Pipes demonstrates the inaccuracy of studies purporting to show lower administrative costs for Medicare, studies that also fail to account for Medicare's enormous hidden costs. For example, unlike the Medicare Trustees report, private healthcare providers include such items as marketing costs and managers' and administrators' salaries as administrative expenses. Additionally, because of its low reimbursement rates, Medicare passes off a huge portion of its costs to private payers.[20]

It was against this disgraceful backdrop that Obama, during a prime-time news conference in July 2009, launched his assault on insurance companies for making too much money. "There have been reports just over the last couple of days of insurance companies making record profits, right now," he declared. "At a time when everybody's getting hammered, they're making record profits, and premiums are going up. What's the constraint on that?...Well, part of the way is to make sure that there's some competition out there."

The entire campaign against insurers was based on a lie—insurance industries profits were *not* at a record high. The *St. Petersburg Times'* fact-checking operation, PolitiFact.com, found that United-Health Group, one of the largest publicly traded health insurance companies, had net income for the previous quarter of $859 million, which was far short of the $1.23 billion it had earned during the same quarter in 2007. Rating Obama's claims as "false," PolitFact reported, "We reviewed the income statements of the other largest publicly traded health insurance companies—WellPoint, Aetna, Cigna, Humana and Coventry Health Care—and found similar trends."[21]

Other evidence refuted Obama's inflammatory claims. Fortune 500's annual ranking of America's largest corporations for 2008 showed "Health Care: Insurance and Managed Care" to be ranked 35th in profitability, with a modest profit of 2.2 percent for 2008.[22] The AP's "Fact Check" likewise threw cold water on Obama's contentions. Obama, according to Fact Check, attacked insurers "as rapacious profiteers making 'immoral' and 'obscene' returns while 'the bodies pile up.' Ledgers tell a different reality. Health insurance profit margins typically run about 6 percent, give or take a point or two. That's anemic compared with other forms of insurance and a broad array of industries, even some beleaguered ones. Profits barely exceeded 2 percent of revenues in the latest annual measure."[23] Yahoo's industry browser also contradicted Obama's claim. It showed in August that "Health Care Plans" ranked 86th in terms of profit margin with 3.3 percent. In other words, eighty-five industries were more profitable."[24]

In early August 2009, the *New York Times* reported that Obama and congressional Democrats were preparing for "an August offensive against the insurance industry as part of a coordinated campaign to sell the public on the need for reform." It would be "a campaign of increasingly harsh rhetoric against the insurance industry" designed "to drive home the message that revamping the health care system [would] protect consumers by ending unpopular insurance industry practices, like refusing patients with pre-existing conditions."

Obviously the administration was unable to sell Obama's plan through the magic of his silver tongue, because facts are stubborn things—facts that he was misrepresenting, as people could easily discover through the Internet and the new media. The public knew he couldn't reduce costs while expanding coverage. They knew he couldn't increase patient choice with a "public option" and government bureaucracies and an official health care czar ("Health Choices Commissioner") who would have control over treatments based on their "cost effectiveness." People also rightfully doubted

Obama's promise that they could keep their own insurance, since his plan would eventually drive private insurers out of business.

Obama had to demonize the insurance companies to divert attention from the facts and replace them with the divisive rhetoric of class warfare. Obama adviser David Axelrod unleashed a harsh salvo, saying, "This is going to give people who have insurance a degree of security and stability, the protection they don't have today against the sort of mercurial judgments of insurance bureaucrats." Despite drawing first blood against the insurance industry, the administration and its congressional allies portrayed insurers as the aggressor in the media battle. House Speaker Nancy Pelosi said there would be a "drumbeat across America" to hit back at the health insurance industry for its "shock and awe, carpet-bombing ... to perpetuate the status quo."[25]

In a *New York Times* op-ed, Obama said the "system" often works better for health insurers than for millions upon millions of Americans. He cited a 2007 national survey that, in his words, showed insurance companies had "*discriminated* against more than 12 million Americans in the previous three years because they had a pre-existing illness or condition." (emphasis added) Thus, Obama used civil rights language to slander private insurance companies simply for enforcing lawful provisions in their contracts excluding coverage for pre-existing conditions. In Obama's America, to enforce a contract is to "discriminate."[26]

Obama soon sharpened his rhetoric, accusing insurers of "denying coverage" to sick people and holding America "hostage. It's wrong. It's bankrupting families. It's bankrupting businesses. And we are going to fix it when we pass health insurance reform this year."[27] Turning up the heat even further, Obama threatened legal action against insurance companies for ostensibly trying to scare seniors into believing they would lose coverage benefits under his reform.[28] The Centers for Medicare and Medicaid sent a notice to Humana and other companies saying, "As we continue our research into this issue, we are instructing you to immediately discontinue all such mailings to beneficiaries and to remove any related materials directed to Medicare enrollees from your Web sites."

Consider the sheer magnitude of this abuse of power: the government threatening legal action against a company for informing policyholders about the likely effect of an administration policy. It would be like the administration threatening a private company for telling its clients that Obama's stimulus package wouldn't create jobs. Surely we haven't strayed so far from our constitutional roots that we find it acceptable for the government to criminalize speech.

The administration's warning came just as ObamaCare was reaching a critical phase in a Senate committee and as public polls revealed seniors were skeptical of the plan. With ObamaCare's fate in doubt, Obama's congressional allies joined the attack on the insurers. Democratic senator Max Baucus proclaimed, "It is wholly unacceptable for insurance companies to mislead seniors regarding any subject—particularly on a subject as important to them, and to the nation, as healthcare reform."[29] Indeed, how dare insurance companies try to get their side of the story out when Obama wanted to dominate the debate with charges of their villainy!

Under criticism that Obama's government was trampling free speech, the administration was forced to back off. It announced private insurers could send seniors information on health-related issues—so long as they permitted recipients to opt out of receiving the communications. Medicare official Teresa DeCaro wrote, "While we feel it is important to protect Medicare beneficiaries from potentially unwelcome marketing and other communications, we also recognize the plan's interest in contacting their enrollees on issues unrelated to the specific plan benefit that they contract with CMS [Centers for Medicare and Medicaid Services] to provide to those enrollees."

But some Republicans were not satisfied with the administration's qualified retreat. Congressman Dave Camp, the senior Republican on the House Ways and Means Committee, stated, "I remain concerned that CMS overstepped in issuing its gag order as a result of undue political pressure to penalize anyone who dare speak out against the Democrats' healthcare bill. We still need to get the answers to how and why this gag order was issued."[30]

The administration was hardly repentant for its Stalinist tactics. At a townhall event in New Orleans, Obama gloated over falling health insurance stocks, declaring, "This is when the insurance companies are really going to start gearing up. Their stock went down when the Senate Finance Committee voted out that bill. Now they're getting nervous and, by the way, they have been wildly profitable over the last decade."[31]

Moreover, in a weekly radio address in October 2009, Obama accused insurers of resorting to "smoke and mirrors" in their "last-ditch" effort to defeat healthcare reform. "There are still those who would try to kill reform at any cost," he said, suggesting insurance companies were unfairly earning extraordinary profits while "enjoying a privileged exception from our anti-trust laws, a matter that Congress is rightfully reviewing."[32] He accused them of "filling the airwaves with deceptive and dishonest ads" and funding "phony studies" to "mislead the American people."[33] "This is the unsustainable path we're on, and it's the path the insurers want to keep us on," he claimed. "In fact, the insurance industry is rolling out the big guns and breaking open their massive war chest—to marshal their forces for one last fight to save the status quo. But what I will not abide are those who would bend the truth—or break it—to score political points and stop our progress as a country."[34] Progress toward socialism, that is.

First lady Michelle Obama joined the assault. In a White House event marking National Breast Cancer Awareness Month, she said, "We have a health care system in this country that simply is not working for too many people with breast cancer and too many people who are surviving with breast cancer. And I'm not just talking about women without insurance . . . I am talking about people in this country who have insurance who have breast cancer—folks who all too often find themselves also paying outrageous out-of-pocket costs."

The *Washington Examiner's* Byron York noted Mrs. Obama was implying "the insurance companies make life miserable even for those with coverage." She said there are "those annual lifetime caps that insurance companies set," with "one recent survey show[ing] that ten percent of all cancer patients report hitting a cap on their benefits." Furthermore, a patient in remission gets stuck "with a target on your back for the rest of your life with a 'preexisting condition,' which means that insurance companies can deny you coverage or charge you higher rates for coverage—sometimes much higher." Women, she said, "are living in fear of losing their jobs or changing jobs or even moving, because they worry they won't be able to find affordable insurance." But of course, she assured her audience, all these problems would be eliminated under ObamaCare. There would be "no more denying coverage to people like women we heard from today because of so-called preexisting conditions like having survived cancer." "But first," she said, "we have to get it passed."[35]

In January 2010, President Obama employed combative language similar to that he would soon use against "Wall Street fat-cat bankers." While scolding Democratic House members who were concerned over the political price they would pay for supporting ObamaCare, he said, "If Republicans want to campaign against what we've done by standing up for the status quo and for insurance companies over American families and businesses, that is a fight I want to have."[36]

In February he unveiled his plan to give the federal government broad authority to restrict "excessive" health insurance rate increases. *Politico* reported that Obama was "seeking to play off voter anger toward recent double-digit increases by Anthem Blue Cross of California." Of course, much of the anger toward insurers was obviously caused by Obama persistently vilifying them.[37]

In his weekly radio address on February 20, 2010, Obama said some Californians buying individual plans from Anthem Blue Cross are "likely to see their rates go up anywhere from 35 to 39 percent." He used the same rhetoric on March 8 at a health reform rally at Arcadia University in Glenside, Pennsylvania. "How much higher do premiums have to rise before we do something about it?" asked Obama. "We can't have a system that works better for the insurance companies than it does for the American people."[38]

The Cato Institute's Alan Reynolds noted Obama was using these figures to justify preempting state regulation "by ensuring that, if a rate increase is unreasonable and unjustified, health insurers must lower premiums, provide rebates, or take other actions to make premiums affordable." So, it was a twofer: Obama demonized the insurers *and* the state governments that failed to crack down on them, thus justifying his intervention on behalf of the wonderfully omniscient federal government to protect consumers.

Reynolds also provided another tidbit about Obama's ploy. "So, how many Californians have actually been faced with a 39 percent increase in their premiums?" Reynolds asked. "Exactly zero. How many are really 'likely' to be faced with even a 35 percent increase after state insurance regulators have their say? My forecast: Zero." As Obama continued to suggest insurers were extorting exorbitant profits from their customers, Reynolds pointed out the profits of Anthem's parent company WellPoint were close to 3 percent—hardly excessive by any standard.[39]

The administration tried, with less and less restraint, to dictate the rates and policies of private insurers. Twice in February, Obama's Health and Human Services secretary Kathleen Sebelius wrote insurance company executives asking them to justify their rate hikes. In a letter to WellPoint, she attacked the company for proposing a 39 percent premium increase in California when the company had taken in more than $2.7 billion in the final quarter of 2009. She said the "extraordinary" proposal would be fifteen times higher than the rate of inflation.

Insurance companies blamed the increases on the recession and fewer insurance purchasers—simple supply and demand. Later in the month Sebelius "asked" top insurance company CEOs to come to Washington to explain their planned premium increases. "I'm concerned about these increases, which make it harder for people to access the health care they need, and eager to hear the justification for these increases and steps we can take to create a more stable system that keeps premium costs down for all Americans," she wrote.[40]

In early March, Obama crashed a meeting between Sebelius and executives from five of the largest insurance companies to intimidate the executives again—this time with more anecdotes about alleged health insurance victims whose premiums went up dramatically in their time of need. Obama told the CEOs, "This clearly is unacceptable and unsustainable."[41] Treating the insurers as if they'd already been reduced into public utilities, Sebelius asked the executives to "follow up with an official letter that they file online their rate requests along with the actuarial data that supports those rate requests: what they're paying out, what they are collecting for overhead costs, what they're collecting for administrative costs." After the meeting, apparently forgetting the administration's betrayal of its own promises for transparency, Sebelius said she wanted "to shine a bright light and hop[ed] that the CEOs respond to the call for putting their information up in public. Put it on a website."[42]

A few weeks later Obama took another swing at the insurers. Two days before the House was planning to vote on the Senate bill—or some modified version of it—Obama warned the bill's failure would allow the insurance industry to "continue to run amok."[43] "At the heart of this debate," he intoned,

is the question of whether we will continue to accept a health care system that works better for the insurance companies than it does for the American people. Because if this vote fails, the insurance industry will continue to run wild in America. They will continue to deny people coverage. They will continue to deny people care. They will continue to jack up premiums 40% or 50% or 60% as they have in the last few weeks without any accountability whatsoever. They know this. That's why their lobbyists are stalking the halls of Congress as we speak. That's why they're pouring millions of dollars into negative ads. That's why they're doing everything they can to kill this bill.[44]

Shortly after ObamaCare was signed into law, the *New York Times* reported that insurance companies were claiming the law, as written, did not require them, prior to 2014, to write insurance for children, including those with pre-existing conditions. No problem for this administration. If there was a loophole in the law, why bother fixing it with an amendment when you could just browbeat insurance companies into submission? Accordingly, Sebelius fired off another letter—this one to Karen Ignagni, chair of America's Health Insurance Plans—warning, "Now is not the time to search for nonexistent loopholes that preserve a broken system."

After denying any loopholes existed, Sebelius immediately announced she planned on issuing regulations that would close the loopholes so that no later than September 2010, children with pre-existing conditions could not be denied access to their parents' health insurance plan.[45] Revealingly, House and Senate staffers on the committees that drafted the bill acknowledged the loophole, though House leaders issued a statement saying it was inadvertent. But Obama doesn't have to concern himself with such trifles. If he can ignore the Constitution and Senate rules on such procedures as "reconciliation," he can certainly use his bully pulpit to write into the law any missing stipulations. And Obama's bullying worked, as health insurers wrote Sebelius the very same day saying they wouldn't resist his efforts to fix the loophole.[46]

Obama's campaign against insurance companies was not simply meant to facilitate passage of his woefully unpopular bill. He wanted to stoke the public's anger enough that they would swallow his scheme for the government ultimately to subsume the private insurance industry. His plan—that the government would assume broad regulatory control over premium increases and preclude insurers from denying coverage based on pre-existing conditions—can only be achieved by turning insurance companies into public utilities.

Of course, this was supposed to occur alongside the introduction of the public option—a measure Obama only dropped from his plan after it became clear it couldn't pass the Senate. But Obama denied his overall goal was to displace private insurers, asking rhetorically, "Why would (the public option) drive private insurance out of business?" If private insurers "tell us that they're offering a good deal, then why is it that the government, which they say can't run anything, suddenly is going to drive them out of business? That's not logical."[47]

What Obama's snarky analysis omits is that the government will stack the deck against private insurers to the advantage of its public plan. If a private insurance company is prohibited from excluding coverage for individuals with pre-existing conditions, it ceases to be a risk management evaluator and becomes a business ward of the state. When it is forced to keep its premiums below a level that would allow it to earn profits, it is a government utility, not an insurer. ObamaCare will force insurance companies to act as welfare agencies, which will eventually drive them out of business. At that point, Obama or his acolytes will ride in on a white horse and save the day with the public option.

Our foot-in-mouth vice president, Joe Biden, let the cat out of the bag in an interview with ABC's Jake Tapper, saying,

> Some of them . . . say, well, Joe, look, man, I mean, you know, you guys haven't massaged this very well. And, you know, this thing has gone on so long, I don't know. And my response is, hey, man, the proof of the pudding is in the eating. I'm telling you, you know, pre-existing, they're going to be covered. *You know we're going to control the insurance companies.* You know people aren't going to lose their health care with their

employer like is being advertised. So you've got to if you really want to make sure that you get the benefit of what you've already done, vote for the bill.[48] (emphasis added)

The lynchpin of ObamaCare is the "individual mandate"—a constitutionally dubious law requiring all Americans to buy health insurance whether they want it or not. This is the mechanism that is supposed to allow health insurers to remain solvent while complying with Obama's mandate to cover pre-existing conditions. At a New Hampshire townhall meeting on February 3, 2010, Obama stumbled into admitting as much. "You can't [demand] insurance companies... take somebody who's sick, who's got a pre-existing condition, if you don't have everybody covered," he said. "And the reason, if you think about it, is simple. If you had a situation where not everybody was covered but an insurance company had to take you because you were sick, what everybody would do is they'd just wait till they got sick and then they'd go buy insurance. Right? And so the potential would be there to game the system." [49]

Thus, Obama tacitly admitted that without the individual mandate, health insurers could not survive financially if they were required to cover pre-existing conditions. Yet for an entire year, before the individual mandate was passed, Obama demonized insurance companies for denying exactly that coverage—when by his own admission they could not afford it.

ATTACKING DOCTORS

At his news conference on July 22, 2009, Obama unleashed a stunning indictment of medical practitioners, revealing his profound ignorance and ill-will toward the medical profession. He declared, "Right now, doctors, a lot of times, are forced to make decisions based on the fee payment schedule that's out there. So if they're looking and—and you come in and you've got a bad sore throat, or your child has a bad sore throat, or has repeated sore throats, the doctor may look at the reimbursement system and say to himself, 'You know what? I'll make a lot more money if I take this kid's tonsils out.'"[50]

In case anyone mistook that for a solitary gaffe, he made a similarly malicious claim against surgeons the following month. At another townhall meeting in New Hampshire he said, "Let's take the example of diabetes.... If a family care physician works with his or her patient to help them lose weight, modify diet, monitors whether they're taking their medications in a timely fashion, they might get reimbursed a pittance, but if that same diabetic ends up getting their foot amputated, that's thirty thousand, forty, fifty thousand dollars immediately the surgeon is reimbursed. Why not make sure we're also reimbursing the care that prevents the amputation?"[51]

Consistent with his usual divide-and-conquer methods, Obama has favored general practitioners while penalizing medical specialists who, in President Obama's Washington, "are slightly more popular than the H1N1 virus," as the *Wall Street Journal* noted.[52] The Obama administration is using Medicare regulations to increase payments to general practitioners, internists, and family physicians, but there would be an 11 percent overall cut in the field of cardiology and 19 percent in radiation oncology. The *Wall Street Journal* editors pointed out these cuts were made on cost considerations alone, because they couldn't be based on sound medical judgment. The editors wrote, "Two-thirds of morbidity or mortality among Medicare patients owes to cancer or heart disease."[53]

Obama's war on specialists is also reflected in ObamaCare. Obama's distant cousin, Dr. Milton R. Wolf, writing in the *Washington Times*, described a financial penalty "aimed at your doctor if he seeks the expert care he has determined you need. If your doctor is in the top 10 percent of primary care physicians who refer patients to specialists most frequently—no matter how valid the reasons—he will face a 5 percent penalty on all their Medical reimbursements for the entire year." This "scheme," wrote Wolf, "is specifically designed to deny you the chance to see a specialist."[54]

Beyond that, experience in government-run healthcare systems shows that access to medical specialists is severely reduced. Stanford University Medical Center professor Scott W. Atlas says that independent, peer-reviewed studies show there are far longer waiting times for patients seeking care from cardiologists, orthopedic surgeons, and neurologists "under government-run health systems."[55]

Obama and his supporters glibly dismiss accusations that the president harbors socialist goals. But looking at the short record he's compiled as president, it's hard to come to any other conclusion. While most United States presidents of our lifetime have reserved their harshest rhetoric for our foreign enemies, Obama delights in bashing American businesspeople—corporate executives, insurers, drug-makers, and even medical professionals. Incessantly denouncing companies for generating "excess profits," he clearly believes making a certain amount of money is immoral. In his view, that money doesn't rightfully belong to those who earned it, but to the government, in other words, to Obama himself, who is responsible for spreading that wealth around to those who supposedly deserve it.

There's plenty of room to debate which branch of socialism he adheres to, but one thing's for sure: Obama can't abide the free market.

Chapter Nine

OBAMA THE IMPERIOUS

CRIMES AGAINST THE PRIVATE SECTOR, PART 2

S hortly after he took office, Obama initiated a campaign that would become a major theme of his presidency: castigating Wall Street bankers. On January 29, 2009, he called them "shameful" for giving themselves $20 billion in bonuses when the economy was dragging and the government was giving them bailout money. "There will be time for them to make profits, and there will time for them to get bonuses," he imperiously declared. "Now's not that time. . . . That is the height of irresponsibility. It is shameful. And part of what we're going to need is for the folks on Wall Street who are asking for help to show some restraint and show discipline and show some sense of responsibility." Not to be outdone, Vice President Biden exclaimed, "I'd like to throw some of these guys in the brig. They're thinking the same old thing that got us here, greed. They're thinking, 'Take care of me.'"[1]

But the following year, Obama told Bloomberg he didn't "begrudge" bonuses worth $17 million and $9 million for J. P. Morgan Chase CEO Jamie Dimon and Goldman Sachs CEO Lloyd Blankfein, respectively. It wasn't hard to figure out why Obama was suddenly singing a different tune. As he stated, "I know both those guys; they are very savvy businessmen."[2] But more than that, Blankfein has given more than $100,000 to Democrats, while Dimon, though donating less, has given exclusively to Democrats, plus he's from Chicago, and he's Obama's personal friend and "favorite banker," as the New York Times called him.

Naturally, it is the prerogative of a potentate to treat his friends differently, but Obama's double standard still raised some eyebrows. New Hampshire Union Leader editorial page editor Andrew Cline pointedly observed, "As Obama has accidentally admitted, taking a big bonus during a recession is not shameful. Pitting Americans against each other for purely political purposes is."[3] Despite forgiving his rich buddies, Obama made clear he hadn't softened his animus toward free enterprise when, at an appearance in Quincy, Illinois, he proclaimed Democrats don't begrudge success that's "fairly earned," but "I do think at a certain point you've made enough money."[4]

It's not clear exactly how much money is "enough," but apparently it's quite a lot—at least for certain special people; the Washington Post website reported that in 2008, as he campaigned for president, Obama reeled in a cool $2.5 million just on his book royalties.[5]

FIGHTING OFF THE PITCHFORKS

At a March 2009 townhall meeting in Costa Mesa, California, after defending the government bailout of AIG, Obama went on to compare AIG and big banks to suicide bombers. "It's almost like they've got a bomb strapped to them, and they've got their hand on the trigger," he said. "You don't want them to blow up. But you've got to kind of talk them, ease that finger off the trigger."[6] Obama also savaged AIG for its "recklessness and greed" as he promised to try to block its executives from collecting multi-million dollar bonuses. "Excuse me," he muttered, "I'm choked up with anger here."[7] And like our wealth, Obama seemed determined to spread his anger around. "I don't want to quell anger," he said angrily. "People are right to be angry. I'm angry. What I want us to do is channel our anger in a constructive way." Obama later deflected an uncomfortable question about whether he regretted his campaign having accepted in excess of $100,000 from AIG executives[8]—perhaps he was too angry to muster an answer.

Obama next summoned bank executives to the White House to make them justify their salaries and bonuses. When J. P. Morgan's Jamie Dimon told Obama his company wanted to pay back the TARP money as soon as practical and asked him to "streamline" that process, Obama insisted that government money remain in the system to generate growth—a position that belied his later, phony condemnation of banks for not repaying TARP monies. Obama said, "This is like a patient who's on antibiotics. Maybe the patient starts feeling better after a couple of days, but you don't stop taking the medicine until you've finished the bottle."

Obama worried that paying the money back too quickly could send a bad signal. But some CEOs at the meeting disagreed, arguing it was their duty to repay the funds now that they no longer needed them and that doing so would inspire the market's confidence.[9] Eventually the administration instituted a "test" to determine whether it would permit banks to repay their TARP loans. If banks had plenty of capital and demonstrated an ability to raise fresh money, they would ostensibly be permitted to repay—providing the administration deemed that repayment would be in the wider economic interest.[10]

There was no mistaking the president's harsh tone toward the bankers. One attendee commented, "The only way they could have sent a more Spartan message is if they had served bread along with the water. The signal from Obama's body language and demeanor was, 'I'm the president, and you're not.'[11] Sounds familiar, does it not?

When the subject turned to the salaries and bonuses, one CEO explained, "We're competing for talent on an international market." But Obama, the self-described "listener," was uninterested. He interrupted them and warned with his signature haughtiness, "Be careful how you make those statements, gentlemen. The public isn't buying that. My administration is the only thing between you and the pitchforks." If that was true, it was only because Obama had stoked the flames against banks and corporate executives in the first place.

More than a half year later, in December 2009, Obama was still blasting Wall Street bank bonuses, declaring on CBS's *60 Minutes*, "I did not run for office to help out a bunch of fat cat bankers on Wall Street. The people on Wall Street still don't get it. They're still puzzled why it is that people are mad at the banks. Well, let's see. You guys are drawing down $10 (million), $20 million dollar bonuses after America went through the worst economic year in decades and you guys caused the problem." He also accused the banks of "fighting tooth and nail with their lobbyists" to oppose financial regulatory control.[12]

But once again, "excessive CEO salaries" were only a problem for certain bankers unconnected to Obama; it came to light in February 2010 that government-run GM was providing its CEO, Ed Whitacre, a pay package valued at $9 million—a package approved by U.S. Treasury pay czar Kenneth Feinberg.[13]

SQUEEZING THE "FAT CATS"

In a December 2009, meeting with the CEOs of large banks, Obama all but ordered them to increase their loans to small businesses and their assistance to troubled homeowners. In a statement, he again referred to the financial collapse being "a predicament largely of their own making, oftentimes because they failed to manage risk properly."

But in fact, with its myriad regulations and programs pressuring banks to offer mortgages almost regardless of the recipient's ability to repay, the government was a greater contributor to the crisis than "Wall Street." Both parties, though Democrats far more than Republicans, embarked on this loose lending policy, placing their "good intentions" above good financial sense, and forced banks to make uncreditworthy loans in the name of compassion.

But when the Bush administration warned as early as 2003 of the systemic risks posed to the entire economy by the expansion of Fannie and Freddie and recommended the creation of a new federal agency to regulate them, Democrats, such as Congressman Barney Frank, would have none of it. Frank said that critics "exaggerate a threat of safety" and "conjure up the possibility of serious financial losses to the Treasury, which I do not see." Frank sneered at the idea that the government's lending policy had been too liberal, saying it had "probably done too little rather than too much . . . to meet the goals of affordable housing."

In June 2004, seventy-six House Democrats, including Barney Frank and Nancy Pelosi, sent President Bush a letter defending Fannie and Freddie and insisting that "an exclusive focus on safety and soundness" would likely come "at the expense of affordable housing." Similarly, in 2007 when the Bush administration discovered some $11 billion of accounting errors on the books of Fannie Mae and Freddie Mac and demanded a "robust reform package" for these companies as a condition to their expanding their mortgage portfolios, Senator Chris Dodd, chairman of the Banking Committee, scoffed that Bush should "immediately reconsider his ill-advised" demand. Dodd continued this reckless obstinacy into July 2008, when he pronounced that Fannie and Freddie were "on a sound footing."[14]

An analysis by George Mason University economics professor Lawrence H. White found the financial crisis and ensuing recession were not the result of "financial deregulation and private-sector greed," but "misguided monetary and housing policies:...the expansion of risky mortgages to underqualified borrowers... encouraged by the federal government." Additionally, "the government-supported mortgage lenders, Freddie Mac and Fannie Mae, grew to own or guarantee about half the United States' $12 trillion mortgage market." This caused monumental distortions in the mortgage market because the guarantees artificially eliminated the risk of purchasing bad mortgages, thus catalyzing their rapid expansion. Congress exacerbated the problem and virtually guaranteed a meltdown by pushing Fannie and Freddie to continue to "promote 'affordable housing' through expanded purchases on nonprime loans to low-income applicants."[15]

However, Obama not only refused to acknowledge the government's role in the collapse, but he took credit for rescuing the dastardly banks from it: "We took difficult and, frankly, unpopular steps to pull them back from the brink, steps that were necessary not just to save our financial system, but to save our economy as a whole."

With that predicate, he told bankers they owed it to the country to help lift the economy out of crisis. He leaned on them to show their gratitude for his magnanimity by making loans he wanted them to make, as opposed to those consistent with managing risk properly. In other words, he pressured them to do more of the very kind of politicized, irresponsible lending for which he was condemning them. Obama said, "So my main message...was very simple: that America's banks received extraordinary assistance from American taxpayers to rebuild their industry, and now that they're back on their feet we expect an extraordinary commitment from them to help rebuild our economy."

"We expect?" The Central Planner in Chief concluded, "That starts with finding ways to help credit-worthy small and medium-size businesses get the loans that they need to open their doors, grow their operations and create new jobs."[16] The next week Obama met with CEOs and other officers of a dozen community banks to pressure them to increase their small-business lending and lobby them to support his regulatory overhaul plans.[17]

Obama continued the executive branch assault on the banks into 2010. In January he unveiled a proposal for a Financial Crisis Responsibility Fee—a euphemism for a bank penalty tax, a version of which he had first suggested months before. The tax would apply to the nation's largest financial institutions (banks, thrifts, and insurance companies with more than $50 billion in assets) for the ostensible purpose of "recover[ing] every single dime the American people are owed" for bailing out the economy. Obama said it would remain in effect until the TARP losses, estimated at $117 billion, were recovered, in ten or twelve years. As if working in tandem with Obama, a number of congressional Democrats proposed a 50 percent tax on bonuses above $50,000 at banks that received bailout money.

After Obama announced his tax proposal, even the *New York Times* admitted he "spoke in some of his harshest language to date about the resurgent financial industry." Obama said, "My determination to achieve this goal is only heightened when I see reports of massive profits and obscene bonuses at the very firms who owe their continued existence to the American people—who have not been made whole, and who continue to face real hardship in this recession."[18] He further claimed,

> We're already hearing a hue and cry from Wall Street suggesting that this proposed fee is not only unwelcome but unfair. That by some twisted logic it is more appropriate for the American people to bear the cost of the bailout rather than the industry that benefited from it, even though these executives are out there giving themselves huge bonuses. What I say to these executives is this: Instead of sending a phalanx of lobbyists to fight this proposal or employing an army of lawyers and accountants to help evade the fee, I suggest you might want to consider simply meeting your responsibilities.[19]

It couldn't have been more disingenuous for Obama to frame this retroactive penalty as an effort to "recover" money "owed" to Americans, when most of the affected banks had already repaid their bailout debts with interest. When the banks protested, the White House responded that the measure was aimed at the institutions whose risk-taking had caused the financial crisis, which was tantamount to an admission that it was, in fact, a retroactive penalty.[20]

It was also dishonest for Obama to call his tax a "fee." As the Heritage Foundation's Retirement Security and Financial Markets guru David C. John said, the "responsibility fee" is neither responsible nor a fee. However, "The White House needs a villain to blame for the nation's continuing economic woes, and Treasury desperately needs revenues to reduce the massive deficits caused by the Obama administration's spending policies." A more candid explanation of the targets of the "fee," suggested John, would mirror Willie Sutton's answer to why he robbed banks: "Because that's where the money is."[21]

Obama didn't cotton to backtalk from the banks, slamming them again in his weekly radio address. "Like clockwork, the banks and politicians who curry their favor are already trying to stop this fee from going into effect. We're not going to let Wall Street take the money and run. We're going to pass this fee into law. . . . If the big financial firms can afford massive bonuses, they can afford to pay back the American people. Those who oppose this fee have also had the audacity to suggest that it is somehow unfair. The very same firms reaping billions of dollars in profits, and reportedly handing out more money in bonuses and compensation than ever before in history, are now pleading poverty. It's a sight to see."[22]

With Obama's proposed tax, we saw, once again, that he was trying to pick the winners and losers, taxing some banks that had paid their debts in full, with interest, and exempting government-connected ones such as Fannie Mae, Freddie Mac, GM, and Chrysler, that still owed billions. Heritage Foundation expert on government regulation James Gattuso observed that while Obama claimed his new tax would "pay back the taxpayers who rescued them in their time of need . . . in truth, the new tax would do nothing of the kind. Mr. Obama knows that almost every major bank has paid back their bailout funds, with interest. Taxpayers made substantial profits on those repayments." Heritage presented a chart, reprinted below, to illustrate Gattuso's point that many banks that paid their debt would be taxed, and many who didn't would be exempted.[23]

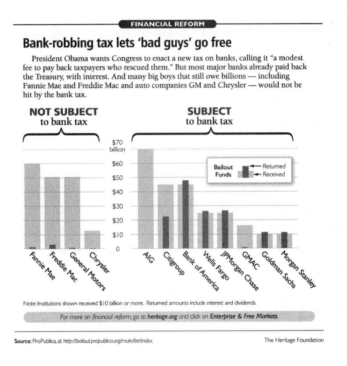

FINANCIAL REFORM

Bank-robbing tax lets 'bad guys' go free

President Obama wants Congress to enact a new tax on banks, calling it "a modest fee to pay back taxpayers who rescued them." But most major banks already paid back the Treasury, with interest. And many big boys that still owe billions — including Fannie Mae and Freddie Mac and auto companies GM and Chrysler — would not be hit by the bank tax.

NOT SUBJECT to bank tax   **SUBJECT** to bank tax

Bailout Funds — Returned / Received

Fannie Mae, Freddie Mac, General Motors, Chrysler, AIG, Citigroup, Bank of America, Wells Fargo, JPMorgan Chase, GMAC, Goldman Sachs, Morgan Stanley

Note: Institutions shown received $10 billion or more. Returned amounts include interest and dividends.

For more on financial reform, go to heritage.org and click on **Enterprise & Free Markets.**

Source: ProPublica, at http://bailout.propublica.org/main/list/index.   The Heritage Foundation

This bank "fee" is manifestly unfair and ill-advised for other reasons as well. It would be imposed irrespective of whether a bank was profitable. Furthermore, the fee would come on top of other new proposed fees on the same institutions and of corporate income taxes they pay. Nor was the fee structured to deter further irresponsible risk taking. And, of course, who can possibly believe the White

House's claim that the fee would sunset after TARP deficits are eliminated a decade from now?[24]

"TARP ON STEROIDS"

Obama's proposed bank tax was eventually rolled into a sweeping plan, unveiled in June 2009, to overhaul the financial system. Treasury secretary Tim Geithner—in keeping with the administration's philosophy that Alinksyites should never let a crisis go to waste—emphasized that the banking system "was fundamentally too fragile and unstable and it did a bad job of protecting consumers and investors.... The damage of the crisis was just too acute. We are trying to move very, very quickly while the memory of the crisis is still in the forefront of people's memory."

It was a stunningly candid admission. Furthermore, as a good central planner, Geithner complained that America's financial system is much less centralized than other "mature" economies, and that we need a more centralized regulatory system to make this vast system accountable. The proposed bill would give a new council of regulators the authority to identify and monitor large financial firms (those "too big to fail") that were in trouble, seize control of them, and wind them down to avoid their collapse, a scenario Geithner claimed would be limited to "extraordinary circumstances."[25] The plan contemplated covering the costs of such dissolutions by imposing a "fee" on firms with assets of $10 billion or more.[26]

Obama and Geithner's plan wasn't initially well received in Congress. At a House Financial Services hearing, Republicans objected, Democrats were skeptical, and regulators were ambivalent. There was bipartisan concern that the plan would give both regulators and the executive branch unprecedented power. "I'm not a man that fears this administration or you," said Democratic congressman Paul Kanjorski. "But I do fear the accumulation of power exercised by someone in the future that can be extraordinary." Labeling the proposal "TARP on steroids," fellow Democrat Brad Sherman told Giethner, "You've got permanent, unlimited bailout authority." Geithner tendentiously objected that "the only authority we would have would be to manage their failure."[27]

In January 2010, Obama refined his "reform" plan, proposing what the *Financial Times* described as "the most far-reaching overhaul of Wall Street since the 1930s."[28] In addition to his new bank tax proposal, Obama proposed new bank regulations that would limit a bank's investments and restrict the total size of financial institutions. The stated purpose of the regulations was to shore up financial institutions against another financial meltdown.

ABC News' Jake Tapper reported that Obama introduced the new regulations with "fiery, populist rhetoric ... almost daring the financial sector to take him on." Castigating profits and the private sector, Obama blamed deregulation and bank speculation for the financial crisis. He said, "As we dig our way out of this deep hole, it's important we not lose sight of what led us into this mess in the first place. This economic crisis began as a financial crisis, when banks and financial institutions took huge, reckless risks in pursuit of quick profits and massive bonuses." He said Wall Street was still operating by the same rules that led to the near-disaster, rules which allow "firms to act contrary to the interests of customers, to conceal their exposure to debt through complex financial dealings, to benefit from taxpayer-insured deposits, while making speculative investments; and to take on risks so vast that they pose threats to the entire system."[29]

Obama denounced the banks with the derogatory and bellicose language he had earlier used against insurance companies, declaring, "Never again will the American taxpayer be *held hostage* by a bank that is 'Too Big to Fail.'" (emphasis added) Wall Street, he said, was "fighting reforms," while there are "soaring profits and obscene bonuses at some of the very firms claiming that they can't lend more to small businesses, they can't keep credit card rates low, they can't pay a fee to refund taxpayers for the bailout without passing on the cost to shareholders or customers—and that's the claims they're making." He then lashed out at the "army" of Wall Street lobbyists who opposed his reform efforts (though it turned out they didn't oppose it much, as described below).

Once again echoing his attacks on insurers, he said, "If those folks want a fight, it's a fight I'm ready to have."[30] He also asserted, "In recent years, too many financial firms have put taxpayer money at risk by operating hedge funds and private equity funds and making riskier investments to reap a quick reward. And these firms have taken these risks while benefiting from special financial privileges that are reserved only for banks."[31]

Not everyone swallowed Obama's cavalier claim that deregulation caused the financial meltdown. The Heritage Foundation's James Gattuso wrote, "Financial services were not deregulated during the Bush administration. If there ever was an 'era of deregulation' in the financial world, it ended long ago. . . . Not only was there little deregulation of financial services during the Bush years, but most of the regulatory reforms achieved in earlier years mitigated, rather than contributed to, the crisis."[32]

Obama's reverse Midas touch kicked in as his ominous financial reform announcement caused the markets to plummet, losing 213 points and 216 points on two consecutive days.[33] Despite the damage to stockholders—or perhaps because of it—leftists applauded the move.[34]

"GET IN OUR WAY, AND WE'LL MOW YOU DOWN"

Meanwhile, the House, led by Democratic congressman Barney Frank, passed its version of financial reform on December 11, 2009, by a margin of 223 to 202. Senator Dodd introduced the Senate version—the Restoring American Financial Stability Act of 2010—the following March, hewing closely to Obama's reworked reform plan. The Senate Committee on Banking, Housing, and Urban Affairs, on a straight party line vote of 13 to 10, rushed the bill through after only a twenty-one-minute markup. Republican senator Bob Corker commented, "It is pretty unbelievable that after two years of hearings on arguably the biggest issue facing our panel in decades, the committee has passed a 1,300 page bill in a 21-minute, partisan markup. I don't know how you can call that anything but dysfunctional." Senator Dodd warned Republicans that if they resisted his bill, they would suffer the same fate they did on the healthcare bill. In other words, as National Legal and Policy Center's Carl Horowitz noted, "Get in our way, and we'll mow you down."[35]

The administration threw its full weight behind the bill, which some began to call the "Dodd–Frank financial reform bill." Treasury secretary Geithner argued the administration's case in the *Washington Post*. He bragged that the Financial Crisis Responsibility Fee would make "the cost to American taxpayers ... zero." So banks that subsidize these losses are not American taxpayers? And they won't pass these penalties on to consumers, who happen to be taxpayers? Why should banks that paid back their loans bear the cost more than anyone else? Indeed, in his piece, Geithner said, "A clear lesson of this crisis is that any strategy that relies on market discipline to compensate for weak regulation and then leaves it to the government to clean up the mess is a strategy for disaster." Translation: free market bad, government good. Geithner closed with the administration's typical Chicago-style machismo. "As the bill moves to the floor, we will fight any attempt to weaken it."[36]

As Geithner promised, the White House pushed the bill aggressively. White House blogger Jen Psaki wrote, "The reality is that there's a clear choice in this debate: to stand with American families or stand on the side of big Wall Street banks and their lobbyists who are defending the status quo. Opponents of reform are protecting the big banks at the expense of American families—so they're going to do whatever they can to keep the present system in place and leave the American taxpayer with the bill."[37]

This was the same Alinskyite strategy the White House employed against insurers when it was pushing ObamaCare, only this time its target was "fat-cat" Wall Street bankers. As was the case with ObamaCare, the administration claimed their opponents were in Wall Street's pocket defending the status quo at the expense of the taxpayers. And whereas Obama called ObamaCare "insurance reform," he called financial reform "Wall Street reform," to capitalize on his demonization of the respective scapegoats of his "reform" efforts. He also deceitfully argued, as he had with ObamaCare, that insufficient regulation led to the problems, although the opposite was much more accurate.

In the campaign against the bill's opponents, the Chamber of Commerce emerged as a key target. Obama attacked the Chamber for "spending millions on an ad campaign" opposing a Consumer Financial Protection Agency that the bill would create. Doing what he loves most, he attacked businesses, profits, "Wall Street" and lobbyists, claiming, "They're doing what they always do—descending on Congress and using every bit of influence they have to maintain the status quo that has maximized their profits at the expense of American consumers . . . We have already seen and lived the consequences of what happens when there is too little accountability on Wall Street and too little protection for Main Street, and I will not allow this country to go back there."[38]

The next week, *Politico* reported that the White House and congressional Democrats were working to circumvent the Chamber of Commerce by going directly to the CEOs of major U.S. corporations. Since June, administration officials had met with executives from more than fifty-five companies. The Chamber accused the administration of launching a "frontal assault against free enterprise and the Chamber of Commerce" and trying to divide the business community in order to weaken opposition to ObamaCare, just as it had done with the cap and trade bill. Democrats painted the Chamber's opposition as ideological rather than a matter of promoting the most favorable business environment.[39] But admittedly, the modern liberal establishment's hostility to the free market makes such a distinction moot.

With Obama's newfound confidence and a new spring in his step following passage of ObamaCare, he proceeded even more aggressively with his statist agenda. In March 2010, he renewed his attack on the Chamber for continuing to resist the financial reform package. Deputy Treasury Secretary Neal Wolin essentially accused the Chamber of lying in its opposition to "reform." Wolin said, "The chamber has every right to oppose those policies with which its members disagree. But as a leading, respected institution, the chamber also has an obligation to be honest with you, its members, and with the American people." It should "engage in a debate on the merits, not on the basis of misinformation."[40] He added, "It is so puzzling that despite the urgent and undeniable need for reform, the Chamber of Commerce has launched a $3 million advertising campaign against it." Following Wolin's remarks, Bruce Josten, the chamber's top lobbyist, issued a statement describing the speech as "political grandstanding and distortion of facts."[41]

Administration officials announced Obama planned on leading a series of outside-the-beltway rallies for his financial regulatory reform efforts and to pressure Senate Republicans to get on board, in the same way he did with ObamaCare. Convinced Obama had regained policy momentum after passing healthcare, his aides believed the push for financial reform would boost his approval ratings. Obama's campaign arm, Organizing for America, would coordinate the effort. "We cannot delay action any longer," said Obama in an e-mail.[42]

Seeking to create a sense of urgency, Obama argued a crisis would recur if all the essentials of his proposal were not passed immediately. In his radio address on April 17, 2010, he declared, "Every day we don't act, the same system that led to bailouts remains in place, with the exact same loopholes and the exact same liabilities. And if we don't change what led to the crisis, we'll doom ourselves to repeat it." If another crisis occurs, he claimed, "taxpayers" would be left "on the hook." Obama also threatened to veto the financial overhaul bill if it didn't include his proposal to authorize the government, for the first time ever, to regulate "derivatives." As with ObamaCare, he paid superficial lip service to a call for bipartisanship, but stated in plain terms that Democrats were prepared to go forward by themselves. "One way or another, we will move forward," he insisted. "This issue is too important."[43]

UNLIMITED BAILOUT AUTHORITY

So what exactly would the Senate bill do? According to Carl Horowitz, it is "an unabashed attempt to bring virtually the entire financial services industry under federal heel—the portion not already under it." The bill would create a new regulatory agency, the Consumer Financial Protection Bureau, that would have rule-making authority and enforcement powers apart from those of the Fed to monitor financial firms that have at least $10 billion in assets. The bill would also codify "the Volcker Rule," which would restrict banks from making certain types of speculative investments, such as hedge funds and derivatives, that are not made on behalf of consumers.

Most important, Dodd's bill would create a new bureaucracy called the Office of Financial Research, which would be the driving force behind a new body called the Financial Stability Oversight Council (FSOC). A nine-member board, the council would be empowered to place risky financial firms—at its discretion—in receivership. It would monitor the entire financial services marketplace to assess threats to financial stability and recommend new regulations to be written by the appropriate federal financial agencies. The FSOC would have subpoena power and the authority to collect any and all information from "any financial company" to analyze whether its business practices might threaten financial stability. In fact, it would monitor the entire financial services marketplace to identify potential risks to the financial stability of the United States.

For its part, the Office of Financial Research could require companies to submit periodic and other reports to assess whether they could be a threat to the financial stability of the United States. This is a dangerous expansion of federal power in an effort that has little hope of success—Heritage Foundation expert James Gattuso notes that no regulators have successfully predicted threats to financial stability in the past. Gattuso dismisses all this "process" in the bill as mere political theater by Dodd and company.[44] Alternatively, Obama and Dodd may have understood the data won't be useful, but that the expansive powers the bill authorizes will make it that much easier for the government to assert control of companies and micromanage them at will based on subjective judgments that they pose an economy-wide threat.

Initially, the bill sought to create a revolving emergency loan fund of up to $50 billion for "emergencies" (as defined by Congress) to use to close or restructure distressed financial firms.[45] Promising the fund would only be used to wind down failing firms, Democrats claimed the regulators would have little flexibility in how it was allocated because its purpose was not to bail out companies, but to keep firms afloat while the government liquidated them. At any rate, the provision authorizing the fund was later removed in an effort to mollify opponents who argued it would amount to a permanent TARP fund since Congress would have the fund at its disposal, without having to pass authorizing legislation each time.

But while many Republican critics argued that this $50 billion fund was the main problem with the bill, others, such as Senator Bob Corker, warned unlimited bailout powers would still exist apart from the fund. In an interview with *National Review Online*, Corker said the real danger is in the fine print, which confers on regulators the power to bail out firms that aren't yet technically insolvent. Even without the fund provision, the government could still exercise its unlimited discretion to break up or bail out firms not yet insolvent via the Fed making loans and accepting "the shadiest of assets (such as subprime-mortgage-backed securities) as collateral," or through FDIC guaranteed loans. *National Review Online*'s Stephen Spruiell commented, "The only difference is that, rather than being able to 'pre-fund' the resolution authority and cap it at $50 billion, the government would 'post-fund' the resolution of a failed firm by borrowing whatever it needs from the Treasury and then sending Wall Street the bill."[46]

"A CURE FAR WORSE THAN THE DISEASE"

Like ObamaCare, the financial reform bill will likely yield results exactly opposite from those Obama promised. He said he wanted to end the "too big to fail" era, but experts believe his reform will enshrine that very concept into law. This new "all-powerful bureaucracy," says Heritage expert David C. John, would "actually make future crises—and bailouts—more likely."[47] The bill makes it "more likely that those same institutions that made risky bad bets before will make the exact same mistakes again." This is because the government's advance promise to bail out companies "too big to fail" reduces the checks creditors naturally exercise over banks by, for example, demanding higher interest rates on loans to banks that are highly leveraged. With the government's backing, creditors would be less cautious about making riskier loans.[48]

Carl Horowitz agrees, noting that the command-and-control model envisioned by the Dodd bill is "a cure far worse than the disease, triggering major misallocations of resources. Rewarding political allies and punishing enemies would become prime criteria for making business decisions."[49] Under this bill, the risk of collapse will intensify, because big financial firms will be spared the risk that encourages them to act responsibly. The Dodd bill, says David John, "does nothing to reduce the systemic risk of today's 'too big to fail' financial institutions or to prevent this risk in the future."[50] What it does do, ironically, is enhance the government's sweetheart protection for the very firms from whom Obama claims he's protecting us—quite the sophisticated hustle.

Heritage's James Gattuso prepared a non-exhaustive list of "14 Fatal Flaws" in Senator Dodd's bill, a bill which, Gattuso argued,

will make "another financial crisis or bailout *more* likely to occur."
According to Gattuso, the bill will:[51]

- Create a protected class of firms that would be subject to "enhanced regulation." This would send a signal that these firms are too big to fail and encourage them to take "undue risk." It "will be like creating Fannies and Freddies in every sector of the economy."
- Provide for seizure of private property without meaningful judicial review.
- Create permanent bailout authority. As David John wrote about Obama's earlier plan—and the same essential arguments would apply to Dodd's bill—the Fed would have power to consider "unspecified factors" in its determination and "exercise discretion" in evaluating those factors, which translates into "open-ended power" that "would be difficult to constrain and should be resisted." Under such a law, investing the government with broad authority to assume control of banks and inject them with cash, coupled with the power to assess penalties on bigger firms to pay for the intervention and cash injections after the fact, just imagine the temptation of a statist like Obama "exercising his discretion" to step in even in marginal cases, knowing that costs could be covered by penalties imposed in the future. What a seamless scheme for further wealth redistribution![52] The bottom line, in John's view, is that Obama's financial plan "would give government regulators almost unlimited powers to take over or micromanage financial institutions."

It's hard to argue with John's conclusion when you consider the words of Senator Dodd, himself: "Cracking down on the biggest players is critical to ending bailouts. And if a Wall Street firm does become too

large or too complex and poses a grave threat to our
financial stability, the Federal Reserve has the power to
restrict its risky activities, restrict its growth, and, Mr.
President, even to break up those institutions."[53]
Obama-finance will mean expanding federal control
over financial institutions in the name of economic stability and preventing future economic catastrophes
caused by firms deemed "too big to fail." Democratic
congressman Brad Sherman, in an interview with
Politico, confirmed, "The Dodd bill has unlimited
executive bailout authority. That's something Wall
Street desperately wants but doesn't ask for. The bill
contains permanent, unlimited, bailout authority."[54]

- Open a "line of credit" to the Treasury for additional
  government funding, which provides additional taxpayer financial support.

- Authorize regulators to guarantee the debt of *solvent*
  banks, if regulators determine there is a liquidity crisis.

- Give the Bureau of Consumer Financial Protection
  broad powers to limit what financial products and services can be offered to consumers. The stated purpose is
  to protect consumers, but the effect would be to reduce
  consumer choice—reminiscent of ObamaCare.

- Give this bureau its own staff and autonomous rule-
  making authority, and the ability to examine financial
  institutions with more than $10 billion in assets. John
  warns with this autonomy it could pass regulations
  that could endanger the stability of the financial system
  with Congress having no ability to veto such regulations in advance—before the damage is done.

- Subject non-financial firms to financial regulations.
  This could lead to "a broad swath of private industry"
  being "ensnared in the financial regulatory net."

- Do nothing to address problems at Fannie and Freddie. "There is still nothing in this bill that addresses the perverse incentives and moral hazard that is created when the federal government sticks its nose into the housing market."[55]

Another major problem with the bill, highlighted by *National Review*'s editors, is that it would give unions "proxy access... under the guise of bolstering shareholder rights." This would "greatly expand Big Labor's influence over American corporations," because it would facilitate consolidated voting by large and politically powerful shareholders, such as union pension funds. "Big labor's agenda will often conflict with the goal of maximizing shareholder value" and "sound corporate management, which the unions would seek to undermine."[56]

Despite the bill's myriad dangerous provisions, the Senate passed it on May 20, 2010, by a 59 to 39 vote with just three Republicans voting for it, after which it was reconciled with the House bill and signed by Obama. Senate majority leader Harry Reid bragged, "When this bill becomes law, the joy ride on Wall Street will come to a screeching halt." After all his savaging of banks, Obama, with a straight face, announced, "Our goal is not to punish the banks."[57] Republican senator Judd Gregg remarked, "This bill is a disaster because it doesn't address the fundamental underlying causes of the economic issue, which were real estate and underwriting." Of the bill's newly formed Consumer Protection Agency, he said, "It's going to become an agency which defines lending on social justice purposes... versus on safety and soundness of purposes."[58]

Gregg couldn't be more correct. Just as with the subprime mortgage fiasco, government bureaucrats will be forcing banks to make loans to people and institutions that are poor credit risks, which will likely have the same disastrous consequences as the Democrats' similar policies toward Fannie Mae and Freddie Mac.

GOLDMAN NEEDS NO PROTECTION FROM ITSELF

For all of Obama's demonizing of banks, it was his party that sided with Wall Street on this issue. Heritage's Conn Carroll wrote, "It is 'the big Wall Street banks' that are supporting the Geithner permanent bailout plan." It was Obama, not some Republican, who "raised about a million dollars from Goldman Sachs employees and executives in 2008, the most any politician has raised from a single company since McCain-Feingold." Indeed, just as Obama's push for his financial overhaul package was intensifying, Goldman Sachs promoted the bill in their annual report to shareholders. Goldman CEO Lloyd Blankfein and President Gary Cohn stated in their introductory letter accompanying the report, "Given that much of the financial contagion was fueled by uncertainty about counter parties' balance sheets, we support measures that would require higher capital and liquidity levels, as well as the use of clearinghouses for standardized derivative transactions."[59]

Goldman's support for the overhaul plan was suspicious, just as was the ultimate support of pharmaceutical companies for Obama-Care. As usual, an element of sleaze appears to have oozed into an Obama "reform" proposal. So what did Goldman have to gain in exchange for folding? According to the *Washington Examiner*'s Timothy Carney, Goldman "want[s] the government to reduce the risk that Goldman's debtors or insurers will run into trouble."

Blankfein's statements lend support to that view. He wrote, "The biggest beneficiary of reform is Wall Street itself. The biggest risk is risk financial institutions have with each other."[60] In other words, Blankfein appears to have no objection to the government propping up his fellow "fat cats." This was, said Carney, an "odd function of government: making Goldman Sachs feel safer in its business dealings." Also enticing to Goldman, noted Carney, was that these stricter government requirements were designed to renew American investors' confidence in the stock market, which would hopefully lead to financial firms lending more and Goldman type firms thriving on the "free-flowing capital."[61] At the time, the Obama administration employed many Goldman alumni-lobbyists, including Chief of Staff Rahm Emanuel, White House economic advisor Larry Summers, and Treasury chief of staff Mark Patterson. "So who," asks Carroll, "is really on the side of the American people and who really is doing the work of Wall Street lobbyists?"[62]

Another wrinkle arose when the government filed civil fraud charges against Goldman. The timing of the suit, just as Senate debate on the Dodd bill was ready to begin, was highly suspicious, though the SEC claimed it was acting entirely independently from the administration. The White House professed not to have known in advance about the SEC's plans to file the suit, but Press Secretary Robert Gibbs nevertheless admitted the complaint helped the cause of financial reform, because it "is a prescient reminder of what's at stake."

The White House's denial of a link between the SEC charges and its efforts to pass the financial reform bill became more suspect when the Democratic National Committee bought online ads capitalizing on the Goldman case.[63] Internet surfers entering "Goldman Sachs SEC" in Google were directed to the president's website by way of a sponsored link titled "Help Change Wall Street." The web page had a photo of Obama with the quote, "We've seen and lived the consequences of what happens when there's too little accountability on Wall Street and too little protection for Main Street. It's time for real change."[64] Even if there was no collusion between the White House and the SEC, the political exploitation of a civil suit by the administration was unconscionable.

Obama's furious attacks on Wall Street were a natural outgrowth of his anti-corporate ideology, but they were also a cynical ploy to whip up public support for his policies by stoking outrage at "fat-cat bankers" and other evil capitalists who seemed to come straight out of a comic book. Amidst all the heated rhetoric, the fact was largely ignored that his signature financial reform bill would benefit the very bankers and other Wall Street veterans who have deep connections to his administration. Denying that government policies and regulations helped spark the financial meltdown in the first place, Obama sought to solve the problems of big government with the only approach he knows: creating more big government. That these policies will depress competition and institutionalize the damaging practices of the past is apparently of little concern to this administration. They don't necessarily want a successful America; they want a *transformed* America—and with the financial reform bill, that is what they're trying to deliver.

Chapter Ten

THE COMMISSAR

CRIMES AGAINST AMERICAN INDUSTRY

Obama has exerted power beyond that of any previous U.S. president. On March 29, 2009, his Treasury secretary Tim Geithner made the Sunday talk show circuit to explain that some banks would have to take new TARP monies against their wishes—which was consistent with Obama preventing J. P. Morgan executives from repaying their TARP funds. Later that same Sunday, Obama made another extraordinary move, firing General Motors CEO Rick Wagoner. As an indication of widespread opposition to federal control over the auto industry, GM's stock fell 25 percent the next day upon news of Wagoner's firing. But Obama and Geithner were unchastened. Geithner told *CBS News*' Katie Couric that "of course" he was open to the option of pressuring CEOs of "troubled banks" to resign as well. The government, he said, "has had to do exceptional things."[1]

Republican senator Bob Corker called the Wagoner firing "a major power-grab by the White House on the heels of another power-grab from Secretary Geithner, who asked last week for the freedom to decide on his own which companies are 'systemically' important to our country and worthy of taxpayer investment, and which are not." He said it was "a marked departure from the past," "truly breathtaking," and "should send a chill through all Americans who believe in free enterprise."[2] CNBC economist Larry Kudlow noted that this was the proper domain of bankruptcy courts, not the executive branch. Corker agreed, telling Kudlow that "today, a bright line was crossed.... Now, in essence, they have taken over these companies." He accurately predicted that soon the executive branch would be deciding which GM plants would stay open and which would close.[3]

A few days after the firing, Obama and Treasury secretary Giethner were reportedly weighing a plan to divide the "good" and "bad" assets of GM and Chrysler before putting them into bankruptcy. This would effectively nationalize a major portion of the auto industry—an action unprecedented in American history and, in the words of the *Wall Street Journal*, one which would "represent one of the biggest-ever government incursions into private enterprise." Obama and his henchmen were deeply immersed in micromanaging a wholesale restructuring of the companies, planning on allowing Chevrolet and Cadillac to remain independent while selling the equity in Chrysler to Fiat SpA. Obama played both ends against the middle, warning the automakers they had only brief windows to formulate plans to justify government support, then saying he would do all he could to salvage the industry. "We cannot, we must not, and we will not let our auto industry simply vanish," he vowed.[4]

Just as Obama would later duplicitously claim his healthcare plan would not interfere with patients' choice of their doctors as he signed into law a bill contradicting his assertion, he insisted he had no intentions of taking over GM at the very same time he was cementing plans to do just that. Obama had another motive to sub-sume the auto industry beyond his claim that automakers were "too big to fail" and jobs had to be preserved. As with his redirection of the space program, he aimed to push his environmental agenda from the inside—to force automakers into producing more energy efficient vehicles.[5] As Peter Kaufman, president and head of restructuring at investment bank Gordian Group LLC, said, "The big question is whether the government, as a shareholder, will be focused on GM making money, or it making clean and green cars, or whatever other political agenda they have for the auto space."[6]

That question was answered when Brent Dewar, Chevrolet vice president, told dealers they should learn to sell small cars, based on projections that smaller cars will overtake trucks and SUVs as GM's best sellers.[7] On the other hand, we saw an interesting glimpse of liberal hypocrisy at work as the "New GM" conspicuously withdrew from an environmental partnership called the End of Life Vehicle Solutions (ELVS). ELVS was created to collect toxic parts from scrapped cars to prevent the release of mercury emissions into the environment when vehicles are crushed and shredded. But the new government managers weren't so concerned about the environment when their own credibility was at stake in making the new company a financially viable entity. New GM basically said the mercury in the old vehicles wasn't its problem, as those vehicles remained with Old GM.

New GM's environmental callousness was rather untimely, as Obama's "cash-for-clunkers" program was expected to lead to the trade-in and recycling of an estimated 750,000 vehicles, some of which contain mercury switches whose destruction could cause mercury pollution. Clearly, it's always easier to preach environmentalism to the other guy than to abide by the rules yourself. ELVS executive director Mary Bills commented, "We're surprised that GM, who wants to have this great green image, would do this." New GM's spokesperson dismissed the company's culpability, claiming the responsibility for participating in the partnership

remained with Old GM. But that was small comfort to other partners, as Old GM was but a composite of GM's liabilities and under-
performing assets.[8]

Without any semblance of constitutional authority, Obama
announced he would unilaterally guarantee federal warranties for
all new GM and Chrysler vehicles. Why should taxpayer dollars
guarantee—retroactively, no less—the quality of a car? Why should
the federal government offer to make such a guarantee without any
inquiry into whether it was a prudent decision? But being a politician with no business experience, Obama unilaterally declared *carte
blanche* responsibility on behalf of the federal government, as if he
had an endless supply of money. Obama also expressed support for
a congressional bid to offer large tax incentives for new-car purchases from stimulus monies, without bothering to justify that
expenditure either. At least he was being consistent: since he didn't
have to justify his use of bank bailout money to keep Chrysler
afloat with emergency loans, why should he have to justify using
"stimulus" funds for a purpose not contemplated by the law?

UAW'S SWEETHEART DEALS

A major supporter of Obama, the United Auto Workers got sweetheart deals in both the GM and Chrysler restructurings. In the case
of GM, the UAW and the bondholders were both unsecured creditors with equal rights under bankruptcy law, although GM contended that it had made a deal in 2007 that gave a preference to the
UAW's unsecured claims. The bondholders, however, reportedly
never agreed that their claims would be subordinated to those of
UAW. Because GM's debt to the UAW (estimated at $20–30 billion)
and to the bondholders ($27 billion) were roughly equal, it would
follow they would each receive a similar percentage of shares in the
new company. But Obama's proposed restructuring contemplated
UAW receiving about 39 percent of the stock while the bondholders would get just 10 percent, with the other 50 percent going to the

government.[9] New York attorney and financial expert Norman Kinel noted, "To say it's unusual is an understatement. The government doesn't ever get involved this way." Dan Seiver, a San Diego State University finance professor, said, "We're in a new era where the government is calling a bunch of shots."

Other experts pointed to the government's conflict of interest as a shareholder on the one hand and, on the other, its interest in protecting jobs and benefits. Some also expressed concerns about the government's heavy-handed tactics and the possible unstated consequences of disobeying its directions. Dartmouth's Tuck School of Business professor Syd Finkelstein noted allegations by Bank of America Chief Executive Ken Lewis that the government had pressured him to complete a merger with Merrill Lynch.[10]

GM Bondholder Advisers issued a statement saying they were "deeply concerned with today's decision by GM and the auto task force to offer only a small, inequitable percentage of stock to its bondholders in exchange for their bonds." Calling the offer "neither reasonable nor adequate," they said it amounted to using taxpayer money "to show political favoritism" for certain creditors over others.[11]

A month later, UAW's proposed share was cut to approximately 20 percent of GM's common stock, with 17.5 percent to be transferred immediately, along with a warrant for an additional 2.5 percent. The bondholders' share was to remain at 10 percent. When GM was asked whether the bondholders' deal would be "sweetened," it responded that the government was preventing it from offering them more than 10 percent.[12] As it happened, a deal could not be consummated, and GM filed for bankruptcy on June 2, 2009.[13] Within a month of the filing, the government was trying to sell the company to a "New GM," the majority share of which would be owned by the government. The bondholders were still objecting, however. Their attorney, Michael Richman, accused the government of being "overbearing" and of circumventing the law. Richman contended that the sale had not been negotiated as an arms-length sale to an independent party because the government, essentially, was dealing with itself and otherwise dictating—not negotiating—the terms of the deal.

The government was allegedly manipulating the deal and determining the price not through good faith negotiations, but by first determining how much its "favored parties" needed from the deal and then backing into the price. The sale, if approved, would result in the union initially owning a 17.5 percent interest, Canadian governmental entities 12 percent, the bondholders 10 percent, and the government 60 percent.[14] Obama, of course, said the government needed such a large stake because the financial health of the auto industry affected the financial health of the nation—the "too big to fail" argument. He insisted he really didn't want to nationalize the companies. "We could have simply offered the company more loans," he said. "But . . . piling on irresponsibly large debt on top of the new GM would mean simply repeating the mistakes of the past."[15] Ultimately the sale proceeded—much to the chagrin of the bondholders, who had made the mistake of lending their money to a private company in the age of Obama.[16]

THE MADMAN THEORY OF THE PRESIDENCY: OBAMA WANTED TO BE FEARED

The Chrysler case was even worse. The creditors competing against the UAW were secured creditors, presumably entitled to priority over the unsecured union workers. But the secured creditors were being heavily pressured to accept just a fraction of the amount of their claims: $2.25 billion of the $6.9 billion they were owed (29 cents on the dollar), while the unsecured UAW was offered some 50 cents on the dollar. The UAW agreed to concessions to freeze wages, cut retiree health benefits, and not to strike for at least six years. Chrysler executives still hoped to avoid bankruptcy and possibly merge with GM. But Obama's inside man, Steven Rattner, the head of Obama's Auto Industry Task Force, had virtually pre-ordained the outcome—bankruptcy—while publicly claiming he was studiously seeking to avoid that result. Chrysler's CFO Ron Kolka said Rattner told him how it would go: bankruptcy, followed by a restructuring with the creditors, the union, and Fiat—not GM, even though Robert Manzo, a financial consultant for Chrysler, said he believed "the valuations of an alliance with GM were higher than those of a deal with Fiat." It didn't matter to Rattner, who had already decided as of March 30 that his task force would only authorize taxpayer money to be used for a deal with Fiat.

In an e-mail to Chairman Bob Nardelli, Vice Chairman Tom LaSorda, and Robert Manzo, Kolka wrote, "We need a deal with Fiat today. We were told to pretty much take it." Nardelli said that Rattner and his politically radical colleague Ron Bloom—Obama's manufacturing czar—"will call the union and tell them what will happen. Then they'll tell the banks, 'Here's the deal: take it or liquidate it.'"[17] In other words, *Don't bother us with valiant efforts to save your sorry company when we have plans to take it over and do with it as we please. And don't try to negotiate better terms—or any different terms—any of you. We are the government and we're calling the shots.*

The four primary creditors, J. P. Morgan Chase, Citigroup, Goldman Sachs, and Morgan Stanley, agreed to the Treasury's plan, but other lenders—mostly hedge funds—weren't on board. Obama maneuvered himself into position to call these shots, because a condition of the TARP loans to GM and Chrysler was that the government would have the right to convert its claim to debtor-in-possession status, which has first priority under bankruptcy law.[18] Reportedly, one of the lawyers on Rattner's team, Matthew Feldman, got his nose out of joint in negotiations with Chrysler and refused to allow Manzo to sweeten the offer to the reluctant investors in a final attempt to avert bankruptcy. Feldman reportedly told Manzo, "I am not talking to you. You went where you shouldn't." Even after Manzo apologized—who knows what for—Feldman highhandedly replied, "It's over. The president doesn't negotiate second rounds. We've given and lent billions of dollars to your team, so your team could manage this properly. I've protected your management and board, and now you're going to put me in a position to have to bend to a terrorist like Lauria. That's B.S."[19]

"Lauria" was Tom Lauria, an attorney representing Perella Weinberg Partners, one of Chrysler's secured creditors unhappy with the proposed deal. He offered an unflattering account of the administration's capricious actions in the process. Lauria, Global Practice Head of the Financial Restructuring and Insolvency Group at White & Case, a highly reputed international law firm, told *ABC News* that Steven Rattner informed an official of Perella Weinberg that the administration would embarrass the firm if it opposed Obama's plan.[20] In an interview with FOX News' Megyn Kelly and Neil Cavuto, Lauria said, "One of my clients was directly threatened by the White House and, in essence, compelled to withdraw its opposition to the deal under the threat that the full force of the White House press corps would destroy its reputation if it continued to fight."

The plot thickened when Perella officials curiously denied Lauria's account, without elaboration. But unnamed witnesses corroborated Lauria's version of events. John Carney, writing for *Business Insider*, reported that the sources, who insisted on anonymity for fear of political reprisals, said they represented creditors of Chrysler and were taken aback by the hardball tactics the Obama administration employed to compel their acceptance of the restructuring plans. One described the White House as the most shocking "end justifies the means" group they had ever encountered. Another source claimed Obama was "the most dangerous smooth talker on the planet—and I knew Kissinger." Both had voted for Obama. Another participant in the negotiations described Obama's tactics as employing a "madman theory of the presidency," where Obama wanted to be feared as someone who was "willing to do anything to get his way." This witness said his firm took the strategy very seriously.[21]

"SHAKING DOWN LENDERS FOR THE BENEFIT OF POLITICAL DONORS"

As had become his practice, Obama attacked his critics personally as well as ungraciously and unpresidentially. Although he didn't name Perella specifically, those following the negotiations knew exactly who he was talking about when he released a statement saying, "While many stakeholders made sacrifices and worked constructively, I have to tell you some did not. In particular, a group of investment firms and hedge funds decided to hold out for the prospect of an unjustified taxpayer-funded bailout. They were hoping that everybody else would make sacrifices, and they would have to make none."[22] Here was the president of the United States, again, attacking the reputation and integrity of a private firm merely for asserting its rights in a negotiation.

The statement also outraged hedge funds which, after all, weren't the ones being bailed out. Hedge fund executive Cliff Asness passionately denounced Obama's bullying in *Business Insider*:

> The president screaming that the hedge funds are looking for an unjustified taxpayer-funded bailout is the big lie writ large. Find me a hedge fund that has been bailed out. Find me a hedge fund, even a failed one, that has asked for one. In fact, it was only because hedge funds have not taken government funds that they could stand up to this bullying. The hedge funds were singled out only because they are unpopular, not because they behaved any differently from any other ethical manager of other people's money. The president's comments here are backwards and libelous.... This is America. We have a free enterprise system that has worked spectacularly for us two hundred plus years. When it fails it fixes itself. Most importantly, it is not an owned lackey of the oval office to be scolded for disobedience by the President.[23]

In his statement, Obama took another thinly veiled swing at Perella and at hedge funds:

I don't stand with them. I stand with Chrysler's employees and
their families and communities. I stand with Chrysler's management, its dealers, and its suppliers. I stand with the millions of
Americans who own and want to buy Chrysler cars. I don't
stand with those who held out when everyone else is making
sacrifices. . . . But it was unsustainable to let enormous liabilities
remain on Chrysler's books, and it was unacceptable to let a
small group of speculators endanger Chrysler's future by refusing to sacrifice like everyone else.[24]

Investment bankers are "speculators?" This was stunningly distorted and abusive language. Obama's use of the first person indicated this was very personal to him. What we were witnessing was
a public temper tantrum from an egomaniac who enjoys a reputation for being cool, calm, and unflappable. Cliff Asness weighed in
on Obama's lecturing hedge funds about "sacrifice," noting that it's
the job of all investment managers to maximize their clients' return.
They may choose to be charitable with their own money, but they
have no right to give away their clients' money in the name of "sacrifice." That, said Asness, is "stealing." He continued, "The managers have a fiduciary obligation to look after their clients' money
as best they can, not to support the president, nor to oppose him,
nor otherwise advance their personal political views." Obama, said
Asness, took money from bondholders and gave it to labor, which
"delivers money and votes for him. Why is he not calling on his
party to 'sacrifice' some campaign contributions, and votes, for the
greater good . . . [S]haking down lenders for the benefit of political
donors . . . is recycled corruption and abuse of power."[25]

The *Economist* had similarly harsh language for the administration. "America's government, keen to protect workers, is providing
taxpayer's cash to keep the lights on at both firms. But in its haste,
it has vilified creditors and ridden roughshod over their legitimate
claims over the carmakers' assets. . . . Bankruptcies involve dividing
a shrunken pie. But not all claims are equal: some lenders provide

cheaper funds to firms in return for a more secure claim over the assets should things go wrong. They rank above other stakeholders, including shareholders and employees. This principle is now being trashed."[26] Even self-described left-leaning author Douglas Rushkoff condemned the administration's "misguided" tactics. "The people who bought GM bonds over the past few years," he said, "were bailing out GM's health plan for very low returns—but a high level of security," he said. "Now, as government continues to bail out the auto giant, those consumer-grade debtors are being pushed to the back of the line. They'll not only pay for GM's bailout through their bond investments, but through their taxes as well."[27]

Tom Lauria said Obama's assertion that "I don't stand with you" sounded like "You're fair game." People, said Lauria, "are scared. They have gotten death threats. Some have been told people are going to come to their houses. God forbid if some nut did something, I'm just wondering how the president would feel." Query: Was Obama's language the type of speech the Left has in mind when it so often accuses conservatives of inciting violence just by registering their dissent with this administration?

Lauria is almost certainly telling the truth. What motive would a widely respected attorney like Lauria have to lie, and especially in a way that would misrepresent what his clients had experienced? And Lauria was not some rock-ribbed Republican. A self-described independent, he donated $10,000 to the Democratic Senatorial Campaign Committee in 2008 and $1,000 to then-Senator Hillary Clinton in 2006.[28] Moreover, given the undisputed facts, the White House acted capriciously by skewing the deal in favor of Obama's labor union allies with utterly no legal justification.

GANGSTER GOVERNMENT

Washington Examiner writer Michael Barone commented on the plausibility of Lauria's claim that the White House threatened to savage Perella in the press unless it cooperated. Barone said that while the threat "sounds just a tad bit bizarre," Rattner's involvement raised the possibility that the principals understood Rattner was a former *New York Times* reporter who was "reputed to be one of the best friends" of the paper's publisher, Arthur Sulzberger, Jr. Barone cites blogger Mickey Kaus's observation that hedge funds (such as Perella) are squeamish about negative publicity or any publicity at all, because it could lead to investors withdrawing their funds. Additionally, investors read the *New York Times* every day.[29]

Rattner abruptly resigned as head of the auto task force after leading GM and Chrysler into and out of bankruptcy. Not unbeknownst to the Obama administration when it appointed him for this position, Quadrangle Group, the investment firm Rattner had founded, had been under a two-year investigation by the Securities and Exchange Commission.[30]

Obama's claim that Perella was unwilling to make any sacrifice was absurd on its face. Lauria said his clients, in fact, were willing to take 50 cents on the dollar from Chrysler. Obama was offering to give his UAW buddies 50 cents on the dollar for their *unsecured debts* while only offering Perella 33 or fewer cents for its *secured debts*, which was both outrageously unfair and contrary to fundamental bankruptcy law. Under the plan, the UAW would eventually own 55 percent of the stock in a restructured Chrysler LLC, Fiat SpA would own 35 percent, and the federal government and Chrylser's secured creditors, together, would own the remaining 10 percent.[31] This was an especially hard pill to swallow when a compelling argument can be made that one of the major factors contributing to the auto dealers' financial difficulties was over-priced labor that put the Big Three at a competitive disadvantage with foreign auto makers.

Perella denied it was being unreasonable; it would have received as much, and probably more, under bankruptcy proceedings. And while Obama accused the firm of helping to bankrupt Chrysler, even the *New York Times* said this "boutique investment bank, a latecomer to Chrysler, played only a small role in the slow-motion wreck of the Detroit carmaker." Indeed, the *Times* quoted certain industry executives who contended that Obama needed "political cover" for the "mess in Detroit"—and "Wall Street provided a handy scapegoat."[32]

Obama picks the winners and losers based on political allegiance and abject cronyism—the rule of law be damned. This is the danger of the government being involved as both a party and an arbiter, in effect, of the final outcome—a flagrant conflict of interest that worked strongly against its ability to be fair and objective. The entire episode was aptly described by Michael Barone as "Gangster Government."[33]

"I HAVE NO INTEREST IN RUNNING GM"

Obama's dealings with General Motors and Chrysler opened some previously skeptical eyes about his statist tendencies. At the end of May 2009, Rasmussen Reports showed only 21 percent of voters nationwide supported a plan for the federal government to bail out GM as part of a bankruptcy reorganization, while 67 percent opposed. The proposal involved the government loaning GM $50 billion in exchange for a whopping 70 percent ownership interest in the business. Poll participants had clearly thought through the consequences of their responses. When asked whether they would still oppose the bailout if it meant GM going out of business, it only brought the support up to 32 percent, with 56 percent opposing. An earlier survey showed 76 percent of voters did not believe the "too-big-to-fail" hype of the political class—that economic recovery depended on GM's survival.[34] Other polls revealed a majority of Americans still distrusted the government. One survey discovered only 18 percent believed the government would do a good job running GM,[35] and another found 57 percent expected the government would use its power to give unfair advantage to companies it owned.[36] Only 12 percent said they would prefer a car from a bailed-out automaker.[37]

But Obama doesn't share the public's affinity for capitalism. When announcing GM's bankruptcy, he laughably said, "What we are not doing—what I have no interest in doing—is running GM." Yet, just the night before, he had called Detroit mayor Dave Bing to reassure him that New GM would be headquartered in Detroit.[38] Furthermore, Obama's auto task force had earlier pressured General Motors Corp. to get rid of the GMC brand,[39] which was an odd move for an administration insisting it had no interest in managing the business. In another odd move for a group appointed by someone disinterested in running car companies, Obama's task force cut in half Chrysler's planned expenditures for its "We're Building a New Car Company" campaign.[40]

The story of Chrysler's government-nudged degeneration into bankruptcy is not a pretty tale. And in the end, Obama prevailed, as the Supreme Court lifted a stay on the sale of Chrysler to the group including Fiat SpA, clearing the way for the sale to proceed. As part of the restructuring ordeal, Obama's auto task force closed down nearly 2,500 GM and Chrysler dealerships at the cost of some 100,000 jobs.

There was much suspicion about Obama's partisan favoritism in his decisions as to which dealerships would be closed and which would remain open.[41] The *Washington Examiner's* Mark Tapscott wrote that "evidence appears to be mounting" that the administration "systematically targeted for closing Chrysler dealers who contributed to Republicans." One example he cited was the closing of a dealership of a GOP congressman as well as competitors of a dealership whose owners included former Clinton chief of staff Mack McLarty.

Tapscott argued the basic issue was how to account for millions of dollars that were contributed to GOP candidates by Chrysler dealers who were being closed, while only one Democrat-contributing dealer had been shuttered. Leonard Bellavia, a lawyer representing a group of Chrysler dealers set to be closed, told Reuters he believed the closings had been forced on the company directly by the White House.

In fairness, Tapscott, in an update to his piece, conceded that certain credible bloggers disputed the notion that partisan considerations determined the closings. It could have just been a result of more dealerships being owned by Republicans. But he also cautioned that suspicion remained because the White House had not made public the criteria it used to make decisions on terminating dealerships. Tapscott also raised this provocative question: even if more dealerships were owned by Republicans, which had not been proven, "If 88 percent of all car dealers were Democratic contributors, rather than GOPers, how likely is it that the Obama folks would be delivering such an egregious economic blow to the group, a blow that put thousands of people out of work and deprives hundreds of Democratic donors of their means of making contributions?"[42]

Later, Congress reversed Obama on many of these dealership closings—over the stringent opposition of his administration. At the time, the White House warned this could set a "dangerous precedent." What—Congress failing to rubber stamp one of the president's edicts? The closings, according to the White House, were "a critical part of their overall restructuring to achieve long-term viability." But nearly a year later, when jobs were created after this new legislation, Obama brazenly took credit for them. Obama told Democratic Party donors in Boston, "A year later, GM is hiring again, on the verge of reopening hundreds of dealerships," which proved his $50 billion bailout of GM "was the right thing to do." Bailey Wood, a spokesman for the National Automobile Dealers Association, remarked, "Now he is touting the fact that jobs were created after dealer arbitration legislation, which his administration opposed, forced GM/Chrysler to reevaluate closing these dealerships." The White House declined to comment.[43]

It was expected that taxpayers would incur enormous losses on the auto bailout. The administration told Congress in December 2009 it expected to lose some $30 billion of the $82 billion used in the bailout. And yet, the administration was bragging about it. Gene Sperling, Treasury secretary Timothy Geithner's senior counsel, said,

"The real news is the projected loss came down to $30 billion from $44 billion."[44] The government also recklessly lost an estimated $6.3 billion of the $17.2 billion bailout of GMAC, a principal financing arm for the auto dealers that needed money to keep the floor plans in place. According to Harvard law professor Elizabeth Warren, chair of the Congressional Oversight Panel, the money was extended to GMAC with far fewer conditions than those imposed on the automakers themselves. "Treasury missed many opportunities to improve accountability and protect taxpayer money," said Warren. She said Treasury did not require GMAC to show how it would return taxpayer money or even how the investment would increase credit to consumers. Warren added, "These decisions mean that Treasury is now struggling to deal with a GMAC that is not financially rehabilitated, Treasury has no exit strategy and taxpayers are not fully protected."[45]

No exit strategy and a lack of taxpayer protection—quite a fitting summary of many of Obama's intrusions into the private sector.

Chapter Eleven

THE CASE OF GERALD WALPIN AND AMERICORPS

CRIMES AGAINST THE PUBLIC INTEREST

O bama campaigned on a promise to protect and empower whistleblowers against government corruption. On his website he said that the best source of information about government waste, fraud, and abuse is often "existing government employee(s) committed to public integrity and willing to speak out." Arguing that these "acts of courage" should be "encouraged rather than stifled," he vowed to ensure that federal agencies "expedite the process for reviewing claims of whistleblowers and that they would have full access to courts and due process."

His actions, however, haven't quite lived up to his promises. The White House counsel's office proposed legislation that would actually weaken whistleblower protection for FBI employees and reduce access to jury trials for national security workers who sue for protection from retaliation.[1] But much more significant was the Obama administration's treatment of AmeriCorps inspector general Gerald

Walpin—a chilling tale of lawlessness, cronyism, and a patent disregard for government transparency and accountability.

ANATOMY OF A SCANDAL

On July 11, 2009, Obama abruptly announced his decision to fire Gerald Walpin. He sent letters to leaders of the Senate and House notifying them of the termination, to take effect in thirty days. His stated reason? He had lost "the fullest confidence" in Walpin, which is "vital" in "the appointees serving as Inspectors General."

This was not your ordinary executive firing of an at-will staffer. The Inspector General is a highly sensitive position that acts as a watchdog against government corruption and must not be occupied by a lapdog who provides cover for wrongdoing. To be fired by the leader of the very branch of government one is assigned to investigate is enough to create a presumption of suspicion.

Obama would have preferred to fire Walpin quietly, but the recently passed Inspectors General Reform Act, designed to enhance the independence of IGs and provide them protection to do their jobs free of undue influence, required him to provide thirty days prior written notice to both Houses of Congress and to explain his decision. (Notably, Obama was among the co-sponsors of the bill.) He provided notice, but it was meaningless because he immediately placed Walpin on paid administrative leave and stripped him of his authority, which is precisely what the notice provision is intended to prevent. Nor did Obama outline his reasons beyond vague generalities.

Obama, in fact, had tried to circumvent the act altogether by nudging Walpin into resigning on his own. Senator Charles Grassley reported that the White House had called Walpin and given him one hour either to resign or be fired. Walpin refused to play.[2] Grassley sent a letter to the president reminding him of the purpose of Inspectors General—to combat "waste, fraud, and abuse and to be independent watchdogs" to ensure that federal agencies

are "accountable"—and that they are to be "free from undue political pressure" so they can operate "independently."

Suspicion immediately arose that Obama was firing Walpin
because of Walpin's investigation of Kevin Johnson, a former NBA
star and the Mayor of Sacramento, California, who is a strong
Obama supporter and personal friend. Before becoming mayor,
Johnson had established a non-profit called St. HOPE to help "revi-
talize inner-city communities through public education, civil leadership, economic development and the arts." After opening an
investigation into whether St. HOPE had misused an $850,000
AmeriCorps grant,[3] Walpin discovered that Johnson had used
AmeriCorps funds to pay volunteers to participate in political activ-
ities involving the school board and to run personal errands for
Johnson like washing his car.[4]

In a letter to Senator Grassley, White House counsel Gregory
Craig offered a few details about Walpin's firing, saying that a U.S.
attorney, while communicating with an integrity committee for
inspectors general, had criticized Walpin's handling of the St. HOPE
investigation. Craig wrote, "We are aware of the circumstances
leading to that referral and of Mr. Walpin's conduct throughout his
tenure and can assure you that the president's decision was carefully
considered." Walpin had referred the case to the U.S. Attorney's
office upon discovering anomalies in grant expenditures. The U.S.
Attorney said Walpin's assessment of misconduct seemed overstated
and did not accurately reflect all the information. St. HOPE's board
chairman, Kevin Heistand, issued a statement saying it was "about
time" Walpin was removed and that his "allegations were meritless
and clearly motivated by matters beyond an honest assessment of
our program."

Nevertheless, something improper had occurred, even in the eyes
of acting U.S. Attorney Lawrence Brown, or his office wouldn't
have worked out a settlement with St. HOPE whereby it would
repay almost half the $850,000 grant money.[5] In addition, the
Integrity Committee of the Council of Inspectors General on

Integrity and Efficiency had issued no negative findings against Walpin, and Walpin had "identified millions of dollars in Ameri-Corps funds either wasted outright or spent in violation of established guidelines." Meanwhile, Kevin Johnson and St. HOPE were temporarily cut off from receiving any new grant monies. As the *Washington Examiner's* Byron York said, "The bottom line is that the AmeriCorps IG accused a prominent Obama supporter of misusing AmeriCorps grant money," and "after an investigation, the prominent Obama supporter had to pay back more than $400,000 of that grant money." Yet, "Obama fired the AmeriCorps IG."[6]

The controversy was just beginning for President Obama. Democratic senator Claire McCaskill, a strong Obama ally, expressed concern that Obama hadn't complied with the law requiring 30-day notice prior of termination (though she later reversed herself).

Norm Eisen, Special Counsel to the President, provided more details on Walpin's termination in a letter to senators Joe Lieberman and Susan Collins, with a copy to Senator McCaskill. Eisen stated that Walpin was terminated following a review that had been unanimously requested by the "bipartisan Board of the Corporation." He wrote that in a board meeting in May 2009, Walpin was "confused, disoriented, unable to answer questions and exhibited other behavior that led the Board to question his capacity to serve." Furthermore, Eisen said acting U.S. Attorney Brown had filed a complaint about Walpin's alleged failure to disclose exculpatory evidence about St. HOPE. Finally, Eisen claimed Walpin had insisted—over the objections of the Board—on working from his home in New York; that he "exhibited a lack of candor in providing material information to decision makers; and that he had engaged in other troubling and inappropriate conduct. Mr. Walpin had become unduly disruptive to agency operations, impairing his effectiveness, and, for the reasons stated above, losing the confidence of the board."[7]

Gerald Walpin refused to go quietly, accusing the White House of "grasping at nonexistent straws" to justify his firing. He said the more diligently he investigated St. HOPE, along with the alleged waste of AmeriCorps money at the City University of New York (CUNY), the more resistance he encountered from the board of the Corporation for National and Community Service, which oversees AmeriCorps. "But that's exactly why the IG position was created," said Walpin.

Walpin argued that far from being confused, he simply gave the board information it didn't want to hear and chastised it for "what appeared to be the board's refusal to perform its duty, independent of management, in overseeing what management was doing, particularly as it regards determining the merits of the two reports I had issued." He told the board it was its duty to evaluate all the evidence objectively and not "just to accept what management says." He claimed the board was "angry" at his "temerity in telling them they should not be acting in the manner of many for-profit boards, which have been recently criticized."[8]

As for his alleged confusion at the May meeting, Walpin said he had not been feeling well that day, and that board members repeatedly interrupted him as he was delivering his prepared presentation. At one point they asked him to leave the room so they could handle unrelated business. When he returned, he found the board had rifled through his papers and left them in disorder, but board members wouldn't allow him time to reassemble his notes. He said the only confusion in the room was that of board members "as to their responsibilities." Besides, as Byron York noted, Walpin's confusion or lack of it would not have excused the president's failure to comply with the statutory 30-day notice period.

Many Republican investigators denied Walpin was mentally impaired at all, finding him instead "collected and coherent." One investigator said, "What the White House described is not the experience that we have had in dealing with him." After talking to Walpin for two hours, Byron York corroborated the GOP investigators' findings, further observing that Walpin had "performed well in recent high-profile media appearances."[9] Walpin also denied he was working from home at the displeasure of the board. He said the CEO and general counsel of the corporation had "expressly approved" the arrangement, and that he had also cleared it with the chairman and vice chairman of the board. Walpin called the charge that he lacked candor in providing material information to decision makers "a total lie." As for the allegation that he had engaged in "other troubling and inappropriate conduct," Walpin retorted, "From their viewpoint, my criticisms of the Corporation's operations and the board of directors' failure to perform its duties is troubling."[10]

A CORROBORATING WITNESS

The *Washington Times* reported that it had located a witness who directly contradicted multiple aspects of the official White House explanation for the firing. "The witness," reported the *Times*, "whose bona fides are unimpeachable, is on the agency's payroll, and thus spoke on grounds of anonymity." The *Times* contacted the witness on its own, without Walpin's input or knowledge. The witness, who claimed to have first-hand knowledge, corroborated Walpin's statement that the agency's general counsel, Frank Trinity, and acting CEO Nicola Goren, had no objection to him working from home. As to the allegation that he was "confused" and "disoriented," the witness said Walpin opened up the meeting by castigating the board for "particularly weak oversight of the grants" for both St. HOPE and CUNY, eliciting "considerable hostility and repeated interruptions" from board members. The witness also confirmed Walpin's account of being denied time to reorder his papers after they had been rifled in his absence. The witness said he had never before or since seen Walpin the slightest bit confused, but he agreed Walpin and the board "weren't connecting" at the meeting after the board badgered him and wouldn't let him reorganize his notes.

The *Times* uncovered another damning tidbit against the White House's claim that Walpin was confused. On June 9, 2009, one day before the White House asked him to step down and several weeks after the fateful May 20 board meeting, the agency asked him to deliver an important speech in San Francisco on June 23 to an expected audience of 2,000 staff members and grantees. Walpin said, "They begged me to come. Why would they do that if they thought I am incapacitated?"[11]

Once again, the MO of the Obama White House was on full display: exploit and abuse executive power to benefit or protect your cronies and political allies, and punish or slander anyone who gets in your way. Walpin was sniffing too close to the stench of corruption.

WHITE HOUSE STONEWALLING

Congressional investigators began to look into the reasons for Walpin's firing. White House special counsel Norman Eisen stonewalled Senator Grassley's investigators, revealing very little and refusing to answer many questions. Grassley followed up with a letter to White House counsel Gregory Craig complaining of Eisen's lack of cooperation. He then restated the unanswered questions in the letter.[12]

Key congressional Republicans accused the White House of providing "incomplete and misleading" information to investigators. But the White House hinted that its documents on the case were privileged, which just added to Republican suspicion; for if the White House had conducted a thorough investigation of the facts before firing Walpin, as it claimed, then why the need for secrecy? It looked more like the White House had fired Walpin for political reasons and built its case after the fact.

Next, a bipartisan group of congressional investigators questioned the general counsel for the Corporation for National and Community Service, Frank Trinity, who also refused to provide any details about Walpin's firing. A congressional aide said Trinity claimed he didn't feel at liberty to discuss the firing because it was the White House's prerogative. When investigators pressed Trinity to justify his refusal to cooperate, reminding him that executive privilege had to be asserted by the president, he declined to respond. The issues Trinity refused to address included details on the contacts between the White House and CNCS prior to or after the firing; which members from CNCS had communicated with which White House officials; and whether CNCS officials had discussed with the White House the specific reasons for the firing.[13] At one point, the White House added new allegations to justify the firing: Walpin supposedly demonstrated racial and gender insensitivity based on a parody newsletter that originated from his office commemorating the retirement of an employee. But there was no indication Walpin had any involvement in the newsletter, which had been published a year earlier, in May 2008.[14]

Walpin fought back by filing a federal lawsuit against the CNCS and some of its corporate officials. Requesting to be reinstated, he alleged he had been unlawfully terminated for political and other reasons in circumvention of the Inspectors General Reform Act of 2008. Walpin argued he was denied his job protections in three instances when the White House attempted to terminate him, once orally on June 10 and twice in writing on June 11 and June 16. He also asserted the White House acted so fast that it didn't even bother to substantiate its own stated reasons for firing him, for example, by interviewing Walpin or any of the board members.[15]

Senator Jeff Sessions, the ranking Republican on the Senate Judiciary Committee, requested that Vermont Democratic chairman Patrick Leahy institute a hearing on the AmeriCorps/Walpin case, and particularly the role of U.S. Attorney Brown and his Department of Justice superiors. What got Sessions' attention was an offhand statement in a TV interview in March by Doris Matsui, the congresswoman representing Sacramento, concerning the likelihood that the investigation into Kevin Johnson could interfere with Sacramento's receipt of stimulus money. Matsui said that upon Johnson's request, she had "been in conversation with officials at the White

House and OMB and others to ensure that we don't lose any money at all."[16]

Fishier still was the government's settlement with Johnson whereby his temporary suspension from participating in federal contracts or grants was lifted, but he and St. HOPE were required to repay part of the AmeriCorps grant. Mayor Johnson had to pay $72,836.50 of the $423,836.50 that St. HOPE was required to refund.[17] Acting U.S. Attorney Brown had issued a press release celebrating the fact that the settlement would remove any cloud over Sacramento that might prevent it from receiving stimulus funds.

It was uncharacteristic and inappropriate of a U.S. attorney to issue that kind of political statement, which had nothing to do with the merits of the case he was investigating. Reacting to Brown's statement, Senate Judiciary Committee Republicans demanded, "We need to hear whether the settlement in this case was tainted in any way by political influence or political factors." House Committee on Oversight and Government Reform ranking Republican Darell Issa, on two occasions, submitted questions to Brown, which were ignored.[18]

Apparently frustrated at the administration's stonewalling, Senator Grassley decided to block the White House's nomination of CNCS chairman Alan Solomont as U.S. ambassador to Spain. He cited the CNCS's lack of transparency and cooperation in the Walpin investigation, including its failure to provide a list of the documents it was refusing to deliver and the reasons for the refusal.[19] Solomont was a major Democratic donor and Obama supporter and, when chairman of CNCS, personally went to the White House to report the board's meeting with Walpin and recommend he be fired.

"AN AFTER-THE-FACT SMEAR CAMPAIGN"

On October 19, 2009, the Integrity Committee of the Council of the Inspectors General for Integrity and Efficiency cleared Walpin of the complaint filed against him by acting U.S. attorney Lawrence Brown. Committee Chairman Kevin L. Perkins wrote, "After carefully considering the allegations described in the complaint together with your response, the IC determined that the response sufficiently and satisfactorily addressed the matter and that further inquiry or an investigation regarding the matter was not warranted." In an interview following the dismissal Walpin said, "It takes away any basis belatedly set forth by the White House as a reason for my termination. So I am certainly looking forward to a final determination by the court and to be reinstated."[20]

The White House had filed a motion to dismiss Walpin's lawsuit, and on November 6, Walpin's attorneys filed a legal brief that the *Washington Times*' editors asserted "convincingly refutes the arguments" contained in the White House's motion to dismiss. Walpin pointed out that one of the bases upon which the White House fired him was that acting U.S. attorney Brown had filed his complaint against Walpin. Now that that complaint had been resolved in Walpin's favor, the White House's justification for terminating him was significantly weakened. About a week later, White House officials met with Senator Grassley to discuss the congressional investigation, but after the meeting the parties were still at odds over the release of documents. The White House had delivered several hundred pages of material but withheld as many, claiming they were protected by various legal privileges.

The *Times* editors opined that beyond the investigation terminating in Walpin's favor, "the rest of Mr. Walpin's brief makes mincemeat of the White House motion to dismiss the lawsuit." The White House's specious defense for circumventing the statutory 30-day notice period for termination was that Walpin was put on paid administrative leave, which did not constitute "removal." As the *Times* editors pointed out, this was quite odd since the entire purpose of the notice was to prevent IGs from being blocked from investigating an administration—exactly what happened here. In addition, Walpin alleged in his brief that even before the White House notified

Congress about its dissatisfaction with Walpin, it "terminated his access to his own e-mail account and office, and denied him access to his staff. Mr. Walpin was prevented from performing even the most rudimentary steps in order to ensure that his termination did not prevent the Office of the Inspector General from performing his duties." Moreover, the White House sent a letter six days later actually saying, "Mr. Walpin was removed." But "removed," according to the administration, does not constitute "removal."[21]

The scandal broadened with the release of a congressional report of the Walpin matter prepared by Senator Grassley and Congressman Issa. The report revealed allegations of sexual misconduct against Kevin Johnson (alleged inappropriate advances toward three young women involved in the St. HOPE program), and that St. HOPE board member and now Johnson's fiancé, D.C. schools Chancellor Michelle Rhee, handled "damage control." (It later came out that Rhee had reportedly visited Walpin to vouch for Johnson and to fish for information on the investigation, though she already knew of the many allegations of Johnson's misconduct and was actively engaged in attempting to put a lid on them.[22])

Among the allegations reported to Walpin's investigators was that Johnson had offered at least one of the three women money to keep quiet. An attorney—mentioned as Johnson's personal attorney—allegedly visited the girl and offered her $1,000 a month for as long as she remained at St. HOPE, which led investigators to "reasonable suspicions about potential hush money payments and witness tampering at a federally funded entity." Walpin included these allegations in his criminal referral to the U.S. Attorney's Office in Sacramento, which went nowhere. Not only did these cover-ups assist Kevin Johnson in his successful mayoral bid in November 2008, but in Sacramento receiving stimulus funds in 2009 despite major abuses of St. HOPE funds.[23]

The congressional report vindicated Walpin, strongly suggesting he was fired not because of any disorientation or confusion, but because of his whistle blowing on St. HOPE and Obama crony

Kevin Johnson. It suggested the White House had indeed "orchestrated an after-the-fact smear campaign to justify" Walpin's firing, adding, "The content of the referral tends to undermine any notion that the [inspector general's] investigation was driven by inappropriate motives on the part of Walpin. Rather it appears to have been driven by non-political, career investigators simply following the facts."[24]

Senator Grassley issued a statement on the report that read, in part, "The allegations uncovered by the inspector general are very serious and they deserve to be investigated, not swept under the rug. It seems a lot of people might have been interested in protecting the AmeriCorps program and the Mayor of Sacramento from an IG who was discovering some unpleasant facts. I'm not sure whether the IG was fired for political reasons. The evidence points in that direction, but since the White House is asserting privilege over its decision-making process, we can't be sure. The report details everything we were able to learn, so people can judge for themselves."[25]

"SERIOUS QUESTIONS ABOUT THE VERACITY OF YOUR TESTIMONY"

Shortly after the congressional report was released, the White House finally produced many of its withheld documents on the Walpin–St. HOPE affair. The *Washington Examiner*'s Byron York reported that the newly released documents support the Republican investigators' conclusion that the White House's version of its firing of Walpin was "a public story cobbled together *after* Walpin was fired, not before." In other words, Walpin wasn't fired because he was incompetent; he was fired because he was *too competent* in investigating misconduct involving Obama's friends and supporters. Walpin was apparently so persistent that the White House couldn't afford even to comply with the statutory notice period; it had to terminate Walpin on the spot and then smear his good name to cover its actions.

Earlier, White House counsel Norman Eisen had told House and Senate staffers that the administration had engaged in an "extensive review" of the complaints against Walpin before making its decision to terminate him. But the new report revealed Eisen had told Congress that "his investigation into the merits of removing Gerald Walpin involved contacting members of the Corporation for National and Community Service [CNCS] board to confirm the existence of a 'consensus' in favor of removal." But, according to York, Republican investigators discovered later that during this so-called "extensive review," the White House didn't even check with the board—so it couldn't have learned of any consensus supporting Walpin's termination.

Moreover, "no member of the CNCS board had any substantive input about whether the removal of Gerald Walpin was appropriate" other than major Democratic donor and Obama supporter Alan Solomont. The White House had called one other board member just prior to Walpin's firing: Stephen Goldsmith, who informed investigators the White House had already made its decision to axe Walpin and wanted Goldsmith's after-the-fact blessing.[26]

It gets worse. The newly released documents reveal the White House was hurrying to coordinate with board members an explanation for the firing that would be presented publicly. Within a day of Eisen's ultimatum to Walpin, board members had conferred by telephone. The following day, Ranit Schmelzer, a member of CNCS's press office, sent out talking points to all board members to use if any reporters called. Among the points: "Indicate that you support the president's decision to remove IG Walpin"; "If asked why he was removed, indicate that the president lost confidence in Mr. Walpin"; "If the reporter continues to press, say that you can't get into details on a personnel matter, but you understand there were some performance-based issues"; and avoid "getting into any specifics about IG Walpin's performance-based issues. The WH has stayed away from this and has counseled us to do the same."

Obviously, the White House's fingerprints were all over this. Scandalously, it wasn't until the next day that the White House actually asked the board members for their views on the matter. About a week after the firing, Solomont, apparently believing CNCS had weathered the storm, wrote an e-mail to board member Eric Tanenblatt saying, "I understand how much work you are doing to prevent and control damage from the IG matter. I want you to know how much I personally appreciate all your efforts."[27] This from the man Obama would nominate to be ambassador to Spain.

Another troubling matter for the administration arose as investigators pored through the recently released White House documents. Alan Solomont had earlier denied to investigators that he had met with First Lady Michelle Obama's chief of staff, Jackie Norris, about the Walpin case, but White House visitor logs show he met with her on June 9, the day before Walpin was fired, and two previous times as well. Solomont attempted to explain away his visit to Norris as a meeting on CNCS business, but when further pressed said he may have mentioned the Walpin matter in passing. Congressman Issa followed up with a letter to Solomont expressing his "serious questions about the veracity of your testimony." Grassley expressed similar concerns. In another bizarre twist, Solomont suddenly claimed he had previously disclosed his meetings with Norris. Issa wrote to Solomont, "This is simply false. The notes and recollections of multiple staff in the room at the time are clearly contrary to your recollection."[28]

Congressional investigators sought to interview Norris about his meetings with Solomont, but the White House counsel's office barred the interview. Issa wrote to Norris, "Our request to meet with you was denied by [CNCS] general counsel Frank Trinity. Mr Trinity told my staff that the White House counsel's office has advised him that they were not permitting the Corporation to make you available for an interview." Issa added, "The White House has averred that you had no role whatsoever in the president's decision to remove Mr. Walpin. In light of these representations, it is hard to understand a decision to prevent your testimony. If the information provided by the White House officials is true, it follows that no colorable claim of executive privilege should impede your cooperation with the committee."[29]

Three months later, new revelations threatened to blow the lid off this seemingly bottomless scandal. For months observers wondered why acting U.S. Attorney Lawrence Brown had so cavalierly dismissed Walpin's prosecutorial referral concerning Kevin Johnson. Brown not only declined to investigate, but virtually appointed himself Johnson's PR man, reporting his investigation results in such a way as to rehabilitate Johnson's reputation and thus his chances for election, and to enhance Sacramento's likelihood of receiving stimulus funds in the wake of the damning allegations against Johnson. Investigators later learned that while Brown had been actively running interference against Walpin's investigation of Johnson, he was also seeking a White House appointment as a permanent U.S. Attorney. In their supplemental report, Republican investigators for the Senate Finance Committee and the House Committee on Oversight and Government Reform said the contents of Brown's letter seeking a presidential appointment raised "new questions about his potential motivations. It would be reasonable for an already skeptical public to wonder whether Brown excluded Inspector General Walpin from negotiations and settled the St. HOPE matter with Johnson in order to curry favor with the White House because Brown wanted the president to appoint him U.S. Attorney."

Investigators also found troubling e-mails between Brown and Kevin Johnson's attorney, Matthew Jacobs, in which Jacobs recommended that Brown "should either (1) call out Walpin publicly, or (2) Tell him to take his case back home." After complaining about Walpin, Jacobs said, "WTF is wrong with this guy! First, he tried to effect [sic] the election; now he's messing around with the entire region's federal funding! Over this case?!" He told Brown he should "stand up and say this isn't right." Within minutes, according to

Byron York, Brown replied, "Message heard loud and clear, Matt. I am at a complete loss and do in fact plan to speak to Gerald." Brown was not appointed for the position, but now serves as a Sacramento Superior Court judge.

The Republican investigators' supplemental report concluded that the e-mails showed Brown "was actually parroting to CIGIE supposed grievances first presented to him by Kevin Johnson's attorney.... Together with his efforts to obtain a political appointment from the president, Brown's communications with Johnson's attorney contribute to the appearance that Walpin's removal was more about his vigorous pursuit of the St. HOPE matter than about any other legitimate, unrelated factors."[30]

Meanwhile, the *Washington Times* editors shined the spotlight on Walpin's investigation of AmeriCorps' teaching fellowship at the City University of New York (CUNY), which Walpin said had wasted "upwards of $80 million in taxpayer money." In the aforementioned e-mail from CNCS's Ranit Schmelzer providing talking points to board members, Schmelzer also briefly addressed the CUNY issue. He said, "If asked whether this was connected to Walpin's action in the CUNY case, say no. The decision was made before Walpin's reports on CUNY were issued."

But that assertion is false, the *Times'* editors pointed out. The timeline irrefutably contradicts the e-mail's claim. Walpin issued his draft report, which was critical of CUNY and the CNCS board, on April 2. CUNY responded on April 30, and the CNCS board on May 4. Walpin shared with Senate staffers on May 5 his concern that CNCS would "retaliate" against him for his report. On May 20 Walpin strongly criticized the board members in the first half of the meeting—before they contend he became "confused" and "disoriented" upon returning to the meeting room. The editors said it was highly suspicious that the e-mail would advise board members to stonewall about an issue that was completely ignored elsewhere in the e-mail. They wrote, "Defensiveness about one issue, and only one, when nobody has yet raised the issue, is often a telltale sign that there is something to hide. This is especially the case when the information provided is demonstrably false."[31]

"THIS NEEDLESS DISTRACTION"

Gerald Walpin was not the only government watchdog that got crossways with President Obama. Neil Barofsky, the special inspector general for the $700 billion TARP program, also ended up in a dispute with Obama's Treasury Department. According to the *Los Angeles Times*, the Treasury Department claimed Barofsky's role as "Sigtarp" was not completely independent from Treasury. There was a "dispute over certain Treasury documents" being withheld from Barofsky by Treasury, over what Senator Charles Grassley called a "specious claim of attorney–client privilege."

When he was appointed, Barofsky was praised for his credentials, being a former prosecutor who would rigorously protect the taxpayer's interest in the bailout funds. But it appears Treasury was withholding information from Barofksy, prompting him to write a memo defending the independence of his position and disputing that attorney–client privilege was a legitimate bar to information he was requesting from Treasury.[32] Grassley observed, "The grassroots is furious about the way TARP dollars have been used and what looks like a lack of accountability for this massive infusion of tax dollars. It's added injury to hear about the Treasury Department putting up hurdles to slow down the work of the watchdog who's supposed to track the money. One of the biggest lessons of the last year is that the public deserves more transparency and, in turn, accountability from New York and Washington."[33] Treasury officials said Sigtarp fell under their domain and sought an opinion from the Justice Department's Office of Legal Counsel.[34]

Eventually Treasury backed down. Barofsky, in a letter to Congress, reported that Treasury had withdrawn an earlier request to the Justice Department seeking a legal opinion on the degree of Sigtarp's independence. Barofksy said, "We view such withdrawal as

Treasury's acknowledgment that Sigtarp is an independent entity within Treasury, and that my office and I are not subject to the supervision of the secretary." He referred to the now-ended dispute as "this needless distraction." The episode led Congressman Issa to argue the incident reflected the "arrogance" of Treasury officials "who are wielding immense power over our economy." While Sigtarp was technically a part of the Treasury Department, there was little genuine legal question as to his access to Treasury documents. Congress, in establishing the office, set clear directives that gave him broad access and placed the burden on Treasury secretary Giethner to explain why he would refuse to follow any of Sigtarp's recommendations.

Secrecy, stonewalling, and spurious claims of executive privilege have become the hallmarks of the Obama administration. Notwithstanding his campaign vows to "restore" openness and transparency to the presidency, Obama has treated the office almost as his personal fiefdom, running roughshod over Congress and willfully ignoring vital checks on his authority.

Gerald Walpin's firing was just one of many such examples, but it has already set a dangerous precedent. Less than a month and a half after Obama fired Walpin, congressional Democrats proposed to give Obama the power to appoint inspectors general at five financial regulatory agencies, a move that could greatly compromise the independent oversight of portions of the federal bureaucracy. The *Washington Times* editors warned this move "would only serve to further politicize these positions": the Federal Reserve, Commodity Futures Trading Commission, National Credit Union Administration, Securities and Exchange Commission, and Pension Benefit Guaranty Corp. Supporters of the move argued, deceitfully, that the IGs' independence would not be undermined because they would not be investigating the president personally. But with

Obama's governmental powers growing every day, this was not the time to be reducing checks and balances against abuses.[35]

Furthermore, in June 2010 a federal judge dismissed Walpin's wrongful termination lawsuit—incredibly, the judge upheld the administration's bogus claim that Obama did not technically fire Walpin when Obama removed his authority and placed him on "administrative leave." As Byron York noted, the decision "means the president can remove future inspectors general immediately, without reason or notice to Congress, simply by placing an inspector general on immediate administrative leave.... The inspector general would be out of his office immediately, stripped of his authority, and the president could claim that he had not actually been fired, and thus the law had not been violated."[36]

In the end, although Obama made room in his administration for everyone from the former Communist Van Jones to the environmental extremist Steven Chu, he could not tolerate the presence of an aggressive watchdog of government malfeasance.

PART III

OFFENSES AGAINST AMERICA'S GENERAL WELFARE AND NATIONAL SECURITY

Chapter Twelve

TAXING AND SPENDING AMERICA INTO BANKRUPTCY

CRIMES AGAINST OUR POSTERITY

I t was ironic that during the very week that Obama was, once more, cynically urging a "bipartisan" effort to control our soaring deficits, a survey of economists revealed their belief that Obama's vaunted stimulus package had not contributed much toward an economic recovery. This "stimulus," which hemorrhaged borrowed money to prime the economy's pump, accomplished little more than political payoffs, expanding the public sector, and proving the government was still the king of colossal waste.

The quarterly survey by the National Association for Business Economics polled sixty-eight of its members who work in economic roles at private-sector firms. About 73 percent of them said employment at their companies was neither higher nor lower as a result of the stimulus act. Backing up their assessment were the hard facts that millions of jobs have been lost since the stimulus bill was passed, and that Obama himself had implicitly admitted its failure when he convened his "Jobs Summit" as a prelude to passing his $17.7 billion jobs bill.[1] The same week economic experts inside the Health and Human Services Department confessed that contrary to Obama's claim, ObamaCare would increase healthcare costs.[2]

As if an innocent bystander observing our exploding national debt, Obama piously warned against the deficits that threaten to erode America's standard of living as he addressed members of the "bipartisan" National Commission on Fiscal Responsibility and Reform. Later he would similarly show his limitless gall in presuming to give Germany's Chancellor Angela Merkel economic advice—that "Europe needed to try something big," implying his own "big" actions had restored America's economy.[3] Then, at the G-20 conference in Toronto in June 2010, when other nations were focusing on deficit reduction, Obama urged them to continue reckless deficit spending. Even the *Washington Post* recognized that Obama's remarks "tempered the Group of 20's headline achievement at the summit, a deficit-reduction target that had been pushed by Canadian Prime Minister Stephen Harper, the host of the meeting and a fiscal conservative."[4]

These remarks came from the same guy who refused to let TARP CEOs pay down their debts; who planned a systematic expansion of our national deficits and debt in order to "spread the wealth around" and shore up his reelection efforts; who wasted billions in the stimulus package and the auto bailouts; who was hell-bent on passing the bankrupting cap and trade bill and the financial overhaul debacle; and who rammed through Cash for Clunkers, the mortgage bailout bill, and ObamaCare. It was becoming cartoonish—in a tragic sort of way.

Obama is the guy who arranged for the U.S. to contribute billions of dollars to an international bailout of Greece over the objections of Congress at a time when we were undergoing the most severe debt crisis in our history. As critics noted, just as with Obama's various domestic bailout schemes, this would encourage other European countries in financial straits to request even larger bailouts from the United States. Calling the bailout "absurd," Newt Gingrich rightly asked, "Why should the American taxpayer put up 14 percent of the money, billions and billions of dollars, to bail out a Greek government... [that] has terrible work rules, has massive corruption, [and] has government employees rioting in the streets over the idea that they're going to lose anything? The Greeks are telling us that they don't want to take care of themselves but they don't mind us sending them more money. I think that's just fundamentally wrong."[5]

But when it comes to proposed bailouts, there is no satiating Democratic appetites. Democratic senator Bob Casey has introduced legislation to bail out troubled union pension funds to the tune of $165 billion—which would be just the beginning. Obama's manipulation of the Chrysler and GM restructurings to benefit the unions was apparently not enough payback for their tireless work in getting Democrats elected and promoting their agenda.

STIMULUS

Vowing to "jump start the economy," Obama unleashed on America his stimulus bill—The American Recovery and Reinvestment Act. He claimed it would cost $787 billion—on the heels of the $700 billion TARP bailout program. Even casual students of government knew it would cost more than promised. Less than a year later, the Congressional Budget Office upped its estimate to $862 billion, though some said that with interest the bill would cost $1.3 trillion. The greatest factor contributing to CBO's miscalculation was its assumption that unemployment would not exceed 9 percent. After all, Obama promised his stimulus would keep unemployment from surpassing 8 percent, but joblessness rose above 10 percent in October and thereafter hovered between 9 and 10 percent. With unemployment numbers dwarfing Obama's predictions, unemployment compensation costs soared far above CBO's estimates.[6]

Although the bill was pitched as a way to stimulate the economy and create jobs, it was actually a disgraceful boondoggle full of waste, pork, political payoffs, temporary green jobs, and other programs designed to further expand government. Obama and his Democratic allies stuffed years' worth of their legislative wish lists into this monstrous vehicle, exploiting the economic crisis to covertly enact legislation as sweeping as reversing the successful welfare reforms of the 1990s.

But even a committed Keynesian would be hard-pressed to describe the stimulus as primarily designed to stimulate. If the only way out of the economic crisis were to infuse nearly a trillion dollars into the economy, then why did Obama intentionally hold back such a great portion of the funds for expenditure in later years? Why did he recklessly waste so much of the money on programs and initiatives that couldn't conceivably have been expected to stimulate anything, other than liberal euphoria over long-awaited spending on their pet projects and Democratic reelection efforts?

In early February 2009, Republicans published a list of some of the wasteful items in the bill. Among the items:

- $2 billion for FutureGen, a near-zero emissions coal power plant in Illinois from which the Department of Energy pulled funding in 2009 after determining the project was inefficient.
- A $246 million tax break for Hollywood movie producers to buy motion picture film.
- $88 million for the Coast Guard to design a new polar icebreaker ship.
- $448 million for constructing the Department of Homeland Security headquarters and $248 million for the building's furniture.
- $600 million to buy hybrid vehicles for federal employees.

- $400 million for the Centers for Disease Control to screen and prevent STDs.
- $1.4 billion for rural waste disposal programs.
- $125 million for the Washington sewer system.
- $150 million for the Smithsonian museum facilities.
- $1 billion for the 2010 Census, which has a projected cost overrun of $3 billion.
- $75 million for "smoking cessation activities."
- $200 million for public computer centers at community colleges.
- $75 million for salaries of FBI employees.
- $25 million for tribal alcohol and substance abuse reduction.
- $500 million for flood reduction projects on the Mississippi River.
- $10 million to inspect canals in urban areas.
- $6 billion to turn federal buildings into "green buildings."
- $500 million for state and local fire stations.
- $650 million for wildland fire management on forest service lands.
- $1.2 billion for "youth activities," including youth summer job programs.
- $88 million for renovating the headquarters of the Public Health Service.
- $412 million for CDC buildings and property.
- $500 million for building and repairing National Institutes of Health facilities in Bethesda, Maryland.
- $160 million for "paid volunteers" at the Corporation for National and Community Service.
- $5.5 million for "energy efficiency initiatives" at the Department of Veterans Affairs National Cemetery Administration.
- $850 million for Amtrak.

- $100 million for reducing the hazard of lead-based paint.
- $75 million to construct a "security training" facility for State Department security officers (who can actually be trained at existing facilities of other agencies).
- $110 million to upgrade computer systems at the Farm Service Agency.
- $200 million to lease alternative energy vehicles for use on military installations.[7]

Is it any wonder this bill was immediately dubbed "Porkulus?" This list illustrates so much of what's wrong with socialism and expanding government into areas never contemplated by the framers of our Constitution. If you submitted this list to the people and itemized how much each taxpayer's share would be, few items would be approved.

There's also a lot of politically correct environmentalism and make-work projects that are obscenely wasteful, especially on the heels of the similarly extravagant TARP bill. This legislative act was unconscionable, considering that it was largely funded by exacerbating our growing debt problem. That the bill passed both chambers of Congress is a testament to how far Democrats will go if possessed, albeit temporarily, of virtually unchecked power.

The stimulus proved to be disorganized, out of control, and beyond the ability of government to account for, despite promises from Obama and Biden that they would vigilantly monitor the money.[8] The federal government's Recovery.org website, which is supposed to have tracked the expenditures, listed some $9.5 million in stimulus money as going to fourteen zip codes in Virginia that did not exist or are in other states, according to Old Dominion Watchdog.[9] New Mexico Watchdog discovered $27 million of federal money went to nonexistent zip codes in New Mexico.[10] In addition to these disgraceful developments, the *Atlanta Journal-Constitution* reported that the stimulus delivered some $2.2 billion in tuition grants to massage and beauty schools, online universities, and other for-profit colleges in Georgia and across the nation.[11]

As detailed in chapter three, the stimulus did not cause a jobs spurt, but an enormous job loss. A Bureau of Labor statistics chart shows, state by state, that through December 2009, 3,179,328 jobs were lost—while the administration claims 638,825 jobs were "created or saved." Veronique de Rugy, a senior research fellow at the Mercatus Center at George Mason University, notes this means that for every job "created or saved"—a concept she mocks as "a completely fictitious and unverifiable metric"—six jobs were lost as shown in this chart:

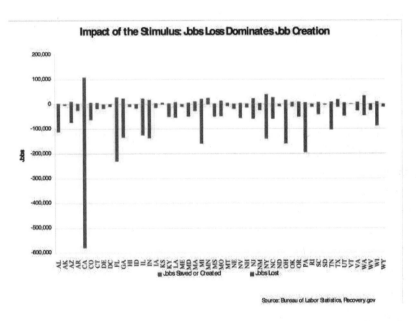

Of the few jobs that were actually created, most were in the public sector, contradicting another administration claim. De Rugy said data from *Stimulus Watch* revealed only 140,765 of the 638,825 jobs the administration claimed to have created or saved with stimulus funds were private sector jobs. To the extent the stimulus was

stimulating anything, it was government—the last thing we need.
Going from bad to worse, the Bureau of Labor Statistics reported
that since the stimulus bill was passed, the private sector had suffered a net loss of 2,610,000 employees, while the government had
only lost 46,000 employees. The number of private jobs lost compared to private jobs created is "far greater than 6." Dr Rugy concluded that since the CBO had recently admitted it was "impossible
to determine how many of the reported jobs would have existed"
without the stimulus, "it seems clear that for the sake of taxpayers
and for the sake of job creation, a second stimulus is absolutely the
wrong idea."[12] Yet such common sense didn't deter Obama and
Congress, which passed the second stimulus bill, offensively called
the "Jobs Bill," on March 17, 2010.[13]

Moreover, the pathetic results of Obama's stimulus did not prevent Vice President Joe Biden from declaring the stimulus an
"absolute success." Nor did it keep Obama from deceitfully boast-
ing in a speech in Wisconsin in June 2010 that without his stimulus the economy would have been much worse—an argument that
is at odds with the evidence and, at any rate, is impossible to con-
clusively prove. He also declared, "Every economist who's looked
at it has said that the [stimulus] did its job." That's quite an interesting claim in light of the Heritage Foundation's statement earlier
that month that "for objective observers the failure of President
Obama's $862 billion stimulus package has become increasingly
difficult to deny."[14]

EXPLODING DEFICITS AND NATIONAL DEBT

It appears that the only thing the stimulus bill created—other than
public sector jobs—was astronomical federal debt. Indeed, the ultimate scandal of the Obama administration—and this is a tough
call, given ObamaCare as well as Obama's virtual surrender in the
war on terror—is its exponential growth of the national debt to
unsustainable levels that put the nation on a path to bankruptcy.

One would have expected that after the extraordinary TARP expenditures, prudent politicians would have pulled the reins in for the sake of the nation's fiscal stability. But Obama did the opposite with his myriad indulgent initiatives, as listed above. He never intended to pull back government spending, but obviously planned on perpetuating the economic crisis and milking it to redistribute every dollar he could from certain citizens and companies to others. While mouthing phony bromides about fiscal stewardship, he is continuing to spend at a breakneck pace, with the apparent strategy to get us into such debt that our only way out will be to increase taxes, possibly even enacting a Value Added Tax (VAT), as noted in chapter three.

A VAT is especially insidious because it is invisible; it's incorporated in the price of goods and services, which makes it easier for government to raise the rates. Every European nation began promising a low VAT rate, but all have raised their rates to at least 15 percent—and some much higher for the ostensible purpose of balancing their budgets. The problem is that the VAT, along with other tax hikes, simply won't extricate us from our fiscal imbalance and unprecedented debt. These tax increases (as the Bush tax cuts expire and the new ObamaCare taxes kick in) would smother an already ailing economy, just as it needs to be unshackled.

The 2009 fiscal year deficit of $1.41 trillion—as compared with the 2008 fiscal year deficit of $454.8 billion—could be blamed largely on TARP and other items, and much of it occurred during President Bush's last year in office, albeit under a Democratic congressional majority. But Obama had no such excuses for his profligacy in FY2010. In February 2009 Obama presented a projected budget deficit of $1.258 trillion for FY2010, and a cumulative, ten-year deficit of $7.107 trillion for FY2010–2019. Just a year later, he had to revise those figures dramatically upward, offering a projected FY2010 deficit of $1.56 trillion, some $300 billion higher. His revised projected cumulative deficit for fiscal years 2010–2019 was $9.086 trillion, almost $2 trillion higher, as shown on the Heritage Chart on the right.

Obama unveiled his FY2011 budget in February 2010, with his Office of Management and Budget (OMB) projecting the cumulative deficit for FY2011–2020 at $8.53 trillion. The CBO projected it would be $9.75 trillion—almost $1.2 trillion higher. This difference in calculation, according to Brian Riedl, "represents an additional debt of $10,000 per household above and beyond the federal debt they are already carrying."[15]

President Proposes $2 Trillion More in 2010–2019 Deficits Than Last Year

Proposed Budget Deficits, in Billions, by Fiscal Year

	Last Year's Budget Proposal	This Year's Budget Proposal
2010	–$1,258	–$1,556
2011	–$929	–$1,267
2012	–$557	–$829
2013	–$512	–$727
2014	–$536	–$706
2015	–$528	–$752
2016	–$645	–$778
2017	–$675	–$778
2018	–$688	–$785
2019	–$779	–$908
Total	–$7,107	–$9,086

Source: Table S–1 of President Obama's FY 2010 and FY 2011 budgets.

The *Washington Times* reported that the federal public debt was $6.3 trillion when Obama took office, amounting to $56,000 per household. By mid-2010 it totaled $8.2 trillion ($72,000 per household) and is headed toward $20.3 trillion by 2020 (more than $170,000 per household and more than triple the debt of $6.3 trillion when Obama took office). According to the CBO, this would increase the national debt to 90 percent of the nation's total economic output by 2020, compared to 40 percent of GDP at the close of fiscal year 2008,[16] as illustrated on the chart on the opposite page.

Some experts believe the forecast is much worse: that if we don't repeal the Obama tax and regulatory policies and reform entitlements substantially we'll end up with a ruinous debt-to-GDP ratio of 104 percent by 2019.[17]

At any rate, this projected tripling of the national debt, though based on Obama's fiscal agenda, wouldn't finally occur until 2020, four years after the end of Obama's second term, should he be re-elected. But Riedl looks at the projections for Obama's hypothetical two terms and finds that just in his eight years, Obama would

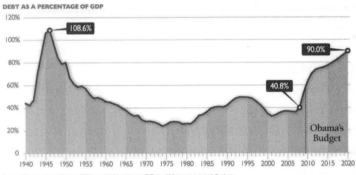

Obama's Budget Would Send Federal Debt to Levels Not Seen Since World War II

In 2008, publicly held debt as a percentage of the economy (GDP) was 40.8 percent, nearly five points below the post-war average. Under President Obama's budget, this figure would more than double to 90 percent by 2020. Continued structural debt poses serious economic risks.

DEBT AS A PERCENTAGE OF GDP

Source: Congressional Budget Office and White House Office of Management and Budget.

more than double the national debt. Riedl notes Obama "harshly criticized" Bush for the $3.3 trillion in budget deficits he accumulated in his eight years in office, but the conservative projected deficits for Obama's eight years total $7.6 trillion (averaging almost $1 trillion per year), which is almost two and a half times Bush's cumulative total and easily more than the total debt to date of $6.3 trillion when Obama took office.[18] And this is without even considering the recent upward revisions to ObamaCare, his cap and tax dream, or a host of other expensive proposals he seeks to enact.

Obama said he wouldn't be able to bring the deficit down "overnight," but claimed he'd be well on his way to reductions once the recovery took hold. But Heritage's Conn Carroll observed, "Not only does President Obama's budget fail to reduce deficits 'overnight,'" it "actually moves them in the opposite direction." Obama's budget would "permanently expand the federal government by nearly 3 percent of GDP *over pre-recession levels*...and leave permanent deficits that top $1 trillion in as late as 2020."[19]

While Obama glibly dismisses his bankrupting deficits as being caused by (and no greater than) those generated by President George W. Bush, nothing could be more misleading. We've already noted Congressman Jeb Hensarling's point that Democrats took control of Congress in 2006 and that CBO numbers show that the Democrats' and Obama's budgets dwarf those of the Republican-controlled congresses of the preceding twelve years. And simply comparing the Bush deficits to the Obama deficits presents a similar picture. Bush's budgets averaged some $300 billion[20]—and it wasn't until his last year in office, when the economic downturn and financial crisis hit hard and sparked the TARP program, that he (and Congress) produced the type of outrageous deficit Obama is routinely generating as far as the eye can see. This Heritage Chart brings this into clear perspective:

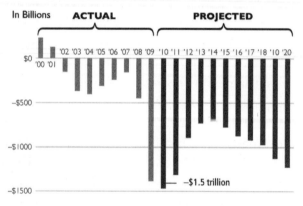

Obama Deficits Will Exceed Previous Deficits

Sources: Congressional Budget Office and Office of Management and Budget.

Obama whines about inheriting a $1.3 trillion deficit "when I walked in the door" and forever uses that as an excuse to crank up spending even further. But as Dick Morris points out, Bush's projected deficit for FY2008 was about $485 billion and grew another $100 billion by the start of the fiscal crisis to about $600 billion. TARP raised it $700 billion to around $1.3 trillion, though revised figures showed the deficit ended up being around $1.41 trillion, as noted. But as Morris correctly observes, most of the TARP money was paid back, so in reality the Bush deficit for that year was much lower, maybe $800 billion.[21]

Regardless, it's absurd to use the $1.3 trillion or $1.41 trillion figure as a baseline, since it included the extraordinary TARP bailout monies, which would hopefully be a one-time occurrence. As Brian Riedl said, "President Obama's pledge to halve the budget deficit by 2013 is hardly ambitious." After quadrupling the deficit in 2009, to cut it in half "would still leave deficits twice as high as under President Bush." Furthermore, three *expected* developments—"the end of the recession, withdrawal of troops from Iraq, and phase-out of temporary stimulus spending—would halve the budget deficit by 2013." But Obama's deficits will more than double, possibly triple Bush's "even after the economy recovers and the troops return home from Iraq." Obama deceitfully used that FY2009 deficit as a baseline when he made the preposterous pledge to cut the deficit in half, a pledge that he still wouldn't be able to fulfill and wouldn't even really try to—because, as mentioned above, his projected annual deficits are $1 trillion for the foreseeable future.

And Obama's budget hits just keep coming. The CBO reported that for just the first five months of FY 2010, the budget deficit was already $655 billion—$65 billion greater than the deficit at that point in the previous budget year, which was horrible enough. Even though bailout spending had decreased, the deficit continued to increase because of lower tax receipts, increased spending on unemployment benefits, interest on the public debt, and increased spending on other programs. The April deficit was $82.7 billion—the largest ever April deficit—compared to last April's deficit of $20 billion.[22]

Riedl also notes before the recession started, annual federal spending totaled $24,000 per household, but under Obama's projected budgets that figure would reach $36,000 per household by 2020—"an inflation-adjusted $12,000 per household expansion of government." The chart on the following page illustrates these increases.

In the *American Thinker*, Steve McCann argued there is a "very high probability" that we'll see a repeat of the financial meltdown that preceded the TARP bailouts in 2008. The current administration, however, has engulfed us in such debt that we won't have a

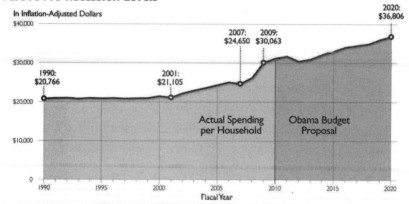

President Obama Would Push Spending $12,000 Per Household Above Pre-Recession Levels

In Inflation-Adjusted Dollars

2020: $36,806

2007: $24,650   2009: $30,063

1990: $20,766

2001: $21,105

Actual Spending per Household

Obama Budget Proposal

Fiscal Year

Source: Office of Management and Budget, Historical Tables, Budget of the United States Government, Fiscal Year 2011 (Washington, D.C.: U.S. Government Printing Office, 2010), p. 22, Table 1.1, and U.S. Office of Management and Budget, Budget of the United States Government, Fiscal Year 2011 (Washington, D.C.: U.S. Government Printing Office, 2010), pp. 146, Table S-1. Spending totals are adjusted to include the House-passed cap-and-trade bill, which President Obama endorsed yet excluded from his budget tables. All figures are then adjusted for inflation and the number of households.

Chart 1 • B 2382 🅷 heritage.org

fallback position. Meanwhile, instead of shoring up our own financial stability to avoid Greece's fate, we are bailing Greece out with money we don't have and pursuing more of the reckless policies that got us into this mess in the first place. McCann remarked, "The Obama administration and its fellow travelers in Congress appear to care little for the long-term survival of this country. They are in the process of squandering the nation's wealth and thus its well-being, in their headlong determination to 'fundamentally change the country.'" [23]

If this pattern continues and our debt-to-GDP ratio does soar into the range of 90 to 104 percent or more by 2019 or 2020, the United States would "become the next Greece," but "unlike Greece, will not have the European Union or the IMF to turn to.... Can we expect our traditional allies, who will find themselves in a similar situation, to come to our aid? As to a dramatic economic downturn, the traditional tools used to come through a recession or depression will not be available."[24] Yet Obama continues to fiddle as he burns our dollars.

As Obama announced his record budget for FY2011 of $3.83 trillion, he declared the federal government could not "continue to spend as if deficits don't have consequences" and that it was unacceptable to act "as if the hard-earned tax dollars of the American people can be treated like Monopoly money."[25] As surreal as those statements were, his excuses were even worse. He blamed the deficit on President Bush, previous Congresses, and on the unavoidable actions his administration had supposedly taken to prevent an economic collapse. He specifically blamed Bush and previous Congresses for creating a new drug program, implementing "tax cuts for the wealthy, and funding two wars."[26]

Obama's Treasury secretary, Timothy Geithner, took the same tack when appearing before Congress—blaming Bush and having no explanation for why the administration was multiplying the spending of its predecessor. Republican congressman Paul Ryan told Geithner that all economists, including those of the administration, say "that the medium and long-run budget deficits have to get below 3% of GDP, yet this budget plan that you're bringing to us doesn't even get close to it." Ryan was saying the administration knew we couldn't afford these budgets but was presenting them anyway, without proposing meaningful reductions. Instead, it was passing off the problem to a "partisan commission, with a 2 to 1 ratio of Democrats and Republicans, that will give us a report after the election."

Geithner responded, á la Obama, by blaming Bush and accepting no responsibility even for future budgets, saying, "We're going to solve our part of the mess we inherited." Ryan shot back, "Why don't you [solve this problem] in your Budget? You guys run the government, if you are going to solve our fiscal situation, why don't you do that? Why don't you give us a budget that actually gets the deficits to a sustainable level?" Giethner pathetically repeated his mantra: "Congressman, we are proposing a budget that takes the huge mess we inherited and cuts the deficit dramatically." But Ryan had the last word. "You can blame Bush only so long," he said. "You obviously inherited a tough situation, [but] you are making it worse by your own admission."[27]

Ryan was exactly right. Obama is tied to a socialist ideology and Keynesian economic theory compelling him to continue outrageous spending in order to transfer wealth from the "rich" to the "poor" regardless of the devastating debt he accumulates. But Keynesian theory doesn't work. The money government spends, to reiterate Brian Reidl's point, "doesn't fall from the sky. The only way Congress can inject spending into the economy is by first taxing or borrowing it out of the economy. No new demand is created; it's a zero-sum transfer of existing demand."[28] So increasing government demand decreases private sector demand.

ENTITLEMENTS

Democrats once acknowledged our entitlements would eventually bankrupt the nation, but when President Bush tried to reform Social Security, they engaged in scaremongering to downplay any problems and successfully shut down reform efforts. The problem is much more urgent now with our economic downturn and rising debt. The first chart on the opposite page shows how dire the situation is. Congressman Paul Ryan has proposed substantial entitlement reform, as shown in the second chart. This could go a long way toward restoring the nation's fiscal solvency, though it is unlikely to gain traction as long as Democrats control the Senate and the White House.

ALMOST $3 TRILLION IN ADDITIONAL TAXES

As noted in chapter three, Obama flagrantly broke his no new taxes pledge on families making less than $250,000 a year. But his real tax punishment is reserved for those making $250,000 or more. He will raise the top two income tax brackets from 33 percent to 36 percent and from 35 percent to 39.6 percent, respectively. He'll raise capital

National Debt Set to Skyrocket

In the past, wars and the Great Depression contributed to rapid but temporary increases in the national debt. Over the next few decades, runaway spending on Social Security, Medicare, and Medicaid will drive the debt to unsustainable levels.

DEBT AS A PERCENTAGE OF GDP

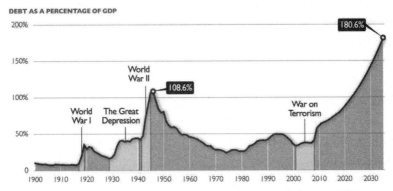

Source: Heritage Foundation compilations of data from U.S. Department of the Treasury, Institute for the Measurement of Worth (Alternative Fiscal Scenario), Congressional Budget Office, and White House Office of Management and Budget.

Entitlement Reform Would Eliminate Long-Term Deficits

In January 2010, Representative Paul Ryan (R–WI) re-introduced the Roadmap for America's Future, legislation that would improve America's long-term budget situation by reforming entitlements. Compared to the current trajectory, the bill would eliminate long-term deficits.

SURPLUS/DEFICIT AS A PERCENTAGE OF GDP

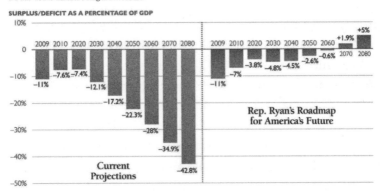

Source: Congressional Budget Office.

gains and dividends tax rates from 15 percent to 20 percent. He'll phase out personal exemptions and limit itemized deductions. He'll reduce the value of tax deductions by about one-fourth.

Collectively, these measures will amount to a $1 trillion tax increase on just 3.2 million tax filers, which is an average of $300,000 per filer over ten years on those who already pay a disproportionate share of the taxes, notwithstanding Obama's demagogic misrepresentations to the contrary. But there's more: businesses and wealthy individuals would pay most of the proposed $743 billion in new taxes imposed by ObamaCare; Obama will institute some $468 billion in new taxes on America's businesses;[29] and cap and tax, if implemented, could cost $843 billion in additional taxes. The following Heritage Chart itemizes the specifics:

The President's $2.9 Trillion Tax Increase

Proposal	Ten-Year Revenue Impact (in Billions)
Cap-and-trade energy tax*	$843
Health reform tax	$743
Tax increase for upper-income families and small businesses	$968
Raise income tax rates for upper-income taxpayers	$361
Raise capital gains and dividends rates for upper-income taxpayers	$105
Reinstate the personal exemption phaseout and limitation on itemized deductions for upper-income taxpayers	$208
Limit itemized tax deductions to 28% value for upper-income taxpayers	$291
Tax Increases for businesses	$469
Reform U.S. international tax system	$122
Bank tax	$90
Other business, financial and energy tax increases	$256
Various tax cuts for families and businesses	–$172
New stimulus tax cuts	–$61
Extensions of expiring tax cuts	–$47
Other proposals	$111
Total Tax Increase	**$2,853**

* Figures represent the cost of House-passed bill, which President Obama endorsed yet excluded from his budget tables.

Note: Policies are net of outlay effects of proposals.

Source: Office of Management and Budget, *Budget of the United States Government, Fiscal Year 2011* (Washington, D.C.: U.S. Government Printing Office, 2010), pp. 146–179, Table S-8.

As Brian Riedl observes, Obama might plausibly argue his $3 trillion in new taxes were necessary to balance the budget. But even if you assume no economic slowdown as a result of these taxes, his numbers don't add up because he is planning on at least $1.6 trillion in new spending for healthcare, cap and trade, another stimulus bill, and additional education entitlements. Riedl concludes, "Simply put, surging spending is driving the budget deficits."[30]

SMOTHERING SMALL BUSINESSES

The "soak the rich" strategy, though appealing to Obama's fellow class warriors, has a proven track record of failure because it depresses the number of high-income producers—these are people, often small business owners, who benefit the economy by creating jobs. Tax economist Curtis Dubay of the Heritage Foundation testified before the House Committee on Small Business, warning that many small businesses are now struggling to survive in this strained economy. Punitive new taxes, he argued, will impede any recovery, while reducing taxes, lifting regulations, and reducing government spending would re-energize small businesses and benefit the overall economy.

But Obama plans on doing the opposite by raising the two top income tax rates. Dubay says it is a myth that only a small percentage of small businesses are affected by such a move. The "number of businesses that pay top rates," he said, "is economically meaningless because so many small businesses represent the part-time efforts of their owners." While 8 percent of small businesses pay the highest two tax rates, those businesses earn 72 percent of all small business income and pay 82 percent of all income taxes paid by small businesses. And those small businesses "employ most workers hired by small businesses."

Furthermore, "It is these businesses that the economy needs to create new jobs and ramp up economic growth after the severe recession. Higher taxes would drain the businesses of cash flow, the lifeblood of any business, and would diminish the incentives to grow and add other workers. Raising rates on these successful businesses would damage the economy at any time, but doing so now when the unemployment rate is starkly elevated and the recovery just underway is stunningly foolish." Dubay also says the resurrection of the death tax will be another major drag on small businesses, as it "will destroy jobs, and lower wages while raising little revenue."[31]

OBAMA'S FORECLOSURE PREVENTION PLAN

The day after Obama signed the stimulus bill, the indefatigable spender announced his $75 billion plan ostensibly to prevent nationwide mortgage foreclosures, a situation he described as a "crisis unlike we've ever known." As with ObamaCare, he billed it as an effort to bring the economy out of recession, but it was actually—like ObamaCare—another enormous wealth redistribution scheme. Declaring another urgent crisis, he proclaimed, "If we act boldly and swiftly to arrest this downward spiral, then every American will benefit." Promises, promises.

The plan was to draw $50 billion from existing bailout money and $25 billion from government-backed entities such as Fannie Mae and Freddie Mac. It directed Fannie and Freddie to automatically approve refinancing at current rates, which was expected to give 4 to 5 million people an immediate reduction in their mortgage payments, according to an administration official. At no time did anyone in the administration explain on what law or constitutional provision they based their authority for such a sweeping move. Nor did they explain how they could force contracting parties to alter the terms of their existing contracts. They just issued the edict. Period. Obama promised the plan would "give millions of families resigned to financial ruin a chance to rebuild." He said it would reward those who played by the rules. The ultimate goal was to save 7 to 9 million mortgages.[32]

One of the primary causes of the financial meltdown in the first place was the government's mania for incentivizing and pressuring lenders to make uncreditworthy loans. But Obama, instead of belt-tightening, applied a little hair of the dog, and the housing industry got drunk all over again. In the end, Obama's extravagant plan didn't quite turn out as he'd predicted. The *New York Times* reported in January 2010 that the plan had "been widely pronounced a disappointment, and some economists and real estate experts now contend it has done more harm than good."[33] The program was believed to have raised false hopes among people that they could keep homes they still couldn't afford, causing them to waste payments on inevitably failed mortgages they could have used to move into cheaper homes or apartments. Many borrowers were surprised to find that participating in the program had damaged their credit ratings.

Despite the manifest failure of the program, Obama's tone-deaf Treasury Department insisted the program was on track and "meeting its intended goal of providing immediate relief to homeowners across the country." It was a crass denial of responsibility for egregious recklessness that not only further damaged the nation's fiscal condition, but harmed the very homeowners it was designed to help—just more liberalism 101. To get an idea of just how miserably the program failed, by mid-December 2009, some 759,000 homeowners had received loan modifications on a trial basis that lasted 3 to 5 months. But only 31,000 received permanent modifications. The administration maintained the temporary users were benefitting, but mortgage experts and lawyers said trial participants often ended up worse off.[34]

And the bad news didn't stop there. In June 2010, it was reported that more than a third of the 1.24 million borrowers who enrolled in the mortgage bailout program had already dropped out. One major reason for this is that the Obama administration pressured banks to sign up borrowers without insisting first on proof of their income and ability to repay.[35] That month CNN Money also reported that "between 65% and 75% of loans that are modified through [Obama's] Home Affordable Modification Program but not backed by the federal government are likely to go bad, according to a report released by Fitch Ratings, a N.Y.-based credit-rating agency."[36]

CAP AND TRADE

Global warming alarmists in the administration and Congress tried to foist on the nation another boondoggle called the American Clean Energy and Security Act of 2009, a.k.a. the "Waxman-Markey bill," the "cap and trade bill," or "cap and tax." This bill, with its Draconian provisions, was based on the increasingly discredited view that man-made global warming will produce catastrophic, even apocalyptic consequences. But accepting the premise for purposes of argument, the salient questions are whether the bill would effect significant improvements and, even assuming it would, whether it would be worth the enormous costs it would generate. The inescapable fact is that the bill would involve colossal de facto tax increases (as documented in chapter three) and other prohibitive expenses while producing negligible results, at best.

Climate scientist Chip Knappenberger of New Hope Environmental Services has calculated that Waxman-Markey would reduce the earth's temperature by just 0.1 to 0.2 degree Celsius by 2100. Ben Lieberman, Senior Policy Analyst for Energy and the Environment at the Heritage Foundation confirms he has seen no "decent refutation of the assertion that the temperature impact (of the bill) would be inconsequential."

But the negative impact of the bill would not be inconsequential—it would be devastating. It would cause estimated *net* "job losses averaging 1,145,000 at any given time from 2012-2030." Some of the jobs would be lost completely and others outsourced to China and India, two nations that have made it quite clear they will not sabotage their own economic growth as we're proposing to do to ourselves with this bill. Projecting the bill would cause a loss in GDP of $9.4 trillion by 2035, Lieberman predicted it would increase each family of four's share of the national debt by 26 percent, or $115,000, and this is irrespective of the other bankrupting programs of bailouts, stimulus, and ObamaCare.[37] Even the liberal Brookings Institution projects the bill would reduce GDP by 1.8 percent by 2035 and 2.5 percent by 2050.

The recklessness of the bill is truly staggering. As Heritage's Foundry blog said, "Economists from liberal think tanks and industry associations agree that Waxman-Markey will reduce income by hundreds of billions of dollars per year." Yet Obama liberals nevertheless tout their coveted transition to a green economy as if it were actually going to be a boon to economic growth. Lieberman said, "If truth-in-advertising laws applied to politics . . . you'd have to replace the word 'clean' with 'costlier'" in the phrase "clean energy economy," and that is why "this agenda is actually very bad news for jobs and the economy."[38]

If all this weren't bad enough, the American Issues Project notes that Section 204 of the bill, called the "Building Energy Performance

Labeling Program," gives the federal government unprecedented authority over our homes. It would mandate that new homes be 30 percent more energy-efficient than under current building codes—starting the very day the bill is signed into law—and the requirement jumps to 50 percent by 2014 and continues to rise until 2030. The bill would also cover existing properties by requiring states to assess their efficiency ratings and make the results public. The ratings could lead to a number of circumstances that would allow the state to inspect a property, such as with planned renovations. Another enormously wasteful provision in the bill sets up a fund that would reward homeowners for making their properties more environmentally friendly—up to $12,200.

Also tucked into Waxman-Markey is another Obama standby: a major redistributionist scheme. The Foundry blog reported Obama is counting on $650 billion in revenues for selling carbon permits (an energy tax by another name) and only $150 billion of that will be assigned to alternate energy production. The rest will be transferred to people "who don't pay income taxes."[39] This isn't as much about the environment as it is about socialism.

And all this for what? As Lieberman contends, "Virtually everything one hears about global warming that sounds terrifying is not true, and what is true is not particularly terrifying. The risks of global warming are outweighed by the risks of ill-advised global warming policy like Waxman-Markey.... The bill would have a trivial impact on future concentrations of greenhouse gases (and)...it only binds the U.S., and trends in the rest of the world clearly show that emissions are rising." It is "free markets," argues Lieberman, "that provide us with the best way forward."[40]

Just as with ObamaCare, Waxman-Markey was so problematic, even for some Democrats, that some holdouts had to be bribed with taxpayer goodies to support it—for example, Ohio Democratic congresswoman Marcy Kaptur was offered a new federal power authority, according to the *Washington Times*, "stocked with up to $3.5 billion in taxpayer money available for lending to renewable energy and economic development projects in Ohio and other Midwestern states." Apparently unable to conjure enough of these bribes, however, the administration watched Waxman-Markey bog down in Congress.

But liberals won't give up easily on such a transformative program. In May 2010, senators John Kerry and Joe Lieberman proposed a new version of cap and tax, The American Power Act (APA). They initially had the support of Republican senator Lindsey Graham, who thankfully retreated from his folly.

According to climate scientist Chip Knappenberger, the new bill, like its predecessors, "will have no meaningful impact on the future course of global warming." The APA has "identical" long-term benchmarks to the Waxman-Markey bill, and while the APA relaxes Waxman-Markey's near-term reduction target slightly from 20 percent to 17 percent below 2005 emissions levels by 2020, both bills include targets of 42 percent below by 2030 and 83 percent by 2050. Moreover, like Waxman-Markey, the "global temperature 'savings' of the Kerry-Lieberman bill is astoundingly small—$0.043°C$ ($0.077°F$) by 2050 and $0.111°C$ ($0.200°F$) by 2100. In other words, by century's end, reducing U.S. greenhouse gas emissions by 83% will only result in global temperatures being one-fifth of one degree Fahrenheit less than they would otherwise be"—a "scientifically meaningless reduction."[41]

Similarly, the Cato Institute's Patrick Michaels argues the APA "mandates the impossible, *will not* produce any meaningful reduction of planetary warming, and it *will* subsidize just about every form of power that is too inefficient to compete today." The bill will allow the average American the same carbon dioxide emissions enjoyed by "the average citizen back in 1867, a mere 39 years from today." The bill's sponsors, he says, have "no idea how to accomplish" their goals. "Instead, they wave their magic wands for noncompetitive technologies like carbon capture and sequestration (clean coal), solar energy and windmills, and ethanol among many others." Ultimately, Michaels says, the bill is "yet another scheme to make carbon-based energy so expensive that you won't use it."[42]

Now that's something our coal industry-destroying president can support—and indeed, he is hyping the bill with the same propaganda flourish he's employed for the rest of his disastrous agenda. Michaels presents two charts, one using his projections for APA climate impact by 2050 and the other by 2100. Each illustrates three different scenarios: the first assumes the APA or its equivalent is not enacted ("business as usual"), the second that it's passed only in the U.S., and the third, that it's passed in "Kyoto countries." Michaels concludes, "As you can plainly see, APA does nothing, even if all the Kyoto-signatories meet its impossible mandates."

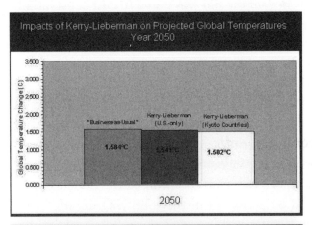

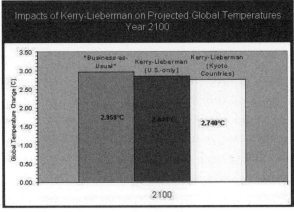

OBAMACARE

Obama promised he would bend the cost curve down with his healthcare reform plan. He promised he would "not sign a plan that adds one dime to our deficits—either now or in the future." Even as he signed ObamaCare in March 2010, he declared it would "lower costs for families and for businesses and for the federal government."

We've already detailed in chapter six the gimmicks and deceits the administration used to secure a favorable, but ultimately fraudulent, CBO scoring for the bill. And lo and behold, we learned a month after the bill was passed that the CBO said the bill would cost an additional $115 billion due to discretionary spending that wasn't counted in the initial scoring. Plus, a study inside his administration showed the bill was going to cost substantially more. The Centers for Medicare & Medicaid Services (CMS) issued a report finding that ObamaCare would not only fail to reduce the deficit, but the bill would actually raise spending by about 1 percent and cause healthcare costs to rise $311 billion over the next decade— and that's without even factoring in the CBO's $115 billion discretionary spending revelation or the other gimmicks and distortions in the administration's accounting.

Another study following the bill's passage estimated ObamaCare will add more than $500 billion to the deficit over the next ten years and $1.5 trillion in the following decade.[43] And, as far as could be determined, none of these follow-up studies were even considering an analysis by the Center for Studying Health System Change, which found another flagrant underestimation of costs: ObamaCare doesn't allocate nearly enough money to cover the estimated 5.6 to 7 million Americans with pre-existing medical conditions who will qualify for temporary high-risk insurance pools. According to MoneyNews.com, "The gap will force policymakers to freeze enrollment in the new pools, limit access and benefits, or increase premiums."[44]

The CMS report also indicated more than 7 million seniors could lose their current Medicare coverage and as many as 15 percent of hospitals, nursing facilities, and home health agencies could be forced out of the Medicare system. Further, the funds derived from the new 3.8 percent Medicare tax (Obama's tax on unearned income) will not be paid into the Medicare trust funds. The report might as well have directly described this provision as fraudulent advertising. It said, "Despite the title of this tax, this provision is unrelated to Medicare; in particular the revenues generated by the tax on unearned income are not allocated to the Medicare trust funds."[45] Instructively, Obama dispatched his hit-squad staff to attack CMS chief actuary Richard Foster and his findings. Both Nancy-Ann DeParle, director of the White House Office of Health Reform, and White House communications director Dan Pfeiffer criticized Foster's analysis on the White House website, but Foster stood by his work.[46]

Following passage of the bill, dozens of companies have reported to the Securities and Exchange Commission—more than just the few that Henry Waxman tried to intimidate—the losses they expect to incur from ObamaCare. Companies that offer drug benefits to their retiring employees will be taxed on the federal subsidies they receive for those retirees. The U.S. Chamber of Commerce has projected that some forty large companies will sustain losses totaling $3.4 billion.[47]

Furthermore, about a month after the bill was signed into law, Senate Democrats debated in the health committee a bill that would confer on states the power to reject premium increases that state regulators deemed to be "unreasonable." This could not be included in the actual ObamaCare bill due to procedural rules. The *Wall Street Journal* editors opined that the reason for this new proposal is that "Democrats are petrified they'll get the blame they deserve when insurance costs inevitably spike" under ObamaCare. "So the purpose of this latest Senate bill is to have a pre-emptive political response on hand. . . . As Democrats are showing by trying to pass a *new* insurance bill, they want all U.S. health care to function like price-controlled Medicare."[48]

But the real shocker was that the administration had this information more than a week before Congress voted on the bill, at a time when Obama and his congressional Democrats were still maintaining what they knew to be false: that their bill would not increase the deficit. The economic report was submitted to HHS secretary Kathleen Sebelius, and she sat on it until after the House vote. Inside sources said that Sebelius's staff refused to review the document beforehand, saying they didn't want to influence the vote. But as the source correctly observed, that's the entire "point of having a review like this." Obama was not going to let anything get in the way of this bill, not least the facts concerning costs.

The analysis was performed by Medicare's Office of the Actuary, a non-political office. An HHS staffer said, "We know a copy was sent to the White House via their legislative affairs staff and there were a number of meetings here almost right after the analysis was submitted to the secretary's office. Everyone went into lockdown, and people here were too scared to go public with the report."[49] So despite knowing full well he was lying through his teeth, Obama declared, as he was signing the bill, that it would "lower costs for families and for businesses and for the federal government."

This is the way the Obama government operates, and this is the kind of fear they strike in civil servants to intimidate them from doing the right thing. Sadly, this was Obama's behavioral pattern throughout the ObamaCare debate. In the beginning, he set up false premises to establish a false need for his particular fix, he distorted the facts all the way through the process, he badgered, bullied, and demonized his opponents, he refused to budge or compromise, and he blamed his opponents for the very tactics he was employing.

Universal healthcare was a crown jewel for Democrats and, in their minds, both a historical jinx and an avenue to political hegemony. In their penchant for misreading and revising history, they have assumed their failure to pass HillaryCare was the primary reason for their loss of Congress in 1994—much more than the

Republicans' Contract with America. In part they were right: HillaryCare did have a lot to do with their thrashing, but not in the way they thought. The lesson the liberals took away from that experience was that if they had succeeded in passing this socialists' dream they would have ushered in a new era of Democratic dominance, if for no other reason than it would have created a major entitlement on which more and more voters had to depend on Democrats to sustain.

Today's Obama liberals weren't about to repeat those mistakes. But liberals, as usual, misread the reality. Voters, whom Democrats characteristically underestimate, *did* understand socialized medicine, and they rejected it, as well as the high-handed and secretive manner by which the Clintons attempted to shove it through—with the same arrogance Obama later evinced.

Sure, Obama succeeded in passing his bill, but it was not because he correctly read the tea leaves. Americans flat out rejected socialized medicine every bit as much as they did in the 1990s, but he was able to hang on to the congressional majority Democrats won in November 2008 long enough to shove the bill through Congress via legislative trickery. Fittingly, Obama's despicable abuse of power in this process played a great part in the Democrats' electoral smackdown of November 2010.

Already state legislators representing half the nation have introduced bills to exempt their residents from the dysfunctions of ObamaCare. Idaho, Utah, and Virginia have passed laws, while Missouri residents approved a referendum to nullify the provision mandating participation in the healthcare system. As the *Washington Times* editors wrote, "It is a testament to the health of our democracy that so many states are fighting back."[50] In addition, attorneys general from twenty-six states as well as the National Federation of Independent Business are challenging the law, arguing that it's unconstitutional for the federal government to force citizens, under penalty of law, to obtain insurance coverage.[51]

EXORBITANT COSTS AND QUALITY OF CARE

One of Obama's central premises in demanding universal health-care was his oft-repeated statement that Americans spend more on healthcare (one and a half times more per person) than citizens of any other country, "but we aren't any healthier for it." His corol-lary statement drips with bitterness toward this country: "We are the only democracy—the only advanced democracy on Earth—the only wealthy nation—that allows such hardships for millions of its people." Do you get that? America is immoral for *allowing* these *hardships*. Almost everything in his two statements is wrong.

While America does spend more on healthcare than any other nation, that's not necessarily a bad thing. We get what we pay for, and we get the best. Of course, there are exorbitant costs in many cases, but as we've demonstrated, these will only increase further under ObamaCare. One major reason medical costs have risen dra-matically in recent decades is that the introduction of employer-pro-vided insurance interfered with market forces. When Americans didn't have to pay out of pocket for their medical care, the costs became invisible to them and demand soared, while the normal functioning of price was taken out of the equation. Further inter-fering with the operation of the market, obviously, was the advent of the various government programs now in place for medical care.

Another major reason Americans have higher medical costs is that we demand the best in medical advancements and in treatment of deadly diseases—and we get it, which is why people from across the world want to come to America for treatment when they get seriously ill. According to Cato's Michael Tanner, most of the world's best doctors, hospitals, and research facilities are located in this country. Eighteen of the last twenty-five Nobel Prize winners in medicine are either U.S. citizens or work here. U.S. companies have developed half of all the major new medicines that have been intro-duced on the market over the last two decades. Americans have played major roles in some 80 percent of the most important med-ical advances of the last three decades.

While Obama happily cites biased statistics showing America to have poorer quality healthcare than it really has, the fact is that comparative statistics on infant mortality rates and life expectancy are skewed and misleading. Other nations often exclude high-risk, low-birth-weight infants in tabulating their statistics on infant mortality, while America includes them, which greatly distorts the numbers in our disfavor. Life expectancy numbers, likewise, are misleading because of extra-medical factors, such as violent crime, poverty, obesity, tobacco, and drug use. But when you isolate and compare—apples to apples—our outcomes on serious illnesses like heart disease and cancer, the United States easily outperforms the rest of the world.[52] America has the best quality healthcare in the world, but ObamaCare will make it worse. As Heritage Foundation expert Robert Moffit says, the uniform experience of other nations proves that you can't deliver universal access to high-quality health care.

Consider Obama's other central reasons for promoting Obama-Care—the numbers of uninsured, the inadequate patient choice, and access to care—and you will see not only the distortions in the premises, but also the fraud in his promises to fix the very problems he mischaracterizes.

THE UNINSURED CANARD

As we noted, Obama finally had to revise his false claim of 47 million uninsured Americans to 30 million because the higher number included millions of non-citizens, among others. Let's look more closely at the actual numbers. In the first place, Obama conflates health insurance coverage with access to healthcare. All Americans, by law, have access to emergency room care. Plus, many of the uninsured lack coverage by choice—they can afford it but choose not get it, as explained below, but they still have access to care if they need it. Finally, the poorest Americans are eligible for government assistance for healthcare.

The Cato Institute's Michael D. Tanner noted that the Census Bureau's latest figures show 45.6 million Americans lack health insurance. But Tanner says we must account for the fact that only some 30 percent of the uninsured lack insurance for more than a year, 16 percent for two years, and less than 2.5 percent for three years or more. About half are uninsured for no more than six months (some have said four months). Much of this, says Tanner, is due to changing jobs and switching coverage through different employers.[53]

Putting aside the issue of the temporarily uninsured, if we begin with the 45.6 million number, we must first subtract 10 million people who are not U.S. citizens, including an estimated 5.6 million illegal immigrants and 4.4 million legal immigrants who are foreign citizens. Additionally, some 12 million are eligible for Medicaid and the State Children's Health Insurance Program (S-CHIP) but haven't enrolled. (For all the handwringing about the millions of uninsured children, this figure includes 64 percent of all uninsured children and 29 percent of parents with children.) Tanner notes if these people went to the hospital for care they'd be instantly enrolled, and thus it's essentially fraudulent to say they're uninsured.

There are also millions among the "uninsured" who can afford health insurance but choose not to buy it. These are referred to as the "young invincibles"—those who have decided to gamble on their good health and forego the expense of health insurance. Healthcare expert Sally Pipes wrote that almost 18 million people fall into this category and earn more than $50,000 annually, and almost 10 million of those make more than $75,000 a year.[54] Former CBO director June O'Neill prepared a study finding that 43 percent of the uninsured have incomes greater than 250 percent of the poverty level ($55,125 for a family of four), and the income of more than a third of them exceeds $66,000. Another study, produced by Mark Pauly of the University of Pennsylvania and Kate Bundorf of Stanford, found that almost 75 percent of the uninsured could afford insurance but choose not to get it. Moreover, writes

Tanner, most of these uninsured are in fact, as noted above, young and healthy: the CBO says some 60 percent are younger than thirty-five, and 86 percent claim to be in good health.

There is overlap among these different categories, making it difficult to determine accurately the number of U.S. citizens who are chronically uninsured and both ineligible for government assistance and unable to afford coverage. Estimates vary, but Sally Pipes estimates the number of these "chronically uninsured working poor" at about 8 million.[55]

If Obama were truly interested in providing health insurance for these people who fall through the cracks, he could do so with dramatically less cost and without wrecking the quality and access of healthcare for the rest of Americans. Many of these chronically uninsured could be aided by portability reform—by tying insurance to the person rather than the job. One Health Affairs study in 2003 found that only 12 percent of the uninsured were chronically so, with the rest falling in and out of coverage. Many experts maintain if you enacted portability reform—like we do in every other insurance market—the number of uninsured would drop drastically at a reasonable cost to taxpayers. As for any remaining uninsured, we could provide aid at a fraction of the cost of ObamaCare, and without destroying the quality, quantity, and choice of care.

CHOICE AND ACCESS TO CARE

In economic terms it is axiomatic that when you increase demand (which ObamaCare will do by force of law, among other things), and control prices (which ObamaCare will do out of necessity and the sheer force of government inertia), you will end up with rationing. In fact, ObamaCare sets up a board that will make decisions about our choices of care, and the bureaucrats will base their reimbursements on obedience to the prescribed choices. As much as anything else, these realities expose the fraud in ObamaCare. It was promoted on the basis of increasing access, as we've detailed. And yet, for all its "fixes," ObamaCare, after forcing people to procure coverage, will reduce access and quality because it will result in rationing. The choices for care will be made by top-down bureaucrats instead of those who know best: the doctors directly treating the patients. Obama said he wouldn't interfere with the relationship between doctors and their patients, just as he was pushing through his bill that would empower bureaucrats to direct these very decisions.

But Obama's own words betray his true intent on controlling healthcare choices. Not only does he favor bureaucratic intervention in intimate decisions between patients and their doctors, he has an embarrassingly unsophisticated perspective concerning it. Recall his statement, "If there's a blue pill and a red pill and the blue pill is half the price of the red pill and works just as well, why not pay half-price for the thing that's going to make you well?"[56] Or how about this gem from Dr. Barack: "We're going to start encouraging paying doctors not based on how many tests they take, but based on the quality of the outcome—does somebody end up healthy.... If you go to the doctor you get one test. Then (you are) referred to a specialist, you get another test. Then maybe you go to a third person, the surgeon, you get a third test—it's all the same test but you're paying three times. So ... we'll pay you for the first test and then e-mail the test to everybody. Right? Or have all three doctors in the room when the test is being taken."[57]

Obama appointed Donald Berwick, CEO of the Institute for Healthcare Improvement, to be the administrator for the Centers for Medicare and Medicaid Services (CMS). According to Robert M. Goldberg of the Center for Medicine in the Public Interest, the role of the CMS will be expanded under ObamaCare to define "the quality of health care for every insurance plan, set reimbursement rates for physicians in Medicare and Medicaid, and decide what treatments are more 'valuable' than others." Goldberg surmises, "Berwick will get control of the practice of medicine."

The CMS will have the sweeping power "to unilaterally write new rules on when medical devices and drugs can be used, and how they should be priced" as part of ObamaCare's strategy of "retaining costs through controls on specialist physicians. Based on the government's premise that they often make wasteful treatment decisions," ObamaCare "will subject doctors to a mix of financial penalties and regulations to constrain their use of the most costly clinical options."[58]

It would be disturbing enough for any person to have such broad authority, but Obama's choice—Donald Berwick—is not just any person. Like Obama, he believes in radical wealth redistribution and that socialized medicine is an ideal vehicle to achieve it. Don't take my word for it, take Berwick's: "Any health care funding plan that is just, equitable, civilized and humane must ... redistribute wealth from the richer among us to the poorer and the less fortunate," he said, adding, "Excellent health care is, by definition, redistributional." Berwick also idealizes the ineffectual, scandal-plagued British healthcare system, condemning America's system for running in the "darkness of private enterprise."[59]

Writing of Britain's National Health Service rationing, Berwick said, "You plan the supply; you aim a bit low; historically, you prefer slightly too little of a technology or service to much too much; and then you search for care bottlenecks, and try to relieve them." Goldberg notes that in 2008 Berwick's pet British system "denied cutting edge cancer drugs to 4,000 people, forcing thousands to remortgage their homes to pay for treatment. Love is blind. With regard to Dr. Berwick's devotion to the NHS, it's deaf and dumb as well."[60]

ObamaCare's architects ultimately intended to ration care because that was the only way these command-control types knew to reduce costs. They are philosophically on board with Obama's idea that a bureaucracy's payment determination can't be influenced by a person's spirit and "that at least we can let doctors know and your mom know that ... this isn't going to help. Maybe you're better off not having the surgery, but taking the painkiller."[61] They believe in substituting their value judgments for the freedom of

choice of American healthcare patients as to whether they need
care. Under a free system, a patient can spend as much or as little
on healthcare as he wishes. But under a government-run plan—for
which ObamaCare lays the groundwork—the government will
reduce, deny, and ration care based on a compassionless bureaucratic chart designed by "compassionate" liberals. So while Obama-
Care may marginally decrease the numbers of uninsured—though
that's not guaranteed—it will greatly reduce access to quality care.

All government-run healthcare systems ration care, either directly,
by denying or limiting certain types of treatment, or indirectly, by
imposing cost constraints through budgets, waiting lines, and/or
limited technology. One million British people are awaiting admission to government-run hospitals at any given time, and shortages
result in the cancellation of some 100,000 operations annually. New
Zealanders experience similar troubles. Swedes can wait for heart
surgery up to twenty-five weeks, and 800,000 Canadian patients are
on waiting lists.[62]

Moreover, an *Investors Business Daily* poll found ObamaCare
will cause up to 45 percent of doctors to retire early. Similarly, the
National Center for Policy Analysis reported that ObamaCare
"could impact physician supply in such a way that the quality of
health care would suffer. The reality is that there may not be enough
doctors to provide quality medical care to the millions of newly
insured patients." Why? Because it would make practicing medicine "more trouble than it's worth." This reduction in the physician
workforce, according to the doctors surveyed, could "result in a significant decline in the overall quality of medical care nationwide."[63]

Perhaps the most ominous predictor of rationing in ObamaCare
involves so-called end-of-life counseling. Sarah Palin took a lot of
flack for arguing that various provisions in the healthcare bill,
including end-of-life counseling, could establish "death panels."
Regardless of whether ObamaCare would lead to death panels, one
is entitled to ask why such a provision is in the bill at all. What
business does the government have insinuating itself into intimate,

end-of-life matters? The answer is quite clear: it has no business at all making such decisions, but as the government takes over more and more of the healthcare system, it gains a bigger interest in containing costs in every part of the system.

Furthermore, ObamaCare, as noted above, also expands the role of the CMS over healthcare decisions. These provisions, together with the fact that a number of the bill's architects, such as Obama's close advisers on the matter, Tom Daschle and Ezekiel Emanuel, firmly believe in rationing care to the elderly, makes speculation about death panels more than plausible. But there's more.

Before ObamaCare was passed, Democrats slipped into the stimulus bill a provision to establish a $1.1 billion fund for a Federal Council for Comparative Effectiveness Research, a brainchild of former Democratic senator Tom Daschle. Former New York lieutenant governor Betsy McCaughey warned about this panel when the stimulus bill was being considered. According to McCaughey, the council was based on ideas Daschle had sketched out in his 2008 book *Critical: What Can We Do about the Health Care Crisis*, in which he explained that such a panel is meant to empower an unelected bureaucracy to make hard decisions about healthcare rationing that elected politicians might lack the courage to make. He suggested Americans would be better served if they passively accepted "hopeless diagnoses" like Europeans do. Daschle's argument, said McCaughey, was that "seniors should be more accepting of the conditions that come with age instead of treating them." Yet Obama claims conservatives are hyperventilating over this issue.[64]

Joseph Ashby, in the *American Thinker*, wrote that Rahm Emanuel's brother, Dr. Ezekiel Emanuel, is on this council. Emanuel's credo concerning rationing to the elderly is: "Unlike allocation by sex or race, allocation by age is not invidious discrimination; every person lives through different life stages rather than being a single age. Even if 25 year olds receive priority over 65 year olds, everyone who is 65 years now was previously 25 years." Some comfort. Some logic. Some values.

It is thus preordained that ObamaCare will ultimately go into cost-cutting mode, saving money by curtailing treatment. As frighteningly long and complex as the ObamaCare legislation is, Ashby warns the regulations promulgated under it could be vastly worse and give regulators enormous power to interpret the law and regulations. This is certainly consistent with our experience in the entire field of administrative law.

Ashby says that if that happens, regulatory czar Cass Sunstein would doubtlessly play a major role in crafting and administering the regulations and thus in controlling medical care. And how does Sunstein view "end of life care?" It should be no surprise, given Obama's chosen cast of macabre characters, that Sunstein once wrote a paper for the AEI-Brookings Joint Center for Regulatory Studies in which he posited that human life varies in value, which is hardly a principle one would find in the Book of Genesis. It gets worse. Sunstein advocates the government employing "statistical methods that give preference to 'quality-adjusted life years,'" as determined by the government. In Ashby's words, "If the government decides the life is not worth living, it is the individual's duty to die to free up welfare payments for the young and productive."[65]

Contrary to Obama's claims, America has the best healthcare system in the world, with far fewer chronically uninsured than he says. If Obama truly wanted to reform the system and bring down costs, he would initiate a series of market-based reforms, such as those offered by conservative Republicans, including expanding health savings accounts, reducing costly government mandates and regulations, permitting health insurance purchases across state lines, amending the tax code's discriminatory treatment militating in favor of employer provided healthcare, tort reform, and portability solutions. As Dr. David Gratzer wrote in his book *The Cure: How Capitalism Can Save American Health Care*, "Capitalism is not the cause of America's health-care problem. It is the cure."

But instead of market-based reforms, Obama has forced through a system that will not ameliorate, but exacerbate the problems of access to care, choice, and quality. Finally, ObamaCare comprised more unsustainable spending on top of all the crushing debt our president has already lassoed onto our children. Nevertheless, he is determined to create a new entitlement to vastly expand the dependency class on whom he and other Democrats increasingly rely for their votes, their careers, and their resulting political power. What this is ultimately about is expanding government control—it's about crimes against our liberties.

Chapter Thirteen

THE ANTI-AMERICAN

CRIMES AGAINST THE NATION

At the April 2010 nuclear summit in Washington, D.C., Obama uttered a single sentence that encapsulated his approach to foreign policy: "Whether we like it or not, we remain a dominant military superpower, and when conflicts break out, one way or another we get pulled into them; and that ends up costing us significantly in terms of both blood and treasure." Outraged, Senator John McCain declared this statement was a "direct contradiction to everything America believes in."[1]

Obama's disdain for American exceptionalism and for America's history—as viewed in his eyes—is palpable. He has made that clear with his manifold apologies on both U.S. and foreign soil. He believes America unfairly consumes a disproportionate share of the world's resources; that we have projected our power imprudently, imperiously, unfairly, arrogantly, and dismissively; and that America has been too nationalistic and too resistant to what he believes are the inevitable forces of globalism.

He believes we must radically change course and share much more of our resources, especially with third world countries. In his view, America should reach out to other nations, adopt more of their enlightened and progressive values, and make amends for our past wrongs. He thinks our already deplorable international record was exacerbated by his predecessor's "cowboy diplomacy." This, coupled with Bush's record in the war on terror—including his invasion of Iraq, his approval of enhanced interrogation techniques, and his enabling of Gitmo—resulted in the proliferation of terrorists. He is convinced that by drawing a line in the sand between the forces of good and evil and by refusing to engage terrorists and terrorist sponsoring states, we have lost ground in the war. His approach to foreign policy and national security can only be understood against this backdrop.

"A SPRAWLING, PROFANE BEAR OF A PREACHER"

How do we know Obama harbors the attitudes we've described? Well, he sat approvingly at the feet of his pastor, Jeremiah Wright, for years. Wright's incendiary sermons were legendary. *ABC News*, in its "review of dozens of Rev. Wright's sermons, offered for sale by the church, found repeated denunciations of America based on what he described as his reading of the Gospels and the treatment of black Americans." How could anyone sit in Wright's pews and be indifferent to his indictments of America, especially a man aspiring to be president of the United States?

Wright's doctrine of choice, Black Liberation Theology, is arguably more Afrocentric and Marxist than Biblical in its orientation. While many have quoted Wright, a few of his statements bear repeating here, not for their inflammatory tone, but for the race-oriented grievance mentality against "White America" that they reveal. If Obama hadn't adopted domestic and foreign policies consistent with this mindset (and with the principles and attitudes ingrained in him by his mother and his Communist mentor Frank Marshall Davis, among others), there would be no point in quoting Wright. But he has.

Wright said in a 2003 sermon, "The government gives them the drugs, builds bigger prisons, passes a three-strike law and then wants us to sing 'God Bless America.' No, no, no, God da** America, that's in the Bible for killing innocent people. God da** America for treating our citizens as less than human. God da** America for as long as she acts like she is God and she is supreme." On the Sunday following the 9/11 attacks, Wright implied America had invited the massacre. "We bombed Hiroshima, we bombed Nagasaki, and we nuked far more than the thousands in New York and the Pentagon, and we never batted an eye. We have supported state terrorism against the Palestinians and black South Africans, and now we are indignant because the stuff we have done overseas is now brought right back to our own front yards. America's chickens are coming home to roost."[2]

Wright has referred to "the U.S. of KKK A"[3] and has declared, "Racism is how this country was founded and how this country is still run. . . . We [in the U.S.] believe in this white supremacy and black inferiority and believe it more than we believe in God." He also wrote in a church-affiliated magazine, "In the 21st century, white America got a wake-up call after 9/11/01. White America and the western world came to realize that people of color had not gone away, faded into the woodwork or just 'disappeared' as the Great White West kept on its merry way of ignoring black concerns."[4]

Given to anti-Israel and anti-Semitic riffs, Wright referred to Nation of Islam leader Louis Farrakhan, with whom Wright traveled to Libya to visit the country's crackpot leader, Muammar al-Gaddafi, as "one of the most important voices in the 20th and 21st centuries." Beyond sympathizing with Palestinians, Wright also frequently condemned Israel directly, as when he said, "The Israelis have illegally occupied Palestinian territories for almost 40 years now," and denounced "the injustice and racism under which the Palestinians have lived because of Zionism."[5] He also once claimed in an interview that "them Jews" were keeping Obama from speaking to him.[6]

Wright had been unleashing these racist, anti-capitalist, anti-Semitic, and anti-American screeds for decades—and certainly as long as Obama had been affiliated with his church. In a much earlier sermon, Wright had claimed we live in "a world where cruise ships throw away more food in a day than most residents of Port-au-Prince see in a year, where white folks' greed runs a world in need, apartheid in one hemisphere, apathy in another hemisphere.... That's the world! On which hope sits!" We learned of this sermon in Obama's autobiography, *Dreams from My Father*,[7] written by a man who later claimed to be unaware of Wright's invective.

Indeed, during his presidential campaign, Obama insisted he "personally" hadn't heard "such incendiary language." Wright, he said, "always preached the social gospel." Had he heard these sermons he "would have quit." Not only did these denials fail the laugh test, but we have independent proof that Obama knew. A *New York Times* story from March 2007 reported that the Obama campaign had rescinded its invitation to Wright to deliver a public invocation at the ceremony announcing Obama's candidacy. Wright reported that Obama called him "fifteen minutes before Shabbos" and told him "one of his members had talked him into uninviting me."

Obama, citing a *Rolling Stone* article about his ties to Wright, reportedly told Wright, "You can get kind of rough in the sermons, so what we've decided is that it's best for you not to be out there in public."[8] The article, titled "The Radical Roots of Barack Obama," described Wright as "a sprawling, profane bear of a preacher, a kind of black ministerial institution," and cited Wright's "10 essential facts about the United States," which were caustic and unflattering, to say the least. As *ABC News*' Jake Tapper later asked with extreme understatement, "This [*Rolling Stone* piece] was more than a year ago. So . . . what did Obama know then and what did he just all of a sudden learn?"[9]

Based on Obama's statements, policies, and performance in office, it is clear he shares Reverend Wright's basic worldview, which is why Wright's statements are still relevant today—they are directly impacting our nation. But Obama knew the public would be mortified if they were aware of his relationship with Wright, which is why he decided it would be "best" for Wright not to be "out there in public."

If Obama hadn't exhibited knee-jerk racism (as in the case of siding with Harvard professor Henry Gates against the Cambridge police before hearing both sides of the story, and as with his stunning protection of the New Black Panther Party); if he hadn't exhibited such obvious hostility to our ally Israel; if he hadn't been doing everything in his power to redistribute wealth among Americans in ways *he* believes are fair; if he hadn't pushed through socialized medicine against the will of the people; if he weren't trying to effect a redistribution of America's resources to other nations to further settle what he perceives as our injustices toward the world; if he hadn't appointed a slew of radicals as czars and advisers; and if he hadn't apologized for and condemned America at almost every turn, we could dismiss his voluntary association with Reverend Wright. But based on what we know, we do so at our peril.

As noted, Obama's worldview leads him to scorn American exceptionalism and American sovereignty in favor of a globalist approach. At a speech at West Point in May 2010, he pledged to shape a new "international order" as part of a national security strategy that emphasizes his faith in global institutions and international cooperation as the best vehicles for securing America's interests.[10] Obama's words caused some to question how much U.S. sovereignty he was willing to cede in exchange for global "cooperation." KT McFarland, former deputy assistant secretary of defense for Ronald Reagan, worried Obama was rejecting American exceptionalism. "It's a very international sense," said McFarland, "that America is just one of many, that we are not going to be a superpower in leading the world and I think it's a very dangerous mindset and trend."[11]

Obama is suspicious of our traditional allies and sympathetic to our rivals and enemies. A simple, three-framed cartoon from the comic strip titled "Hope n' Change," by Stilton Jarlsberg, placed it in graphic perspective. All three frames depict a smiling Obama with these captions: 1) Obama: "Okay, I admit that I've backed down from Russia, Iran, and North Korea. But I got really tough with Israel." 2) An un-pictured questioner: "Isn't Israel our ally?" 3) Obama. "Define 'our'"...

WE'RE SO SORRY

Once sworn in, Obama wasted little time in making amends for what he viewed as America's many sins against the world. He couldn't trot the globe fast enough to apologize on behalf of America. Having dealt almost exclusively in the world of words throughout his life, he thought his utterances alone could move diplomatic mountains. Whether delivered on American or foreign soil, his message was the same: *America has been bad in the past, including the recent past. I had nothing to do with it, of course, but as its current leader I apologize. And I expect the slate to be wiped clean because I'm in charge now.*

Thus, on April 2, 2009, at the G20 meeting in London, he declared, "I would like to think that with my election and the early decisions that we've made, that you're starting to see some restoration of America's standing in the world." Similarly, White House press secretary Robert Gibbs said, based on Obama's apologetic rhetoric, Obama had "changed the image of America around the world" and made the United States "safer and stronger."

Patronizingly, Obama told the CIA it had made "mistakes" in its Bush-era counter-terrorism policies. He told the Arabic-language *Al Arabiya* TV network that America "dictates" without knowing "all the factors involved." He told the G20 group America needs to account for "inadequacies" in its "regulatory system." He accepted blame and "responsibility" on our behalf for the economic crisis having begun in the United States—"even if I wasn't president at the time." He told the French that America failed "to appreciate Europe's leading role in the world," and that we'd shown "arrogance" and been "dismissive" and "derisive."

And the apologies kept on coming. He apologized to Latin America for our failure to pursue "sustained engagement with our neighbors." He repeated in Trinidad that we had been "disengaged" and "dictatorial."[12] Echoing Reverend Wright, he said in Prague America had "a moral responsibility to act" on arms control because we were the only nation that had ever "used a nuclear weapon."[13] Then in May 2010, the administration went so far as to apologize for Arizona's immigration law to the Communist Chinese, whose civil rights violations are legendary. Assistant Secretary of State Michael Posner reported that during a meeting with Chinese leaders, U.S. representatives, on their own initiative, repeatedly denounced the Arizona law as a "troubling trend in our society, and an indication that we have to deal with issues of discrimination or potential discrimination."[14]

Likewise, Obama, in a Rose Garden press conference with Mexican president Felipe Calderón, declined to reply after Calderón blasted Arizona for its immigration law—a reticence widely interpreted as signaling agreement. If anything, Obama should have encouraged Calderón to reform the dismal conditions in Mexico that lead his people to storm our borders. Or perhaps Obama could have addressed Mexico's brutal treatment of its own illegal aliens, who Amnesty International found are subject to "extortion, beatings, kidnap, rape and murder by officials or criminal gangs that often [operate] with the complicity of local authorities."[15]

The Rose Garden event was remarkable, for as one writer noted, this might have been the first time "a foreign head of state who is promoting an ongoing, aggressive, illegal, and often violent invasion of America came to our country, met with our president, and, from the White House itself, received our president's implicit but obvious public support for that invasion."[16]

With such a warped view of America, Obama doesn't seem familiar with America's benevolent actions toward other nations, such as fighting the spread of Communism, liberating peoples—including many Muslims—from oppressive governments, helping to defeat the Imperial Japanese and the Nazis in World War II, or rebuilding vanquished nations through the Marshall Plan.

Through abject apologies, Obama aims to rectify the damage President Bush supposedly caused to our image. As he tilts at diplomatic windmills, he believes he is showing the world he is not the unsophisticated rube his predecessor was.

IRAN

The antiwar Left regularly mocked President Bush for viewing Iran as a nuclear threat. They smugly claimed vindication when the now-discredited National Intelligence Estimate reported in 2007, "We judge with high confidence that in fall 2003, Tehran halted its nuclear weapons program."[17] Fast forward to 2009 and the Left's hand-picked president, Barack Obama, was desperately searching for a way to end Iran's supposedly non-existent nuclear program. He had unleashed his negotiators in Vienna to try to strike a deal with the Iranians that would delay the mullahs' ability to build a nuclear weapon for about a year, "buying more time for President Obama to search for a diplomatic solution to the Iranian nuclear standoff."

The proposed deal contemplated Iran sending three-quarters of its uranium fuel, which it claimed it needed for peaceful purposes, to Russia for further enrichment. Russia would return it to Iran in the form of metal fuel rods, which could only be used for nuclear reactors, not for weapons. This depletion of uranium would slow down any Iranian plans to produce a nuclear weapon. The *New York*

Times reported that administration officials were cautiously optimistic they could reach a "broader diplomatic accord" with Iran.[18]

It didn't take long for Iran to renege and for Obama's enlightened method of engagement to prove a failure. And as this charade
unfolded, Iran bought more time to advance its nuclear program
and earned U.S. diplomatic engagement—all for violating UN Security Council declarations and giving nothing in return. *Investors
Business Daily's* editors asked, "How can a theocratic government
with a stone-age worldview take the most sophisticated, modern,
industrialized nation in the world for a ride, as if we just fell of the
turnip truck?" Answer: "Because those who run Iran realize they
are engaged in a global war. Those who now run American foreign
policy, on the other hand, think 'war on terror' is passé." Obama's
approach sounds nice, "but it is the naïveté of Neville Chamberlain
and the piece of paper he waved bearing Hitler's autograph."[19]

Obama added failure on top of failure as he doggedly clung to
his engagement strategy. Playing bad cop to his good cop, Secretary
of State Hillary Clinton had issued Iran an ultimatum in March
2009 to disband its nuclear program by year's end, warning of "real
consequences" unless Iran complied.[20] No response. In July she
threatened to beef up the military capabilities of our Persian Gulf
allies if Iran continued to develop its nuclear program.[21] Again, no
response. Obama had said in May, in his "diplomatic" way, "The
important thing is to make sure there is a clear timetable, at which
point we say these talks don't seem to be making any serious
progress. By the end of the year, we should have some sense
whether or not these discussions are starting to yield significant benefits, whether we are starting to see serious movement on the part
of the Iranians."[22]

Iran contemptuously dismissed Obama's end-of-year deadline.
On December 22, 2009, Iranian president Mahmoud Ahmadinejad
asked defiantly, "Who are they to set us a deadline? We set them a
deadline that if they do not correct their attitude and behavior and
literature we will demand from them the Iranian nation's historic

rights. . . . They must know that the Iranian nation and all the world's nations will continue resisting until the complete (nuclear) disarmament of America and all arrogant powers."[23]

The Obama administration cravenly responded by disavowing its own deadlines. Hillary Clinton said, as if the administration's previous words meant nothing, "Now, we've avoided using the term 'deadline' ourselves. That's not a term that we have used, because we want to keep the door to dialogue open." Tellingly, she even admitted the administration's efforts at "engagement" had not succeeded.[24] Iran triumphantly acknowledged the administration's abandonment of its deadline. An Iranian foreign ministry spokesman crowed, "We share the same idea with [Clinton]. Deadlines are meaningless. We hope other countries return to their natural path, too."[25]

Obama claimed there was a method to his engagement madness. If his efforts ultimately failed, he argued, countries previously resistant to sanctions—Russia, China, and Germany—would come on board. Secretary Clinton said, "We actually believe that by following the diplomatic path we are on, we gain credibility and influence with a number of nations who would have to participate in order to make the sanctions regime as tight and as crippling as we would want it to be."

But by all indications, that strategy was not working too well, either. While Germany might have been playing lip service to supporting sanctions, Russia, which has considerable economic interests in Iran and is helping to build Iran's nuclear reactors, resisted all but the most toothless sanctions. Similarly, with "a rapidly growing stake in Iran's energy sector," China had decreed that Iran's nuclear program did not represent a threat and therefore diplomacy should be given more time. China declined to send a high ranking official to talks among the United States, Britain, France, Russia, and Germany, and it even stopped using the word "sanction." Without Russia or China's cooperation, the prospect of meaningful sanctions was negligible because, among other things, both countries have a Security Council veto at the United Nations. Thus, the only sanctions to emerge from the UN—and greeted with mocking contempt by the Iranians—have been largely symbolic measures that Russia and China allow to pass only because of their meaninglessness.

As both prongs of Obama's Iran strategy—engagement and sanctions—were failing, even some of his defenders, such as an anonymous "Hill Democrat" quoted by *Time*, were asking, "What exactly did your year of engagement get you?" According to Obama-friendly *Time*, "The very fact that the U.S. and its allies are even thinking of going it alone is a sign of just how much trouble Obama's policy is in."[26]

Columnist Charles Krauthammer wrote that Iran's thuggish president, Mahmoud Ahmadinejad, didn't simply reject Obama's "feckless floating nuclear deadline...he spat on it." Krauthammer sighed, "So ends 2009, the year of 'engagement,' of the extended hand, of the gratuitous apology—and of spinning centrifuges, two-stage rockets and a secret enrichment facility that brought Iran materially closer to becoming a nuclear power."[27]

In May, Iran announced it had reached an accord with Turkey and Brazil to exchange a portion of its low enriched uranium to more highly enriched uranium to fuel its medical research reactor in Tehran. It was a clever move on Ahmadinejad's part: it wouldn't satisfy the UN Security Council's demands to halt Iran's uranium enrichment processes, but it could further undermine Obama's efforts to impose sanctions, demonstrating yet again the futility of his engagement efforts.[28]

As the *Washington Times* editors observed, during the campaign Obama

> made light of what he saw as his [Bush's] lack of diplomatic skills. As Wednesday's U.N. Security Council vote on sanctions over Iran's nuclear program showed, Mr. Obama's team could learn a few things about diplomacy from George W. Bush.... President Obama is losing the international consensus that Mr.

Bush once had. . . . Talk is cheap, but true diplomacy is difficult. . . . Perhaps [Obama] should take a trip to Dallas to pick up
a few pointers from Mr. Bush about how to rally the world
behind the policies that are in America's best interests.[29]

MUSLIM OUTREACH

A centerpiece of Obama's foreign policy and national security policy strategy has been to improve our relationship with the Muslim
world. Obama seems obsessed with the idea that Muslims believe
we are at war with them instead of with radical Islamists. Perhaps
more accurately, *he* believes it—and is intent on rectifying it.

President George W. Bush, on countless occasions, declared we
are not at war with Muslims. But Obama's insistence that he needed
to correct the record lent credence to the notion that we are. Obama
also seems to believe he has a certain duty to engage on this issue,
given his childhood in Indonesia and his lineage from Muslim family members. He can relate to Muslims—and he wanted to tell them
so in a forum where the entire world was watching. In his vaunted
Cairo speech of June 2009, he apologized for America again, gave
legitimacy to Muslim grievances, inflated the number of Muslims
in America three-fold, and exaggerated Islamic accomplishments in
world history and in American history. He implied the war in Iraq
was an unjustified act of aggression by the United States and that
we had earned our poor reputation among Arab and Muslim peoples, and assured his audience that we were not at war with Islam.

After all this pandering, what did Obama have to show for it? In
November 2009, one Saudi academic in Jeddah who had previously
been enamored with Obama said of him, "He talks too much."
Fouad Ajami, a professor at Johns Hopkins School of Advanced
International Studies, thought the Obama mystique had already
worn off. "He has not made the world anew, history did not bend
to his will, the Indians and Pakistanis have been told that the matter of Kashmir is theirs to resolve, the Israeli-Palestinian conflict is

the same intractable clash of two irreconcilable nationalisms, and the theocrats in Iran have not 'unclenched their fist,' nor have they abandoned their nuclear quest."

Moreover, Pew polling confirmed that for all his posturing, Obama hadn't improved our Muslim relations at all. Only 15 percent of those in the Palestinian territories had a favorable view of the United States, while 82 percent had an unfavorable one. In Turkey—after Obama gave a speech in Ankara—14 percent favorable and 69 percent unfavorable. In Egypt, 27 percent favorable, 70 percent unfavorable. In Pakistan things got worse, with unfavorables rising from 63 percent in 2008 to 68 percent in 2009,[30] which is an ominous sign given Pakistan's nuclear capability and the precariousness of Pakistan's current leadership. "There were a lot of illusions about Obama because he has African and Muslim roots," said Aya Mahmoud, a Cairo University student. "Turns out the [Cairo] speech was all just hype."[31]

Obama's primary failure here lies not in his inability to cure this region of its endemic anti-Americanism, but in his profoundly naïve assumption that he could, and in wrongly castigating the Bush administration for causing Middle East animus toward the United States, which predated Obama's presidency by decades, is thriving during his term, and will last long after he vacates the Oval Office.

Under Obama, America is no longer proud of its liberty. Instead, we are peddling American guilt and doing penance. Professor Ajami says this approach has been ill-advised. "No one," says Ajami, "told Mr. Obama that [in] the Islamic world, where American power is engaged and so dangerously exposed, it is considered bad form, nay a great moral lapse, to speak ill of one's own tribe in the midst, and in the lands, of others."[32]

THUG OUTREACH

Rejecting the Bush administration's focus on supporting international democratic movements, Obama adopted a policy of appeasing the

world's tyrants and dictators—also with no dividends to show for
it. At the Americas Summit in April 2009, he boasted that reaching
out to U.S. enemies "strengthens our hand" and claimed the notion
that his approach projects weakness "doesn't make sense."[33] Illustrating his new tack, he snuggled up to anti-American Venezuelan
dictator Hugo Chavez at the summit, graciously accepting Chavez's
gift—a book by Uruguayan author Eduardo Galeano, *Open Veins
of Latin America: Five Centuries of the Pillage of a Continent*—
which is a scathing attack on American and European involvement
in Latin America. Galeano wrote, "Our defeat was always implicit
in the victory of others; our wealth has always generated our
poverty by nourishing the prosperity of others."[34] Was Reverend
Jeremiah Wright also Chavez's mentor?

Also at the summit, following a nearly hour-long tirade against
the United States by far-left Nicaraguan president Daniel Ortega,
Obama elected not to defend his own country, instead saying he
was "grateful that President Ortega did not blame me for things
that happened when I was three months old." In other words,
America might be terrible, but it's not my fault. And anyone who
thought Obama might at least have his secretary of state rebuke
Ortega and stand up for America was mistaken. As FOX News
reported, "Secretary of State Hillary Clinton ignored two questions
about Ortega's speech, instead offering lengthy praise of a cultural
performance of dance and song opening the summit."[35]

Besides Ortega and Chavez, other Latin American leaders took
swipes at Obama at the summit. Then-Brazilian president Luis
Inácio Lula da Silva warned Obama that another summit without
Cuba's Communist leaders would be unacceptable, and Argentine
president Cristina Fernandez de Kirchner detailed a host of grievances against America, from the drug war to U.S. support for coun-
terinsurgencies during the 1980s.[36]

After a full year of Obama's enlightened diplomacy, Chavez did-
n't seem to warm up any further. At the Copenhagen summit in
December 2009, he called the United States "the great polluter,"

which was responsible "for having threatened, for having killed, for genocide as well." Having called President George W. Bush a "devil" whose podium "still smells of sulfur" in 2006, Chavez said of Obama in 2009, "I still smell sulfur. I still smell sulfur in this world." He referred to Obama's recently received Nobel Peace Prize as the "Nobel prize of war" and called Washington's offer to contribute $10 billion to an annual fund for developing countries "laughable."[37]

THE ANTI-DEMOCRAT

Like most leftists, Obama sees himself as a champion of democracy but proves otherwise, not just on domestic policy, where he routinely thwarts the people's will, but on the world stage as well, where he instinctively sides with tyrants, thugs, and dictators, and turns his back on true democratic movements. Nowhere was this on clearer display than with Obama's appalling handling of the Iranian uprising of 2009.

Here it was not just his leftist instinct toward tyranny, but also his fear that showing any sympathy to the people might displease the dictator he was trying to court. When outraged Iranians took to the streets in summer 2009 to protest the corrupt "election" of President Mahmoud Ahmadinejad, Obama largely remained neutral, even in the face of the regime's widespread beatings and killings of peaceful protestors. The administration's initial response was not to stand with the Iranian people and denounce the fixed election, but rather to insist the engagement policy would continue regardless of the election's outcome.[38]

Everyone knew the election was disgracefully fraudulent. As Senator Joe Lieberman declared, "Through intimidation, violence, manipulation and outright fraud, the Iranian regime has once again made a mockery of democracy and confirmed its repressive and dictatorial character." Senator John McCain urged Obama to "speak out forcefully" against the "sham, corrupt election" and the "depravation of [the Iranian people's] fundamental rights," and to "speak up for the people of Iran" and "make sure the world knows America leads."[39]

But Vice President Joe Biden said on *Meet the Press*, "We're going to withhold comment. . . . I mean we're just waiting to see." Secretary of State Hillary Clinton offered the same, saying, "The United States has refrained from commenting on the election in Iran." White House press secretary Robert Gibbs, unwittingly approaching *Saturday Night Live* absurdity, said the administration was "impressed by the vigorous debate and enthusiasm this election generated."

The administration's feckless response brought derision from critics around the world. British political commentator Nile Gardiner called America's response "cowardly, lily-livered and wrong" and said it was "undermining America's standing as a global power." He denounced it as a "cynical exercise in appeasement that will all end in tears. . . . As blood flows on the streets of Tehran, the United States government remains as silent as a Trappist Monk." Even the German government, he said, was "showing more backbone than the White House."[40]

But Iranian democratic protestors persisted. They turned the pressure up a notch on November 4, the thirtieth anniversary of the Iranian leadership's takeover of the U.S. embassy in Tehran, when they gathered in the streets and called Obama out. "Obama, Obama, you are either with us or with them," they yelled. He answered them again, emphatically, with his silence.

That very day Obama was scorned by the brutal leaders whose favor he was seeking. Iran's supreme leader, Ayatollah Ali Khamenei, spurned Obama's numerous direct overtures to him and warned that negotiating with the United States would be "naïve and perverted," and that Iranian political leaders must not be "deceived" into engaging in negotiations. Khamenei acknowledged Obama's outreach, but dismissed it as, essentially, empty rhetoric. He said Obama had "said nice things. . . . He has given us many spoken and written messages and said: 'Let's turn the page and create a new situation. Let's cooperate with each other in resolving world problems.'" However, "What we have witnessed is completely the opposite of what they have been saying and claiming. On the face of things, they say, 'Let's negotiate.' But...they threaten us and say that if these negotiations do not achieve a desirable result, they will do this and that." Unmoved by Obama's acclaimed personal charm, Khamenei said, "Whenever they smile at the officials of the Islamic revolution, when we carefully look at the situation, we notice that they are hiding a dagger behind their back. They have not changed their intentions."[41]

Obama employed the same hapless, morally bankrupt approach toward the true democratic forces in Honduras. He instinctively sided with the country's socialist thug president, Manuel Zelaya, when Zelaya launched a referendum without the backing of his Congress to organize an assembly to draft a new constitution. The move, which was declared illegal by the Honduran Supreme Court, was a clear attempt to extend his power beyond the constitutionally prescribed term—a tactic previously employed by his ally, Hugo Chavez. Lawlessly, Zelaya and his supporters seized millions of ballots from a military base, but before he could implement his scheme, the Supreme Court ordered his arrest. He was then sent to Costa Rica, and Congress appointed an interim successor.

Although Zelaya's leftwing sympathizers denounced his removal as a coup, it was nothing of the sort. The military acted under color of law, by order of the Supreme Court. If anyone was attempting a coup it was Zelaya, who had even terminated a top military leader, General Romeo Vasquez, because he wouldn't join the conspiracy to commandeer the crooked referendum.

The Obama administration, which had refused to "meddle" in the internal affairs of Iran, was all too pleased to inject itself into the Honduran crisis, and as usual, on the side of the thug. Secretary of State Hillary Clinton fretted that the situation had "evolved into a coup." She stated, "It's important that we stand for the rule of law"—just as she was siding with the very forces who were defying the rule of law in Honduras.

Obama continued to violate his own admonition against meddling by pressuring the interim regime to restore Zelaya to power. Claiming Zelaya's ouster could set a "terrible precedent," he joined with other Latin American countries—Costa Rica, Peru, Panama, and Colombia—to condemn the move as an illegal coup. To add some teeth to his declarations, Obama slashed military aid by $16.5 million to Honduras, cut off various kinds of economic aid, and suspended issuing most visas to Honduran citizens.

The interim Honduran government, however, refused to yield to the pressure, even after Zelaya snuck back into the country and took refuge in the Brazilian embassy. Four months after Zelaya's removal, the Honduran Congress decided by an overwhelming 98 to 12 majority not to reinstate him.[42] Honduras instead held a presidential election that, in a shocking turnabout from America's historic support for democracy, the Obama administration had repeatedly threatened not to recognize unless Zelaya presided over it.

Zelaya was granted safe passage out of the country by newly elected Honduran president Porfirio Lobo, who allowed Zelaya to return after about a year.[43] In the end, Honduran democracy proved strong enough to resist anti-democratic pressure from most of the international community, including, shamefully, the United States.

THE INSPECTOR CLOUSEAU OF FOREIGN POLICY

Obama's foreign policy failures have not been limited to his inability to convert jihadists into America-lovers. They've been much broader than that. The Left assured us Obama would restore class and dignity to the Oval Office after they had to endure eight years of embarrassment with Cowboy George. Finally, America could hold its head high again. The trouble is, like most everything else from this pseudo messiah, the reality didn't quite square with the hype. Obama managed to offend leader after leader through awkward, insensitive, clueless, and sometimes rude and boorish behavior—as if oblivious to proper protocol.

Obama promised he would "repair" our relations with Europe, but he's succeeded only in alienating the continent. When British prime minister Gordon Brown visited Washington in March 2009, Obama so blatantly disrespected him that British newspapers decried Obama's "rudeness" and "appalling" behavior. Removing a bust of Winston Churchill from the Oval Office was Obama's initial misstep. Then, he gave embarrassingly trite gifts to the Brown family. Brown had given Obama a penholder made from the timbers of the nineteenth-century British warship HMS *Gannet*. (The Oval Office desk is made from the wood of its sister ship, HMS *Resolute*.) Obama reciprocated with twenty-five DVDs of Hollywood movies, prompting one *Daily Telegraph* staffer to remark, "Oh, give me strength. We do have television and DVD stores on this side of the Atlantic." The *Times of London* found Michelle Obama's "solipsistic" and "inherently dismissive" gifts to the Browns' two little boys—toy models of Marine One, the president's helicopter—just as insulting.[44]

Beyond the gifts, which many Brits interpreted as a calculated snub, the world noticed Obama acted distinctly indifferent toward the leader of our closest ally. Not even bothering to deny the slight, the administration casually passed off Obama's rudeness on his being "too tired" to give Brown a proper welcome because of his focus on the economic crisis. Obama was reportedly so busy with domestic issues that he had little time to deal with international matters, "let alone the diplomatic niceties of the special relationship," according to the *Sunday Telegraph*. One source told the *Telegraph* he was concerned that Obama had failed to "even fake an interest in foreign policy."[45] Obama also offended our ally yet again by turning down five requests from the Brits in September 2009 to hold a bilateral meeting, either at the UN building in New York or at the G20 summit in Pittsburgh.[46]

Obama's distaste for Britain was also evident in his West Point speech on Afghanistan, of which Nile Gardiner wrote, "One subject was conspicuous by its total absence . . . there wasn't a single mention of America's main ally in the region, Britain. Never mind that we have 10,000 troops on active service there—far more than any other of America's so-called allies—and never mind that 237 of our brave soldiers have already lost their lives there, Great Britain wasn't even a footnote." Condemning what he called "the most extraordinary and insulting oversight," Gardiner noted this wasn't just a one-time occurrence, which "might have been overlooked as a careless mistake," but in all of Obama's speeches "neither Britain nor the special relationship have merited a single mention"—a relationship, said Gardiner, that is "certainly dying."[47]

But nothing has alienated Brits from America as much as Obama's relentless bullying of BP over the Gulf Oil spill. At one point in June 2010, Obama's public trashing of BP had helped to erase nearly half the market value of BP stock—a serious problem for Britain's elderly, since almost every pension fund in the UK owns BP shares. The *Financial Times* suggested Obama's "attack on BP" and "increasingly aggressive rhetoric" could damage transatlantic relations.[48]

Summing up the state of U.S.–British relations, the *London Daily Telegraph*'s Alex Singleton wrote, "Let me be clear: I'm not normally in favour of boycotts, and I love the American people. I holiday in their country regularly, and hate the tedious snobby sneers against the United States. But the American people chose to elect an idiot who seems hell bent on insulting their allies, and something must be done to stop Obama's reckless foreign policy, before he does the dirty on his allies on every single issue."[49] So much for recasting America's global image—with Britain, anyway.

Aside from the Brits, Obama miffed the Europeans when he promised the Russians to cancel a planned anti-missile system in Poland and the Czech Republic. This unsettled Eastern Europe, given its history under Russian domination, but more than that, it signaled to these nations and others that under Obama, the United States cannot be relied on to honor its commitments. In the naïve, false hope that Russia would cast aside its security, nuclear, economic, and military interests in Iran and repay us by helping us thwart Iran's nuclear program, Obama effectively threw under the bus two emphatically pro-American allies who had supported the anti-missile system in the face of thinly veiled threats from Russia.

Nor has French president Nicholas Sarkozy been spared Obama's insolence. When Sarkozy met with Obama in April, he told Obama France and the United States were "the same family." He had been strongly pro-America during the Bush presidency, even being nicknamed at one point "Sarko the American." But as time passed Sarkozy began to lose respect for Obama. When the Obamas went to Paris in June 2009 for the sixty-fifth D-Day anniversary, they embarrassed the Sarkozys by declining their dinner invitation. Nor was it particularly beneficial to their relationship when the French media mocked Sarkozy over Obama's "coolness" toward him.

Perhaps Obama was getting back at Sarkozy for what the *Times of London* characterized as his grabbing "the limelight at the G20 summit in April" and talking "condescendingly" of Obama in private. Mr. Sarkozy reportedly had told colleagues he found Obama to be inexperienced and uninformed, particularly on climate change.[50] He also reportedly said Obama was naïve in his call for a world free of nuclear weapons.[51] Though doubtless of little consolation to Sarkozy, Obama proved to be an equal opportunity snubber when he avoided Berlin during his trip to Germany—a sign of disrespect for German chancellor Angela Merkel.[52]

The Sarkozy–Obama freeze continued as Sarkozy appeared to have little patience for what one writer aptly described as Obama's "apology tour of weakness."[53] After Obama outlined his childlike ideas on international cooperation in an address to the UN, Sarkozy came close to mocking him, saying, "We live in a real world not a virtual world. And the real world expects us to make decisions. President Obama dreams of a world without weapons . . . but right in front of us two countries are doing the exact opposite." Sarkozy was referring to Iran and North Korea—countries whose nuclear proliferation programs are advancing despite Obama's urgent pleas for them to stop.

Sarkozy hit Obama in a particularly sensitive spot when he indicted his engagement policy. Sarkozy said, "I support the extended hand of the Americans, but what good has proposals for dialogue brought the international community? More uranium enrichment and declarations by the leaders of Iran to wipe a UN member state off the map."[54] It is doubtful that Obama's snubs were the only reason for Sarkozy's disrespect, for during the presidential campaign Israeli sources reported that Sarkozy viewed Obama as "arrogant" and his stance on Iran as "utterly immature" and comprised of "formulations empty of all content."[55]

Obama has even managed to turn altruistic offers of assistance from our allies into sources of contention and distrust. Three days after the Deepwater Horizon oil rig exploded off the Louisiana coast, the Dutch offered, free of charge, to send ships to help suck up the polluted water. Although each ship had more cleanup capacity than all the ships combined that the U.S. then had in the Gulf, the Obama administration refused the offer—and similar offers of assistance from twelve other nations—claiming the Dutch ships' operations violated environmental regulations. After they realized the monumental stupidity of this decision, the administration partly relented. However, they delayed the operation to cater to labor unions—instead of simply allowing the Dutch ships to come and help, they insisted the Dutch equipment be retrofitted onto U.S. ships and that U.S. crews be trained to operate it.

Similarly, although the Dutch offered to build sand berms to protect coastal areas—a task they can accomplish twice as fast as U.S. firms can—Obama once again put his union pals first, insisting, as the oil slick spread every day, that the Dutch burn valuable time training U.S. workers to do the job. A spokesman for the Dutch embassy in Washington observed, "Given the fact that there is so much oil on a daily basis coming in, you do not have that much time to protect the marshlands." According to the *Financial Post*, the spokesman was "perplexed that the U.S. government could be so focused on side issues with the entire Gulf Coast hanging in the balance."[56]

As it turns out, resentment of Obama's high-handedness is quite widespread in international circles. The *New Delhi Sunday Pioneer* called Obama "arrogant," in a headline no less, because he "alienates friends," i.e., Israel, with his "abrasive style of diplomacy, which has become the signature tune of the Obama administration." The *Pioneer* noted it might have been understandable had Obama's abrasiveness been directed toward Iran and Venezuela, who always "take swipes at the U.S." But instead, "Obama appears to have reserved his acid tongue for those who are considered close allies of the US."

Then came the zinger, the crowning judgment on Obama's brand of diplomacy: "How Obama chooses to turn his machismo into political advantage in his battle with the Republicans is a matter best left to the American voters. It is of academic concern to India. But when his combativeness is transferred to the global stage and, furthermore, is accompanied by gratuitous discourtesy, it is time for a country like India to consider diplomatic alternatives to over-dependence on the U.S. The experiences of Netanyahu and Karzai are clear writings on the wall."[57]

It would be hard to devise a more concise indictment of Obama's foreign policy: his treatment of U.S. allies is so feckless that nobody wants to become one anymore. More than halfway into Obama's term, one thing is clear about his foreign policy: for all his talk about rehabilitating America's image in the world and "resetting" our relationships with other nations—which he never proved were as strained as he said they were—Obama is visibly failing throughout the globe, from France, Britain, and Germany to Iran, Venezuela, and North Korea. He is finding—or more accurately, Americans are finding—that talking has its limitations, and talking about talking even more so.

Chapter Fourteen

BETRAYING ISRAEL

CRIMES AGAINST AMERICA'S ALLY

During the presidential campaign, many feared Obama had an anti-Israel bias because of his Muslim family roots, his reported ties to pro-Palestinian groups, and his overall leftist orientation. The mainstream media dutifully ignored any and all suspicious Obama ties, including a reported connection to Islamic extremist Khalid Al Mansour, which the Obama campaign denied.

But the media went the extra mile in covering up his relationship with Rashid Khalidi. Having served as a PLO operative at a time when the group was a designated terrorist organization, Khalidi is a virulent critic of Israel who, just days after the 9/11 attacks, denounced the media's "hysteria about suicide bombers."[1]

The *Los Angeles Times* reportedly was in possession of a damning video of Obama effusively toasting Khalidi at a dinner. Despite acknowledging thousands of phone calls and e-mails requesting the release of the video, they refused. Responding to demands from the

McCain campaign to release it, the *Times* said it was ethically bound to honor a promise to a confidential source not to share the video. Reportedly, the dinner featured heavy Israel bashing, including one young woman who accused the Israeli government of committing terrorism. Obama reportedly "adopted a different tone and called for finding common ground," yet the *Times* wouldn't release the video to verify his statement.[2]

Apart from the video, however, *Times* staff writer Peter Wallsten had already written about Obama's ties to Khalidi and the mysterious dinner toast. According to Wallsten, Obama, "Khalidi's friend and frequent dinner companion," gave a "special tribute" to Khalidi at a send off dinner when Khalidi was about to leave Chicago for New York. Wallsten said Obama "reminisced about meals prepared by Khalidi's wife, Mona, and conversations that had challenged his thinking." Obama said the talks were "consistent reminders to me of my own blind spots and my own biases."

Despite Obama's claims during his presidential campaign that he was a strong supporter of Israel, according to Wallsten, some Palestinian-American leaders believed he was "more receptive to their viewpoint than he is willing to say," based on his "warm embrace" of Khalidi and his dinner toast. Wallsten wrote, "Their belief is not drawn from Obama's speeches or campaign literature, but from comments that some say Obama made in private and from his association with the Palestinian American community" in Chicago, "including his presence at events where anger at Israeli and U.S. Middle East policy was freely expressed." Wallsten obviously wasn't referring to Reverend Wright's Trinity Church there.[3]

Speaking of Obama's long-time church, *WorldNetDaily* reported that in its newsletter *Pastor's Page*, the Trinity United Church of Christ published a terror manifesto by Hamas "that defended terrorism as a legitimate resistance, refused to recognize the right of Israel to exist and compared the terror group's official charter—which calls for the murder of Jews—to America's Declaration of Independence." Hamas, of course, is listed as a terrorist group by the U.S. State Department.[4] Similarly, Trinity's *Trumpet* newsletter reportedly expressed the church's strong support of the terrorist group Hezbollah during Israel's incursion into Lebanon in 2006.[5]

OMINOUS SIGNS

Some Israel supporters were also troubled that candidate Obama assembled a group of foreign policy advisers who signaled that, as president, "Obama would likely have an approach towards Israel radically at odds with those of previous presidents" of both parties. A group of experts cited by the Israeli newspaper *Haaretz* deemed Obama to be the candidate least likely to support Israel, and that he was the one most favored by the Arab-American community.[6]

In June 2008, someone purporting to represent Socialists for Obama published an article on Organizing for America, Obama's official campaign website, titled, "How the Jewish Lobby Works." The article was later removed, but *NewsBusters* posted some of the content, which included shockingly anti-Semitic language, such as the following:

> NO LOBBY IS FEARED MORE or catered to by politicians than the Jewish Lobby. If a politician does not play ball with the Jewish Lobby, he will not get elected, or re-elected, and he will either be smeared or ignored by the Jewish-owned major media.
>
> All Jewish lobbies and organizations are interconnected and there are hundreds upon hundreds of them. The leaders of the numerous Jewish Lobby Groups go to the same synagogues, country clubs, and share the same Jewish investment bankers. And this inter-connectedness extends to the Jews who run the Federal Reserve Bank, US Homeland Security, and the US State Department.
>
> In other words, "Jews stick together." Americans must know how extremely powerful the Jewish Lobby is and how it operates to undermine America's interests both at home and abroad. At

350 CRIMES AGAINST LIBERTY

home—by corrupting America's political system, and abroad—
by dictating American Foreign Policy against America's best
interests.[7]

This was no one-off event; *NewsBusters* provided links to other
anti-Jewish posts on the website.[8] While some may be reluctant to
hold Obama responsible for what others posted on his website, one
wonders how these apparent anti-Semites got posting privileges,
assuming Obama's own people didn't write these missives themselves. The MSM, unsurprisingly, declined to investigate the question; Obama always gets a presumptive pass, whether for Jeremiah
Wright, William Ayers, or anti-Semitic contributors to his website.

"CAN ISRAEL STILL CALL THE UNITED STATES
ITS BEST INTERNATIONAL FRIEND?"

After winning the presidential election, Obama made moves even
before he assumed office that cast doubt on his campaign pose as a
friend of Israel. In December 2008 he appointed as his national
security adviser James Jones, a man, according to reports, who is
"not known as a friend of the Jewish State." In his new position,
Jones lived up to his reputation, assembling Brent Scowcroft and
Carter-era anti-Israel stalwart Zbigniew Brzezinski to meet with
Obama and urge him to impose a solution on Israel. Furthermore,
in a keynote speech at the Washington Institute for Near East Policy, Jones kicked off his remarks with a joke invoking stereotypes
about greedy Jewish merchants. As *Red State*'s Jeff Dunetz pointed
out, the White House tried to whitewash the joke by omitting it
from the transcript it sent to reporters.[9]

From its inception, the Obama administration treated Israel not
as a sovereign nation and an ally, but as a pawn to be ordered
around in pursuit of their vision of a Middle East peace agreement.
In his first week in office, Obama signaled his Palestinian sympathies
by authorizing $20 million in aid to help the Hamas-ruled Gaza

Strip recover from damage caused in an Israeli offensive provoked by Hamas rocket fire into Israel.[10] In his second week, Palestinian Authority officials, after meeting with Obama's Mideast envoy, George Mitchell, said they believed that under Obama the Palestinians could extract from Israel much bigger concessions than under previous administrations, and that Obama wanted to see Israel withdraw from nearly the entire West Bank.[11]

This indicated Obama sought even more Israeli concessions than were made at Bill Clinton's Camp David summit in 2000—concessions which then-Palestinian leader Yassir Arafat rejected in favor of a new war against Israel. A few months later, as a further sign Obama was moving the goalposts on Israel, the State Department ducked the question of whether it would honor a promise by the George W. Bush administration to former Israeli prime minister Ariel Sharon that Israel would retain sovereignty over large Jewish areas in Judea and Samaria (the West Bank) if a new Palestinian state were created.[12]

A little over a month in office, Obama pledged more than $900 million—not just $20 million—to rebuild Gaza[13] and to shore up the Palestinian Authority. The stated purpose was to strengthen Palestinian moderates to facilitate the Israeli–Palestinian peace process, but experts warned the aid could be diverted to Hamas and other terrorist groups. Additionally, UNRWA, the main UN body administering this aid, is widely considered corrupt, it operates without internal or external audits, and it is known to be infiltrated by Hamas supporters and other radicals. As Republican congressman Mark Kirk noted, "To route $900 million to this area, and let's say that Hamas was only able to steal 10 percent of that, we would still become Hamas's second-largest funder after Iran."[14]

Shortly thereafter, in an abrupt change of tone from her pro-Israel declarations when she was senator of New York, Secretary of State Hillary Clinton angered Jewish leaders by denouncing Israel's treatment of Palestinians in Gaza. For some observers, Clinton's condemnation brought back memories of her controversial kiss of

Yassir Arafat's wife Suha, after Suha had unleashed a shocking anti-Israel tirade, including outlandish accusations that Israel was poisoning the Palestinian water supply and attacking Palestinians with poison gas. Some Jewish leaders wondered out loud "who the real Hillary Clinton is." One said, "She is pro-Palestinian 100 percent, really. Of course, we always knew it."[15]

In March, the United States returned to the UN Human Rights Council, which it had left nine months earlier primarily because the Bush administration objected to its obsessive focus on denouncing Israel while overlooking the horrific abuses that occur every day in the Middle East's assorted dictatorships.[16] Also in March, tension arose between the United States and Israel following a surprise visit by Hillary Clinton to Israel, where she was once again "highly critical" of the Jewish state, this time over the demolition of Palestinian homes in Eastern Jerusalem. Israel strongly defended its actions, insisting they were a matter of law enforcement that had been approved following a hearing at the Israeli Supreme Court.

By April, reporters were asking the question, "Can Israel still call the United States its best international friend?" Israel's primary security threat is Iran's ambition to get a nuclear weapon—a logical focus in light of the Iranian president's vow to wipe Israel off the map—but White House chief of staff Rahm Emanuel told Israeli leaders if they wanted to defuse the Iranian threat they better start evacuating settlements in the West Bank. This drew accusations that the Obama administration was exploiting Israeli anxiety about Iran's nuclear ambitions to pressure Israel into making more concessions to the Palestinians.

Meanwhile, the administration canceled a scheduled meeting between Obama and Israeli prime minister Benjamin Netanyahu and announced it would end Bush's tradition of hosting Israeli prime ministers whenever they were in town. Adding to Israel's unease, Obama demanded a complete settlement freeze in the West Bank and reversed the Bush policy of opposing Hamas' inclusion in a future Palestinian government.[17]

The administration's dictatorial tone continued with Mideast envoy George Mitchell's assertion, after meeting with Palestinian president Mahmoud Abbas, that a "two-state solution is the only solution" to the Israeli-Palestinian conflict. This was an unmistakable rebuke of Netanyahu, who had shortly beforehand expressed his misgivings to Mitchell about Palestinian statehood. More significant, Mitchell adopted the controversial 2002 Arab peace initiative, which called for Israel to withdraw from Eastern Jerusalem, the entire West Bank, and the Golan Heights, and to accept the influx of millions of foreign Arabs as Israeli citizens as part of the "right of return," in exchange for promises of peace with the Arab world. Mitchell proclaimed, as if wholly ignoring any Israeli aspirations or security concerns, "The U.S. is committed to the establishment of a sovereign, independent Palestinian state, where the aspirations of the Palestinian people to control their own destiny are realized. We want the Arab peace initiative to be a part of the effort to reach this goal."[18]

Unsurprisingly, a PA negotiator reportedly declared that President Obama was intent on creating a Palestinian state "more quickly than anybody could imagine."[19] The administration also irked Israel when they cavalierly rejected Netanyahu's insistence that the Palestinians recognize Israel as the state of the Jewish people as a condition to renewing peace talks.[20]

Administration demands on Israel persisted with the U.S. State Department's command that Israel engage in negotiations with Syria, one of the primary sponsors (along with Iran) of the Hezbollah terrorist group. This was just two days after Syrian foreign minister Walid Muallem praised a speech by Mahmoud Ahmadinejad in which the Iranian leader called the Israeli government "the most cruel and repressive racist regime."[21]

INTENSE AND UNPRECEDENTED PRESSURE

In May, Rahm Emanuel upped the ante against Israel. Whereas the administration had been linking U.S. pressure against Iran to Israel's discontinuation of West Bank settlements, it now took the position that America's ability to confront Iran was solely dependent on progress toward creating a Palestinian state.[22]

Reports also surfaced in May that Obama's nuclear arms reduction efforts "threatened to expose and derail a 40-year-old secret U.S. agreement to shield Israel's nuclear weapons from international scrutiny by pressuring Israel to join the Non-Proliferation Treaty, which would require Israel to declare and relinquish its nuclear arsenal."[23] The United States joined Britain, Russia, France, and China in voicing support for making the Middle East a nuclear-weapons-free zone. This would ultimately force Israel to surrender what is perhaps its biggest deterrent against another Arab invasion—its never-declared nuclear arsenal.[24]

Identifying the apparent goal underlying all of Obama's policy reversals, journalist Caroline Glick reported in the *Jerusalem Post* on May 8 that U.S. national security adviser James Jones "told a European foreign minister that the US is planning to build an anti-Israel coalition with the Arabs and Europe to compel Israel to surrender Judea, Samaria and Jerusalem to the Palestinians." *Haaretz*, wrote Glick, had quoted Jones in a classified foreign ministry cable as saying, "The new administration will convince Israel to compromise on the Palestinian question. We will not push Israel under the wheels of a bus, but we will be more forceful toward Israel than we have been under Bush."

This was consistent with earlier reports that the United States supported the 2002 Arab peace initiative, whose "right of return" clause, Glick observed, would mean "Israel would effectively cease to be a Jewish state."[25] This, of course, is precisely the Palestinians' goal, which is why they refused Netanyahu's insistence on recognizing Israel as a state of the Jewish people.

Author Joel Rosenberg similarly reported that his sources were telling him the Obama administration had been "applying intense and unprecedented pressure on the Netanyahu government to make huge unilateral concessions to the Palestinians even before direct peace talks begin." Obama had even contacted the leaders of Germany, Britain, and France to get each to agree to the strategy. But Netanyahu held his ground.[26] Indeed, in a speech marking the annual Jerusalem Day, Netanyahu insisted that Jerusalem would always remain united under Israeli sovereignty—a contradiction of the 2002 Arab peace plan, which called for Israel to surrender Eastern Jerusalem to the Palestinians. "United Jerusalem is Israel's capital," said Netanyahu. "Jerusalem was always ours and will always be ours. It will never again be partitioned and divided."[27]

Meanwhile, as his efforts to end Iran's nuclear program foundered, Obama sternly warned Netanyahu against Israel's exercising its own self-defense by attacking Iran's nuclear facilities.[28]

A few weeks later, Hillary Clinton delivered another harsh warning from Obama for Israel to halt all construction in settlements on the West Bank. "He wants to see a stop to settlements—not some settlements, not outposts, not 'natural growth' exceptions," said Clinton, who indicated she had communicated that message "very clearly." This was an in-your-face rebuke to Israel, which had recently told the administration it wanted to preserve the right to undertake some limited new construction in West Bank settlements.[29] Aaron David Miller, who served under both Democratic and Republican administrations, told AFP that Obama's toughness against Israel was "almost unprecedented" and represented "something of a radical break with past administrations."[30]

WorldNetDaily reported that just days after Netanyahu's speech, the Obama administration told the Palestinian Authority Jerusalem could not remain united under Israeli sovereignty. A top PA official said the United States was cooperating with the PA to "thwart Israel's plans in Jerusalem." This report was consistent with the State Department, just one day earlier, saying the future status of Jerusalem would be determined through peace negotiations—a contradiction of Netanyahu's vow that Jerusalem would "never be divided."[31]

Obama then met with Palestinian president Abbas, whose adviser, Nimer Hamad, reported that Obama "was very friendly to the position of the PA" and had told Abbas that the United States foresees the creation of a Palestinian state with Jerusalem as its capital, which Obama said was "in the American national and security interest." Another PA official reportedly said that Obama informed Abbas that he would not let Netanyahu "get in the way" of normalizing U.S. relations with the Arab and greater Muslim world.[32]

Obama's hostility toward Israel continued as his administration reportedly blocked the sale of six AH064D helicopters to Israel while approving twelve for Egypt. This was revealed in a January 2010 Jewish Institute for National Security Affairs report concluding that the Obama administration had refused for the past year to approve any major Israeli weapons requests while approving more than $10 billion in arms sales to Arab League states.[33] Caroline Glick had confirmed the administration's limitations on arms sales to Israel in a June 2009 interview with *National Review Online*. Should the Palestinian army attack Judea and Samaria, said Glick, and the U.S. side with the Arabs against Israel, "Israel will have to move quickly to find other suppliers."[34]

"I CONDEMN THE DECISION
BY THE GOVERNMENT OF ISRAEL"

As the months ticked by, Obama's pressure on Israel was unrelenting. Showing its enthusiasm for dictating the most minute aspects of Israeli domestic policy—even in Israel's own capital city—the State Department in July warned Israel not to permit construction of a 20-apartment building on a piece of privately owned land in Eastern Jerusalem. Netanyahu flatly rejected the demand, saying Israeli sovereignty meant that any Jerusalem resident, whether Jewish or Arab, could choose to live in any part of the city. "Jerusalem," he said, "is not a settlement." Another Israeli official called the Obama demand "odd," saying he'd never heard of a similar demand against an Arab citizen building in Jerusalem.[35]

Relations between the United States and Israel reached a low in March 2010, when Israel announced its plan to build 1,600 homes in an Israeli settlement in Eastern Jerusalem—the announcement occurring when Vice President Joe Biden was in Jerusalem for meetings with Prime Minister Netanyahu. After he heard of the announcement, a petulant Biden kept Netanyahu waiting ninety minutes before dinner as the administration contemplated how to respond. They decided to use the harsh word "condemn," which is rarely used by countries when discussing their own allies. "I condemn the decision by the government of Israel to advance planning for new housing units in East Jerusalem," Biden said. "The substance and timing of the announcement, particularly with the launching of proximity talks, is precisely the kind of step that undermines the trust we need right now and runs counter to the constructive discussions that I've had here in Israel."[36]

The relationship continued to deteriorate from there. Biden delivered a speech a few days later in Tel Aviv looking as though he were seeking an approving pat on the head from Obama. After paying lip service to our "unbreakable bond" with Israel, he again scolded Israel over the housing project. By marked contrast, he lauded Palestinian president Abbas and prime minister Fayyad as willing partners for peace and again accused Israel of having "undermined the trust required for productive negotiations." As Leo Rennert wrote in *American Thinker*, Biden's slamming Israel while not mentioning "anything about Abbas's multiple impediments to advancing the peace process makes a mockery of Obama-Biden pledges to hold all sides equally accountable when they get out of line." If they had, said Rennert, Biden would have condemned "Abbas's incitement campaign against Israel in Palestinian Authority media, schools and mosques; and Abbas's retention of clauses in the PLO/Fatah charter that call for the total elimination of the Jewish state. He also might have 'condemned' Fayyad for joining Abbas in legitimizing terrorist murderers. Doesn't such conduct also 'undermine trust required for productive negotiations?'"[37]

UNFORESEEN CONSEQUENCES

Many astute observers, including Rennert, have noted that Obama's bias toward the Palestinians and against the Israelis has been counterproductive to his stated goal of peace. By highlighting and magnifying any and all alleged Israeli infractions and wholly ignoring those of the Palestinians, Obama left the Palestinians with no incentive for cooperating toward peace, effectively encouraging them to remain intransigent and allow Obama to do their negotiating for them. Although Obama's strategy has proven counterproductive, we can't expect anything else from him, for that's Obama's typical MO: he must have his way, and he will bully anyone that gets in his way, including our longest and most loyal Middle East ally.

Even the reliably pro-Palestinian *New York Times* chided the "rare and decidedly undiplomatic language" with which Obama and Biden condemned Israel's housing policies, though it said the administration was "understandably furious." The *Times* acknowledged "Obama seriously miscalculated last year" in demanding the complete halt of all new settlements, and faulted Obama and Mitchell for failing to extract any concessions from Arab leaders in exchange for Obama's demanded Israeli settlement freeze.[38]

For all Obama's posturing about bringing a new era of diplomatic relations, he has single-handedly made a royal mess of our relationship with Israel—and for nothing. The peace process was, if anything, set back by his antics. Israel's ambassador to the United States Michael Orin said ties between Israel and the United States were the worst they'd been since 1975. But Obama was unrepentant, demanding a monopoly on the claim to being offended. His aide David Axelrod reiterated that Israel's housing announcement was an "affront" and an "insult" to the United States.[39]

ISRAEL: A BIPARTISAN CAUSE NO MORE

Caroline Glick argued that "bipartisan support for Israel has been one of the greatest casualties of U.S. President Barack Obama's assault on the Jewish state." Today, said Glick, Republican support for Israel is at an all-time high, but it is a minority position among Democrats. She cited evidence demonstrating a remarkable change in the Democratic attitude pre- and post-Obama. Eleven days before Obama's inauguration, the House passed Resolution 34, which sided with Israel against Hamas during Operation Cast Lead—the Israeli offensive to stop Hamas from firing rockets into Israel. Of the 390 yea votes, five nays, and thirty-seven abstentions, Democrats cast four nays and twenty-nine abstentions. In November 2009, Congress passed a resolution urging Obama to disregard a report that falsely accused Israel of committing war crimes during Cast Lead. There were 344 yea votes. Of the thirty-six nay votes, thirty-three were Democrats, and forty-four of the fifty-two abstentions were from Democrats.

In February 2010, fifty-four congressmen—all Democrats—sent Obama a letter encouraging him to pressure Israel to open the borders of Hamas-ruled Gaza and also accusing Israel of engaging in collective punishment. Moreover, when Obama was berating Israel over the Jerusalem construction issue, 327 congressmen signed a letter to Secretary of State Clinton demanding the administration quit publicly attacking Israel. Of the 102 refusing to sign the appeal, ninety-four were Democrats. Glick concluded that the numbers point to a 13-point decline in the number of congressmen supporting Israel, with the entire decrease coming from the Democratic side. Meanwhile, the number of Democratic congressmen willing to attack Israel has tripled. Even the pro-Israel initiatives the other Democrats do support are "less meaningful than those they supported before Obama entered office."[40]

BACKLASH

Eventually, Obama's mistreatment of Israel began to backfire, as there is just so much good will a fallen messiah can squander. Conservative and even some liberal commentators criticized Obama's dogmatic position against Israeli settlements. The left-leaning *Washington Post*, while also critical of Netanyahu, said that by insisting on "a total construction ban" in the settlements, the administration risked "bogging itself down in a major dispute with its ally, while giving Arab governments and Palestinians a ready excuse not to make their own concessions."[41]

Reminding Obama that he has always insisted the United States not "dictate" to other countries (as he alleged his predecessor did), columnist Charles Krauthammer noted he was doing just that with Israel, especially in demanding it stop the settlements. No "natural growth," wrote Krauthammer, meant "strangling to death the thriving towns close to the 1949 armistice line ... no babies. Or if you have babies, no housing for them—not even *within* the existing town boundaries. Which means for every child born, someone has to move out. No community can survive like that." All that would be required for both Jews and Arabs to stay in their existing homes, noted Krauthammer, is for the 1949 armistice line to be "shifted slightly into the Palestinian side to capture the major close-in Jewish settlements" and "then shifted into Israeli territory to capture Israeli land to give to the Palestinians."

This was agreed to by both Democratic and Republican administrations for the past decade, said Krauthammer, and agreed to in writing by Israel and the United States in 2004 and endorsed by a congressional resolution. Yet Obama wouldn't even promise to honor the agreement when he is constantly berating politicians for not living up to their commitments. Krauthammer also criticized Obama's Cairo speech for stating that the Palestinian people's "situation" is "intolerable." Yes, but it is not intolerable because of Israel, implied Krauthammer, but because of "60 years of Palestinian leadership that gave its people corruption, tyranny, religious intolerance and forced militarization; leadership that for three generations rejected every offer of independence and dignity, choosing destitution and despair rather than accept any settlement not accompanied by the extinction of Israel."[42]

The American Jewish Committee also spoke up, urging the administration to halt its public denunciations of the Israeli government and return to using language befitting close allies. It wasn't just Obama's demands that were distasteful, the AJC noted, but that he was making such a public spectacle of the issue and attempting to humiliate Israel.

The AJC said, "Ideally, differences with allies, which do occur even between the closest of friends, should be discussed and resolved in private. We urge the White House to reconsider its latest, repeated verbal assaults on the Israeli government. It is not beneficial to pummel Israel with language that has rarely been used in U.S. foreign policy. And it may, however unintentionally, send the wrong signal to Israel's adversaries in the region, further complicating an already complex landscape."[43]

Obama's betrayal of Israel also earned a stunning denunciation from Democratic former New York City mayor Ed Koch, who wrote,

> I weep as I witness outrageous verbal attacks on Israel. What makes these verbal assaults and distortions all the more painful is that they are being orchestrated by President Obama....I weep today because my president, Barack Obama, in a few weeks has changed the relationship between the U.S. and Israel from that of closest of allies to one in which there is an absence of trust on both sides. The contrast between how the president and his administration deals with Israel and how it has decided to deal with the Karzai administration in Afghanistan is striking.

According to Koch, Obama treats the "corrupt and opiate producing state" with complete respect but, "on the other hand, our closest ally—the one with the special relationship with the U.S., has been demeaned and slandered, held responsible by the administration for our problems in Afghanistan and Iraq and elsewhere in the Middle East." Koch said he supposed Obama's plan was to "weaken the resolve" of Israel to make it easier to impose on it a peace plan that will ultimately leave "Israel's needs for security and defensible borders in the lurch." Koch concluded by expressing his "shock" at "the lack of outrage on the part of Israel's most ardent supporters," including "members of Congress in both the House and Senate" who "have made pitifully weak statements against Obama's mistreatment of Israel, if they made any at all."[44]

In another op-ed, Koch called out by name New York Democratic senator Chuck Schumer, a pro-Israel stalwart who had kept noticeably quiet about Obama's Israel policies. Koch wrote, "President Obama's abysmal attitude toward the State of Israel and his humiliating treatment of Prime Minister Benjamin Netanyahu is shocking. . . . I have nor heard or read statements criticizing the president by New York Senators Charles Schumer and Kirsten Gillibrand or many other supporters of Israel for his blatantly hostile attitude toward Israel and his discourtesy displayed at the White House" as well as his berating and "degrading" attitude toward Netanyahu. "It is one thing to disagree with certain policies of the Israeli government," wrote Koch. "It is quite another to treat Israel and its prime minister as pariahs, which only emboldens Israel's enemies and makes the prospect of peace even more remote."[45]

Schumer may have been keeping silent out of loyalty to Obama, but he eventually reached his breaking point. He joined with a majority of members of the House and Senate in urging Obama to keep his disagreements with Israel private. *Politico*, however, reported that his tone was "dramatically" sharper on a radio talk show where he called the White House stance "counter-productive," and said he had threatened to "blast" the administration if the State Department did not refrain from further "terrible" tough talk toward Netanyahu. Schumer rightly noted that "Palestinians don't really believe in a state of Israel."[46]

Unsurprisingly, Obama's popularity among U.S. Jews overall has plummeted. He garnered 78 percent of Jewish voters in the presidential election, but *Arutz Sheva* reported that a poll by the

McLaughlin Group found that today only 42 percent said they would vote to re-elect him.[47] Caroline Glick reported that American and European Jews are "belatedly awakening to the threat of divestment from Israel." They are now seeing that Israel's constant compromising of its rights in exchange for promises of support and peace have made matters worse—where Israel's peace is in greater jeopardy and its "very legitimacy is being called into question throughout the world." As Glick correctly observes, "It is impossible to reconcile the rights of the Jewish people and the demands of the Obama administration and the alliance of the international Left and the Islamic world it leads in their common campaign to undermine Israeli control over Jerusalem."[48]

The Obama administration's heavy-handed treatment of Israel, especially its wildly exaggerated reaction to Israel's housing policies and its demands for a complete freeze in settlement construction, bespeaks a pre-planned policy. Obama's approach to the Israeli–Palestinian issue has been completely one-sided and strikingly unfair—as if he has inflexible, preconceived notions about the conflict and is impervious to the facts and history.

How can an objective witness to Obama's behavior fail to conclude that he has bought into Palestinian propaganda and its skewed view of history? What else would account for his meting out harsher treatment to one of our best allies and the world's finest and most honorable democratic societies than to the world's dictatorial regimes that are not only enemies of freedom, but hostile to the United States? What is it that Obama resents so much about Israel?

In light of his constant apologies for American history and his endless flattery of third world grievances, it's clear that for Obama, a distant outpost of Western, democratic values like Israel is not something worthy of admiration. Instead, he seems to believe the Jewish state is just another Western imposition on noble, innocent Muslim societies for which we must apologize and make amends.

Chapter Fifteen

SEE NO EVIL

CRIMES AGAINST NATIONAL SECURITY

I n keeping with his view that America, not Islamic extremism, is the world's agitator, President Obama is deeply ambivalent about the war he now leads. From his perspective, if we hadn't historically behaved so badly toward the Muslim world by supporting Israel, invading Iraq in a "war of choice," and "abusing," torturing," and "illegally detaining" enemy prisoners, al Qaeda might not be attacking us. But our excessive, misguided response to the 9/11 attack, in his view, alienated the entire Muslim world and swelled the terrorist ranks. Only he, with his unique background and proper understanding of the real America, can rectify our missteps and restore our relationship with Muslims, repair our damaged world image, and ultimately redeem this nation.

As columnist and military expert Ralph Peters, wrote, "The Obama administration has ducked all unwelcome evidence that such appeasement doesn't work. Instead, it goes to absurd lengths

to convince Muslim radicals that we respect their views. Our coun-
terfactual assumption is that, if we're really, really nice, the fanat-
ics will stop being grumpy and blowing us up. But Islamic
extremists haven't read our actions (or inactions) as an admirable
exercise in tolerance. They view our bowing and scraping and apologizing as weakness."[1] Victor Davis Hanson had a similar take:

> To paraphrase the president himself, "words matter.". . . Our
> enemies are simultaneously also waging a symbolic war in which
> imagery, vocabulary, and perceptions matter as much as battle-
> field realities. So when Obama and his team were dreaming up
> euphemisms like "overseas contingency operations". . . and mag-
> nifying our own past misdemeanors while downplaying the
> felonies of Islam . . . perhaps a subtle message was delivered to
> radical Islamists that we either would not or could not any
> longer wage war against them. . . . Words matter. . . . Our enemies
> may look far more to words than deeds—and see in them a rad-
> ical loss of our deterrence ability. So the Hasans, Abdulmutal-
> labs, and Shahzads of the world interpret our new philological
> magnanimity as weakness, regardless of whether it is or not. And
> that seems to me very dangerous indeed.[2]

With these instincts for appeasing our enemies, it's a small step
to trivializing the horror of terrorist attacks—even the 9/11
attacks. Incredibly, Obama's nominee for the number two man at
the Justice Department, James Cole, takes exactly this approach,
writing in a 2002 op-ed, "Our country has faced many forms of
devastating crime, including the scourge of the drug trade, the
reign of organized crime, and countless acts of rape, child abuse,
and murder. The acts of Sept. 11 were horrible, but so are these
other things."[3]

In other words, *terrorism is bad, but so is crime and many other
things, so let's not get caught up in spending too much time and
energy fighting terrorists.*

PAPER TIGER

Obama's worldview blinds him to the facts and to human nature. Osama bin Laden himself said our feckless reaction to the massacre of U.S. soldiers in Somalia by al Qaeda terrorists emboldened him to attack us. In 1996 he declared, "You have been disgraced by Allah and you withdrew. The extent of your impotence and weaknesses became very clear. When people see a strong horse and a weak horse, by nature they will like the strong horse." He repeated this argument in 1998: "Muslim fighters . . . were surprised at the low morale of the American soldiers and realized, more than before, that the American soldier was a paper tiger and after a few blows . . . would run in defeat."[4]

In April 2010, we heard from a former bin Laden associate that bin Laden was stunned that the United States—the "paper tiger"—reacted with such force following the 9/11 attacks. Norman Benotman, head of the Libyan Islamic Fighting Group, said, "I'm 100 percent sure they had no idea about what was going to happen. What happened after the 11th of September was beyond their imagination." Benotman reported that al Qaeda leader Ayman Al-Zawahiri laughed when Benotman told him the United States would react ferociously to the attack. Since we responded to the bombings of their embassies in East Africa with seventy-five cruise missiles, Zawahiri predicted we would simply respond with 200 after 9/11.[5]

Obama has pursued an ostentatious policy of retreat from the War on Terror. Despite all we've learned about our vulnerabilities prior to the September 11 attacks, Obama made a conscious decision to revert to our pre-9/11 mindset and approach the war as a criminal law enforcement matter. Henceforth, we would no longer treat terrorists as the enemy. We wouldn't even treat them as criminals, but more like criminal *suspects*.

Attempting to definitively reject Bush-era policies and reclaim the "moral high ground" in the War on Terror, Obama issued three executive orders on January 22, 2009, his second day in office. He said the United States does not have "to continue with a false choice between our safety and our ideals," as he issued an order to close the prison in Guantanamo Bay.

"Guantanamo became a symbol," said Obama, "that helped al Qaeda recruit terrorists to its cause." Closing the facility would "restore the standards of due process and the core constitutional values that have made this country great even in the midst of war, even in dealing with terrorism." His second order formally banned "torture" by requiring the Army field manual to guide terrorism interrogations, which would preclude controversial enhanced inter- rogation techniques such as waterboarding. Obama declared, "We can abide by a rule that says we don't torture, but . . . still effectively obtain the intelligence that we need." His third order established an interagency task force to systematically review detention policies and individual detainees' cases.[6]

Obama also undertook other actions, symbolic as well as con- crete, that further signaled our retreat in the war. By April 2009, the administration had ordered an end to the use of the phrase "Global War on Terror"—another infernal reminder of the Bush adminis- tration—and replaced it, per Defense Department memo, with "Overseas Contingency Operation." Perhaps the administration was responding to pressure from the International Commission of Jurists, which argued the phrase "war on terror" had given the Bush administration "spurious justification to a range of human rights and humanitarian law violations," such as controversial detention practices and enhanced interrogation techniques.[7]

Another casualty of Obama's vernacular purge was the Bush-era phrase "enemy combatants." But there was more to this move than mere symbolism. As if acting as advocate for the constitutional rights of our nation's enemies, Obama and Attorney General Eric Holder said the term was too broad and allowed the government to detain almost any terrorism suspect indefinitely. Holder said we would only seek to hold suspects who "substantially supported" the groups against us and not those who "provide unwitting or insignificant support" to al Qaeda and the Taliban.[8] Next, Secretary of Homeland Security Janet Napolitano told the German newspaper *Der Spiegel* that she was abandoning use of the word "terrorism" because it "perpetuates the politics of fear"—as if fearing jihadists is an irrational thing. She would replace it with the meaningless, widely ridiculed locution "man-caused disasters."[9] Finally, Obama made the mind-numbing decision to Mirandize terrorists on the battlefield, claiming this unprecedented, woefully impractical legalism would help "to preserve the quality of the evidence obtained."[10]

A THWARTED ATTACK

For all his posturing, Obama didn't have a plan to close our expensive, state-of-the-art detention facility at Gitmo, nor for relocating its terrorist detainees or funding the relocation. He also failed to substantiate his claim that we could obtain the same information without enhanced interrogation and be just as safe. Though Obama dismisses the reliability of information obtained through such means because the victims will allegedly say anything to stop the procedures, our experience teaches differently. In fact, we indisputably extracted life-saving information from 9/11 mastermind Khalid Sheikh Mohammed via waterboarding, the most "controversial" technique of all.

Before he was waterboarded, KSM defiantly told CIA interrogators that "soon you will know" about planned attacks on the United States. But the CIA has repeatedly confirmed that after undergoing enhanced interrogation techniques, KSM sang a different tune, producing information that helped prevent a planned attack that would use "East Asian operatives to crash a hijacked airliner into a building in Los Angeles."[11] The *Chicago Tribune* reported that KSM offered so much information it took 100 footnotes to reference it all in the final report of the 9/11 investigative commission. Much of the information was corroborated through other captured al Qaeda prisoners.[12]

For all the Left's sanctimonious sermonizing on waterboarding, the United States reportedly only administered the technique against three al Qaeda terrorists: KSM, Abu Zubaydah, and Abd al-Rahim al-Nashiri. According to a May 30, 2005 Justice Department memo, the CIA applied very restrictive rules on waterboarding and did not operate like the lawless cabal the Left has depicted. It only used the technique against "high value" detainees if it had "credible intelligence that a terrorist attack is imminent." This is the ticking time bomb scenario, when there are "substantial and credible indicators that the subject has actionable intelligence that can prevent, disrupt or deny this attack, and [o]ther interrogation methods have failed to elicit this information within the perceived time limit for preventing the attack." In the memo, a Justice Department official named Bradbury told a CIA official, "Your office has informed us that the CIA believes that 'the intelligence acquired from these interrogations has been a key reason why al Qa'ida has failed to launch a spectacular attack in the West since 11 September 2001.'"[13]

Obama continued to bend over backward to accommodate terrorists, this time in his decision to declassify and release the opinions of the Bush Justice Department's Office of Legal Counsel (OLC) on the legality of the CIA's interrogation techniques. There was no legal requirement that they be released, and there were considerable damaging national security consequences in doing so, including the revelation of the precise techniques themselves. Even Obama's CIA chief, Leon Panetta, objected to the release, as did former Homeland Security secretary Michael Chertoff. In an op-ed, former CIA director Michael Hayden and former Attorney General Michael Mukasey noted that the disclosure compromised the techniques by assuring that "terrorists are now aware of the absolute limit of what the U.S. government could do to extract information from them, and can supplement their training accordingly." Well aware of the partisan nature of this exercise, former vice president Dick Cheney argued the memos didn't tell the whole story and urged the administration to release other classified documents that detailed the success of the enhanced interrogation techniques.

Whether Obama's primary motive was to embarrass the Bush administration or to attempt to further prove to terrorists he would take a softer approach toward them, the net effect of the disclosures was to subject the United States to yet further bashing from foreign and domestic detractors and to enhance terrorists' intelligence on us. The notion that this reckless gesture would earn us good will from Islamic extremists—especially in view of the jihadists' redoubled resolve upon any display of our weakness—is pathetically absurd. As Hayden and Mukasey wrote, "It seems unlikely that the people who beheaded Nicholas Berg and Daniel Pearl, and have tortured and slain other American captives, are likely to be shamed into giving up violence by the news that the U.S. will no longer interrupt the sleep cycle of captured terrorists even to help elicit intelligence that could save the lives of its citizens."[14]

"MY DUTY IS TO EXAMINE THE FACTS AND TO FOLLOW THE LAW"

The administration was seriously considering prosecuting Bush-era CIA operatives for administering enhanced interrogation techniques as well as Bush officials for their legal opinions approving them. But as they released the "torture memos," Obama and Attorney General Eric Holder said they wouldn't prosecute the CIA officials, as long as they were acting according to the legal advice they were given.[15] A few days later, White House chief of staff Rahm Emanuel indicated that "those who devised the policies" also "should not be prosecuted."

But Obama's left hand must not have known what his right hand was doing, for the *New York Times* reported that White House aides "did not rule out legal sanctions for the Bush lawyers who developed the legal basis for the use of the techniques." Indeed, when AP's Jennifer Loven put the question directly to Obama, he would not rule out the possibility of prosecuting those who "formulated those legal decisions," and he passed the buck to Holder.[16] He proclaimed, "With respect to those who formulated those legal decisions, I would say that this is going to be more of a decision for the attorney general within the parameters of various laws, and I don't want to prejudge that. I think that there are a host of very complicated issues involved there."[17]

A few months later, Holder threw yet another curveball, announcing he would appoint a prosecutor, John H. Durham, to investigate CIA interrogators and contractors over nearly a dozen alleged interrogation abuses. Holder said, "As attorney general, my duty is to examine the facts and to follow the law."[18] Holder maintained his decision to reconsider prosecution of the CIA interrogators and operatives was not a reversal of the administration's position against prosecuting those interrogators who followed guidelines written by their superiors. He insisted he was basing his decision to open the investigation on troubling abuse allegations from a CIA inspector general's report. The only problem was that this report was five years old, and congressional leaders had been aware of it for years. Moreover, professional prosecutors had already investigated the allegations and declined (per "declination memos") to prosecute all but one of the cases—and that one resulted in an acquittal.

Obama pretended he had nothing to do with this decision as well, a decision that reportedly provoked CIA director Leon Panetta to consider resigning.[19] Given the political nature of this White House, however, many didn't believe the attorney general operated with the autonomy the two were implying. Seven former CIA directors, from both Democratic and Republican administrations, wrote Obama a letter urging him to heed his own promise to look forward, not backward. They expressed concern that Holder's decision would "seriously damage the willingness of intelligence officers to take risks to protect the country." Furthermore, they argued, "Attorney General Holder's decision to re-open the criminal investigation creates an atmosphere of continuous jeopardy for those whose cases the Department of Justice had previously declined to prosecute." They added, "Those men and women who undertake difficult intelligence assignments in the aftermath of an attack such as September 11 must believe there is some permanence in the legal rules that govern their actions."[20]

What's more, Holder did not open the investigation based on any alleged flaw in the work of the professional prosecutors who had already refused the cases, nor had any newly discovered evidence emerged.[21] What had changed was that this Justice Department likely had political motivations to reopen the case. Former federal prosecutor Andy McCarthy called Holder's probe "a nakedly political, banana republic-style criminalizing of policy differences and political rivalry."

McCarthy theorized that Holder's reversal might have to do with the administration's bent toward transnationalism—"a doctrine of post-sovereign globalism in which America is seen as owing its principal allegiance to the international legal order rather than to our own Constitution and national interests." McCarthy cited Obama's appointment of Yale Law School dean Harold Koh—"the country's leading proponent of transnationalism"—as the State Department's legal adviser. Holder had hinted to the German press he would consider cooperating with efforts by foreign or international tribunals to prosecute U.S. officials who carried out the Bush-era post-9/11 counterterrorism policies. "Obviously," said Holder, "we would look at any request that would come from a court in any country and see how and whether we should comply with it."

When you "put it all together," said McCarthy, transnationalists in the United States and other countries "have been ardent supporters of prosecutions against American officials" who carried out the Bush counterterrorism policies that protected this nation after 9/11. While Obama and Holder may not want to risk the political fallout from directly prosecuting these people—despite Obama's adamant advocacy for such during the campaign and the hard Left's pressure to hold him to his promise—they have a way out of this dilemma, said McCarthy. The Justice Department will continue investigating and churning up "new disclosures," which can be used by detainees' lawyers to press the UN and European authorities to file charges. Then, if these international and foreign authorities issue formal requests to the administration for evidence, "Holder will piously announce that the 'rule of law' requires him to cooperate with these 'lawful requests' from 'appropriately created courts.' Finally, the international and/or foreign courts will file criminal charges against American officials."[22] Whether or not this scenario plays out, careful observers understand McCarthy has accurately pegged where Obama and Holder's sympathies lie.

Six months later, House Democrats tried to sneak a provision into the intelligence authorization bill to criminalize the use of certain interrogation tactics. After the plot was exposed largely through McCarthy's efforts, however, Democrats pulled the entire bill.[23]

In his next extravagant gesture to atone for Bush's supposed sins, Obama issued an edict to transfer KSM and others to New York to stand trial in our civilian courts without any consideration of the costs and security implications, and without consulting New York officials on the matter. (The Bloomberg administration later placed the price for security operations for the trials at more than $200 million a year). Aside from the enormous expense and security problems, legal experts warn that in the trial, prosecutors will be forced to reveal valuable U.S. intelligence concerning KSM's relationships with fellow al Qaeda members. This will inform terrorist groups which of their plans have been compromised, and will also give them further insight into our intelligence gathering processes. Amidst popular outrage and bipartisan opposition in Congress, the administration backed off its plan for a KSM trial in New York. Eventually, Obama reluctantly signed a congressional bill effectively barring civilian trials for Guantanamo detainees, forcing an infuriated Eric Holder to convene a military trial for KSM.[24]

Obama's plan to close Gitmo was similarly impulsive, compulsive, and was formulated without fully considering the costs, consequences, or complications, and without any plan for relocating the prisoners. As a symbol of Bush-era policies, not to mention all the chest-thumping Obama had engaged in about closing it, Gitmo had to be shut down. He asked Congress for $80 million to close the facility by early 2010. But just as with so many other policy initiatives, Obama had no plan to present to Congress. Details are not his strong suit; only pre-written speeches.

And once again he ran into opposition from Congress, which initially wouldn't agree to have any of the 240 prisoners relocated in U.S. prisons. But that prohibition risked sparking resistance from European nations, which might refuse to accept any prisoners on their soil if the U.S. banned any from its own prisons. Objections from both sides of the aisle were also beginning to resurface against closing Gitmo at all. Democratic senator James Webb remarked, "We spent hundreds of millions of dollars building an appropriate facility with security precautions on Guantanamo to try these cases. I do not believe they should be tried in the United States."[25]

But Obama was not to be denied. Just a month after he had made the precipitous decision to give KSM a civilian trial in New York, he announced his plan in December to purchase the Thomson Correctional Center in northwestern Illinois and transfer some of the prisoners there. Illinois Democratic senator Dick Durbin strongly supported the move, even claiming it would be good for the local job market. Durbin said, "We have an opportunity to bring thousands of good-paying jobs to Illinois where we need them the most."[26] Tennessee Republican senator Lamar Alexander, by contrast, declared, "I have yet to hear one good reason why moving these terrorists from off our shores right into the heart of our country makes us safer."[27] But liberals don't need reasons or evidence; they just need their good intentions.

Eventually, however, the relocation problems forced Obama to admit he couldn't close Gitmo by the end of the year—another broken campaign promise over which we should rejoice.

"THE PUBLIC IS VERY, VERY SAFE"

Obama's ill-conceived plan to close Gitmo and the disastrous consequences it could bring were brought into full relief when news broke of the Christmas Day "underwear bombing" attempt on a Northwest Airlines flight approaching Detroit. *ABC News* reported that two of the jihadist leaders behind the failed attack were released Gitmo prisoners, which was hardly an eye-opener—it's not as though there's any such thing as a moderate jihadist. Indeed, we learned a month later from Congressman Mark Kirk, a veteran of the war in Afghanistan, that "all of the major leaders of the Taliban in the south of Afghanistan are former Gitmo releasees—all of them."[28] Additionally, the *Times of London* reported that at least a dozen former Gitmo prisoners had rejoined al Qaeda to fight in Yemen.[29] Democratic senator Dianne Feinstein estimated seventy-four Gitmo detainees "have gone back into the fight."[30] Then again, this might not have been as offensive to some as the fact that four released Chinese Uighurs were sent to the island paradise of Bermuda at considerable U.S. taxpayer expense.

It turns out Homeland Security secretary Janet Napolitano was just as clueless in the aftermath of the Christmas Day bombing attempt as she had been in announcing new terms for our politically correct lexicon. Ignoring what the *New York Daily News* called "the glaring mistakes that allowed a Nigerian bomber onto a U.S.-bound plane," Napolitano claimed security functioned "like clockwork" and that the "system worked" to foil the attack. "The public is very, very safe," she insisted, with a deer in the headlights expression. This was despite the authorities' ignoring a warning from the terrorist's father that his son might be plotting an attack, and the screening flaws that permitted the bomber to board the plane with his weapon.

Dismissing the administration's fantastic rationalizations, Republican congressman Pete King told CBS's *Face the Nation* what had really happened: "The fact is the system did not work. He got to the one-yard line." Indeed, the plot almost killed 289 people that day. Making matters worse, instead of treating Umar Farouk Abdulmutallab like the enemy combatant he was, the administration allowed the Christmas bomber to lawyer up after only fifty minutes of interrogation, which guaranteed, many believe, we would extract no further information from him. Only after the fortuitously failed Times Square bombing plot in May did Attorney General Holder finally announce he wanted to work with Congress on possible limitations on constitutional rights afforded to terrorism suspects—even for U.S. citizens—to make sure law enforcement agents had the "necessary flexibility" to gather information.[31]

The administration continues to promote their dangerous fable that America is safer under their retreat-and-surrender approach to the war. Meanwhile, Americans are beginning to notice, despite the White House's best efforts to deny it, that incidents of terrorism are rising on U.S. soil. In addition to the Christmas Day and Times Square bombing attempts, there was the fatal shooting at an Army recruiting station in Arkansas; an attempted jihadist car bombing in Dallas; an attempted bombing of a federal building in Springfield, Illinois, by an American convert to Islam; the Fort Hood massacre; the arrest of five Virginians in Pakistan for terrorist activities; the arrest of Pennsylvania's Jihad Jane and Colorado's Jamie Paulin-Ramirez; the arrest of a Brooklyn-born man along with twelve others for supporting an al Qaeda-affiliated group and for plotting several attacks in New York; another New York plot to blow up a synagogue; a planned suicide attack at Grand Central Station; and others.[32] Nor does Obama's Muslim outreach seem to be impressing Pakistan jihadist leader Hakimullah Mehsud who, according to the Middle East Media Research Center, recently released a

YouTube video declaring, "From now on, the main targets of our Fidaeen [armed fighters] are American cities."[33]

ADMINISTRATION ROADBLOCKS

As part of his pandering to the Muslim world, Obama has increasingly refused to identify obvious acts of terrorism by Islamist extremists for what they are. After radical Muslim U.S. Army major Hadal Malik Hasan gunned down twelve U.S. soldiers and a security guard and wounded thirty-one others while shouting "Allahu Akbar," Obama could not bring himself to call the Fort Hood massacre "terrorism," much less Islamist terrorism. This, despite his awareness of these important facts about Hasan:

- He had business cards marked "SoA," or "Soldier of Allah."
- He had e-mail communications with Anwar al-Awlaki, an al Qaeda recruiter who inspired at least two other North American terror plots and was a fugitive from U.S. justice. He had been Hasan's "spiritual leader at two mosques," and later praised Hasan for the massacre.
- Hasan had routinely signed his e-mails with "Praise Be to Allah," and reportedly said that infidels should be beheaded and have boiling oil poured down their throats.
- Key psychiatric authorities at Walter Reed reportedly met to discuss whether Hasan was psychotic because his Islamist proclivities were so undeniable that one such official reportedly feared "that if Hasan deployed to Iraq or Aghanistan, he might leak secret military information to Islamic extremists."
- He had contacted jihadist websites through various e-mail addresses and screen names.

Obama simply would not declare the obvious, claiming, "We cannot fully know what leads a man to do such a thing."[34] On this point the administration is pathetically consistent. Eric Holder outdid himself in his congressional testimony following the attempted terrorist car bombing in Times Square. Despite leading questions, he repeatedly refused to acknowledge that radical Islam had inspired the attack. Agents, he said, were trying to understand Faisal Shahzad's motivation. "There are a variety of reasons why I think people have taken these actions," he stammered. "I think you have to look at each individual case. . . . I don't want to say anything negative about a religion."[35]

Throughout the investigations of both the Christmas bomber and the Fort Hood massacre, the administration was particularly secretive, not so much to protect national security, it seemed, but to cover up the Islamist role at play in both. Congressman Pete Hoekstra, the top Republican on the House Intelligence Committee, released a statement on January 7 welcoming the release of the administration's report on the Christmas bomber, but criticizing it for refusing to release its reports on Guantanamo Bay terrorist detainee recidivism or the Fort Hood attack. "Congress needs the analysis of both attacks," said Hoekstra, "to help prevent the next attack." But the administration, he said, "continues to put up roadblocks and hurdles to prevent us from getting information or answers to even basic questions."

He laid these roadblocks squarely at the feet of the White House, pointing to its "absolute refusal . . . to meet the requirement that Congress be kept fully and currently informed." Instead, the administration was employing a "go-it-alone approach after the Fort Hood attack" that "did not work before and it will not work now." He said that our national security depends on the executive and legislative branches working together, "but the president and congressional Democrats have to be willing to reach out and accept our repeated offers of help."[36] Hoekstra added, "The White House review on the attacks was completed on November 30th. Despite our requests, the administration has yet to brief us on the findings of that report. This is inexcusable and contradicts the many promises from you and the Intelligence Community to brief us in a timely manner."[37]

REFUSING TO CONNECT THE DOTS

It wasn't until January 15, 2010, that the administration finally released its report on the Fort Hood attack and an Obama administration official called the murders "an act of terrorism." But even then, it was a diluted description focusing on the tactic that was used. As for the theological or ideological motivation, the report professed ignorance, claiming, "We are still acquiring knowledge about different people involved, and whether or not there was any type of direction, control, inspiration that led to the events of the day."[38]

Tellingly, the 86-page report did not once mention the shooter, Major Nidal Hasan, by name, or make any reference to his strong Islamic faith. As *Time* magazine asked, "The Fort Hood Report: Why No Mention of Islam?" *Time*'s Mark Thompson wrote, "The apparent lack of curiosity into what allegedly drove Hasan to kill isn't in keeping with the military's ethos; it's a remarkable omission for the U.S. armed forces, whose young officers are often ordered to read Sun Tzu's *The Art of War* with its command to know your enemy." Yet the heads of the review, former Army Secretary Togo West and the Navy's former top admiral, Vernon Clark, simply refused responsibility for investigating Hasan's motives, claiming, "Our concern is with actions and effects, not necessarily with motivations. . . . We certainly do not cite a particular group."

Whether it was a matter of the politically correct culture or of a top-down edict from the White House to whitewash Islam lest Obama's theories of appeasement be compromised, one thing is for certain: this type of willful denial is suicidal to our homeland security and represents a mindset toward Islamist terrorism that is perhaps even more reckless than our pre-9/11 orientation.

The administration's report, according to Thompson, lumped in radical Islam with other fundamentalist religious beliefs and, contrary to all evidence, even asserted that "religious fundamentalism alone is not a risk factor," and that "religious-based violence is not confined to members of fundamentalist groups." These people may be fooling themselves, but they're not fooling the American people, or even less, adequately protecting us. Thompson noted that many believe this attitude means that the lessons of 9/11, Afghanistan, and Iraq, "where jihadist extremism has driven deadly violence against Americans, are being not merely overlooked but studiously ignored."[39]

As a further striking example of the administration's mentality, Eric Holder compared Osama bin Laden to mass murderer Charles Manson[40]—as if the al Qaeda leader is just another maniac, with no particular affiliation or motivation worth discussing. Another example was the government's acceptance of a UN decision to send some 6,000 Somali refugees from Uganda to the United States in 2010, despite our recession, the ever growing national debt, and the even grimmer reality that these refugees are reportedly turning into jihadist fighters throughout many cities in the world. The reason they are being moved is even more ominous: their failure to integrate with other refugee groups.[41]

The administration goes to great pains to narrowly describe our enemy—when it will even concede having an enemy—as only "al Qaeda and its affiliates," thus ignoring the inconvenient fact that many branches of Islamist terrorists beyond the al Qaeda network are warring against us. The administration also refuses to acknowledge that jihadists can operate independently, without direct orders from some hierarchical authority and without affiliation with al Qaeda or any other outside group. The *Washington Times* cited the example of Lloyd R. Woodson, who was arrested on January 25 in rural New Jersey with "a cache of weapons, body armor, a map of a military installation and jihadist personal effects." Most Americans, argued the *Times*, "assume the situation is terrorist-related. The Obama administration said otherwise."[42]

Does anyone remember all the Democratic posturing and hand-wringing following the 9/11 attacks over the Bush administration's failure "to connect the dots?" Here we have not just a failure, but an adamant refusal.

Still, there are a few individuals in the administration who do suspect jihadists can become self-radicalized. Defense secretary Robert Gates, in announcing the Defense Department report on the Fort Hood shooting, admitted, "Military supervisors are not properly focused on the threat posed by self-radicalization and need to better understand the behavioral warning signs."

Walid Phares, author and terrorism expert, warned it is ideology that is behind the radicalization. But our government is reluctant to recognize that for fear of "theological entanglement." Phares wrote, "Washington disarmed its own analysts when bureaucrats of the last two years banned references to the very ideological indicators that would enable our analysts to detect the radicalization threat." Ironically, he said, the very fact that Hasan "fully displayed the narrative of Jihadism" is why he "was not spotted as a jihadist."[43]

In April, Congressman Hoekstra voiced his concern that the administration was withholding information on the Fort Hood attack. But Defense secretary Gates denied it, claiming, "What [is] most important is the prosecution, and we will cooperate with the committee in every way with that single caveat—that whatever we provide does not impact the prosecution. That is the only thing in which we have an interest."[44] Considering this massacre was an act of war by a jihadist, one would think the administration would be interested in the factors behind Hasan's radicalization, his contacts with Anwar al-Awlaki and any other Islamists, and other relevant information. It takes a stunning willful blindness to believe the government's only interest should be in criminal prosecution.

THE NO-NUKE COMMITMENT

On the campaign trail, our appeasement-oriented president, in addition to vowing not to weaponize space and to cut investments in "unproven" missile defense systems, said he would "slow our development in future combat systems," and in pursuing his goal of a world without nuclear weapons he "will not develop new nuclear weapons."[45]

For once Obama has been true to his word, as he has been hell-bent on unilaterally disarming the United States of its nuclear arsenal. He doesn't present it as unilateral, but given the absence of verification measures with the Russians in his recently signed START agreement, it might as well be. In early April, Obama announced he was reformulating our nuclear strategy to substantially narrow the conditions under which the United States would use nuclear weapons. The *New York Times* reported that "for the first time, the United States is committing not to use nuclear weapons against nonnuclear states that are in compliance with the Nuclear Nonproliferation Treaty, even if they attacked the United States with biological or chemical weapons or launched a crippling cyberattack." His strategy, of a piece with his naïve fantasy that being kind to terrorists will tame them, was to make nuclear weapons obsolete by incentivizing nations not to develop them. Apparently, our scaling back of our own nuclear deterrent would encourage them not to do so.

Amidst charges that the policy was recklessly destructive to our national security, the administration claimed it has carved out exceptions for certain rogue states like Iran and North Korea, and reserved the option of reconsidering the use of nuclear retaliation against a biological attack. Obama announced this "Nuclear Posture Review" just over a week before he signed the new Strategic Arms Reduction Treaty (START) with Russia in Prague.[46] In that treaty, Obama agreed with Russia to reduce our nuclear arsenal by historic amounts: nuclear warheads would be reduced by one-third and the missiles and other delivery vehicles would be cut in half. Senators from both parties called the agreement troublesome.[47] Obama also disclosed details about the size and scope of our atomic stockpile—5,113 nuclear warheads—as part of his campaign to get other nuclear nations to be more forthcoming, which he believed would improve his bargaining position against Iran's pursuit of nuclear capabilities. Once again, Obama's recklessly childlike naïveté was on full display.

Retired Army lieutenant colonel Robert Maginnis, a national security expert, warned that by reducing our nuclear umbrella, Obama could prompt other nations that have relied on us to produce their own arsenal—the opposite of his stated intent. Meanwhile, Russia gets the deal of a lifetime: we unilaterally reduce our nuclear stockpile to equal Russia's, and they get to save money by reducing a stockpile they can scarcely afford anyway. It also leaves Russia with thousands more tactical nuclear weapons than we have. Former Czech president Vaclav Havel had warned Obama we should not make too many concessions to Russia based on a narrow understanding of Western interests[48]—but as with almost every other issue falling within his ideological orbit, Obama knew better.

It soon became apparent that the administration and Russia had dramatically different interpretations of the treaty's stipulations on missile defense. The White House released a fact sheet on March 26, 2010, saying the agreement "does not contain any constraints on testing, development or deployment of current or planned U.S. missile defense programs." But Russian foreign minister Sergei Lavrov said on April 6 that Russia would opt out of the treaty if "the U.S. build-up of its missile defense strategic potential in numbers and quality begins to considerably affect the efficiency of Russian strategic nuclear forces. . . . Linkage to missile defense is clearly spelled out in the accord and is legally binding."

In an April 8 fact sheet, the State Department affirmed the U.S. position, but on April 21, State's new fact sheet showed considerable movement toward Russia's interpretation, proclaiming, "The New START Treaty does not constrain the United States from deploying the most effective missile defenses possible." While this may sound definitive, experts believe there is a big difference between the administration's initial position that the treaty "does not contain any constraints on testing, development or deployment of current or planned

U.S. missile defense programs," and its new view that the treaty "does not constrain the United States from deploying the most effective missile defenses possible."[49] And the revised fact sheet is certainly a far cry from Secretary of State Hillary Clinton's statement that "nothing in the treaty will constrain our missile defense efforts."[50] It's just more smoke and mirrors from an administration whose chief, President Obama, has repeatedly expressed his disapproval of America's pursuit of robust missile defense systems.

In May 2010, as Obama was puffing himself up over his progress toward a nuclear free world, we were treated to a real-time, bird's eye glimpse of the "success" of that policy as well as his strategy of engagement. Just as Obama and Russia were agreeing the United States should disarm, Iranian president Mahmoud Ahmadinejad spoke in New York at the beginning of the UN conference reviewing the Nuclear Nonproliferation Treaty. Ahmadinejad openly defied the United States and the entire world, going so far as to advocate America's suspension from the UN. The *Wall Street Journal*'s editors put it quite poignantly: "The truly humiliating spectacle is the sight of the world's leading powers devoting a month to updating a treaty designed to stop nonproliferation even as Mr. Ahmadinejad makes a mockery of that effort before their very eyes."[51]

Anyone who thinks Obama is a conventional, pragmatic politician should take a hard look at his national security policies. He certainly does not want America to suffer another terrorist attack, but his slavish adherence to ideology results in policies that make that horrifying outcome much more likely. These policies flow naturally from a worldview that holds America responsible for many, if not most, of the world's ills. Because we are historically a brutal exploiter of other nations, in Obama's view, the animus terrorists hold toward us is at least somewhat deserved. Therefore, by apologizing to the world; by treating captured terrorists better and sympathizing with their grievances; by refusing to acknowledge any connection between Islam and Islamic terrorism; and by unilaterally reducing America's strategic defense capabilities, Obama believes he is making America safer by proving our new good will under his enlightened, benevolent presidency.

Judging solely by the string of terrorist attacks—both successful and unsuccessful—that have occurred during his presidency, however, the terrorists seem unimpressed by his overtures and sycophancy. Tragically, Obama doubtlessly interprets this result as an indication he has not taken his appeasement policies far enough.

CONCLUSION

n July 2010, I came across a heartbreaking post on *Free Republic*, a popular conservative forum visited by thousands upon thousands of patriots every day. The author wrote,

In the 55 years of my life as a proud citizen of the United States of America, this is the first time I've felt that a president of our country holds his fellow Americans and the United States in contempt. I don't think I've ever felt such an overwhelming feeling of rejection as I do with this administration. It's as though everything that I was raised so proudly to hold dear and true has been denigrated. Every single day we hear something else that is a slap in the face of every patriot. I pray that we will see relief in November because I know that I'm not the only American who feels the frustration. It is unimaginable to me what might happen if we cannot find some relief in November.

It seems to me these sentiments are now widely held in this country. My friends and acquaintances, and even strangers I meet during my travels, often don't want to talk about politics anymore. Some say they can't bear to watch the news because of Obama's daily assaults on all we hold dear. And yet he continues, deliberately and unapologetically, to force his abject will on the nation.

This book has meticulously documented Obama's efforts to systematically undermine America's founding principles and its heritage of liberty in his quest to transform our economy and very form of government. The facts speak for themselves, as does Obama's destructive record.

For all his posturing about bipartisanship and his openness to all ideas, this book has shown just how partisan, close minded, and determined he is to implement his agenda at any cost. And it has detailed the deplorably corrupt and high-handed tactics he has used in the process.

Obama doesn't listen to the people; he brazenly ignores our wishes, indeed our pleas, that he cease and desist from his reckless course. But far from showing the normal concern a politician—even a statesman—would have toward his own rising unpopularity, Obama moves forward at double-time pace, never looking back and never revealing the slightest inkling of self-doubt—an alleged trait of President George W. Bush that earned him the Left's everlasting contempt.

In his monomania for socialism, Obama will brook no challenge. In response to the miserable results of his economic charlatanism, he maintains things would have been much worse without his initiatives. And after he failed to keep his grandiose promises to improve American diplomacy, he gave us more of the same: weak-kneed engagement and Chamberlainesque appeasement. In the meantime he continues to insult and sell out our allies and coddle our enemies, as Iran races unimpeded to cross the nuclear threshold.

Does it worry him that America is in decline under his leadership? Obviously not, as he voices contempt for American exceptionalism and pledges to rectify our allegedly unfair consumption of the world's resources. In fact, one can't help but notice that a declining America actually meshes with his ideology quite well.

His colossally wasteful stimulus and mortgage bailout packages, along with his foisting nationalized healthcare on this nation, are just the beginning. He is hell-bent on passing a cap and trade bill that will further destroy our prospects for economic recovery and future growth. His plan to boost taxes, including a possible VAT, is also on the front burner, and we shouldn't be surprised if he ultimately tries to enact a wealth tax whereby he taxes not just our income and sales transactions, but our constitutionally protected private property. Many reasonably fear their pension funds are vulnerable and ripe for the taking. If that happens, you can be sure the debt-exploding Obama will insist he's doing us a favor by confiscating our life's earnings to rectify the debt crisis for which he himself is largely responsible. Small businesses and producers everywhere wait in anxiety for the next series of shoes to drop from the socialist centipede of Obama's agenda.

If all this weren't bad enough, his "urgent" push for comprehensive immigration reform is now underway. Expect this initiative to be loaded with more than the normal amount of demagoguery and populism, as this supposedly post-racial president plays the race card on steroids en route to decimating the rule of law and what remains of America's unique culture.

Some maintain Obama is intentionally wreaking havoc on America as part of a Cloward-Piven or Alinskyite strategy to manufacture a crisis in order to destroy the nation as we know it and rebuild it in a socialist image. Others argue Obama just believes so deeply in socialist dogma that he is impervious to the manifest evidence of its failure. Regardless of which scenario may be correct, the outcome would be the same.

Americans, even former skeptics on the right side of the aisle, should now understand how committed Obama is to his far-left agenda. They should finally grasp how far the Left is willing to go when they're in power. Their talk of moving past divisive partisanship is a veneer designed to cover their radical designs. They are precisely the opposite of what they hold themselves out to be: freedom-loving, compassionate, pro-economic growth, bullish on America, democratic, tolerant, and compromising.

America is in a dangerously rapid nosedive under Obama's navigation. The key to our delivery from this systematic assault is for the American people to understand Obama's extremist agenda, to get engaged, and to do everything we can to peaceably remove him and his supporters from office at election time and replace them with constitution-revering, liberty-loving public servants who respect the rule of law.

No matter how bleak conditions look now, we have reason for optimism, as the American people, like no other people in world history, love and appreciate the liberty bestowed upon us by our founding fathers and preserved by the blood of our patriotic ancestors.

God bless America.

ACKNOWLEDGMENTS

I want to thank everyone at Regnery Publishing with whom I've had a wonderful working relationship. I especially want to thank Marji Ross for her continued support and confidence and for her wisdom in all aspects of the publishing business. I am also indebted to Harry Crocker for always being there from the beginning through the conclusion of every project. His encouragement, advice, and creative ideas are always first rate and invaluable. Also, I am very grateful to Jack Langer, the primary editor of the book, for his 20/15 vision, his insight, his extraordinary wordsmithing, and his temperament, which made this a thoroughly painless and enjoyable process.

Many thanks as well to my buddy Greg Mueller and his team at Creative Response Concepts for quarterbacking the promotion and marketing of this book along with the excellent marketing staff at Regnery. Greg is the guy who initially prodded me into nonfiction authorship, for which I'm eternally grateful.

I also wish to thank Heritage Foundation scholars Brian Riedl and David John, who not only educated me (and countless others) through their prodigious research and writings, but freely gave their time to discuss, explain, and clarify their work in phone conversations, receiving nothing but a heartfelt thank you in return. Many thanks also to Heritage folks Ralph Buglass, Jim Weidman, John Fleming, and others who made special efforts to make available high resolution charts for inclusion in this book.

A sincere thank you to my very good friends and NRO heavy-weights Kathryn Lopez (K-LO) and Andy McCarthy for their friendship, support, and counsel. Andy was particularly helpful in clarifying some of the complex factual and legal issues involved in the administration's wrongheaded and muddled approach to prosecuting the war on terror.

I am humbled and honored by my friendship with Sean Hannity and Mark Levin and abundantly appreciative of the support they always lend to my books and to me personally. The same is true for my good friend Ann Coulter, who gave me the best idea I've ever received in book writing, which made all the difference on my first book and the ones thereafter, including this one. If you are a beginning author and ever find yourself floundering in anxiety in anticipation of the seemingly overwhelming task at hand, and find that the more you research the more overwhelmed you become, follow her advice to me: just begin writing and you will necessarily acquire your focus.

Once again I must thank my brother Rush for personally inspiring me, for opening up doors for me directly and indirectly, for leading the charge for American conservatives, and for truly making an immeasurable and positive impact on this nation and the preservation of its Constitution and freedom tradition.

NOTES

Introduction to the Paperback

1. "Bush to ask for TARP; Obama to 'rebrand' it," *ABC News*, January 12, 2009; available at http://abcnews.go.com/GMA/Economy/story?id=6626721&page=1.

2. "Obama, US viewed less favorably in Arab world, poll shows," *Boston Globe*, July 13, 2011; available at http://www.boston.com/Boston/politicalintelligence/2011/07/obama-viewed-less-favorably-arab-world-poll-shows/yIVn6f6PueWbdhZutglhoJ/index.html.

Introduction

1. Ben Wallace-Wells, "Destiny's Child, No candidate since Robert F. Kennedy has sparked as much campaign-trail heat as Barack Obama. But can the one-term senator craft a platform to match his charisma?" *Rolling Stone*, February 22, 2007.

2. "Partisan Gap in Obama Job Approval Widest in Modern Era," Pewresearch.org, April 2, 2009; available at: http://pewresearch.org/pubs/1178/polarized-partisan-gap-in-obama-approval-historic [accessed July 2, 2010].

3. Jeffrey M. Jones, "Obama's Approval Most Polarized for First-Year President," Gallup.com, January 25, 2010; available at: http://www.gallup.com/poll/125345/obama-approval-polarized-first-year-president.aspx [accessed July 2, 2010].

4. Andy McCarthy, "A New Dawn?" *National Review Online*, The Corner, March 4, 2010; available at: http://corner.nationalreview.

com/post/?q=yjgyMGRjZWUzZjQ30GY5MDJ1M2RjMzd
[accessed July 7, 2010].

5. Ibid.

6. Karen Travers, "Exclusive: President Obama: We Lost Touch with American People Last Year," ABCNews.go.com, January 20, 2010; available at: http://abcnews.go.com/WN/Politics/president-obama-lost-touch-american-people-year/story?id=9613462 [accessed July 2, 2010].

7. Quin Hillyer, "Not the American Way," *American Spectator*, March 5, 2010; available at: http://spectator.org/archives/2010/03/05/not-the-american-way [accessed July 2, 2010].

8. "Book: Rahm 'Begged' Obama for Days Not to Pursue Ambitious Health Reform," *Washington Post*, May 14, 2010; available at: http://voices.washingtonpost.com/plum-line/2010/05/book_rahm_spent_week_aggressiv.html [accessed July 2, 2010].

9. Mark Knoller, "Obama Has Given 54 Speeches on Health Care," CBSNews.com, March 19, 2010; available at: http://www.cbsnews.com/8301-503544_162-20000825-503544.html [accessed July 2, 2010].

10. Transcript: "George Stephanopoulos' Exclusive Interview with President Obama," ABCNews.com, January 20, 2010; available at: http://blogs.abcnews.com/george/2010/01/transcript-george-stephanopoulos-exclusive-interview-with-president-obama.html [accessed July 2, 2010].

11. Anne E. Kornblut, "Obama's 17-minute, 2500-word Response to Woman's Claim of Being 'Over-taxed,'" *Washington Post*, April 2, 2010; available at: http://voices.washingtonpost.com/44/2010/04/obamas-17-minute-2500-word-res.html [accessed July 2, 2010].

12. Video available at: http://www.youtube.com/watch?v=ZlKIfzoC8D0.

13. "Team O: Incoherent on Iran," *New York Post*, February 17, 2010; available at: http://www.nypost.com/p/news/opinion/editorials/team_incoherent_on_iran_JrMOBaVv159w6StvVzGMOJ [accessed July 2, 2010].

Chapter 1

1. Charles Krauthammer, "The Audacity of Vanity," *Washington Post*, July 18, 2008; available at: http://www.washingtonpost.com/wp-dyn/content/article/2008/07/17/AR2008071701839.html [accessed June 28, 2010].
2. Greta Van Susteren, "Interview With Rick Santorum, Jack Kelly," FOX News Network, *On the Record With Greta Van Susteren,* September 29, 2009.
3. Ryan Lizza, "Battle Plans, How Obama Won," *The New Yorker*, November 17, 2008; available at: http://www.newyorker.com/reporting/2008/11/17/081117fa_fact_lizza [accessed June 28, 2010].
4. "Sen. Reid Says Obama Told Him, 'I Have a Gift,'" Associated Press, April 28, 2009; available at: http://www.foxnews.com/politics/2009/04/28/sen-reid-says-obama-told-gift/ [accessed June 28, 2010].
5. President Barack Obama, "Obama's Speech to the United States General Assembly," *New York Times*, September 23, 2009; available at: http://www.nytimes.com/2009/09/24/us/politics/24prexy.text.html [accessed June 28, 2010].
6. Jeff Jacoby, "Obama's Swelling Ego," *Boston Globe*, November 14, 2009; available at: http://www.boston.com/bostonglobe/editorial_opinion/oped/articles/2009/11/14/obamas_swelling_ego/ [accessed June 28, 2010].
7. Major Garrett, "Obama Endures Ortega Diatribe, Nicaraguan President Daniel Ortega Lashes Out at a Century of what he called terrorist aggression in Central America," FOX News, April 18, 2009.
8. Ed Carson, "Obama to Dems: 'Don't Worry, You've Got Me,'" Investors.com, January 25, 2010; available at: http://blogs.investors.com/capitalhill/index.php/home/35-politics/1233-obama-to-dems-dont-worry-youve-got-me [accessed June 28, 2010].
9. Kevin Hall, "A Numbers Breakdown of the SOTU: Obama Refers to Himself 114 Times," *Des Moines Conservative Examiner*, January 28, 2010; available at: http://209.157.64.200/focus/f-news/2439024/posts [accessed June 28, 2010].
10. Dan Gainor, "Obama's Speeches—Obama Mentions Self Nearly 1,200 Times," FOXNews.com, September 23, 2009; available at:

http://www.foxnews.com/opinion/2009/09/23/dan-gainor-obama-speeches-ego/ [accessed June 28, 2010].

11. Judi McLeod, "Obama's West Point Address," *Canada Free Press*, December 3, 2009; available at: http://www.foxnews.com/politics/2010/05/22/obama-focus-wars-abroad-speech-west-point-graduates/ [accessed June 28, 2010].

12. Jim Hoft, "Obama Refers to Himself 132 Times In One Speech" (Video), Gateway Pundit Blog, First Things, January 26, 2010; available at: http://gatewaypundit.firstthings.com/2010/01/obama-refers-to-himself-132-times-in-one-speech-video/ [accessed June 28, 2010].

13. Mark Finkelstein, "Oh the Sacrifices Obama Has Made: I Didn't Get Into This for Fame or Fortune," NewsBusters.org, February 3, 2010; available at: http://newsbusters.org/blogs/mark-finkelstein/2010/02/03/oh-sacrifices-obama-has-made-i-didnt-get-fame-or-fortune [accessed June 28, 2010].

14. Linda Matchan, "A Law Review Breakthrough," *Boston Globe*, February 15, 1990; available at: http://www.boston.com/news/politics/2008/articles/1990/02/15/a_law_review_breakthrough/ [accessed June 28, 2010].

15. Caroline Kim, "Obama Visits U. Illinois Campus in Final Leg of Campaign," *University Wire*, November 2, 2004.

16. Renee Montagne, Steve Inskeep, "Obama Draws a Big Crowd in New Hampshire," National Public Radio, December 11, 2006; available at: http://ww.npr.org/templates/story/storyComments.php?storyId=6607687 [accessed June 28, 2010].

17. Kim Ahern, "Barack is on the Ballot!" Rhode Island's Future, December 10, 2007; available at: http://rifuture.org/barack-is-on-the-ballot-.html?blogger=Kim+Ahern [accessed June 28, 2010].

18. "Democratic Presidential Debate," Federal News Service, December 13, 2007.

19. Kevin Chappell, "A Moment in History," *Jet*, September 15, 2008; available at: http://findarticles.com/p/articles/mi_m1355/is_10_114/ai_n28572804/?tag=content;col1 [accessed July 7, 2010].

20. "Obama: 'This Inauguration is Not About Me. It's About All of Us,'" *Washington Post*, Inauguration Watch, January 14, 2009; available at: http://voices.washingtonpost.com/inauguration-watch/

2009/01/obama_this_election_is_not_abo.html [accessed June 28, 2010].

21. "Stephanie Condon, "Obama on Health Care: 'This Isn't About Me,'" CBS News Political Hotsheet, July 20, 2009; available at: http://www.cbsnews.com/8301-503544_162-5175035-503544.html [accessed June 28, 2010].

22. Alister Bull and Steve Holland, "Feisty Obama: 'I won't stop fighting for you,'" Reuters, January 22, 2010; available at: http://www.reuters.com/article/idUSTRE60L4MC20100122 [accessed June 28, 2010].

23. "Gibbs: Obama Willing To Be One-Term President To Pass His Agenda," BreitbartTV.com, August 21, 2009; available at: http://www.breitbart.tv/gibbs-obama-willin-to-be-one-term-president-to-pass-his-agenda [accessed July 7, 2010].

24. Kyle-Anne Shiver, "Danger Ahead: Obama Jumped the Shark, But Didn't Drown," Pajamas Media, March 25, 2010; available at: http://pajamasmedia.com/blog/danger-ahead-obama-jumped-the-shark-but-didn%E2%80%99t-drown/ [accessed June 28, 2010].

25. Byron York, "For Obama and Pelosi, Health Care is Ego Trip," *Washington Examiner*, March 2, 2010; available at: http://www.washingtonexaminer.com/politics/For-Obama-and-Pelosi_-health-care-is-ego-trip-85871962.html [accessed June 28, 2010].

26. Byron York, "For Obama and Pelosi, Health Care is Ego Trip," *op. cit.*

27. Valerie Jarrett, "Americans are Idiots, Obama Too Intelligent For Words," *The Lid*, February 23, 2010; available at: http://yidwith-lid.blogspot.com/2010/02/blog-post_23.html [accessed June 28, 2010].

28. Tom Brokaw, "Interview with David Axelrod," NBC, *Meet the Press*, March 14, 2010; available at: http://www.msnbc.msn.com/id/29209460/ [accessed June 28, 2010].

29. Larry King, "Interview with Bill Maher," CNN, *Larry King Live*, February 16, 2010; available at: http://quiz.cnn.com/TRANSCRIPTS/0406/02/lkl.00.html [accessed June 28, 2010].

30. Jacob Weisberg, "Down With the People," *Slate*, February 6, 2010; available at: http://www.slate.com/id/2243797 [accessed June 28, 2010].

31. Joe Klein, "Too Dumb to Thrive," Time.com, Swampland Blog, January 25, 2010; available at: http://swampland.blogs.time.com/2010/01/25/too-dumb-to-thrive/ [accessed June 28, 2010].

32. Mathhew Yglesias, "Reframing Public Ignorance," *Yglesias*, January 25, 2010; available at: http://yglesias.thinkprogress.org/2010/01/reframing-public-ignorance/ [accessed June 28, 2010].

33. Sarah Lai Stirland, "McCain Campaign Yanks 'Obama Love' Web Video," Wired.com, July 25, 2008; available at: http://www.wired.com/threatlevel/2008/07/mccain-campai-1/ [accessed June 28, 2010].

34. Karen Travers and Jake Tapper, "President Beekcake? D.C. Magazine to Feature Shirtless Obama on Cover," ABCNews.com, *Political Punch*, April 20, 2009; available at: http://blogs.abcnews.com/politicalpunch/2009/04/president-beefc.html [accessed June 28, 2010].

35. Scott Whitlock, "ABC Heavily Promotes New HBO Documentary on Obama: He's so 'Zen' and 'Normal,'" Media Research Center, October 27, 2009; available at: http://www.mrc.org/biasalert/2009/20091027051654.aspx [accessed June 28, 2010].

36. Transcript: "How is the World Reacting to President Obama's Speech to the Muslim World?" MSNBC, *Hardball*, June 5, 2009; available at: http://www.msnbc.msn.com/id/31173133/ns/msnbc_tv-hardball_with_chris_matthews/ [accessed June 28, 2010].

37. Peter Wehner, "Joe Klein's *Almost* Pathological Love Affairs," *Commentary Magazine*, February 2, 2010; available at: http://www.commentarymagazine.com/blogs/index.php/wehner/229776 [accessed June 28, 2010].

38. Fouad Ajami, "The Obama Spell is Broken," *Wall Street Journal*, January 31, 2010; available at: http://online.wsj.com/article/SB10001424052748704094304575029110104772360.html [accessed June 28, 2010].

39. "MSNBC's Ed Schultz Says the West Wing of the White House is a 'Shrine' to Obama—Audio," FreedomsLighthouse.com, February 4, 2010; available at: http://www.freedomslighthouse.com/2010_02_04_archive.html [accessed June 28, 2010].

40. "Narcissist Alert! Obama Clutching the Obama GQ Magazine with his face on the cover!" rashmanly.wordpress.com, November 25,

2009; available at: http://rashmanly.wordpress.com/2009/11/25/nar-cissist-alert-obama-clutching-the-obama-gq-magazine-with-his-face-on-the-cover/ [accessed June 28, 2010].

41. "Obama Has Name Stitched to Suit Jacket," *Real Clear Politics* Video, March 25, 2010; available at: http://www.realclearpolitics. com/video/2010/03/25/ [accessed June 28, 2010].

42. Mark Knoller, "Obama's First Year: By the Numbers," CBSNews. com, January 20, 2010; available at: http://www.cbsnews.com/8301-503544_162-6119525-503544.html [accessed June 28, 2010].

43. Brent Baker, "'Paging Dr. Obama' Makes it Seven Time Mag Covers Since Election for Obama," Newsbusters.org, July 31, 2009; available at: http://newsbusters.org/blogs/brent-baker/2009/07/31/pag-ing-dr-obama-makes-it-seven-time-mag-covers-election-obama [accessed June 28, 2010].

44. Domenico Montanaro, "Obama Appeared on Half of Time Covers," MSNBC, *First Read*, December 17, 2008; available at: http:// firstread.msnbc.msn.com/_news/2008/12/17/4432215-obama-appeared-on-half-of-time-covers [accessed June 28, 2010].

45. Howard Kurtz, "The Media Elites Secret Dinners," *Washington Post*, April 27, 2009; available at: http://www.washingtonpost.com/ wp-dyn/content/article/2009/04/27/AR2009042700891.html [accessed June 28, 2010].

46. Mail Foreign Service, "Obamamania or Overkill? President marks his first 100 days in office with three hundred photos...all of him," Dailymail.co.uk, April 30, 2009; available at: http://www.daily-mail.co.uk/news/worldnews/article-1174828/Obamamania-overkill-President-marks-100-days-office-THREE-HUNDRED-photos—him. html [accessed June 28, 2010].

47. Matthew Sheffield, "Primetime Obama Costing Network Millions," *Washington Examiner*, April 24, 2009.

48. Don Irvine, "Obama Breaking Media Appearance Records," Accuracy in Media, July 30, 2009; available at: http://www.aim.org/don-irvine-blog/obama-breaking-media-appearance-records/ [accessed June 28, 2010].

49. Mark Leibovich, "Obama the Omnipresent," *New York Times*, September 17, 2009; available at: http://www.nytimes.com/2009/09/18/ us/politics/18memo.html [accessed June 28, 2010].

50. "Obama To Appear on America's Most Wanted's 1000th Episode," TV Shark.com, March 4, 2010; available at: http://www.tvshark. com/read/?art=arc4842 [accessed June 28, 2010].

51. Mark Leibovich, "Obama the Omnipresent," *op. cit.*

52. Howard Kurtz, "If It's Sunday, It Must Be Obama," *Washington Post*, September 17, 2009; available at: http://www.washingtonpost. com/wp-dyn/content/article/2009/09/17/AR2009091701077.html [accessed June 28, 2010].

53. Ibid.

54. James Poniewozik, "Obama to Appear on Everything, Everywhere. Except FOX," Time.com, September 15, 2009; available at: http:// tunedin.blogs.time.com/2009/09/15/obama-to-appear-on-every- thing-everywhere-except-fox/?utm_source=feedburner&utm_ medium=feed&utm_campaign=Feed%3A+time%2Ftunedin+% 28TIME%3A+Tuned+In%29 [accessed June 28, 2010].

55. "Obama: Regrets of Year One," ABCNews.com, January 20, 2010; available at: http://blogs.abcnews.com/george/2010/01/obama- regrets-of-year-one.html [accessed June 28, 2010].

56. David Zurawik, "He's baaack: TV Obama is everywhere—again," *The Baltimore Sun*, February 3, 2010; available at: http:// weblogs.baltimoresun.com/entertainment/zontv/2010/02/barack_ obama_tv_president_mich.html [accessed June 28, 2010].

57. David A. Patten, "New York Times Buries Bad Poll for Obama," Newmax.com, July 30, 2009; available at: http://www.newsmax. com/Headline/obama-poll-times-health/2009/07/30/id/331970 [accessed June 28, 2010].

58. Allahpundit, "Revealed: Who Else Was At that Secret Obama Brief- ing with Olby and Maddow?" HotAir.com, October 21, 2009; available at: http://hotair.com/archives/2009/10/21/revealed-who- else-was-at-that-secret-obama-briefing-with-olby-and-maddow/ [accessed June 28, 2010]; see also, "Obama meets with McChrystal in Denmark," *Washington Times*, October 2, 2009; available at: http://www.washingtontimes.com/news/2009/oct/02/obama-meets- mcchrystal-copenhagen [accessed June 28, 2010].

59. Scott Rasmussen, "Daily Presidential Tracking Poll," Rasmussen Reports, December 14, 2009; available at: http://www.rasmussenre-

ports.com/public_content/politics/obama_administration/daily_
presidential_tracking_poll [accessed June 28, 2010].

60. Sean Hannity, Bob Beckel, "Obama Grades Himself," FOX News
Network, *Hannity*, December 14, 2009; available at: http://
forums.hannity.com/showthread.php?t=1759271 [accessed June 28,
2010].

61. Gabriel Sherman, "End of the Affair, Barack Obama and the press
break up," *New Republic*, August 13, 2008; available at: http://
www.huffingtonpost.com/2008/07/25/end-of-the-affair-press-b_n_
114925.html [accessed June 28, 2010].

62. Ibid.

63. Helene Cooper, "We're Not Keeping Score, but..." *New York
Times*, April 1, 2009; available at: http://thecaucus.blogs.nytimes.
com/2009/04/01/were-not-keeping-score-but/ [accessed June 28,
2010].

64. Gabriel Sherman, "End of the Affair, Barack Obama and the press
break up," *op. cit.*

65. Dana Milbank, "President Obama Continues Hectic Victory Tour,"
Washington Post, July 30, 2008; available at: http://www.washing-
tonpost.com/wp-dyn/content/article/2008/07/29/
AR2008072902068.html [accessed June 28, 2010].

66. Jim Hoft, "After Obama Tells America 'Everyone Must Sacrifice,'
the White House Throws 1 Party Every 3 Days in First Year," First
Things Blog, January 13, 2010; available at: http://gatewaypun-
dit.firstthings.com/2010/01/after-first-family-tells-america-everyone-
must-sacrifice-they-hold-white-house-party-every-3rd-day-in-first-
year/ [accessed June 28, 2010].

67. Dee Dee Myers, "Memo to Obama: Get Back in Touch," *Politico*,
March 12, 2010; available at: http://www.politico.com/news/stories/
0310/34280.html [accessed June 28, 2010].

68. Ibid.

69. Robert A. George, "Obama's Frightening Insensitivity Following
Shooting, A bad week for Democrats compounded by an awful
moment for Barack Obama," NBC News Chicago, January 20,
2010; available at: http://www.nbcchicago.com/news/politics/A-
Disconnected-President.html [accessed June 28, 2010].

70. Toby Harnden, "Bloodless President Barack Obama Makes Americans Wistful for George W. Bush," Telegraph.co.uk, November 7, 2009; available at: http://www.telegraph.co.uk/news/worldnews/ northamerica/usa/barackobama/6520286/Bloodless-President- Barack-Obama-makes-Americans-wistful-for-George-W-Bush.html [accessed June 28, 2010].

71. Bill Sammon, "George W. Bush Secretly Visits Fort Hood Victims," FOXNews.com, November 7, 2009; available at: http://www. foxnews.com/politics/2009/11/07/george-w-bush-secretly-visits-fort- hood-victims/ [accessed June 28, 2010]; see also, Andrew Malcolm, "George W. Bush Makes Secret Visit to Mourning Families at Fort Hood; Laura Bush goes too," *Los Angeles Times* Blogs, November 7, 2009; available at: http://latimesblogs.latimes.com/washington/ 2009/11/george-w-bush-laura-bush-fort-hood-nidal-malik-hasan. html [accessed June 28, 2010].

72. Jim Hoft, "Sick. Obama Says Daniel Pearl's Beheading 'Captured the World's Imagination,'" Gateway Pundit, May 18, 2010; available at: http://gatewaypundit.firstthings.com/2010/05/sick-obama- says-daniel-pearls-beheading-captured-the-worlds-imagination-video / [accessed June 28, 2010].

73. Sarah Palin, "Mr. President: Please Try, 'I'm Listening, People,' Instead of 'Listen Up, People!'" Facebook, January 25, 2010; available at: http://www.facebook.com/note.php?note_id=267042703434 [accessed June 28, 2010].

74. Ernest Istook, "Obama Fails to Listen," The Foundry, January 27, 2010; available at: http://blog.heritage.org/2010/01/27/sotu-a-view- from-inside-the-chamber/ [accessed June 28, 2010].

75. Joseph Curl, "At Summit, Obama Mostly Hears Obama," *Washington Times*, February 26, 2010; available at: http://www.washington- times.com/news/2010/feb/26/obama-listens-at-health-summit-but- mostly-hears-fr/ [accessed June 28, 2010].

76. Ibid.

77. Barack Obama, "President Obama on Health Care's Passage," *Real Clear Politics*, March 21, 2010; available at: http://www.realclear- politics.com/articles/2010/03/21/barack_obama_transcript_health_ care_passage_104866.html [accessed June 28, 2010].

78. Jennifer Rubin, "Trying to Reinvent Obama," Commentary, Contentions Blog, March 12, 2010; available at: http://www.commentarymagazine.com/blogs/index.php/rubin/255411 [accessed June 28, 2010].

79. Byron York, "Obama: 'She insisted she's going to be buried in an Obama t-shirt,'" *Washington Examiner*, February 2, 2010; available at: http://www.washingtonexaminer.com/opinion/blogs/beltway-confidential/Obama-She-insisted-shes-going-to-be-buried-in-an-Obama-t-shirt-83645132.html [accessed June 28, 2010].

80. Anne Reynolds, "Sobbing Kindergarteners Snubbed for Steelers?" NBC Washington, May 22, 2009; available at: http://www.nbcwashington.com/news/local-beat/Kindergarteners-Snubbed-for-Steelers.html [accessed June 28, 2010].

81. Katarina Andersson, "Obama Snubs the King," *The Daily Beast*, December 9, 2009; available at: http://www.thedailybeast.com/blogs-and-stories/2009-12-09/obamas-oslo-snub/full/ [accessed June 28, 2010].

82. Eric Werner, "Senator Says Obama 'Got Nerve' to Push Lawmakers," Breitbart.com, June 7, 2009; available at: http://topics.breitbart.com/Chuck+Grassley/ [accessed June 28, 2010].

83. Glenn Thrust, "Dems Ducking Obama's Reform Calls," *Politico*, March 19, 2010; available at: http://www.politico.com/politico44/perm/0310/busy_signal_79e06a9d-554a-495b-9d4b-cbbf5f75160f.html [accessed June 28, 2010].

84. John McCormick, "Obama's Air Force One Flight to Chicago and back Monday to Cost $236,00," *Chicago Tribune*, June 15, 2009; available at: http://www.chicagotribune.com/news/local/chi-air-force-one-15-jun15,0,2483578.story [accessed June 28, 2010].

85. Data available from the *Encyclopedia Britannica* Online.

86. "Narcissism," Healthline.com; available at: http://www.healthline.com/galecontent/narcissism [accessed June 28, 2010].

87. Joy Tiz, "America's Crash Course in Narcissism 101," Joy Tiz.com; available at: http://joytiz.com/2010/americas-crash-course-in-narcissim-101/ [accessed June 28, 2010].

88. Robin of Berkeley, "Is Obama a Narcissist?" *American Thinker*, September 16, 2009; available at: http://www.americanthinker.com/

2010/03/obamas_malignant_narcissism.html [accessed June 28, 2010].

89. Ibid.

90. M. Scott Peck, *People of the Lie* (New York: First Touchstone, Simon & Schuster, 1985), 66, 76, 77.

91. James Lewis, "Obama's Malignant Narcissism," *American Thinker*, March 4, 2010; available at: http://www.americanthinker.com/2010/03/obamas_malignant_narcissism.html [accessed June 28, 2010].

92. Noel Sheppard, "CNN Shows Faces Obama Was Making During Healthcare Summit," *NewsBusters*, February 28, 2010; available at: http://newsbusters.org/blogs/noel-sheppard/2010/02/28/cnn-shows-faces-obama-was-making-during-healthcare-summit [accessed June 28, 2010].

93. Lamar Alexander, "Alexander: ObamaCare the Most Brazen Act of Political Arrogance Since Watergate," Breitbart TV, March 15, 2010; available at: http://www.breitbart.tv/alexander-obamacare-the-most-brazen-act-of-political-arrogance-since-watergate/ [accessed June 28, 2010].

94. Mark Knoller, "Obama's $3M Chicago Olympics Pitch Falls Short of the Gold," CBS News, Political Hotsheet, October 2, 2009; available at: http://www.cbsnews.com/8301-503544_162-5359359-503544.html [accessed June 28, 2010].

95. Ibid.

Chapter 2

1. Brian Friel, Richard E. Cohen, and Kirk Victor, "Obama: Most Liberal Senator in 2007," *National Journal*, January 31, 2008; available at: http://news.nationaljournal.com/articles/voteratings/.

2. Peter Wehner, "Why Republicans Like Obama," *The Washington Post*, February 3, 2008; available at: http://www.washingtonpost.com/wp-dyn/content/article/2008/02/01/AR2008020102663.html.

3. Tony Campbel, "Why Some Conservatives will Vote for Barack Obama," *Republicans for Obama*, July 14, 2008; available at: http://www.republicansforobama.org/?q=node/1513.

4. Jitendra Joshi, "Obama's Strange Appeal to High Priests of US Conservatism," *Agence France-Presse*, June 21, 2008; available at:

http://afp.google.com/article/ALeqM5hTmPa3TKWcnYhN5dNGm
P7AWgtmIA.

5. Christopher Buckley, "Sorry, Dad, I'm Voting for Obama," *The Daily Beast*, October 10, 2008; available at: http://www.thedaily-beast.com/blogs-and-stories/2008-10-10/the-conservative-case-for-obama.

6. Doug Kmiec, "Endorsing Obama," *Slate*, Convictions, March 23, 2008; available at: http://www.slate.com/blogs/blogs/convictions/archive/2008/03/23/endorsing-obama.aspx.

7. Danny Shea, "David Brooks: Sarah Palin 'Represents A Fatal Cancer to the Republican Party'" *The Huffington Post*, October 8, 2008; available at: http://www.huffingtonpost.com/2008/10/08/david-brooks-sarah-palin_n_133001.html.

8. "Fukuyama Backs Obama for US Presidency," ABC News, May 27, 2008; transcript available at: http://www.abc.net.au/worldtoday/content/2008/s2257118.htm.

9. Mary Lu Carnevale, "Obamacons: Prominent Republicans Line Up Behind Obama," *Washington Wire, Wall Street Journal Blogs*, October 24, 2008; available at: http://blogs.wsj.com/washwire/2008/10/24/obamacans-prominent-republicans-line-up-behind-obama/.

10. George Packer, "First Colin Powell, Now…" *The New Yorker*, October 20, 2008; available at: http://www.newyorker.com/online/blogs/georgepacker/2008/10/not-quite-colin.html.

11. Ibid.

12. Adam Levy, "Former Reagan Adviser Endorses Obama," *CNN's Political Ticker*, October 31, 2008; available at: http://politi-calticker.blogs.cnn.com/2008/10/31/former-reagan-adviser-endorses-obama/?fbid=dTM8OJzYU_J.

13. "Eisenhower Appointees for Obama," *Republicans for Obama Blog*, November 3, 2008; available at: http://my.barackobama.com/page/community/post/GOP/gGg8zW.

14. Editorial, "It's Time," *The Economist*, October 30, 2008.

15. "How He Did It," *Newsweek*, November 5, 2008.

16. Ibid.

17. Ben Domenech, "Conservatives to Obamacons; A rose is not always a rose," *The Washington Times*, June 13, 2008.

18. Robert Novak, "Two Big Obamacons?" *Mississippi Press*, June 26, 2008.
19. Bruce Bartlett, "Mr. Right?" *The New Republic*, June 25, 2008; available at: http://www.tnr.com/article/technology/mr-right.
20. Christine Allison, "Why this Republican is Voting for Obama," *Dallas Morning News*, February 23, 2008; available at: http://www.dallasnews.com/sharedcontent/dws/dn/opinion/viewpoints/stories/DN-allison_23edi.ART.State.Edition1.45e0862.html.
21. Christopher Buckley, "Sorry, Dad, I'm Voting for Obama," *The Daily Beast*, October 10, 2008; available at: http://www.thedailybeast.com/blogs-and-stories/2008-10-10/the-conservative-case-for-obama.
22. George Packer, "First Colin Powell, Now…" *The New Yorker*, October 20, 2008; available at: http://www.newyorker.com/online/blogs/georgepacker/2008/10/not-quite-colin.html.
23. Kenneth P. Vogel, "Obama Had Greater Role on Liberal Survey," *Politico*, March 31, 2008; available at: http://www.politico.com/news/stories/0308/9269.html; Ed Morrissey, "Politico: Obama Lied About Survey," Hot Air.com, March 31, 2008; available at: http://hotair.com/archives/2008/03/31/politico-obama-lied-about-survey/.
24. Kenneth P. Vogel, "Obama Had Greater Role on Liberal Survey," *op. cit.*
25. Peter S. Canellos, "Just Don't Call Barack Obama Liberal, Okey Doke?" *The Boston Globe*, February 26, 2008; available at: http://www.boston.com/news/nation/articles/2008/02/26/just_dont_call_barack_obama_liberal_okey_doke/.
26. Mark Schmitt, "The 'Theory of Change' Primary," *The American Prospect*, December 21, 2007; available at: http://www.prospect.org/cs/articles?article=the_theory_of_change_primary.
27. Ibid.
28. Jonathan Chait, "The Case For Bush Hatred, Mad About You," *The New Republic*, September 23, 2003; available at: http://www.tnr.com/article/mad-about-you.
29. Jonathan Chait, "The Obama Method And The Health Care Summit," *The New Republic*, February 9, 2010; available at: http://www.tnr.com/blog/jonathan-chait/the-obama-method-and-the-health-care-summit.

30. Ibid.

31. Bill Clinton, "Transcript: Remarks to the Democratic Leadership Council," December 6, 1993; available at: http://findarticles.com/p/articles/mi_m2889/is_n48_v29/ai_14891633/.

32. Julie Mason, "He's No Charmer: Obama's Personal Appeal Not Delivering Results," *The Washington Examiner*, February 28, 2010; available at: http://www.washingtonexaminer.com/politics/he_s-no-charmer_-Obama_s-personal-appeal-not-delivering-results-85569262.html [accessed July 7, 2010].

Chapter 3

1. Ernest S. Christian and Gary A. Robbins, "Denying Truth and Rewriting a Dictionary," Investors.com, October 6, 2009; available at: http://www.investors.com/NewsAndAnalysis/Article/508150/200910061830/Denying-Truth-And-Rewriting-The-Dictionary.aspx.

2. Macon Phillips, "Change Has Come to WhiteHouse.gov," The White House Blog, January 20, 2009; available at: http://www.whitehouse.gov/blog/2009/01/20/change-has-come-whitehousegov.

3. Jim Harper "A Flagging Obama Transparency Effort," The Cato Institute, April 9, 2009; available at: http://www.cato-at-liberty.org/2009/04/09/a-flagging-obama-transparency-effort/.

4. Chelsea Schilling, "Obama Racks Up List Of Broken Promises," WorldNetDaily.com, March 12, 2009; available at: http://www.wnd.com/?pageId=91286.

5. Jim Harper "A Flagging Obama Transparency Effort," The Cato Institute, April 9, 2009; available at: http://www.cato-at-liberty.org/2009/04/09/a-flagging-obama-transparency-effort/.

6. "The C-Span Lie? See Eight Clips of Obama Promising Televised Healthcare Negotiations," Breitbart.tv, January 6, 2010; available at: http://www.breitbart.tv/the-c-span-lie-did-obama-really-promise-televised-healthcare-negotiations/.

7. President Barack Obama, "Interview of the President by YouTube," White House Documents and Publications, February 1, 2010; available at: http://www.whitehouse.gov/the-press-office/interview-president-youtube.

8. Angie Drobnic Holan, "Obama Said He'd Televise Health Reform Negotiations on C-SPAN," PolitiFact.com, July 10, 2009; available at: http://www.politifact.com/truth-o-meter/promises/promise/517/health-care-reform-public-sessions-C-SPAN/.

9. "Obama Asked About Broken Health Care Debate on C-SPAN Promise," C-Span Video, February 3, 2010. [Can't find video]

10. Lynn Sweet, "Obama Finally Admits He Broke C-SPAN Transparency Promise," *Chicago Sun-Times*, January 26, 2010; available at: http://blogs.suntimes.com/sweet/2010/01/obama_finally_admits_he_broke.html.

11. Joseph Ashby, "'Death Panel' is not in the bill... it already exists," *American Thinker*, August 15, 2010; available at: http://www.americanthinker.com/2009/08/death_panel_is_not_in_the_bill.html; The Editors, "Ending Welfare Reform as We Knew It," *National Review Online*, February 12, 2009; available at: http://article.nationalreview.com/385671/ending-welfare-reform-as-we-knew-it/the-editors.

12. "Obama Admin. Withholds 'Clunkers' Data," CBSNews, August 4, 2009; available at: http://www.cbsnews.com/stories/2009/08/04/politics/main5212863.shtml.

13. Phil Kerpen, "Obama's Secret Slush Fund," FOX News, February 2, 2010; available at: http://www.foxnews.com/opinion/2010/02/02/phil-kerpen-obama-budget-cap-trade-tax-deficit-black-box/.

14. Bill Adair, Angie Drobnic Holan, "A Year Later, Lots of Partisanship," PolitiFact.com, January 10, 2010; available at: http://www.politifact.com/truth-o-meter/promises/promise/522/bring-democrats-and-republicans-together-pass-agen/.

15. Robert Pear and David M. Herszenhorn, "Obama Hails Vote on Health Care as Answering 'the Call of History,'" *The New York Times*, March 21, 2010; available at: http://www.nytimes.com/2010/03/22/health/policy/22health.html?scp=1&sq=Obama%20Hails%20Vote%20on%20Health%20Care%20as%20Answering%20%E2%80%98the%20Call%20of%20History&st=cse.

16. Darren Samuelsohn, "Sen. Rockefeller Criticizes Obama Over Coal Policy," *The New York Times*, February 4, 2010; available at: http://www.nytimes.com/gwire/2010/02/04/04greenwire-sen-rockefeller-criticizes-obama-over-coal-poli-5739.html

17. Fred Lucas, "Rep. Issa: Was Obama 'Just Lying to Congress' on Tort Reform Pledge?" CNSNews.com, February 9, 2010; available at: http://www.cnsnews.com/news/article/61100.

18. Ashby Jones, "On Tort Reform and the Health-Care Bill: Where'd We End Up?" *Wall Street Journal* Law Blog, March 23, 2010; available at: http://blogs.wsj.com/law/2010/03/23/on-tort-reform-and-the-health-care-bill-whered-we-end-up/.

19. "The Vast Majority of the Money I got was from Small Donors All Across the Country," PolitiFact.com, April 21, 2010; available at: http://www.politifact.com/truth-o-meter/statements/2010/apr/22/barack-obama/obama-campaign-financed-large-donors-too/.

20. Hank, "Obama: Commissions a 'Stunt,' Unless I Propose Them," *Federal Review*, February 22, 2010; available at: http://federalreview.com/wp/?p=235.

21. James Rosen, "Obama Administration Steers Lucrative No-Bid Contract for Afghan Work to Dem Donor," FoxNews.com, January 25, 2010; available at: http://www.foxnews.com/politics/2010/01/25/obama-administration-steers-lucrative-bid-contract-afghan-work-dem-donor/.

22. James Rosen, "State Department Admits No-Bid Contract 'Violates' Obama Campaign Pledges," FoxNews.com, January 31, 2010; available at: http://www.foxnews.com/politics/2010/01/31/state-department-admits-bid-contract-violates-obama-campaign-pledges/.

23. Jake Tapper and Sunlen Miller, "President Obama to Sign Pork-Laden Omnibus Spending Bill," *Political Punch*, March 2, 2009; available at: http://blogs.abcnews.com/politicalpunch/2009/03/president-obama.html.

24. "Barack Obama Campaign Promise No. 431: Reduce Earmarks to 1994 Levels," PolitiFact.com, February 19, 2010; available at: http://www.politifact.com/truth-o-meter/promises/promise/431/reduce-earmarks-to-1994-levels/.

25. "Obama Says Lobbyists Have Been Excluded From Policy-Making Jobs," PolitiFact.com, January 27, 2010; available at: http://www.politifact.com/truth-o-meter/statements/2010/jan/27/barack-obama/obama-says-lobbyists-have-been-excluded-policy-mak/.

26. Jake Tapper, "Obama White House Discloses Two More Lobbyist Waivers Granted," *ABC News* Political Punch, March 10, 2010;

available at: http://blogs.abcnews.com/politicalpunch/2009/03/
obama-white-hou.html.

27. Erick Erickson, "Breaking News: Obama Lies About Lobbyists."
Human Events, January 27, 2010; available at: http://www.human-
events.com/article.php?id=35376.

28. Peter Wehner, "An Agent of Cynicism," *Commentary*, undated;
available at: http://www.commentarymagazine.com/viewarticle.cfm/
an-agent-of-cynicism-15097?search=1.

29. David Brooks, "The Emotion of Reform," *The New York Times*,
March 8, 2010; available at: http://www.nytimes.com/2010/03/09/
opinion/09brooks.html.

30. Mike Dorning and Juliana Goldman, "Obama Says He's 'Fierce
Free-Market Advocate,' Rejects Critics," Bloomberg.com, February
11, 2010; available at: http://www.bloomberg.com/apps/news?pid=
20601070&sid=aDLk0lPYaSa0.

31. President Barack Obama, "Transcript: Obama Wall Street Speech on
Financial Reform," ABCNews.com, April 22, 2010; available at:
http://abcnews.go.com/Politics/transcript-obama-wall-street-speech-
financial-reform/story?id=10446690.

32. Senator Barack Obama, "Sen. Barack Obama's Remarks On Taxes
As Prepared for Delivery at a Campaign Event," *CQ Transcriptions*,
September 12, 2008.

33. Brad Schiller, "Obama's Poor Tax," *The Wall Street Journal*, April
1, 2009; available at: http://online.wsj.com/article/
SB123854056373275583.html [accessed June 28, 2010].

34. John Kartch, "Obama's $250,000 Tax Pledge Timeline," Americans
for Tax Reform, November 2, 2009; available at: http://www.atr.
org/obamas-tax-pledge-timelinebr-descending-read-a3897#
[accessed June 28, 2010].

35. Jim Hoft, "Stunner. Obama Now Says He's 'Agnostic' On Raising
Taxes On Those Making Less Than $250,000," *Gateway Pundit*,
February 11, 2010; available at: http://gatewaypundit.firstthings.
com/2010/02/stunner-obama-now-says-hes-indifferent-on-raising-
taxes-on-those-making-less-than-250000/ [accessed June 28, 2010].

36. John Kartch, "Obama Floats a VAT: Admission Explains Attempt to
Alter Tax Pledge," Americans for Tax Reform, April 21, 2010;

available at: http://www.atr.org/obama-floats-vat-br-admission-explains-a4814 [accessed June 28, 2010].

37. Steny Hoyer, "Easy Way vs. Correct Way on Budget," *The Hill*'s Congress Blog, June 22, 2010; available at: http://thehill.com/blogs/congress-blog/economy-a-budget/104679-easy-way-vs-correct-way-on-budget [accessed June 28, 2010].

38. "Obama Calling 'Bluff' of Those Complaining about Deficits and Debt," *Real Clear Politics*; video available at: http://www.realclear-politics.com/video/2010/06/27/obama_calling_bluff_of_those_complaining_about_debt_he_created.html [accessed June 28, 2010].

39. John Kartch, "Obamacare: By the Numbers," Americans for Tax Reform, March 18, 2010; available at: http://www.atr.org/oba-macare-numbers-a4664 [accessed June 28, 2010].

40. Rep. Dave Camp, "Democrats Have Increased Taxes by $670 Billion and Counting...," Committee on Ways & Means Republicans, undated.

41. Ben Lieberman, "The Economic Impact of the Waxman-Markey Cap-and-Trade Bill," The Heritage Foundation, June 22, 2009; available at: http://www.heritage.org/Research/Testimony/The-Economic-Impact-of-the-Waxman-Markey-Cap-and-Trade-Bill.

42. John Kartch, "Obama Floats a VAT: Admission Explains Attempt to Alter Tax Pledge," Americans for Tax Reform, April 21, 2010; available at: http://www.atr.org/obama-floats-vat-br-admission-explains-a4814.

43. Jake Tapper, "President Obama: Not Playing 'Old Washington Game' of What's In, What's Out When it Comes to Deficit Reduction," *ABC News,* Political Punch, April 27, 2010; available at: http://blogs.abcnews.com/politicalpunch/2010/04/president-obama-not-playing-old-washington-game-of-whats-in-whats-out-when-it-comes-to-deficit-reduction.html.

44. Chelsea Schilling, "Obama Racks Up List of Broken Promises," WorldNetDaily.com, March 12, 2009; available at: http://www.wnd.com/?pageId=91286.

45. Jim Angle, "Tax Week: President Obama Plans Tax Increases on Investment Income," FoxNews.com, April 12, 2010; available at: http://congress.blogs.foxnews.com/2010/04/12/tax-week-president-obama-plans-tax-increases-on-investment-income/.

46. Publius, "Obama Admits HealthCare-Not Jobs or the Economy–Is 'Most Important Domestic Priority,'" Biggovernment.com, March 21. 2010; available at: http://biggovernment.com/publius/2010/03/21/obama-admits-healthcare-not-jobs-or-the-economy-is-most-important-domestic-priority/.

47. Stephen Gandel, "Obama's Stimulus Plan: Failing By Its Own Measure," Time.com, July 14, 2009; available at: http://www.time.com/time/business/article/0,8599,1910208,00.html.

48. Hans Nichols, "Obama Says U.S. Must Act Swiftly to Address Economy," Bloomberg.com, January 3, 2009; available at: http://www.bloomberg.com/apps/news?pid=newsarchive&sid=aeLGXDu_0Qiw.

49. "Fact Check: How State of the Union Compares with Reality," *Associated Press* January 27, 2010.

50. Cato Editors, "State of the Union Fact Check," The Cato Institute, January 28, 2010; available at: http://www.cato-at-liberty.org/2010/01/28/state-of-the-union-fact-check/.

51. "Is Obama's Underwhelming Spending Freeze A Fakeroo?" *The Foundry* Blog, January 26, 2010; available at: http://blog.heritage.org/2010/01/26/is-obamas-underwhelming-spending-freeze-a-fakeroo/.

52. "Fact Check: How State of the Union Compares with Reality," *Associated Press* January 27, 2010.

53. James C. Capretta, "Obamacare's Cooked Books and the 'Doc Fix,'" *Critical Condition*, May 24, 2010; available at: http://www.nationalreview.com/critical-condition/55996/obamacare-s-cooked-books-and-doc-fix/james-c-capretta.

54. John C. Goodman, "Goodbye, Employer-Sponsored Insurance," *The Wall Street Journal*, May 21; available at: http://online.wsj.com/article/SB10001424052748703880304575236602943319816.html, 2010.

55. Dr. Scott Gottlieb, "No, You Can't Keep Your Health Plan," *The Wall Street Journal*, May 18, 2010; available at: http://online.wsj.com/article/SB10001424052748703315404575250264210294510.html.

56. Examiner Editorial, "Public Option is Alive and Well, but Hidden," *Washington Examiner*, May 17, 2010; available at: http://www.

washingtonexaminer.com/opinion/Examiner-Editorial-Public-option-is-alive-and-well-but-hidden-93930519.html.

57. Brian Riedl, "Obama's Faith-Based Economics," *National Review Online, The Corner*, February 17, 2010; available at: http://corner.nationalreview.com/post/?q=MmQxMDA3ZDFiZmMzMWE 2YWQ2YTQzMTMzNzVlNmU5Yjg=.

58. Editors, "Lying About Jobs," Investors.com, April 21, 2010; available at: http://www.investors.com/NewsAndAnalysis/Article.aspx?id =530994.

59. Cato Editors, "State of the Union Fact Check," *op. cit.*

60. Terrence P. Jeffrey, "Obama Told House Democrat He Wasn't Talking About House Health Bill When He Told Congress 'Our Plan' Doesn't Fund Abortion," CNSNews.com, October 26, 2009, available at: http://www.cnsnews.com/news/article/56109.

61. Matt Cover, "Obama's New Claim That 30 Million 'Cannot' Get Health Insurance Not Supported by Census Bureau," CNSNews.com, September 22, 2009; available at: http://www.cnsnews.com/news/article/54329.

62. Philip Klein, "Obama Lies on Single-Payer, Disses Post Office," *The American Spectator*, August 11, 2009; available at: http://spectator.org/blog/2009/08/11/obama-lies-on-single-payer-dis.

63. Scott Wilson, "Obama Lists Financial Rescue as 'Most Important Thing' of His First Year," *The Washington Post,* December 23, 2009; available at: http://www.washingtonpost.com/wp-dyn/content/article/2009/12/22/AR2009122202101.html.

64. "Uncovered Video: Obama Explains How His Health Care Plan Will 'Eliminate' Private Insurance," Breitbart.tv, August 3, 2009; available at: http://www.breitbart.tv/uncovered-video-obama-explains-how-his-health-care-plan-will-eliminate-private-insurance/.

65. Zaid Jilani, "Flashback: Obama Repeatedly Touted Public Option Before Refusing to Push For It In The Final Hours," *Think Progress Blog*, December 22, 2009; available at: http://thinkprogress.org/2009/12/22/obama-repeatedly-touted-public/.

66. Examiner Editorial, "Public Option is Alive and Well, but Hidden," *Washington Examiner*, May 17, 2010; available at: http://www.washingtonexaminer.com/opinion/Examiner-Editorial-Public-option-is-alive-and-well-but-hidden-93930519.html.

67. "Barack Obama Campaign Promise No. 71: Allow Imported Pre-scription Drugs," PolitiFact.com, April 8, 2010; available at: http://www.politifact.com/truth-o-meter/promises/promise/71/allow-imported-prescription-drugs/.

68. "Jerusalem Must Remain the Undivided Capital of Israel: Obama," Breitbart.com, June 4, 2008; available at: http://www.breitbart.com/article.php?id=080604153023.crgzcbw7&show_article=1.

69. Robert Burns, "Clinton, Israel PM to Meet," The Associated Press, March 20, 2010.

70. Chelsea Schilling, "Obama Racks Up List of Broken Promises," WorldNetDaily.com, March 12, 2009; available at: http://www.wnd.com/?pageId=91286.

71. Jonathan Gurwitz, "After One Year, Obama's Trail of Broken Prom-ises," *San Antonio News*, January 16, 2010; available at: http://www.mysanantonio.com/opinion/columnists/jonathan_gurwitz/After_one_year_Obamas_trail_of_broken_promises.html.

72. Jonathan Gurwitz, "After One Year, "Obama's Trail of Broken Promises," *San Antonio News*, January 16, 2010; available at: http://www.mysanantonio.com/opinion/columnists/jonathan_gurwitz/After_one_year_Obamas_trail_of_broken_promises.html.

73. Ibid.

74. "Barack Obama Campaign Promise No. 511: Recognize the Armen-ian Genocide," PolitiFact, March 5, 2010; available at: http://politifact.com/truth-o-meter/promises/promise/511/recognize-armenian-genocide/.

75. "Senator Obama's Voting Record," BornAliveTruth.org, undated; available at: http://bornalivetruth.org/obamarecord.php; Andrew C. McCarthy, "Why Obama Really Voted for Infanticide," *National Review Online*, August 22, 2008; available at: http://article.nationalreview.com/367248/why-obama-really-voted-for-infanticide/andrew-c-mccarthy.

76. Douglas Johnson, "Obama Cover-Up on Born-Alive Abortion Sur-vivors Continues to Unravel After Sen. Obama Says NRLC is 'Lying'," National Right to Life, August 18, 2008; available at: http://www.nrlc.org/ObamaBaipa/Obamacoveruponbornalive.htm.

77. Nicholas Ballasy, "Obama Justified in Votes Against Born Alive Infant Protection Bill, Say Democrats," CNSNews.com, October 24, 2008; available at: http://www.cnsnews.com/news/article/38079.

78. Cliff Kincaid, "Damaging Disclosures in Van Jones Scandal," Accuracy in Media, October 21, 2009; available at: http://www.aim.org/aim-column/damaging-disclosures-in-van-jones-scandal/.

79. Michelle Malkin, "Van Jones. Valerie Jarrett, Barack Obama & do-it-yourself vetting Updated," MichelleMalkin.com, September 3, 2009; available at: http://michellemalkin.com/2009/09/03/van-jones-valerie-jarrett-barack-obama-do-it-yourself-vetting/.

80. Kevin Hall, "CBS Exposes Obama Administration Lies About Blocking FOX News," AIP News, October 24, 2009; available at: http://www.aipnews.com/talk/forums/thread-view.asp?tid=9331&posts=6.

81. Simon Walters, "No 10 Turns On Obama and Clinton for Criticising Decision to Release Lockerbie Bomber," *Daily Mail*, September 6, 2009; available at: http://www.dailymail.co.uk/news/article-1211495/No-10-turns-Obama-Clinton-criticising-decision-release-Lockerbie-bomber.html.

Chapter 4

1. Natasha T. Metzler, "Obama Prays for Civility in Washington," Associated Press, February 4, 2010; available at: http://www.washingtonpost.com/wp-dyn/content/article/2010/02/04/AR2010020401728.html [accessed June 29, 2010].

2. Sunlen Miller, "President Obama to Speak at Both Republican, and Democratic Conferences," *ABC News,* Political Punch, January 12, 2010; available at: http://blogs.abcnews.com/politicalpunch/2010/01/president-obama-to-speak-at-both-republican-and-democratic-conferences-.html [accessed June 29, 2010].

3. "Obama Ad Touts Work with GOP," *Boston Globe*, January 22, 2008; available at: http://www.boston.com/news/nation/articles/2008/01/22/obama_ad_touts_work_with_gop/ [accessed June 29, 2010].

4. Judy Berman, "Obama Reaches Across the Aisle on Abortion," Salon.com, May 7, 2009; available at: http://www.salon.com/life/

broadsheet/feature/2009/05/07/abortion_compromise [accessed June 29, 2010].

5. "Transcript: Karl Rove on 'FNS,'" *FOXNews Sunday*, March 15, 2010; available at: http://www.foxnews.com/story/ 0,2933,589242,00.html [accessed June 29, 2010].

6. "'Bipartisan' White House Super Bowl party to feature . . . one Republican," HotAir.com, February 5, 2010; available at: http:// hotair.com/archives/2010/02/05/bipartisan-white-house-super-bowl-party-to-feature-one-republican/ [accessed June 29, 2010].

7. Matt Spetanick, "White House says Republicans Rotting Against Recovery," Reuters, December 11, 2009; available at: http://www. reuters.com/article/idUSTRE5B20TI20091211 [accessed June 29, 2010].

8. Amy Chozick, "Obama: 'If They Bring a Knife to the Fight, We Bring a Gun,'" Washington Wire, *Wall Street Journal*, June 14, 2008; available at: http://blogs.wsj.com/washwire/2008/06/14/ obama-if-they-bring-a-knife-to-the-fight-we-bring-a-gun/ [accessed June 29, 2010].

9. Barack Obama, "Obama Says 'Argue With Neighbors, Get In Their Face,'" YouTube, September 18, 2008; available at: http://www. youtube.com/watch?v=ZCMDur9CDZ4 [accessed June 29, 2010].

10. "Obama 2007 Accused Bush Of A Photo-Op With The Troops," HotAirPundit, November 3, 2009; available at: http://www.hapblog. com/2009/11/obama-2007-accused-bush-of-photo-op.html [accessed June 29, 2010].

11. Steven Ertelt, "House GOP Demands Probe of Obama Admin Report Saying Pro-Lifers Extremists," LifeNews.com, May 7, 2009; available at: http://www.lifenews.com/nat5030.html [accessed June 29, 2010].

12. Larry Kudlow, "One Giant Government Leap Backwards," Townhall.com, March 5, 2010; available at: http://townhall.com/colum-nists/LarryKudlow/2010/03/05/one_giant_government_leap_ backwards [accessed June 29, 2010].

13. Erick Erickson, "Obama Administration Intends to Purge Republi-cans From the Civil Service," Redstate.com, November 12, 2009; available at: http://www.redstate.com/erick/2009/11/12/obama-

administration-intends-to-purge-republicans-from-the-civil-service/
[accessed June 29, 2010].

14. Pamela Geller, "Obama Pays Off: Nominates Vocal Palin Foe Persily To Alaska Pipeline Job," *Atlas Shrugs*, December 9, 2009; available at: http://atlasshrugs2000.typepad.com/atlas_shrugs/ [accessed June 29, 2010].

15. Jim Angle, Trish Turner, and Judson Berger, "Republicans Claim Top Lawmakers Were in the Loop on Interrogations," FOXNews. com, April 23, 2009; available at: http://www.foxnews.com/politics/ 2009/04/23/republicans-claim-lawmakers-loop-interrogations/ [accessed June 29, 2010].

16. David A. Patten, "Report: W.H. Engineered NY-23 Endorsement," *Newsmax*, November 2, 2009; available at: http://freerepublic.com/ focus/f-news/2377184/posts [accessed June 29, 2010].

17. Sunlen Miller, "President Obama to Speak at Both Republican, and Democratic Conferences," *ABC News,* Political Punch, January 12, 2010; available at: http://blogs.abcnews.com/politicalpunch/2010/ 01/president-obama-to-speak-at-both-republican-and-democratic-conferences-.html [accessed June 29, 2010].

18. Karl Rove, "The President's GOP Outreach Comes Too Late," *The Wall Street Journal*, February 3, 2010; available at: http://online.wsj. com/article/SB10001424052748704259304575043342489432552. html [accessed June 29, 2010].

19. Connie Hair, "Republicans Shut out of Stimulus Conference Negotiations," *Human Events*, February 11, 2009; available at: http:// www.humanevents.com/article.php?id=30667 [accessed June 29, 2010].

20. David Herszenhorn, "Senate Clears Path for Vote on $838 Billion Stimulus," *The New York Times*, February 9, 2009; available at: http://www.nytimes.com/2009/02/10/washington/10stimulus-web. html [accessed June 29, 2010].

21. Kara Rowland, "WH Defends Reid Move to Scuttle Bipartisan Bill," *Washington Times*, February 12, 2010; available at: http:// www.washingtontimes.com/news/2010/feb/12/wh-defends-reid-move-scuttle-bipartisan-bill/ [accessed June 29, 2010].

22. Kara Rowland, "Critics Not Invited to White House 'Jobs Summit,'" *Washington Times*, December 2, 2009; available at: http://

www.washingtontimes.com/news/2009/dec/02/obama-policy-critics-not-invited-to-jobs-summit/ [accessed June 29, 2010].

23. J. Taylor Rushing, "White House Snubs Budget Panel Leaders in Health Summit Invites," *The Hill*, February 13, 2010; available at: http://thehill.com/homenews/senate/81025-white-house-snubs-budget-panel-leaders-in-bipartisan-summit-invites [accessed July 8, 2010].

24. "Obama Calls On Parties To Transcend 'Petty Politics,'" *Real Clear Politics* Video, February 9, 2010; available at: http://infidelsarecool.com/2010/02/09/obama-calls-on-parties-to-transcend-petty-politics-meanwhile-gibbs-mocks-palin-from-the-white-house-podium/ [accessed June 29, 2010]

25. Stephen Dinan, "Exclusive: Cantor: Obama's not met with GOP leaders since May," *Washington Times*, October 1, 2009; available at: http://www.washingtontimes.com/news/2009/oct/01/cantor-obama-muted-gop-voices-on-health-care/ [accessed June 29, 2010].

26. Molly K. Hooper, "Boehner: GOP Leaders Haven't Met Obama for Health Talks Since April," *The Hill*, September 9, 2009; available at: http://thehill.com/blogs/blog-briefing-room/news/57859-boehner-gop-leaders-havent-met-obama-for-health-talks-since-april [accessed June 29, 2010].

27. Tom Price, "Now Obama Discovers GOP Health Care Proposals?" Big Government.com, February 12, 2010; available at: http://big-government.com/tprice/2010/02/12/oh-the-president-must-be-really-desperate/ [accessed June 29, 2010].

28. Richard Wolf, "Obama Draws Line on Stimulus Compromise," *USA Today*, February 4, 2009; available at: http://www.ourfuture.org/news-headline/2009020604/obama-draws-line-stimulus-com-promise [accessed June 29, 2010].

29. Stephen Dinan and Kara Rowland, "Obama Denounces Hold Tactic He Used As Senator," *Washington Times*, February 3, 2010; available at: http://www.washingtontimes.com/news/2010/feb/03/obama-denounces-tactic-he-used-senator/ [accessed June 29, 2010].

30. Jake Tapper, "First President in US History to Have Voted to Fili-buster a Supreme Court Nominee Now Hopes for Clean Process," ABC News, *Political Punch*, May 30. 2009; available at: http://blogs.abcnews.com/politicalpunch/2009/05/first-president-in-us-

history-to-have-voted-to-filibuster-a-supreme-court-nominee-now-hopes-for-clea.html [accessed June 29, 2010].

31. Frank James, "Obama Warns Mayors: 'Will Call Them Out,'" *Chicago Tribune*, February 20, 2009; available at: http://www. chicagotribune.com/news/nationworld/chi-obama-mayorsfeb21,0, 4764964.story [accessed June 29, 2010].

32. President Barack Obama, "Remarks By The President To A Joint Session Of Congress On Health Care," White House.gov, September 9, 2009; available at: http://www.whitehouse.gov/the_press_office/ remarks-by-the-president-to-a-joint-session-of-congress-on-health-care/ [accessed June 29, 2010].

33. Ceci Connolly and Michael D. Shear, "Obama Implores Congress to Act, In Arguing for a Public Option, He Emphasizes It's 'Only One Part of My Plan,'" *Washington Post*, September 10, 2010; available at: http://www.washingtonpost.com/wp-dyn/content/article/2009/09/ 09/AR2009090901771.html [accessed June 29, 2010].

34. "Flashback: Democrats Boo Bush at 2005 State of the Union," *Real Clear Politics* Video, September 10, 2009; available at: http://www. realclearpolitics.com/video/2009/09/10/flashback_democrats_boo_bush_at_2005_state_of_the_union.html [accessed June 29, 2010].

35. Mark Krikorian, "Obama Admits Joe Wilson Was Right," *National Review Online*, September 14, 2009; available at: http://corner. nationalreview.com/post/?q=MDgzZWQ2ZGU1NDJkZTBkNDMy Y2FmZWQ2MTI2ZWQxNWI= [accessed June 29, 2010].

36. President Barack Obama, "Remarks By The President To A Joint Session Of Congress On Health Care," September 9, 2009.

37. Editors, "On Presidential Rhetoric, Obama's ad hominem method and the politics of polarization," *Wall Street Journal*, April 22, 2010; available at: http://online.wsj.com/article/SB10001424052748 704448304575196121075748664.html [accessed June 29, 2010].

38. President Barack Obama, "Text: State of the Union 2010," January 27, 2010; available at: http://abcnews.go.com/Politics/State_of_the_Union/state-of-the-union-2010-president-obama-speech-transcript/ story?id=9678572 [accessed June 29, 2010].

39. Karl Rove, "The President's GOP Outreach Comes Too Late," *Wall Street Journal*, February 3, 2010; available at: http://online.wsj.com/

article/SB10001424052748704259304575043342489432552.html [accessed June 29, 2010].

40. Bridget Johnson, "Rep. Hensarling Fires Back at Obama in the Rumble Over Deficits," *The Hill*, January 30, 2010; available at: http://thehill.com/blogs/blog-briefing-room/news/78901-hensarling-fires-back-at-obama-in-the-deficit-rumble [accessed June 29, 2010].

41. Jeb Hensarling, "Press Release: Hensarling Statement on the President's Appearance At GOP Retreat," Hensarling.house.gov, January 29, 2010; available at: http://hensarling.house.gov/list/press/tx05_hensarling/morenews/Hensarling_Fact_Check_Release.shtml [accessed June 29, 2010].

42. Kenneth R. Bazinet, "President Obama to GOP Leaders: Stop 'Grandstanding' and Get to Work on Jobs Legislation," *New York Daily News*, February 9, 2010; available at: http://www.nydailynews.com/news/politics/2010/02/09/2010-02-09_president_obama_to_gop_leaders_stop_grandstanding_and_get_to_work_on_jobs_bill.html [accessed June 29, 2010] ; see also, "Obama Pleads for Bipartisanship, Calls for End to 'Grandstanding,'" Associated Press, February 9, 2010; available at: http://www.foxnews.com/politics/2010/02/09/obama-pleads-bipartisanship-calls-end-grandstanding/ [accessed June 29, 2010].

43. "At Deeds Rally, Obama Knocks GOP Critics," *Real Clear Politics*, August 6, 2009; available at: http://www.realclearpolitics.com/politics_nation/2009/08/at_deeds_rally_obama_knocks_go.html [accessed June 29, 2010].

44. Steve Holland, "Obama's 2010 Strategy Taking Shape," Reuters, February 7, 2010; available at: http://www.reuters.com/article/idUS-TRE6160PJ20100207 [accessed June 29, 2010].

45. "Obama" Republicans 'Do What They're Told,'" *Real Clear Politics* Video, October 22, 2009; available at: http://www.realclearpolitics.com/video/2009/10/22/obama_republicans_do_what_theyre_told.html [accessed June 29, 2010].

46. David M. Herszenhorn, "Updated: Obama Urges Democrats Forward On Health Care," *New York Times*, February 3, 2010; available at: http://prescriptions.blogs.nytimes.com/2010/02/03/obama-we-have-to-finish-the-job/ [accessed June 29, 2010].

47. Gary L. Bauer, "2-4-10 End of Day," February 4, 2010, *Politico*.

48. Michael D. Shear, "White House Revamps Communications Strategy," *Washington Post*, February 15, 2010; available at: http://www.washingtonpost.com/wp-dyn/content/article/2010/02/14/AR2010021403550.html [accessed June 29, 2010].

49. "Obama Camp: Swiftboaters Behind Health Care Attacks," Newsmax.com, May 16, 2009; available at: http://www.newsmax.com/InsideCover/health-care-swiftboat/2009/05/16/id/330163 [accessed June 29, 2010].

50. Jake Tapper, "Obama Political Arm Says GOP House Members Caved to Insurance Lobby Pressure," ABC News, *Political Punch*, November 8, 2009; available at: http://blogs.abcnews.com/politicalpunch/2009/11/obama-political-arm-says-gop-house-members-caved-to-insurance-lobby-pressure.html [accessed June 29, 2010].

51. Michael O'Brien, "Dems Plan 'Pain' For GOP If They Drag Out Health Debate," *The Hill,* Blog Briefing Room, March 4, 2010; available at: http://thehill.com/blogs/blog-briefing-room/news/84893-dems-plan-pain-for-gop-if-they-drag-out-health-debate [accessed June 29, 2010].

52. Chris Cillizza, "Ten Facts You Need to Know About Rahm Emanuel," *Washington Post*, November 6, 2008; available at: http://voices.washingtonpost.com/thefix/eye-on-2008/top-10-facts-you-need-to-know.html [accessed June 29, 2010]; see also, Sara Jarman, "Rahm Emmanuel: Con," *BYU Political Review*, January 27, 2010.

53. Steve Clemons, "Movement Left Has Stroke: Rahm Emanuel Accepts Obama's Chief of Staff Offer," *Washington Note*, November 5, 2008; available at: http://www.thewashingtonnote.com/archives/2008/11/movement_left_h/ [accessed June 29, 2010].

54. Camille Paglia, "Obama's Early Stumbles," Salon.com, January 14, 2009; available at: http://www.salon.com/news/opinion/camille_paglia/2009/01/14/obama [accessed June 29, 2010].

55. Peter Baker and Jeff Zeleny, "Emanuel Wields Power Freely, and Faces the Risks," *New York Times*, August 15, 2009; available at: http://www.nytimes.com/2009/08/16/us/politics/16emanuel.html [accessed June 29, 2010].

56. Jake Tapper, "Rahm Apologizes for Privately Calling Liberal Activists 'Retarded,'" ABC News, *Political Punch*, February 2, 2010; available at: http://blogs.abcnews.com/politicalpunch/2010/

02/rahm-apologizes-for-privately-calling-liberal-activists-retarded.
html [accessed June 29, 2010].

57. Carol E. Lee, "Handling Problems the Obama Way," *Politico*,
December 29, 2009; available at: http://www.politico.com/news/sto-
ries/1209/31021.html [accessed June 29, 2010].

58. "Sen. Gregg Withdraws as Commerce Secretary Nominee, Citing
Conflicts," FOXNews.com, February 12, 2009; available at: http://
www.foxnews.com/politics/2009/02/12/sen-gregg-withdraws-com-
merce-secretary-nominee-citing-conflicts/ [accessed June 29, 2010].

59. Jake Tapper, "WH: Some Critics 'Serving the Goals of al Qaeda,'"
ABC News, *Political Punch*, February 9, 2009; available at: http://
blogs.abcnews.com/politicalpunch/2010/02/wh-some-critics-serving-
the-goals-of-al-qaeda.html [accessed June 29, 2010].

60. Jonathan Martin, "Obama 'Gearing Up for a Fight,'" *Politico*, February 28, 2008; available at: http://www.politico.com/news/stories/
0209/19434.html [accessed June 29, 2010].

61. Camille Paglia, "Obama's Early Stumbles," Salon.com, January 14,
2009; available at: http://www.salon.com/news/opinion/camille_
paglia/2009/01/14/obama [accessed June 29, 2010].

62. Peter Beinart, "Democrats, Forever Changed," *The Daily Beast*,
March 15, 2010; available at: http://www.thedailybeast.com/blogs-
and-stories/2010-03-15/the-decision-that-changed-the-dems/full/
[accessed June 29, 2010].

63. Steven Ertelt, "Notre Dame President Defends Pro-Abortion Obama
Invite Despite Bishops' Rules," *LifeNews.com*, April 9, 2009; available at: http://www.lifenews.com/state4046.html [accessed June 29,
2010]; see also, Steven Ertelt, "Former Vatican Ambassador Won't
Speak at Notre Dame Over Obama Controversy," LifeNews.com,
April 27, 2009; available at: http://www.lifenews.com/state4082.
html [accessed June 29, 2010].

64. Dan Gilgoff, God & Country, "Notre Dame Critics Tally $8.2 Mil-
lion in Denied University Donations Over Obama," *U.S. News &
World Report*, April 27, 2009; available at: http://politics.usnews.
com/news/blogs/god-and-country/2009/04/27/notre-dame-critics-
tally-82-million-in-denied-university-donations-over-obama.html
[accessed June 29, 2010].

Chapter 5

1. Transcript, *Hardball With Chris Matthews*, Thursday, October 22, 2009.

2. "Alexander: 'Unpresidential' For Obama To Bring 'Street Fighting' In WH," *Real Clear Politics Video*, October 23, 2009; available at: http://www.realclearpolitics.com/video/2009/10/23/alexander_unpresidential_for_obama_to_bring_street_fighting_in_wh.html.

3. Jim Vandehei and Mike Allen, "Obama Strategy: Marginalize Most Powerful Critics," *Politico*, October 21, 2009; available at: http://www.politico.com/news/stories/1009/28532.html.

4. Michael Barone, "Obama Hits Opponents with Chicago Brass Knuckles," *Washington Examiner*, October 21, 2009; available at: http://www.washingtonexaminer.com/politics/Obama-hits-opponents-with-Chicago-brass-knuckles-8415163-65077847.html.

5. Sam Youngman, "Obama to McCain on Iran: 'I'm the President,'" *The Hill*, June 23, 2009; available at: http://thehill.com/homenews/news/47261-obama-to-mccain-on-iran-im-the-president.

6. Glenn Greenwald, "Creepy, Revealing Quote from White House staffer," Salon.com, Jun 30, 2009; available at: http://www.salon.com/news/opinion/glenn_greenwald/2009/06/30/white_house.

7. President Barack Obama, "Homosexuality—Obama Hopes to Persuade All Americans to accept Homosexuality," YouTube.com, November 9, 2009; available at: http://www.youtube.com/watch?v=dOvNUqf81Do.

8. "Obama Mocks GOP's Health Care 'Armageddon' Claims: Six Months From Now 'You Can Check It Out, We'll Look Around,'" *Huffington Post*, March 23, 2010; available at: http://www.huffingtonpost.com/2010/03/23/obama-mocks-gops-health-c_n_510371.html.

9. President Barack Obama, "President Barack Obama Remarks As Prepared For Delivery At A Health Care Rally, *CQ* Transcriptions, April 1, 2010.

10. Editors, "On Presidential Rhetoric, Obama's ad hominem method and the politics of polarization," *Wall Street Journal*, April 22, 2010; available at: http://online.wsj.com/article/SB10001424052748704448304575196121075748664.html.

11. Dennis Loo, "DOD Training Manual: Protests are 'Low-Level Terrorism,'" Salon.com, blog, June 14, 2009; available at: http://open.salon.com/blog/dennis_loo/2009/06/14/dod_training_manual_protests_are_low-level_terrorism.
12. "Federal Agency Warns of Radicals On Right," *Washington Times*, April 14, 2009; available at: http://www.washingtontimes.com/news/2009/apr/14/federal-agency-warns-of-radicals-on-right/.
13. Steven Ertelt, "Obama Admin Used Pro-Abortion, Conspiracy Sites to Say Pro-Lifers Extremists," LifeNews.com, August 12, 2009; available at: http://www.lifenews.com/nat5348.html.
14. Audrey Hudson and Eli Lake, "Legion Objects to Vets as Terror Risk," *Washington Times*, April 15, 2009; available at: http://www.washingtontimes.com/news/2009/apr/15/legion-objects-to-vets-as-terror-risk/.
15. Audrey Hudson, "Homeland Agency Pulled Back Extremism Dictionary," *Washington Times*, May 5, 2009; available at: http://www.washingtontimes.com/news/2009/may/05/homeland-pulled-back-extremism-dictionary/.
16. Steven Ertelt, "Obama Admin Terrorism Dictionary Calls Pro-Life Advocates Violent, Racist," LifeNews.com, May 5, 2009; available at: http://www.lifenews.com/nat5019.html.
17. Michelle Malkin, "Confirmed: The Obama DHS Hit Job on Conservatives is Real," MichelleMalkin.com, April 14, 2009; available at: http://michellemalkin.com/2009/04/14/confirme-the-obama-dhs-hit-job-on-conservatives-is-real/.
18. "Obama's Team Crosses the Rhetorical Line," The Foundry Blog, September 1, 2009; available at: http://blog.heritage.org/2009/09/01/obamas-team-crosses-the-rhetorical-line/.
19. Jackie Calmes, "Lawmakers Detail Obama's Pitch," *New York Times*, November 7, 2009; available at: http://prescriptions.blogs.nytimes.com/2009/11/07/lawmakers-detail-obamas-pitch/ [accessed June 29, 2010].
20. "Robert Gibbs: Town Hall Protests 'Good T.V. And That's About It,'" HotAirPundit, August 16, 2009; available at: http://www.hapblog.com/2009/08/robert-gibbs-town-hall-protests-good-tv.html [accessed June 29, 2010].

21. "Democrats Accuse Brown of 'Radical' Ties as Senate Election Nears," FOXNews.com, January 15, 2010; available at: http://www.foxnews.com/politics/2010/01/15/democrats-accuse-brown-radical-ties-senate-election-nears/ [accessed June 29, 2010].

22. Jim Hoft, "Awesome... Scott Brown Responds to Elitist Obama's Attack on Truck Owners," *Gateway Pundit*, January 17, 2010; available at: http://gatewaypundit.firstthings.com/2010/01/elitist-obama-bashes-truck-owners-anybody-can-buy-a-truck-scott-brown-responds-unfortunate-in-this-economy-its-no-longer-true/ [accessed June 29, 2010].

23. "Axelrod: Tea Party Anger is Misdirected," FOXNews.com, April 19, 2009; available at: http://www.foxnews.com/politics/2009/04/19/axelrod-tea-party-anger-misdirected/ [accessed June 29, 2010].

24. "'Let's Not Play Games,': Obama Takes Swipe At Tea Party Protestors," Breitbart TV, April 29, 2009.

25. Rep. Dave Camp, "Democrats Have Increased Taxes by $670 Billion and Counting...," Committee on Ways & Means Republicans, undated.

26. Mark Halperin, "Thin Skinned Obama Claims the Press is Against Him," YouTube, January 26, 2010; available at: http://www.youtube.com/watch?v=cNHOAMDHmzA [accessed June 29, 2010].

27. Michael Calderone, "Garrett on White House 'Retribution' Against Fox," *Politico*, May 1, 2009; available at: http://www.politico.com/blogs/michaelcalderone/0509/Garrett_on_White_House_retribution_against_Fox.html [accessed June 29, 2010].

28. Michael Scherer, "Calling 'Em Out: The White House Takes on the Press," Time.com, October 8, 2009; available at: http://www.time.com/time/politics/article/0,8599,1929058,00.html [accessed June 29, 2010].

29. Jesse Lee, "Reality Check: Turning a Point of Pride into a Moment of Shame," The White House Blog, September 30, 2009; available at: http://www.whitehouse.gov/blog/2009/09/30/reality-check-turning-a-point-pride-a-moment-shame [accessed June 29, 2010].

30. Peter Nicholas, "White House Communications Chief Anita Dunn to Depart," *Los Angeles Times*, November 11, 2009; available at: http://articles.latimes.com/2009/nov/11/nation/na-dunn11 [accessed June 29, 2010].

31. "White House Attacks FOX News As 'Research Arm Of The Republican Party,'" Breitbart TV, October 11, 2009; available at: http://www.breitbart.tv/fox-news-lays-out-facts-after-white-house-escalates-war-on-network/ [accessed June 29, 2010].

32. Michael Scherer, "Calling 'Em Out: The White House Takes on the Press," *op. cit.*

33. Noel Sheppard, "Obama Advisor Tells CNN Fox Is Biased, Won't Comment On MSNBC," NewsBusters.org, October 27, 2009; available at: http://newsbusters.org/blogs/noel-sheppard/2009/10/27/obama-adviser-tells-cnn-fox-biased-wont-comment-msnbc [accessed June 29, 2010].

34. Michael Goldfarb, "White House Saying: 'We Love MSNBC,'" *Weekly Standard*, May 4, 2009.

35. David A. Patten, "White House Keeps Up War on FOX News," Newsmax.com, January 18, 2010; available at: http://www.newsmax.com/InsideCover/obama-fox-ailes-hannity/2010/01/18/id/346719 [accessed June 29, 2010].

36. Jim Hoft, "White House Blames FOX News For Their Safe Schools Czar's Slimy Past that Includes Hiding Pedophilia From the Authorities," (Video), Gatewaypundit.firstthings.com, October 5, 2009.

37. "White House Tries to Bar FOX News From Interviewing Pay Czar," *Real Clear Politics* Video, October 22, 2009; available at: http://www.realclearpolitics.com/video/2009/10/22/white_house_tries_to_bar_fox_news_from_intervewing_pay_czar.html [accessed June 29, 2010].

38. "Administration Loses Bid to Exclude FOX News From Pay Czar Interview," FOXNews.com, October 23, 2009; available at:

39. Lynn Sweet, "Obama Rips TV News for Making Rudeness the Road to Stardom," *Politics Daily*, September 20, 2009; available at: http://www.foxnews.com/politics/2009/10/23/administration-loses-bid-exclude-fox-news-pay-czar-interview/ [accessed June 29, 2010].

40. Josh Gerstein, "Gibbs Rebukes CNBC's Santelli," Politico.com, February 20, 2009; available at: http://www.politico.com/news/stories/0209/19083.html [accessed June 29, 2010].

41. Phil Rosenthal, "Rant by CNBC's Rick Santelli Puts Pundit at Odds With Obama Administration," *Chicago Tribune*, February 22,

2009; available at: http://www.chicagotribune.com/business/colum-nists/chi-sun-phil-rosenthal-22feb22,0,7002362.column.

42. Josh Gerstein, "Gibbs Rebukes CNBC's Santelli," *op. cit.*

43. Jeff Poor, "Gibbs Does It Again—Responds Directly to Media Criti-cism of Obama, This Time CNBC's Cramer," NewsBusters.org, March 3, 2009; available at: http://newsbusters.org/blogs/jeff-poor/2009/03/03/gibbs-does-it-again-responds-directly-media-criticism-obama-time-cnbcs-cr.

44. Rowan Scarborough, "White House Attack Machine," *Human Events*, March 20, 2009; available at: http://www.humanevents.com/article.php?id=31148.

45. Frank James, "Edmunds.com Cash For Clunkers Analysis Riles Obama Team," NPR.org, October 29, 2009; available at: http://www.npr.org/blogs/thetwo-way/2009/10/edmundscom_cash_for_clunkers_a.html.

46. Macon Phillips, "Busy Covering Car Sales on Mars, Edmunds.com Gets It Wrong (Again) on Cash for Clunkers," The White House Blog, October 29, 2009; available at: http://www.whitehouse.gov/blog/2009/10/29/busy-covering-car-sales-mars-edmundscom-gets-it-wrong-again-cash-clunkers.

47. Frank James, "Edmunds.com Cash For Clunkers Analysis Riles Obama Team," *op. cit.*

48. Charles Hurt, "Prez Zings GOP Foe in a Stimulating Talk," *New York Post*, January 23, 2009; available at: http://www.nypost.com/p/news/politics/item_wrDZCVt0TdhQPpY2VuPgnN.

49. "Obama, Dems Continue Rush Limbaugh Attacks," WorldNet-Daily.com, January 31, 2009; available at: http://www.wnd.com/?pageId=87546.

50. Jonathan Martin, "Are You With Obama or Rush?" *Politico*, Janu-ary 29, 2009; available at: http://www.politico.com/news/stories/0109/18194.html.

51. Michael Scherer, "Team Obama's Petty Limbaugh Strategy," Time.com, March 4, 2009; available at: http://swampland.blogs.time.com/2009/03/04/team-obamas-petty-limbaugh-strategy/ [accessed June 29, 2010].

52. Ibid.

53. David Von Drehle, "Criticizing Rush Limbaugh: Over the Line?" Time.com, March 4, 2009; available at: http://www.time.com/time/politics/article/0,8599,1883032,00.html [accessed June 29, 2010].

54. David Hogberg, "None Dare Call Them Unpatriotic," *American Spectator*, May 6, 2003.

55. The Editors, "Rush Rammed," *National Review*, October 16, 2009; available at: http://article.nationalreview.com/410299/rush-rammed/the-editors [accessed June 29, 2010].

56. Transcript: Part III Of a FOX News Channel "The O'Reilly Factor Interview With Senator Barack Obama," *Federal News Service*, September 9, 2008.

57. Paul Ibrahim, "Rush Limbaugh Is Only the First Target of Obama's 'New' Politics," Paulibrahim.com, January 26, 2009; available at: http://www.ronaldreagan.com/forums/showthread.php?p=196479 [accessed June 29, 2010].

58. Rush Limbaugh, "Obama Is Stoking Racial Antagonism," *Wall Street Journal*, September 19, 2008; available at: http://online.wsj.com/article/SB122178554189155003.html [accessed June 29, 2010].

59. Ibid.

60. Noel Sheppard, "New Anti-Limbaugh-Beck Group Tied To Ex-Obama Czar Van Jones," NewsBusters.org, November 1, 2009; available at: http://newsbusters.org/blogs/noel-sheppard/2009/10/31/limbaugh-bashing-group-has-ties-ex-obama-czar-van-jones [accessed June 29, 2010].

61. Jim Geraghty, "Barack Obama Calls Out National Review on Michelle," *National Review Online*, The Campaign Spot, July 17, 2008; available at: http://www.nationalreview.com/campaign-spot [accessed June 29, 2010].

62. Jim Vandehei and Mike Allen, "Obama, Dems Sharpen Personal Attacks on Palin," *Politico*, September 9, 2008; available at: http://www.politico.com/news/stories/0908/13315.html [accessed June 29, 2010].

63. Nick Sabloff, "Obama Takes First Direct Shot At Palin," *Huffington Post*, October 7, 2008; available at: http://www.huffingtonpost.com/2008/09/06/obama-takes-first-direct_n_124507.html [accessed June 29, 2010].

64. Toby Harnden, "Barack Obama Using 'Dangerous' Sarah Palin to Raise Cash," Telegraph.co.uk, November 20, 2009; available at: http://blogs.telegraph.co.uk/news/tobyharnden/100017412/barack-obama-using-sarah-palin-to-raise-cash/ [accessed June 29, 2010].

65. Robert Gibbs, "Gibbs Blames Palin For Spreading Misinformation About Health Reform," Real Clear Politics Video, August 12, 2009; available at: http://www.realclearpolitics.com/video/2009/08/12/gibbs_blames_palin_for_spreading_misinformation_about_health_reform.html [accessed June 29, 2010].

66. Greg Sargent, "Dem Strategists: Sarah Palin Is The New Rush Limbaugh," The Plum Line, March 30, 2009; available at: http://theplumline.whorunsgov.com/republican-party/dem-strategists-sarah-palin-is-the-new-rush-limbaugh/ [accessed June 29, 2010].

67. Jim Rutenberg, "Behind the War Between White House and Fox," *New York Times*, October 22, 2009; available at: http://www.nytimes.com/2009/10/23/us/politics/23fox.html [accessed June 29, 2010].

68. Michael Scherer, "Team Obama's Petty Limbaugh Strategy," Time.com, March 4, 2009; available at: http://swampland.blogs.time.com/2009/03/04/team-obamas-petty-limbaugh-strategy/ [accessed June 29, 2010]; see also, Jonathan Martin, "Obama 'Gearing Up for a Fight," *Politico*, February 28, 2009; available at: http://www.politico.com/news/stories/0209/19434.html [accessed June 29, 2010].

69. Dave Cook, "Robert Gibbs Calls Senator Jim Bunning Irrational," Christian Science Monitor, March 2, 2010; available at: http://www.csmonitor.com/USA/Politics/The-Vote/2010/0302/Robert-Gibbs-calls-Senator-Jim-Bunning-irrational [accessed June 29, 2010].

70. Benjamin Spillman, "Obama Draws Ire Over Vegas Junket Criticism," Las Vegas Review-Journal, February 11, 2009; available at: http://www.lvrj.com/news/39420937.html [accessed June 29, 2010].

71. "President Obama Refuses to Meet With Governor Gibbons About Tourism Comments," KTVN.com, May 18, 2009; available at: http://www.ktnv.com/Global/story.asp?S=10383051 [accessed June 29, 2010].

72. Benjamin Spillman, "Mayor Upset By Questions About Criticism of Obama," Las Vegas Review-Journal, February 5, 2010; available at:

http://www.lvrj.com/news/mayor-upset-by-questions-about-criti-cism-of-obama-83623837.html [accessed June 29, 2010].

73. Stephen Dinan, "Holder Hasn't Read Arizona Law He Criticized," *Washington Times*, May 13, 2010; available at: http://www.wash-ingtontimes.com/news/2010/may/13/holder-hasnt-read-ariz-law-he-criticized/ [accessed June 29, 2010].

74. Transcript: On the Record with Greta Van Susteren, "Ariz. Governor to Obama, Napolitano: 'Do Your Job!'" FOX News, May 21, 2010; available at: http://www.foxnews.com/story/ 0,2933,593302,00.html [accessed June 29, 2010].

75. Margaret Talev, "Most Americans Approve of Arizona's Law on Illegal Immigrants," McClatchy Newspapers, May 12, 2010; available at: http://www.mcclatchydc.com/2010/05/12/94050/most-americans-approve-of-arizonas.html [accessed June 29, 2010].

76. "Gov. Brewer very disappointed in Obama Snub, Vows to Beat Feds in Court Over Illegal Immigraiton Law," FOXNews.com, June 18, 2010; available at: http://www.foxnews.com/story/0,2933,594862, 00.html [accessed June 29, 2010].

77. Press Release, "Governor Jan Brewer Learns of President's Directive to Sue Arizona via Ecuadorean Television Interview," press release, Office of the Governor of Arizona, June 17, 2010; available at: http://azgovernor.gov/dms/upload/PR_061710_BrewerResponse-ClintonAnnouncement.pdf [accessed June 29, 2010].

78. "Obama tells Kyl in private Oval Office meeting: I won't secure border b/c then Republicans will have no reason to support 'compre-hensive immigration reform,'" Redstate.com, June 20, 2010; available at: http://www.redstate.com/coldwarrior/2010/06/20/ obama-tells-kyl-in-private-oval-office-meeting-i-wont-secure-border-bc-then-republicans-will-have-no-reason-to-support-comprehensive-immigration-reform/ [accessed June 29, 2010].

79. Ed Morrissey, "Is Obama Avoiding Red States?" Hot Air, March 29, 2010; available at: http://hotair.com/archives/2010/03/29/is-obama-avoiding-red-states/ [accessed June 29, 2010].

80. Editors, "On Presidential Rhetoric, Obama's ad hominem method and the politics of polarization," *Wall Street Journal*, April 22, 2010; available at: http://online.wsj.com/article/SB10001424052748 704448304575196121075748664.html [accessed June 29, 2010].

81. Jordan Fabian, "Obama Slams Decision on Campaign Finance in His Weekly Address," The Hill, January 23, 2010; available at: http://thehill.com/homenews/administration/77633-obama-targets-campaign-finance-decision-in-weekly-address [accessed June 29, 2010].

82. Andrew Malcolm, "'Very Troubling': Chief Justice Roberts on Obama's Court Criticism to Joint Session of Congress," *Los Angeles Times*, Top of the Ticket, March 9, 2010; available at: http://latimesblogs.latimes.com/washington/2010/03/john-roberts-obama-.html [accessed June 29, 2010].

83. Ibid.

84. "President Obama Says 'BP Will be Paying the Bill' for Oil Spill," Associated Press, May 2, 2010; available at: http://blog.al.com/live/2010/05/president_obama_vows_to_do_wha.html [accessed June 29, 2010].

85. Stephen Collinson, "White House Keeps 'Boot' on BP's Throat," Associated Press, May 3, 2010; available at: http://rawstory.com/news/afp/White_House_keeps_boot_on_BP_s_thro_05032010.html [accessed June 29, 2010].

86. "An Offer BP Couldn't Refuse," Heritage Foundation; available at: http://blog.heritage.org/2010/06/17/morning-bell-an-offer-bp-couldnt-refuse/ [accessed June 29, 2010].

87. Sam Reilly, "Obama: Overhaul of Minerals Management Service on the Way in Wake of Gulf Oil Spill," Associated Press, May 14, 2010; available at: http://topics.signonsandiego.com/article/01Ad6 114AO0Cn?q=Interior+Department [accessed June 29, 2010].

88. Mark Silva, "Obama Criticizes Cheney's Approach to Terrorism in '60 Minutes' Interview, *Los Angeles Times*, March 22, 2009; available at: http://www.huffingtonpost.com/2009/03/21/obama-60-minutes-intervie_n_177660.html [accessed June 29, 2010].

89. Sam Youngman, "Gibbs on Bush Criticism, 'We won,'" *The Hill*, June 18, 2009; available at: http://thehill.com/homenews/news/47183-gibbs-on-bush-criticism-we-won [accessed June 29, 2010].

90. Ryan Lizza, "Battle Plans, How Obama Won," *The New Yorker*, November 17, 2008; available at: http://www.newyorker.com/reporting/2008/11/17/081117fa_fact_lizza [accessed June 29, 2010].

91. Charles Krauthammer, "Blaming Bush At Every Turn Is Getting Old," Investors Business Daily, October 12, 2009; available at: http://www.investors.com/NewsAndAnalysis/Article/510723/200910291820/Blaming-Bush-At-Every-Turn-Is-Getting-Old.aspx [accessed June 29, 2010].

92. Ann Scott Tyson, "Support Troops Swelling U.S. Force in Afghanistan, Additional Deployments Not Announced and Rarely Noted," *Washington Post*, October 13, 2009; available at: http://www.washingtonpost.com/wp-dyn/content/article/2009/10/12/AR2009101203142.html [accessed June 29, 2010].

93. Mark Silva, "Obama Criticizes Cheney's Approach to Terrorism in '60 Minutes' Interview," *op. cit.*

94. Caren Bohan and Richard Cowan, "High U.S. Budget Deficits Not Obama's Fault-Orszag," Reuters, May 11, 2009; available at: http://www.reuters.com/article/idUSWBT01121120090511 [accessed June 29, 2010]; see also, Peter R. Orszag, Director, "Last but Not Least—The Final Installment of the FY 2010 Budget," Office of Management and Budget Blog, May 11, 2009; available at: http://www.whitehouse.gov/omb/blog/09/05/11/LastbutNotLeastTheFinalInstallmentoftheFY2010Budget/ [accessed June 29, 2010].

95. Mike Soraghan, "Administration Blames Bush for GM Crisis," *The Hill*, June 6, 2009; available at: http://thehill.com/homenews/administration/19996-administration-blames-bush-for-gm-crisis [accessed June 29, 2010].

96. Jim Geraghty, "Obama: Stop Blaming Me for the Economy, I Just Got Here in January," *National Review Online*, The Campaign Spot, July 2, 2009; available at: http://corner.nationalreview.com/ [accessed June 29, 2010].

97. Joseph Curl, "Obama Still Cashing In On Bush's Failings," *Washington Times*, July 29, 2009; available at: http://www.washingtontimes.com/news/2009/jul/29/obama-still-cashing-in-on-bushs-economic-failings/ [accessed June 29, 2010].

98. Barack Obama, "Obama's Townhall in Shaker Heights, Ohio," Real Clear Politics, July 23, 2009; available at: http://www.realclearpolitics.com/articles/2009/07/23/obama_townhall_in_shaker_heights_ohio_97593.html [accessed June 29, 2010].

99. Steve Benen, "Obama Tells Dems: I'm Not Tired; I'm Just Getting Started," *Washington Monthly*, October 16, 2009; available at: http://www.washingtonmonthly.com/archives/individual/2009_10/020475.php [accessed June 29, 2010].

100. President Barack Obama, "Text: Obama's Address on the War in Afghanistan," *New York Times*, December 1, 2009; available at: http://www.nytimes.com/2009/12/02/world/asia/02prexy.text.html [accessed June 29, 2010].

101. Vice President Joseph Biden, "NBC 'Meet the Press' Host: David Gregory," Federal News Service, February 14, 2010.

102. "'Blame Bush' Strategy Wears Thin as Obama Enters Second Year," FOXNews.com, January 25, 2010; available at: http://www.foxnews.com/politics/2010/01/25/obama-administration-blaming-bush-president-enters-second-year/ [accessed June 29, 2010].

103. Mark Finkelstein, "Time Cover Story: Bush Decade 'Hell,' Obama Decade Better," Newsbusters.org, November 25, 2009; available at: http://newsbusters.org/blogs/mark-finkelstein/2009/11/25/time-cover-story-bush-decade-hell-obama-decade-better [accessed June 29, 2010].

104. Ibid.

105. "FOX News Poll: 66% Say Obama Should Stop Blaming Bush," HotAirPundit, April 22, 2010; available at: http://www.hapblog.com/2010/04/foxnews-poll-66-say-obama-should-stop.html [accessed June 29, 2010].

Chapter 6

1. Aaron Klein, "Obama's Supreme pick has love affair with social-ism," WorldNetDaily, May 10, 2010; available at: http://www.wnd.com/?pageId=152133 [accessed June 24, 2010].

2. Ed Whelan, "Kagan: Constitution as Charter of 'Positive Liberties,'" *National Review Online*, Bench Memos, May 17, 2010; available at: http://www.nationalreview.com/bench-memos/55696/kagan-constitution-charter-positive-liberties/ed-whelan [accessed June 24, 2010].

3. Tomoeh Murakami Tse and Peter Whoriskey, "Obama Standing By Rattner; White House Knew of Probes," *The Washington Post*, April 18, 2009; available at: http://www.washingtonpost.com/wp-

dyn/content/article/2009/04/17/AR2009041701908.html [accessed June 24, 2010].

4. Edwin Chen, "Obama Open to Partisan Vote on Health-Care Overhaul, Aides Say," Bloomberg, July 14, 2009; available at: http://www.bloomberg.com/apps/news?pid=newsarchive&sid=a4.kYDWV 9erc [accessed June 24, 2010].

5. Nicholas Ballasy, "Pelosi to Aspiring Musicians: Quit Your Job, Taxpayers Will Cover Your Health Care," CNSNews.com, May 14, 2010; available at: http://www.cnsnews.com/news/article/65950 [accessed June 24, 2010].

6. George Will, "Tincture of Lawlessness," Townhall.com, May 14, 2009; available at: http://townhall.com/columnists/GeorgeWill/ 2009/05/14/tincture_of_lawlessness [accessed June 24, 2010].

7. Ian Talley, "Steven Chu: Americans Are Like 'Teenage Kids' When It Comes to Energy," The *Wall Street Journal*, September 21, 2009; available at: http://blogs.wsj.com/environmentalcapital/2009/09/21/ steven-chu-americans-are-like-teenage-kids-when-it-comes-to-energy/ [accessed June 24, 2010].

8. Ibid.

9. Lee Cary, "Obama's Plan for NASA," *American Thinker*, April 22, 2008; available at: http://www.americanthinker.com/2008/04/ obamas_plan_for_nasa.html [accessed June 24, 2010].

10. Loretta Hidalgo Whitesides, "Obama Pits Human Space Exploration Against Education," *Wired Science*, November 21, 2007; available at: http://www.wired.com/wiredscience/2007/11/obama-pits-huma/ [accessed June 24, 2010].

11. Mark Whittington, "Barack Obama Pits Space Explorers Against School Children," Associated Content, December 2, 2007; available at: http://www.associatedcontent.com/article/465985/barack_ obama_pits_space_explorers_against.html?cat=9 [accessed June 24, 2010].

12. Editorial, "Losing it in Space," *The Washington Times*, April 13, 2010; available at: http://www.washingtontimes.com/news/2010/ apr/13/losing-it-in-space/ [accessed June 24, 2010].

13. "Obama Clarifies His Space Policy," Space Politics, January 2, 2008.

14. Stella Paul, "America's Surrender of Space," *American Thinker*, April 10, 2010; available at: http://www.americanthinker.com/blog/2010/04/americas_surrender_of_space.html [accessed June 24, 2010].

15. Kenneth Chang, "Obama Calls for End to NASA's Moon Program," *The New York Times*, February 1, 2010; available at: http://www.nytimes.com/2010/02/02/science/02nasa.html [accessed June 24, 2010].

16. Robert Block, "NASA Cancels KSC Contract Leading to Charge 'Obama Broke Law,'" *Orlando Sentinel*, The Write Stuff Blog, February 12, 2010; available at: http://blogs.orlandosentinel.com/news_space_thewritestuff/2010/02/nasa-cancels-ksc-contract-prompting-angry-response.html [accessed June 24, 2010].

17. Congressman Bill Posey, "Press Release: Administration Plan to Terminate Constellation Contract Without Congressional Approval in Violation of Law," Posey.house.gov, February 12, 2010; available at: http://posey.house.gov/News/DocumentSingle.aspx?DocumentID=170176 [accessed June 24, 2010].

18. Mark Matthews, "Bolden: NASA legit as it readies to end moon program," *Orlando Sentinel*, February 23, 2010; available at: http://blogs.orlandosentinel.com/news_space_thewritestuff/2010/02/bolden-nasa-legit-as-it-readies-to-end-moon-program.html [accessed June 24, 2010].

19. Jeff Sessions, "Jeff Sessions: LeMieux, Sessions Introduce Effort to Stop NASA from Canceling Constellation," Facebook, Jeff Sessions, March 18, 2010; available at: http://www.facebook.com/note.php?note_id=373175967686 [accessed June 24, 2010].

20. Jackqui Goddard, "Boldly going nowhere: NASA ends plan to put man back on Moon," Times Online, June 14, 2010; available at: http://www.timesonline.co.uk/tol/news/science/space/article7149543.ece [accessed June 24, 2010].

21. Michael Griffin and others, "Griffin, NASA Luminaries Urge Obama to Change Space Policy," *Orlando Sentinel*, April 12, 2010; available at: http://blogs.orlandosentinel.com/news_space_thewritestuff/2010/04/griffin-nasa-luminaries-urge-obama-to-change-space-policy.html [accessed June 24, 2010].

22. "Lockheed Martin Responds To The FY2011 NASA Budget Proposal To Cancel Orion," Lockheed Martin; available at: http://www.lockheedmartin.com/news/press_releases/2010/02_03_Orion.html [accessed June 24, 2010].

23. Andy Pasztor, "NASA Plans Face Turbulence in House," The *Wall Street Journal*, February 4, 2010; available at: http://online.wsj.com/article/SB10001424052748704259304575044381122142378.html [accessed June 24, 2010].

24. Joel Acheinbach, "NASA's Moon Plan Too Ambitious, Obama Panel Says," *Miami Herald*, August 14, 2009.

25. Mark Whittington, "No, We Should Not Cut NASA Funding," Associated Content, April 10, 2010; available at: http://www.associatedcontent.com/article/2880660/no_we_should_not_cut_nasa_funding.html?cat=15 [accessed June 24, 2010].

26. Rachel Martin and Karen Travers, "On the Defensive, President Obama Pledges Commitment to NASA, Space Exploration," ABCNews.com, April 15, 2010; available at: http://abcnews.go.com/WN/president-obama-touts-billion-budget-boost-nasa-potential/story?id=10387427 [accessed June 24, 2010].

27. Ibid.

28. Frank Morring, Jr., "U.S. Space Leadership Seen At Risk," Aviation Week, May 3, 2010; available at: http://www.aviationweek.com/aw/generic/story_channel.jsp?channel=space&id=news/asd/2010/05/03/11.xml [accessed June 24, 2010].

29. Byron York, "Democrats Threaten Companies Hit Hard by Health Care Bill," *The Washington Examiner*, March 28, 2010; available at: http://www.washingtonexaminer.com/politics/Democrats-threaten-companies-hit-hard-by-health-care-bill-89347127.html [accessed June 24, 2010].

30. Michelle Malkin, "The Obamacare Inquisition Is on Hold...for Now," Creators Syndicate, April 16, 2010; article available at: http://www.creators.com/opinion/michelle-malkin/the-obamacare-inquisition-is-on-hold-for-now.html [accessed June 24, 2010].

31. Jed Babbin, "Waxman Cancels Healthcare Show Trial," Big Government, April 16, 2010; available at: http://biggovernment.com/jbabbin/2010/04/16/waxman-cancels-healthcare-show-trial/ [accessed June 24, 2010].

32. Rep. Joe Barton, "Rep. Joe Barton on Democratic Intimidation Tactics," YouTube.com, April 14, 2010; video available at: http://www. youtube.com/watch?v=O0foQVNFVWQ [accessed June 24, 2010].

33. Staff, "A Message From Congress: No One Questions Our Authority," CNSNews.com, February 3, 2010; available at: http://www. cnsnews.com/news/article/60932 [accessed June 24, 2010].

34. *Clinton v. City of New York*, 524 U.S. 417 (1998).

35. Peter Baker, "Obama Making Plans to Use Executive Power," *The New York Times*, February 12, 2010; available at: http://www. nytimes.com/2010/02/13/us/politics/13obama.html [accessed June 24, 2010].

36. Jake Tapper, "Thinly-Veiled Threats? White House Suggests Arizona Republicans Put Up or Shut Up," *ABC News,* Political Punch, July 14, 2009; available at: http://blogs.abcnews.com/politicalpunch/ 2009/07/thinly-veiled-threats-white-house-suggests-arizona-republicans-put-up-or-shut-up.html [accessed June 24, 2010].

37. Ed Morrissey, "Kyl, McCain to White House: Threats 'patently offensive,'" HotAir.com, July 15, 2009; available at: http://hotair. com/archives/2009/07/15/kyl-mccain-to-white-house-threats-patently-offensive/ [accessed June 24, 2010].

38. Jake Tapper, "Thinly-Veiled Threats? White House Suggests Arizona Republicans Put Up or Shut Up," *op. cit.*

39. George Will, "Tincture of Lawlessness," *op. cit.*

40. Ed Morrissey, "Why Did Obama Meet with the CBO?" HotAir. com, July 21, 2009; available at: http://hotair.com/archives/2009/07/ 21/why-did-obama-meet-with-the-cbo/ [accessed June 24, 2010].

41. Walter Alarkon, "Orszag: CBO Lowballs Savings From Obama's Healthcare Reform," *The Hill*, April 11, 2010; available at: http:// thehill.com/homenews/administration/91527-orszag-cbo-underestimates-savings-from-obamas-healthcare-bill [accessed June 24, 2010].

42. Chris Edwards, "Government Schemes Cost More Than Promised," Cato Institute, Tax & Budget Bulletin, September 2003; available at: http://www.cato.org/pubs/tbb/tbb-0309-17.pdf [accessed June 24, 2010].

43. Scott Rasmussen and Doug Schoen, "Why Obama Can't Move the Health-Care Numbers," *Wall Street Journal*, March 9, 2010; avail-

able at: http://online.wsj.com/article/SB100014240527487047849045751119935591742112.html [accessed June 24, 2010].

44. Douglas Holtz-Eakin, "The Real Arithmetic of Health Care Reform," *New York Times*, March 20, 2010; available at: http://www.nytimes.com/2010/03/21/opinion/21holtz-eakin.html [accessed June 24, 2010].

45. Major Garrett, "Administration Threatens to Veto Any Deficit Spending Tied to New Health Law," FOX News, May 12, 2010; available at: http://www.foxnews.com/politics/2010/05/12/health-overhaul-law-potentially-costs-billion/ [accessed June 24, 2010].

46. Douglas Holtz-Eakin, "The Real Arithmetic of Health Care Reform," *op. cit.*

47. Representative Paul Ryan, "New CBO Analysis: Health Legislation Increases Deficits," Republican Caucus Committee on the Budget, March 19, 2010; available at: http://www.house.gov/budget_republicans/press/2007/pr20100319healthdeficits.pdf [accessed June 24, 2010].

48. Edwin Feulner, "The Claw-Back Calamity," The Heritage Foundation, March 31, 2009; available at: http://www.heritage.org/Research/Commentary/2009/03/The-Claw-Back-Calamity [accessed June 24, 2010].

49. Mark Impomeni, "Senate Shelves AIG Bonus Tax Bill," *Politics Daily*, March 24. 2009; available at: http://www.politicsdaily.com/2009/03/24/senate-shelves-aig-bonus-tax-bill/ [accessed June 24, 2010].

50. Bill Bartel, "Tax on Bonuses Gets Shunted Aside," The Virginian-Pilot, March 10, 2010; available at: http://hamptonroads.com/2010/03/tax-bonuses-gets-shunted-aside [accessed June 24, 2010].

51. Brady Dennis and Tomoeh Murakami Tse, "Pay Czar Quietly Meets With Rescued Companies," *The Washington Post*, August 9, 2009; available at: http://www.washingtonpost.com/wp-dyn/content/article/2009/08/08/AR2009080802532.html [accessed June 24, 2010].

52. Robert Schmidt and Ian Katz, "Feinberg Wants All Companies to Adopt Pay-Cut Model (Update 1)," Bloomberg, October 22, 2009; available at: http://www.bloomberg.com/apps/news?pid=newsarchive&sid=a16icsH1pzGE [accessed June 24, 2010].

53. Frank Ahrens and David Cho, "Government Widens Control Over Paychecks," *The Washington Post*, October 23, 2009; available at: http://www.washingtonpost.com/wp-dyn/content/article/2009/10/22/AR2009102202670.html [accessed June 24, 2010].

54. Robert Schmidt and Rebecca Christie, "Obama Administration to Seek New Power for SEC on Executive Pay," Bloomberg, June 10, 2009; available at: http://www.bloomberg.com/apps/news?pid=newsarchive&sid=aV0wrDNqSfck [accessed June 24, 2010].

55. Client Memorandum, "Dodd Bill Would Affect Corporate Governance and Executive Compensation Processes for All US Public Companies," DavisPolk, November 17, 2009; available at: http://www.davispolk.com/files/Publication/9bcf3eac-b311-4cec-82ef-8fcf20111303/Presentation/PublicationAttachment/a50f0417-4ae3-406c-843f-9605eba8b21f/111709_dodd_bill.pdf [accessed June 24, 2010].

56. "Senate Banking Committee Amendments to Dodd's Bill: Two Big Governance Changes," *The Corporate Counsel* Blog, March 24, 2010; available at: http://www.thecorporatecounsel.net/Blog/2010/03/this-recent-washington-post-article-1.html [accessed June 24, 2010].

57. Associated Press, "S.E.C. Approves Tougher Rules on Executive Pay," *New York Times*, December 16, 2009; available at: http://www.nytimes.com/2009/12/17/business/17pay.html [accessed June 24, 2010].

58. "SEC Approves Enhanced Disclosure About Risk, Compensation and Corporate Governance," U.S. Securities and Exchange Commission, December 16, 2009; available at: http://www.sec.gov/news/press/2009/2009-268.htm [accessed June 24, 2010].

59. Floyd Norris, "A Window Opens On Pay for Bosses," *The New York Times*, January 14, 2010; available at: http://dealbook.blogs.nytimes.com/2010/01/15/a-window-opens-on-pay-for-bosses/ [accessed June 24, 2010].

60. Deborah Solomon and Damian Paletta, "U.S. Eyes Bank Pay Overhaul," *The Wall Street Journal*, May 13, 2009; available at: http://online.wsj.com/article/SB124215896684211987.html [accessed June 24, 2010].

61. Client Memorandum, "Dodd Bill Would Affect Corporate Governance and Executive Compensation Processes for All US Public Companies," *op. cit.*

62. Frank Ahrens and David Cho, "Government Widens Control Over Paychecks," *op. cit.*

Chapter 7

1. Editors, "Presto: Another $750 Billion, How Treasury Will Conjure that New Money for the IMF," *The Wall Street Journal*, April 14, 2009; available at: http://online.wsj.com/article/ SB123966688949701 5459.html [accessed June 25, 2010].

2. Anne Flaherty, Associated Press writer, "Democrats Irked by Obama Signing Statement," Breitbart, July 21, 2009; available at: http:// www.breitbart.com/article.php?id=D99J11POO [accessed June 25, 2010].

3. Kate Phillips, "Obama Signs Financial Bill, Creating Investigative Panel," *The New York Times*, May 20, 2009; available at: http:// thecaucus.blogs.nytimes.com/2009/05/20/obama-signs-financial-bill-creating-investigative-panel/ [accessed June 25, 2010].

4. "Obama administration spends $1.2 billion on cycling and walking initiatives," *Daily Telegraph*, June 16, 2010; available at: http:// www.telegraph.co.uk/news/worldnews/northamerica/usa/7834334/ Obama-administration-spends-1.2-billion-on-cycling-and-walking-initiatives.html [accessed June 25, 2010].

5. Terrence P. Jeffrey, "Obama's Transportation Secretary Says He Wants to 'Coerce People Out of Their Cars," CNSNews.com, May 26, 2009; available at: http://www.cnsnews.com/news/article/48578 [accessed June 25, 2010].

6. Ibid.

7. George F. Will, "Ray Lahood, Transformed," *Newsweek*, May 16, 2009; available at: http://www.newsweek.com/2009/05/15/ray-lahood-transformed.html [accessed June 25, 2010].

8. Scott McCartney, "LaHood to Airlines: Get Onboard the High-Speed Train," *The Wall Street Journal*, March 9, 2010; available at: http://blogs.wsj.com/middleseat/2010/03/09/lahood-to-airlines-get-onboard-the-high-speed-train/ [accessed June 25, 2010].

9. "Obama Getting Heat for Turning Up the Oval Office Thermostat," Foxnews.com, February 3, 2009.

10. Frederic J. Frommer, Associated Press writer, "Obama Launches 'Great Outdoors' Initiative," CBS News, April 16, 2010; available at: http://www.cbsnews.com/stories/2010/04/16/politics/main64028 05.shtml [accessed June 25, 2010].

11. Barack Obama, "Executive Order Establishing the National Prevention, Health Promotion, and Public Health Council," White-House.gov, June 10, 2010; available at: http://www.whitehouse.gov/the-press-office/executive-order-establishing-national-prevention-health-promotion-and-public-health [accessed June 25, 2010].

12. Review and Outlook, "California's Man-Made Drought," *The Wall Street Journal*, September 2, 2009; available at: http://online.wsj.com/article/SB10001424052970204731804574384731898375624.html [accessed June 25, 2010].

13. "The Interagency Ocean Policy Task Force," WhiteHouse.gov, June 12, 2009; available at: http://www.whitehouse.gov/administration/eop/ceq/initiatives/oceans [accessed June 25, 2010].

14. Jason Dearen, Associated Press writer, "Obama Task Force Calls for National Ocean Council," ABC News, September 17, 2009; available at: http://abcnews.go.com/US/wireStory?id=8602664 [accessed June 25, 2010].

15. Ibid.

16. Frank Miniter, "Gone Fishing?" *National Review Online*, March 11, 2009.

17. Ibid.

18. David Wright, "EPA Determines Greenhouse Gases Harmful to People and Environment," ABC News, December 7, 2009; available at: http://abcnews.go.com/WN/epa-declares-greenhouse-gases-hazardous-peoples-health-environment/story?id=9272194 [accessed June 24, 2010].

19. Ibid.

20. P. J. Gladnick, "Audio: Obama Tells SF Chronicle He Will Bankrupt Coal Industry," NewsBusters.org, November 2, 2008; available at: http://newsbusters.org/blogs/p-j-gladnick/2008/11/02/hidden-audio-obama-tells-sf-chronicle-he-will-bankrupt-coal-industry [accessed June 25, 2010].

21. Erica Werner and Ken Thomas, Associated Press writers, "Obama Orders New Fuel Standards for Future," ABC News, May 21, 2010; available at: http://abcnews.go.com/Business/wireStory?id= 10707368 [accessed June 25, 2010].

22. George Allen and Marlo Lewis, "The EPA's Shocking Power Grab," *Forbes*, May 18, 2010; available at: http://www.forbes.com/2010/ 05/18/epa-environment-power-congress-opinions-contributors-allen-lewis.html [accessed June 25, 2010].

23. J. P. Freire, "16,500 More IRS Agents Needed to Enforce Obamacare," *The Washington Examiner*, March 18, 2010; available at: http://www.washingtonexaminer.com/opinion/blogs/beltway-confidential/16500-more-IRS-agents-needed-to-enforce-Obamacare-88458137.html [accessed June 25, 2010].

24. David A. Patten, "Obamacare Grants IRS Perilous Power, GOP Says," Newsmax.com, March 18, 2010; available at: http://www.newsmax.com/InsideCover/Obamacare-Democrats-healthcare-IRS/2010/03/18/id/353209 [accessed June 25, 2010].

25. J. P. Freire, "Obamacare Expands IRS Authority, May Cause Greater Tax Non-compliance," *The Washington Examiner*, January 4, 2010; available at: http://www.washingtonexaminer.com/opinion/blogs/beltway-confidential/Obamacare-expands-IRS-authority-may-cause-greater-tax-non-compliance-80644757.html [accessed June 25, 2010].

26. Ibid.

27. J. P. Freire, "Obamacare Expands IRS Authority, May Cause Greater Tax Non-compliance," *op. cit.*

28. Yuval Levin, "Finding Out What's In It," *National Review Online*, The Corner, May 6, 2010; available at: http://corner.nationalreview.com/post/?q=NWRiNGY1NjcyMDk1ZjY3MGQ2MmYzOGEwM GIzMDEzMWU= [accessed June 25, 2010].

29. Timothy P. Carney, "Student Loans get the Obamacare Treatment," *op. cit.*

30. Stephen Spruiell, "Takeover on Campus," *National Review Online*, October 29, 2009; available at: http://article.nationalreview.com/411849/takeover-on-campus/stephen-spruiell [accessed June 25, 2010].

31. Eileen AJ Connelly, Associated Press writer, "2,500 Sallie Mae Jobs Fall to New Student Loan Law," ABC News, April 22, 2010; available at: http://abcnews.go.com/Business/wireStory?id=10446879 [accessed June 25, 2010].

32. "Transcript: Diane Sawyer Interviews Obama," ABCNews.go.com, January 25, 2010; available at: http://abcnews.go.com/WN/Obama/abc-world-news-diane-sawyer-diane-sawyer-interviews/story?id=9659064 [accessed June 25, 2010].

33. Katie Couric, "Rahm Emanuel on the State of the Union," CBSNews.com, January 27, 2010; available at: http://www.cbsnews.com/stories/2010/01/27/eveningnews/main6148413.shtml [accessed June 25, 2010].

34. Chris Frates, "Payoffs for states get Harry Reid to 60 votes," *Politico*, December 19, 2009; available at: http://www.politico.com/news/stories/1209/30815.html [accessed June 25, 2010].

35. Michelle Malkin, "Cash for Cloture: Demcare Bribe List, Pt. II," MichelleMalkin.com, December 21, 2009; available at: http://michellemalkin.com/2009/12/21/cash-for-cloture-demcare-bribe-list-pt-ii/ [accessed June 25, 2010].

36. Dick Morris and Eileen McGann, "Obamacare Endorsements: What the Bribe Was," *The Hill*, Pundit's Blog, November 6, 2009; available at: http://thehill.com/blogs/pundits-blog/healthcare/66717-obamacare-endorsements-what-the-bribe-was [accessed June 25, 2010].

37. "Other Tax Shoes Begin to Drop," *Investor's Business Daily*, March 23, 2010; available at: http://www.investors.com/NewsAndAnalysis/Article.aspx?id=528198 [accessed June 25, 2010]

38. Dick Morris and Eileen McGann, "Obama Taxes Pacemakers, Heart Valves," *The Hill*, Pundit's Blog, October 26, 2009; available at: http://thehill.com/blogs/pundits-blog/healthcare/64493-obama-taxes-pacemakers-heart-valves [accessed June 25, 2010].

39. "Medical Device Tax," HealthScienceTechology HSTE Project, April 9, 2010; available at: http://healthsciencetechnology.wikispaces.com/Medical+Device+Tax [accessed June 25, 2010].

40. Paul Hsieh, "The Deadly Tax on Medical Innovation," Pajamas Media, April 11, 2010; available at: http://pajamasmedia.com/blog/the-deadly-tax-on-medical-innovation/ [accessed June 25, 2010].

41. John McCormack, "Obama Now Selling Judgeships for Health Care Votes?" *Weekly Standard*, March 3, 2010; available at: http://www.weeklystandard.com/blogs/obama-now-selling-appeals-court-judgeships-health-care-votes [accessed June 25, 2010].

42. Connie Hair, "Republicans Will Force Vote on Slaughter Rule," *Human Events*, March 17, 2010; available at: http://www.human-events.com/article.php?id=36065 [accessed June 25, 2010].

43. Chris Frates, "Payoffs for States get Harry Reid to 60 Votes," *op. cit.*

44. Jennifer Liberto, "Obama: Use TARP for job creation," CNN-Money.com, December 8, 2009; available at: http://money.cnn.com/2009/12/07/news/economy/tarp_jobs/index.htm [accessed June 25, 2010].

45. Editors, "The White House's Illegal Piggy Bank," *Investors Business Daily*, February 3, 2010; available at: http://www.investors.com/NewsAndAnalysis/Article.aspx?id=520060 [accessed June 25, 2010].

46. Macon Phillips, "Facts Are Stubborn Things," The White House Blog, August 4, 2009; available at: http://www.whitehouse.gov/blog/facts-are-stubborn-things/ [accessed June 25, 2010].

47. Molly Henneberg, "White House Draws Fire for Requesting 'Fishy' Information From Supporters on Health Reform," FoxNews.com, August 5, 2009.

48. Sammy Benoit, "The White House Gets Sued for Its Fishy E-mail Program," *American Thinker* Blog, August 31, 2009; available at: http://comments.americanthinker.com/read/1/408458.html [accessed June 25, 2010].

49. Fred Lucas, "White House Seeks to Capture and Archive Citizens' Comments on its Facebook, YouTube, MySpace Sites," CNSNews.com, September 1, 2009; available at: http://www.cnsnews.com/news/article/53363 [accessed June 25, 2010].

50. Mike Allen, "Barack Obama Urges Backers to Fight Health 'Lies," *Politico*, August 5, 2009; available at: http://www.politico.com/news/stories/0809/25824.html [accessed June 25, 2010].

51. Richard Grenell, "Crossing a Line in the Health Care Debate?" CBNNews.com, March 19, 2010; available at: http://www.cbsnews.

com/stories/2010/03/19/opinion/main6313300.shtml [accessed June 25, 2010].

52. Glenn Greenwald, "Obama confidant's spine-chilling proposal," *Salon*, January 15, 2010; available at: http://www.salon.com/news/ opinion/glenn_greenwald/2010/01/15/sunstein [accessed June 25, 2010].

53. Erick Erickson, "Is the Obama Administration Behind An Astroturf Anti-Tea Party Website?" RedState.com, April 18, 2010; available at: http://www.redstate.com/erick/2010/04/18/is-the-obama-adminis- tration-behind-an-astroturf-anti-tea-party-website/ [accessed June 25, 2010].

54. Hans von Spakovsky, "The Most Transparent Administration Ever? Not at DOJ," *National Review Online*, The Corner, October 6, 2009; available at: http://corner.nationalreview.com/post/?q= MWViM2IwMmUzMDUxNjdjZjcxYmVlMzc4ZGEwYjNhZDI= [accessed June 25, 2010].

55. Gary Locke, "Health Reform and America's Businesses: The Bottom Line," The White House Blog, March 25, 2009; available at: http:// www.whitehouse.gov/blog/2010/03/25/health-reform-and-america-s- businesses-bottom-line [accessed June 25, 2010].

56. Henry Blodget, "White House Blasts Companies For Saying That ObamaCare Will Jack Up Their Costs," *Business Insider*, March 29, 2010; available at: http://www.businessinsider.com/henry-blodget- white-house-blasts-companies-for-saying-that-obamacare-will-jack- up-their-costs-2010-3 [accessed June 25, 2010].

57. Kenneth R. Bazinet, "Obama and the White House Speak Directly to the People with Twitter and Other Social Media Outlets," *New York Daily News*, April 18, 2010; available at: http://www.nydai- lynews.com/news/national/2010/04/18/2010-04-18_bams_image- makers_staying_all_atwitter.html [accessed June 25, 2010].

58. Editors, "Editorial: Obamacare's Secret," *The Washington Times*, April 3, 2010; available at: http://www.washingtontimes.com/news/ 2010/apr/03/obamacares-secret-surveillance/ [accessed June 25, 2010].

59. "Robert Gibbs Gets Very Defensive When Pressed Why Obama Has Held No Press Conferences Since July – Video 5/3/10," *Freedom's Lighthouse*, May 3, 2010; available at: http://www.freedomslight-

house.com/2010/05/robert-gibbs-gets-very-defensive-when.html [accessed June 25, 2010].

60. "CBS's Chip Reid: A Little Ironic For Obama Not To Answer Questions at a Freedom of the Press Signing," HotAirPundit, May 17, 2010; available at: http://www.hapblog.com/2010/05/cbss-chip-reid-little-ironic-for-obama.html [accessed June 25, 2010].

61. Peter Baker, "Obama Turns His Back On the Press," *The New York Times*, May 19, 2010; available at: http://thecaucus.blogs.nytimes.com/2010/05/19/obama-turns-his-back-on-the-press/ [accessed June 25, 2010].

62. Byron York, "Fawning press now gets cold shoulder from Obama," *The Washington Examiner*, May 25, 2010; available at: http://www.washingtonexaminer.com/politics/Fawning-press-now-gets-cold-shoulder-from-Obama-94783304.html [accessed June 25, 2010].

63. John Bresnahan and Jake Sherman, "DOJ nixes Sestak special counsel," *Politico*, May 24, 2010; available at: http://www.politico.com/news/stories/0510/37713.html [accessed June 25, 2010].

64. "Obama Criticizes New Media, iPads, Rumors," RealClearPolitics, May 9, 2010; available at: http://www.realclearpolitics.com/video/2010/05/09/obama_criticizes_new_media_ipads_rumors.html [accessed June 25, 2010].

65. Nick Baumann, "Obama 'Committed' To Net Neutrality Despite Court Ruling," *Mother Jones*, April 6, 2010; available at: http://motherjones.com/mojo/2010/04/obama-committed-net-neutrality-despite-court-ruling [accessed June 25, 2010].

66. "Senators propose granting president emergency Internet power," CNET, June 10, 2010; available at: http://news.cnet.com/8301-13578_3-20007418-38.html [accessed June 25, 2010].

67. Andrew R. Hickey, "Broadband Providers Peeved With FCC Internet Regulation Plans," CNN.com, June 18, 2010; available at: http://www.crn.com/networking/225700593 [accessed June 25, 2010].

68. Mark Hyman, "Shutting Down Free Speech," *The American Spectator*, May 3, 2010; available at: http://spectator.org/archives/2010/05/03/shutting-down-free-speech [accessed June 25, 2010].

69. "Elena Kagan vs. that 1st Amendment thing," World Net Daily, May 19, 2010; available at: http://www.wnd.com/index.php?pageId=155657 [accessed June 25, 2010].

70. Seton Motley, "SCOTUS Nominee Kagan for 'Redistribution of Speech' (Diversity Czar Must be Thrilled)," NewsBusters.org, May 12, 2010; available at: http://newsbusters.org/blogs/seton-motley/2010/05/12/scotus-nominee-kagan-redistribution-speech-diversity-czar-lloyd-must-b.

71. Editorial, "Kagan Speech Rationing," *The Washington Times*, May 17, 2010.

72. Seton Motley, "Fraud-Proof Ratings System Reveals Talk Radio's Higher Numbers, So Left Of Course Cries Foul," NewsBusters.org, April 9, 2009; available at: http://newsbusters.org/blogs/seton-motley/2009/04/09/fraud-proof-ratings-system-reveals-talk-radios-higher-numbers-so-left- [accessed June 25, 2010].

73. Seton Motley, "Citing 'Diversity,' Obama Admin Sides with Leftist Grievance Group and Investigates More Accurate Arbitron Ratings System," NewsBusters.org, May 19, 2009; available at: http://newsbusters.org/blogs/seton-motley/2009/05/19/citing-diversity-obama-admin-sides-leftist-grevance-group-investigates [accessed June 25, 2010].

74. Quinn Hillyer, "Civil Rights Commissioner: DoJ Was 'Racist,'" *The Washington Times*, May 14, 2010; available at: http://www.washingtontimes.com/weblogs/watercooler/2010/may/14/civil-rights-commissioner-doj-was-racist/ [accessed June 25, 2010].

75. J. P. Freire, "Congressman: Why is Justice Department refusing to allow its career attorneys to testify before civil rights commission?" *The Washington Examiner*, April 26, 2010; available at: http://www.washingtonexaminer.com/opinion/blogs/beltway-confidential/congressman-why-is-justice-department-refusing-to-allow-its-career-attorneys-to-testify-before-civil-rights-commission-92104409.html [accessed June 25, 2010].

76. J. P. Freire, "DOJ Voting Rights Attorney Resigns Over Black Panthers Stonewalling," *The Washington Examiner*, May 18, 2010; available at: http://www.washingtonexaminer.com/opinion/blogs/beltway-confidential/doj-voting-rights-attorney-resigns-over-black-panthers-stonewalling-94202249.html [accessed June 25, 2010].

77. "Former Justice Department Lawyher Accuses Holder of Dropping New Black Panther Case for Racial Reasons," Foxnews.com, June 30, 2010; available at: http://www.foxnews.com/politics/2010/06/

30/justice-dept-lawyer-accuses-holder-dropping-new-black-panther-case-political/ [accessed July 7, 2010].

Chapter 8

1. "Obama's Rebukes of MNC's Worry Corporates," Associated Press, May 16, 2009; available at: http://www.indianexpress.com/news/obamas-rebukes-of-mncs-worry-corporates/460314/2.
2. Ed Morrissey, "WaPo: Hey, Did You Know Obama's Statements Had Expiration Dates?" HotAir.com, December 16, 2009; available at: http://hotair.com/archives/2009/12/16/wapo-hey-did-you-know-obamas-statements-had-expiration-dates/.
3. Michael A. Fletcher and Ceci Connolly, "Obama Announces Agreement With Drug Companies," *Washington Post*, June 22, 2009; available at: http://www.washingtonpost.com/wp-dyn/content/article/2009/06/22/AR2009062200349.html.
4. Ed Morrissey, "WaPo: Hey, Did You Know Obama's Statements Had Expiration Dates?" HotAir.com, December 16, 2009; available at: http://www.huffingtonpost.com/2009/08/13/internal-memo-confirms-bi_n_258285.html.
5. Ryan Grim, "Internal Memo Confirms Big Giveaways In White House Deal With Big Pharma," *Huffington Post*, August 13, 2009; available at: http://www.nytimes.com/2009/08/06/health/policy/06insure.html.
6. David D. Kirkpatrick, "White House Affirms Deal on Drug Cost," *New York Times*, August 5, 2009; available at: http://www.nytimes.com/2009/08/06/health/policy/06insure.html [accessed July 12, 2010]
7. Ibid.
8. Ibid.
9. Jake Tapper, "What Did the White House Know About the PhRMA Deal?" *ABC News*, Political Punch, August 8, 2009; available at: http://blogs.abcnews.com/politicalpunch/2009/08/what-did-the-white-house-know-about-the-phrma-deal.html.
10. Ibid.
11. Derrick Z. Jackson, "Drug Firms' Tired Song and Dance on Reform," *Boston Globe*, November 21, 2009; available at: http://www.boston.com/bostonglobe/editorial_opinion/oped/articles/2009/11/21/drug_firms_tired_song_and_dance_on_reform/.

12. Ibid.

13. "Drug Companies Resist White House Call to Reduce Rights to Exclusive Drug Data," FOXNews.com, August 13, 2009; available at: http://www.foxnews.com/politics/2009/08/13/drug-companies-resist-white-house-reduce-rights-exclusive-drug-data/.

14. Alicia Mundy, "Deal Breaker? White House, Drug Companies Fight Over Exclusivity," *Wall Street Journal*, January 15, 2010; available at: http://blogs.wsj.com/washwire/2010/01/15/deal-breaker-white-house-drug-companies-fight-over-exclusivity/.

15. "Pay-For-Delay' Ban Dropped From Health Care Reconciliation Bill," *FDA Week*, March 19, 2010.

16. Charles Babbington, "Analysis: Obama Rebukes Insurance Critics," Breitbart.com, June 23, 2009; available at: http://www.breitbart.com/article.php?id=D990K59O0&show_article=1&catnum=3.

17. Calvin Woodward, "Fact Check: Health Insurer Profits Not So Fat," *ABC News* Money, October 25, 2009; available at: http://abcnews.go.com/Business/wireStory?id=8910507.

18. Sean Lengell, "Sebelius Calls for More Insurance Oversight," *The Washington Times*, May 7, 2009; available at: http://www.washingtontimes.com/news/2009/may/07/sebelius-calls-for-more-insurance-oversight/.

19. Charles Babbington, "Analysis: Obama Rebukes Insurance Critics, GOP," Breitbart.com, June 23, 2009.

20. Sally Pipes, *The Top Ten Myths of American Health Care: A Citizen's Guide* (San Francisco, CA: Pacific Research Institute, 2008), pp. 13, 14.

21. "One Health Insurance Company Turned a Profit, But Not A Record," *St. Petersburg Times*, PolitiFact.com, July 22, 2009; available at: http://www.politifact.com/truth-o-meter/statements/2009/jul/23/barack-obama/health-insurance-company-turned-profit-not-rec/.

22. "Top Industries: Most Profitable," *Fortune* Magazine, May 4, 2009; available at: http://money.cnn.com/magazines/fortune/fortune500/2009/performers/industries/profits/.

23. Calvin Woodward, "Fact Check: Health Insurer Profits Not So Fat," *ABC News* Money, October 25, 2009.

24. Ezra Klein, "Profit and the Insurance Industry," *Washington Post*, September 9, 2009; available at: http://voices.washingtonpost.com/ ezra-klein/2009/09/profit_and_the_insurance_indus.html.

25. Sheryl Gay Stolberg and David Herszenhorn, "Two Sides Take Health Care Debate Outside Washington," *New York Times*, August 2, 2009; available at: http://www.nytimes.com/2009/08/03/ health/policy/03healthcare.html.

26. Barack Obama, "Why We Need Health Care Reform," *New York Times*, August 15, 2009; available at: http://www.nytimes.com/ 2009/08/16/opinion/16obama.html.

27. Jeff Mason and Matt Spetalnick, "Obama Says Insurance Companies Holding US Hostage," Reuters, August 14, 2009; available at: http://www.reuters.com/article/idUSTRE57D47P20090814.

28. Ricardo Alonso-Zaldivar, "HHS Investigates Humana for Medicare Mailer Warning Seniors on Health Overhaul," Associated Press, September 21, 2009; available at: http://www.startribune.com/ lifestyle/health/59990947.html.

29. Ricardo Alonso-Zaldivar, "HHS Investigates Humana for Medicare Mailer Warning Seniors on Health Overhaul," Associated Press, September 21, 2009.

30. "Obama Administration Drops 'Gag Order' on Private Health Insurer," FOXNews.com, October 17, 2009; available at: http:// www.foxnews.com/politics/2009/10/17/obama-administration- drops-gag-order-private-health-insurer/.

31. Sandra Maier, "Obama: Firms Nervous that Health Reform May Pass," Reuters, October 15, 2009; available at: http://www.reuters. com/article/idUSTRE58T43G20091015.

32. Patricia Zengerle, "Obama; Health Insurers 'Deceptive and Dishonest,'" Reuters, October 17, 2009; available at: http://www.reuters. com/article/idUSN17525473.

33. Cathy Arnst, "Obama Attacks Health Insurance Industry," *Business Week*, Money and Politics Blog, October 17, 2009; available at: http://www.businessweek.com/blogs/money_politics/archives/2009/ 10/obama_attacks_h.html.

34. "Obama Attacks Insurance Companies," United Press International, October 17, 2009.

35. Byron York, "Michelle Obama Turns Breast Cancer Awareness Month into Attack on Insurance Companies," *Washington Examiner*, October 23, 2009; available at: http://www.washingtonexaminer.com/opinion/blogs/beltway-confidential/Michelle-Obama-turns-Breast-Cancer-Awareness-Month-into-attack-on-insurance-companies-65818422.html.

36. Jake Tapper and Sunlen Miller, "President Obama Takes on Big Banks: 'If They Want a Fight, That's a Fight I'm Willing to Have,'" *ABC News*, Political Punch, January 21, 2010; available at: http://blogs.abcnews.com/politicalpunch/2010/01/president-obama-takes-on-big-banks-if-they-want-a-fight-thats-a-fight-im-willing-to-have.html.

37. Carrie Budoff Brown, "Barack Obama Seeks Control Over Insurance Rate Hikes," *Politico*, February 21, 2010; available at: http://www.politico.com/news/stories/0210/33258.html.

38. "Obama Health Reform Speech Rallies Pa. Audience, Challenges Insurers," *Kaiser Health News*, March 8, 2010; available at: http://www.kaiserhealthnews.org/Daily-Reports/2010/March/08/Obama-speech.aspx.

39. Alan Reynolds, "The Truth about Health Insurance Premiums and Profits" Cato Institute, March 15, 2010; available at: http://www.cato.org/pub_display.php?pub_id=11447.

40. Alisa Ulferts, "Obama Administration Summons Health Care Insurance Companies to Washington," Justmeans.com, February 25, 2010; available at: http://www.justmeans.com/Obama-administration-summons-health-care-insurance-companies-Washington/9577.html.

41. Jake Tapper and Sunlen Miller, "President Obama Tells Insurance Execs of Constant Premium Hikes," *Politico*, March 4, 2010; available at: http://blogs.abcnews.com/politicalpunch/2010/03/president-obama-tells-insurance-execs-of-constant-premium-hikes-this-is-unacceptable-and-unsustainab.html.

42. Jake Tapper and Sunlen Miller, "President Obama Tells Insurance Execs of Constant Premium Hikes," *Politico*, March 4, 2010.

43. Jill Dougherty, Ed Henry, Evan Glass and Alan Sliverleib, "Obama Targets Insurers for Final Health Care Push," CNN.com Politics,

March 19, 2010; available at: http://www.cnn.com/2010/POLITICS/03/19/health.care.main/index.html.

44. Mark Halperin, "Remarks: Obama on Health Reform at George Mason University March 19, 2010." *Time*, The Page, March 19, 2010; available at: http://thepage.time.com/remarks-obama-on-health-reform-at-george-mason-university-march-19-2010/.

45. Steve Holland, "Obama Administration Has Blunt Message for Insurers," Reuters, March 29, 2010; available at: http://www.reuters.com/article/idUSN2017888120100329.

46. Ricardo Alonso-Zaldiver, "Insurance Industry Agrees to Fix Kids Coverage Gap," Associated Press, March 30, 2010; available at: http://www.foxnews.com/politics/2010/03/29/insurance-industry-agrees-fix-kids-coverage-gap/.

47. Charles Babbington, "Analysis: Obama Rebukes Insurance Critics, GOP," Breitbart.com, June 23, 2009; available at: http://www.breitbart.com/article.php?id=D990K59O0&show_article=1&catnum=3.

48. Jake Tapper, "Exclusive: Vice President Biden Says President Obama's Rescheduled Trip Not a Bad Sign for Health Care Bill's Prospects," *ABC News*, Political Punch, March 18, 2010; available at: http://blogs.abcnews.com/politicalpunch/2010/03/exclusive-vice-president-biden-says-obamas-cancelled-trip-not-a-bad-sign-for-health-care-bills-prosp.html.

49. John E. Calfee, "Obama's Misleading Assault on the Insurance Industry," *Wall Street Journal*, March 12, 2010; available at: http://online.wsj.com/article/SB10001424052748703625304575115540074840182.html.

50. President Barack Obama, "Obama's Fifth News Conference," *New York Times*, July 22, 2009; available at: http://www.nytimes.com/2009/07/22/us/politics/22obama.transcript.html.

51. "Obama: Doctors Choose Amputation Because Surgeons Get Paid More Than Physicians," Breitbart TV, August 11, 2009; available at: http://www.breitbart.tv/obama-doctors-choose-amputation-because-surgeons-get-paid-more-than-physicians/.

52. Editorial, "The War on Specialists, Obamacare Punishes Cardiology and Oncology to Finance GPs," *Wall Street Journal*, October 6,

2009; available at: http://online.wsj.com/article/
SB10001424052748704471504574443472658898710.html.

53. Editorial, "The War on Specialists, Obamacare Punishes Cardiology
and Oncology to Finance GPs," *Wall Street Journal*, October 6,
2009.

54. Dr. Milton R. Wolf, "Wolf: Obama Family Health Care Fracas,"
Washington Times, March 11, 2010; available at: http://www.
washingtontimes.com/news/2010/mar/11/obama-family-health-care-
fracas/.

55. Scott Atlas, "ObamaCare: Kiss Your Access Goodbye," *Real Clear
Politics*, June 23, 2009; available at: http://www.realclearpolitics.
com/articles/2009/06/23/obamacare_kiss_your_access_goodbye_
97122.html.

Chapter 9

1. Sheryl Gay Stolberg and Stephen Labaton, "Obama Calls Wall
Street Bonuses 'Shameful,'" *New York Times*, January 30, 2009;
available at: http://www.nytimes.com/2009/01/30/business/
30obama.html [accessed June 29, 2010].

2. Julianna Goldman and Ian Katz, "Obama Doesn't 'Begrudge'
Bonuses for Blankfein, Dimon," Bloomberg.com, February 10,
2010; available at: http://www.bloomberg.com/apps/news?pid=
newsarchive&sid=aKGZkktzkAlA [accessed June 29, 2010].

3. Andrew Cline, "Obama Plays Favorites," *The American Spectator*,
February 12, 2010; available at: http://spectator.org/archives/2010/
02/12/obama-plays-favorites [accessed June 29, 2010].

4. Ed Morrissey, "Obama: 'I do think at a certain point you've made
enough money,'" HotAir.com, April 29, 2010; available at: http://
hotair.com/archives/2010/04/29/obama-i-do-think-at-a-certain-
point-youve-made-enough-money/ [accessed June 29, 2010].

5. "Obama Earned Nearly $2.5 Million in Book Royalties in
2008," *Washington Post*, March 19, 2009; available at: http://www.
washingtonpost.com/wp-dyn/content/article/2009/03/19/
AR2009031903521.html [accessed June 29, 2010].

6. Jake Tapper, "President Obama Compares Big Banks, AIG, to Suicide Bombers," ABCNews.com, Political Punch, March 18, 2009;

available at: http://blogs.abcnews.com/politicalpunch/2009/03/president-ob-14.html [accessed June 29, 2010].

7.   "Obama Attacks AIG for 'Recklessness and Greed,'" Associated Press, March 17, 2009.

8.   Jeff Zeleny, "As the Public Simmers, Obama Lets Off Steam," *New York Times*, March 20, 2009; accessed June 29, 2010]; see also, "Obama: 'I Don't Want to Quell Anger,' Over AIG," *USA Today*, The Oval blog, March 18, 2009; available at: http://content.usatoday.com/communities/theoval/post/2009/03/64320451/1 [accessed June 29, 2010].

9.   Eamon Javers, "Inside Obama's Bank CEO's Meeting," *Politico*, April 3, 2009; available at: http://www.politico.com/news/stories/0409/20871.html [accessed June 29, 2010].

10. Jui Chakravorty Das, "U.S. to Put Conditions on TARP Repayment: Report," Reuters, April 20, 2009; available at: http://www.reuters.com/article/idUSTRE53J03720090420 [accessed June 29, 2010].

11. Eamon Javers, "Inside Obama's Bank CEO's Meeting," *Politico*, April 3, 2009; available at: http://www.politico.com/news/stories/0409/20871.html [accessed June 29, 2010].

12. "Obama Complains About 'Fat-cat Bankers,'" Reuters, December 11, 2009; available at: http://www.reuters.com/article/idUS-TRE5BA4IF20091211 [accessed June 29, 2010].

13. Sharon Terlep, "GM Chief to Get $1.7 Million Pay," *Wall Street Journal*, February 20, 2010; available at: http://online.wsj.com/article/SB10001424052748703787304575075843943185642.html [accessed June 29, 2010].

14. Thomas Sowell, *The Housing Boom and Bust* (New York: Basic Books, 2009), 44–52.

15. Lawrence H. White, "Housing Finance and the 2008 Financial Crisis," The Cato Institute, August 2009; available at: http://www.downsizinggovernment.org/hud/housing-finance-2008-financial-crisis [accessed June 29, 2010].

16. MarketWatch, "Full Text of President Obama's Remarks," Marketwatch.com, December 14, 2009; available at: http://www.marketwatch.com/story/obama-calls-bankers-fat-cats-before-meeting-them-2009-12-14 [accessed June 29, 2010].

17. Kate Andersen Brower, "President Will Meet with Community Bankers," *Houston Chronicle*, December 21, 2009; available at: http://www.chron.com/disp/story.mpl/headline/biz/6781944.html [accessed June 29, 2010].

18. President Barack Obama, "President Obama Proposes Financial Crisis Responsibility Fee to Recoup Every Last Penny for American Taxpayers," WhiteHouse.gov, January 14, 2010; available at: http://www.whitehouse.gov/the-press-office/president-obama-proposes-financial-crisis-responsibility-fee-recoup-every-last-penn [accessed June 29, 2010].

19. Jackie Calmes, "Taxing Banks for the Bailout," *New York Times*, January 14, 2010; available at: http://dealbook.blogs.nytimes.com/2010/01/15/taxing-banks-for-the-bailout/ [accessed June 29, 2010].

20. Ibid.

21. David C. John, "Obama's 'Financial Crisis Responsibility Fee': Not Responsible, Not a Fee," Heritage Foundation, January 21, 2010; available at: http://www.heritage.org/Research/Reports/2010/01/Obamas-Financial-Crisis-Responsibility-Fee-Not-Responsible-Not-a-Fee [accessed June 29, 2010].

22. Alister Bull, "Obama Chides Banks' 'Audacity' for Fighting Fee," Reuters, January 16, 2010; available at: http://www.reuters.com/article/idUSN1514552120100116 [accessed June 29, 2010].

23. Ken McIntyre, "Bank-Robbing Tax Lets 'Bad Guys' Go Free," Heritage Foundation, March 3, 2010; available at: http://www.heritage.org/Multimedia/InfoGraphic/Bank-Robbing-Tax-Lets-Bad-Guys-Go-Free [accessed June 29, 2010].

24. David C. John, "Obama's 'Financial Crisis Responsibility Fee': Not Responsible, Not a Fee," Heritage Foundation, January 21, 2010; available at: http://www.heritage.org/Research/Reports/2010/01/Obamas-Financial-Crisis-Responsibility-Fee-Not-Responsible-Not-a-Fee [accessed June 29, 2010].

25. Catherine Clifford, "Obama to Offer Broad Market Overhaul," CNNMoney.com, June 15, 2009; available at: http://money.cnn.com/2009/06/15/news/economy/market_reorganization/index.htm?postversion=2009061512 [accessed June 29, 2010].

26. Jim Kuhnhenn and Anne Flaherty, "Financial Overhaul Bill Gets Wary Reception," Associated Press, October 29, 2009; available at:

http://www.gopusa.com/news/2009/october/1030_financial_regs1.shtml [accessed June 29, 2010].

27. Ibid.

28. Tom Braithwaite and Francesco Guerrera, "Obama Hammers Wall Street Banks," *Financial Times*, January 21, 2010; available at: http://ftalphaville.ft.com/thecut/2010/01/22/132081/obama-hammers-wall-street-banks/ [accessed June 29, 2010].

29. Jake Tapper and Sunlen Miller, "President Obama Takes on Big Banks: 'If They Want a Fight, That's a Fight I'm Willing to Have,'" *ABC News*, Political Punch, January 21, 2010; available at: http://blogs.abcnews.com/politicalpunch/2010/01/president-obama-takes-on-big-banks-if-they-want-a-fight-thats-a-fight-im-willing-to-have.html [accessed June 29, 2010].

30. Ibid.

31. Tom Braithwaite and Francesco Guerrera, "Obama Hammers Wall Street Banks," *Financial Times*, January 21, 2010; available at: http://ftalphaville.ft.com/thecut/2010/01/22/132081/obama-hammers-wall-street-banks/ [accessed June 29, 2010].

32. James Gattuso, "President Obama and The War on Banks," The Foundry Blog, Heritage Foundation, January 22, 2010; available at: http://blog.heritage.org/2010/01/22/president-obama-and-the-war-on-banks/ [accessed June 29, 2010].

33. Ibid.

34. Neil K. Shenai, "Obama's Plan Finally Attacks 'Too Big to Fail,'" Huffington Post, January 21, 2010; available at: http://www.huffingtonpost.com/neil-k-shenai/obamas-plan-finally-attac_b_432462.html [accessed June 29, 2010].

35. Carl Horowitz, "Dodd's Financial Services 'Reform' Would Mean More Bailouts," National Legal and Policy Center, March 25, 2010; available at: http://www.nlpc.org/stories/2010/03/25/sen-dodds-financial-services-reform-bill-would-escalate-federal-bailouts-control [accessed June 29, 2010].

36. Timothy Geithner, "How to Prevent America's Next Financial Crisis," *Washington Post*, April 13,. 2010; available at: http://www.washingtonpost.com/wp-dyn/content/article/2010/04/12/AR2010041203341.html [accessed June 29, 2010].

37. Jen Psaki, "False Criticisms to Obscure Choices," White House Blog, April 13, 2010; available at: http://www.whitehouse.gov/blog/2010/04/13/false-criticisms-obscure-clear-choices [accessed June 29, 2010].

38. "Obama Slams US Chamber of Commerce for Anti-reform Ad," Agence France-Presse, October 9, 2009; available at: http://rawstory.com/2009/10/obama-slams-us-chamber-of-commerce-for-anti-reform-ad/ [accessed June 29, 2010].

39. Lisa Lerer, "White House Plan: Neuter the Chamber," *Politico*, October 19, 2009; available at: http://www.politico.com/news/stories/1009/28445.html [accessed June 29, 2010].

40. Jim Puzzanghera, "Obama Official Slams U.S. Chamber Over Opposition to Financial Overhaul," *Los Angeles Times*, March 25, 2010; available at: http://articles.latimes.com/2010/mar/25/business/la-fi-obama-uschamber25-2010mar25 [accessed June 29, 2010].

41. "Administration Pushes for New Wall Street Rules," *Cleveland Ohio Business News*, March 24, 2010; available at: http://www.cleveland.com/business/index.ssf/2010/03/official_attacks_us_chamber_of.html [accessed June 29, 2010].

42. Major Garrett, "Obama to Launch Public Campaign for Wall Street Crackdown," FOXNews.com, April 18, 2010; available at: http://www.foxnews.com/politics/2010/04/18/obama-launch-public-campaign-wall-street-crackdown/ [accessed June 29, 2010].

43. Darlene Superville, "Obama: Fresh Crisis Without New Financial Rules," Associated Press, April 17, 2010.

44. Matt Cover, "Obama-Backed Financial Reform Bill Would Create New Bureaucracy with Power to Subpeona 'Any Data' from 'Any Financial Company,'" CNSNews.com, April 6, 2010; available at: http://www.cnsnews.com/news/article/63756 [accessed June 29, 2010].

45. Carl Horowitz, "Dodd's Financial Services 'Reform' Would Mean More Bailouts," National Legal and Policy Center, March 25, 2010; available at: http://www.nlpc.org/stories/2010/03/25/sen-dodds-financial-services-reform-bill-would-escalate-federal-bailouts-control [accessed June 29, 2010].

46. Stephen Spruiell, "Corker vs. the Real Bailouts," *National Review Online*, April 22, 2010; available at: http://article.nationalreview.

com/432208/corker-vs-the-real-bailouts/stephen-spruiell [accessed June 29, 2010].

47. David C. John, "Dodd Financial Regulation Bill: Super Regulators Not the Answer," Heritage Foundation, March 23, 2010; available at: http://www.heritage.org/Research/Reports/2010/03/Dodd-Financial-Regulation-Bill-Super-Regulators-Not-the-Answer [accessed June 29, 2010].

48. Conn Carroll, "Wall Street Bailouts Forever," Heritage Foundation, Morning Bell, April 14, 2010; available at: http://blog.heritage.org/2010/04/14/morning-bell-wall-street-bailouts-forever/ [accessed June 29, 2010].

49. Carl Horowitz, "Dodd's Financial Services 'Reform' Would Mean More Bailouts," *op. cit.*

50. David C. John, "Dodd Bill Fails to Fix Too Big to Fail,'" *op. cit.*

51. James Gattuso, "Senator Dodd's Regulation Plan: 14 Fatal Flaws," Heritage Foundation, April 22, 2010; available at: http://www.heritage.org/research/reports/2010/04/senator%20dodds%20regulation%20plan%2014%20fatal%20flaws [accessed June 29, 2010].

52. "David C. John, "The Obama Financial Regulatory Reform Plan: Poor Policy and Missed Opportunities," Heritage Foundation, July 15, 2009; available at: http://www.heritage.org/Research/Reports/2009/07/The-Obama-Financial-Regulatory-Reform-Plan-Poor-Policy-and-Missed-Opportunities [accessed June 29, 2010].

53. Sen. Chris Dodd, "Senate Session," C-SPAN Video Library, April 14, 2010; available at: http://www.c-spanvideo.org/videolibrary/clip.php?appid=597986649 [accessed July 7, 2010].

54. "Brad Sherman, "Interview with Politico's David Mark," The Arena, April 19, 2010; available at: http://www.politico.com/arena/perm/Brad_Sherman_5DAC0573-548C-4953-8FF3-5F771F55E323.html [accessed July 7, 2010].

55. "Dodd Bill is Just the Beginning of 'Too Big to Fail,'" Heritage Foundation, May 22, 2010; available at: http://blog.heritage.org/2010/05/20/morning-bell-dodd-bill-is-just-the-beginning-of-too-big-to-fail/ [accessed June 29, 2010].

56. The Editors, "The Case Against the Dodd Bill," *National Review Online*, April 26, 2010; available at: http://article.nationalreview.

com/432504/the-case-against-the-dodd-bill/the-editors [accessed June 29, 2010].

57. Brady Dennis, "Senate Passes Financial Regulation Bill," *Washington Post*, May 21, 2010; available at: http://www.washingtonpost.com/wp-dyn/content/article/2010/05/20/AR2010052003503.html [accessed June 29, 2010].

58. Jay Jeflin, "Gregg Declares Wall Street Bill a Disaster," *The Hill*, May 24, 2010; available at: http://thehill.com/blogs/on-the-money/banking-financial-institutions/99477-gregg-declares-wall-street-bill-a-disaster [accessed June 29, 2010].

59. Timothy P. Carney, "Goldman Rallies for Obama in Wall Street 'Reform,'" *Washington Examiner*, April 16, 2010; available at: http://www.washingtonexaminer.com/opinion/columns/Goldman-rallies-for-Obama-in-Wall-Street-_reform_-90957879.html [accessed June 29, 2010].

60. Vicki Needham, "Blankfein Supports Financial Reform Bill," *The Hill*, On the Money, April 27, 2010; available at: http://thehill.com/blogs/on-the-money/banking-financial-institutions/94735-blankfein-supports-financial-reform-legislation [accessed June 28, 2010].

61. Timothy P. Carney, "Goldman Rallies for Obama in Wall Street 'Reform,'" *op. cit.*

62. Conn Carroll, "Wall Street Bailouts Forever," *op. cit.*

63. Robert Gibbs, "Briefing by White House Press Secretary Robert Gibbs," The White House, April 19, 2010; available at: http://www.whitehouse.gov/the-press-office/briefing-white-house-press-secretary-robert-gibbs-41910 [accessed June 28, 2010].

64. Brendan Scott, "Dem Web War on Sachs," *New York Post*, April 20, 2010; available at: http://www.nypost.com/p/news/national/dem_web_war_on_sachs_KFbf4AqtQR2tMo2rYKyZTO [accessed June 28, 2010].

Chapter 10

1. Stephen W. Smith, "Geithner on Ousting CEOs, Reviving Economy," CBNNews.com, April 1, 2009; available at: http://www.cbsnews.com/8301-503983_162-4911030-503983.html.

2. Larry Kudlow, "Does Wagoner's Fate Signal Obama Power Grab?" CNBC.com, March 30, 2009.

3. Larry Kudlow, "My Interview with Sen. Bob Corker on Pres. Obama's 'Power Grab," CNBC.com Money Politics, March 31, 2009; available at:http://www.cnbc.com/id/29977623/ My_Interview_w_Sen_Bob_Corker_on_Pres_Obama_s_ Power_Grab.

4. Jeffrey McCracken, John D. Stoll and Neil King Jr., "U.S. Threatens Bankruptcy for GM, Chrysler," *Wall Street Journal*, March 31, 2009; available at:http://online.wsj.com/article/ SB123845591244871499.html.

5. Ibid.

6. Neil King and Jeffrey McCracken, "Control of GM Would Create Conflicts for Government," *Wall Street Journal*, April 28, 2009; available at:http://online.wsj.com/article/SB124087977542 061821.html.

7. "GM to Remaining Dealers: Learn to Sell Small Cars," Car Dealer News, August 31, 2009; available at:http://www.cardealerreviews. org/?p=117117.

8. Ken Thomas, "AP NewsBreak: GM Pulls Out of Mercury Partnership," ABCNews.com, August 10, 2009; http://abcnews.go.com/US/ wireStory?id=8297598.

9. Robert Schoenberger, "Government, UAW to own 89% of GM if Restructuring Deal Works," *Cleveland Ohio Business News*, April 27, 2009; available at:http://www.cleveland.com/business/index.ssf/ 2009/04/government_uaw_to_own_89_perce.html.

10. Tom Suhadolnik, "Obama's Pinstripe Revolution," *American Thinker*, May 6, 2009; available at:http://www.americanthinker. com/2009/05/obamas_pinstripe_revolution.html.

11. WSJ Staff, "Statement from GM Bondholder Committee's Advisers," *Wall Street Journal*, April 27, 2009; available at: http:// blogs.wsj.com/autoshow/2009/04/27/statement-from-gm-bond-holder-commitees-advisers/.

12. "UAW Trust to Get Large Chunk of GM Shares, Deal among concessions between company and union as GM restructures," Associated Press, May 26, 2009; available at: http://www.msnbc.msn.com/ id/30938307/.

13. Chris Isidore, "GM Bankruptcy: End of an Era," CNNMoney.com, June 2, 2009; available at: http://money.cnn.com/2009/06/01/news/companies/gm_bankruptcy/.

14. Emily Chasan and Phil Wahba, "Dissenting Bondholders Argue Agaisnt GM Asset Sale," Reuters, July 2, 2009; available at: http://www.reuters.com/article/idUSN024529220090702.

15. "GM Has Chance to 'Rise Again' Under Restructuring, Obama Says," FOXNews.com, June 1, 2009; available at: http://www.foxnews.com/politics/2009/06/01/gm-chance-rise-restructuring-obama-says/.

16. Roger Mezger, "GM Emerges From Bankruptcy After 40 Days," *Cleveland Ohio Business News*, July 10, 2009; available at: http://www.cleveland.com/business/index.ssf/2009/07/gm_emerges_from_bankruptcy_rep.html.

17. Greg Gardner, "Obama Forced Chrysler Into Bankruptcy," Sweetness and Light Blog, June 7, 2009; available at: http://sweetness-light.com/archive/obama-forced-chryslers-bankruptcy.

18. Tom Suhadolnik, "Obama's Pinstripe Revolution," *American Thinker*, May 6, 2009.

19. Eric Morath, "Auto Taskforce: We Don't Negotiate With Terrorists," *Wall Street Journal* Bankruptcy Beat Blog, May 28, 2009; Greg Gardner, "Obama Forced Chrysler Into Bankruptcy," Sweetness and Light Blog, June 7, 2009; available at: http://blogs.wsj.com/bankruptcy/2009/05/28/auto-taskforce-we-dont-negotiate-with-terrorists/.

20. Jake Tapper, "White House Denies Charge By Attorney that Administration Threatened to Destroy Investment Firm's Reputation," ABCNews.com Political Punch, May 2, 2009; available at: http://blogs.abcnews.com/politicalpunch/2009/05/bankruptcy-atto.html.

21. John Carney, "New Allegations Of White House Threats Over Chrysler," *Business Insider,* May 5, 2009; available at: http://www.businessinsider.com/new-allegations-of-white-house-threats-over-chysler-2009-5.

22. President Barack Obama, "Remarks by the President on the Auto Industry," WhiteHouse.gov, April 30, 2009; available at: http://www.whitehouse.gov/the_press_office/remarks-by-the-president-on-the-Auto-Industry/.

23. Clifford S. Asness, "Hedge Funds Outraged At Obama Bullying But Also Cowering in Fear," *Business Insider*, May 5, 2009; available at: http://www.businessinsider.com/henry-blodget-this-hedge-fund-managers-not-afraid-of-big-bad-obama-2009-5.

24. President Barack Obama, "Remarks by the President on the Auto Industry," WhiteHouse.gov, April 30, 2009.

25. Clifford S. Asness, "Hedge Funds Outraged At Obama Bullying But Also Cowering in Fear," *Business Insider*, May 5, 2009.

26. Editorial, "Mismanaging the Collapse of Detroit's Giants, *The Economist*, May 7, 2009.

27. Douglas Rushkoff, "The Economist Gets Something Right," Boingboing.net, May 7, 2009; available at: http://boingboing.net/2009/05/07/the-economist-gets-s.html.

28. Jake Tapper, "White House Denies Charge By Attorney that Administration Threatened to Destroy Investment Firm's Reputation," ABCNews.com Political Punch, May 2, 2009.

29. Michael Barone, "Steve Rattner and 'Gangster Government,'" *The Washington Examiner*, May 8, 2009; available at: http://www.washingtonexaminer.com/opinion/blogs/beltway-confidential/Steve-Rattner-and-Gangster-Government-44599032.html.

30. Peter Whoriskey and Tomoeh Murakami Tse, "Rattner Resigns as Obama's Point Man on the Auto Industry," *The Washington Post*, July 14, 2009; available at: http://www.washingtonpost.com/wp-dyn/content/article/2009/07/13/AR2009071302411.html.

31. Alex P. Kellogg and Kris Maher, "UAW to Get 55% Stake in Chrysler for Concessions," *Wall Street Journal*, April 28, 2009; available at: http://online.wsj.com/article/SB124087751929461535.html.

32. Zachery Kouwe, "The Lenders Obama Decided to Blame," New York Times, April 30, 2009; available at: http://www.nytimes.com/2009/05/01/business/01hedge.html.

33. Michael Barone, "White House Puts UAW Ahead of Property Rights," *Washington Examiner*, May 6, 2009; available at: http://www.washingtonexaminer.com/politics/White-House-puts-UAW-ahead-of-property-rights-44415057.html.

34. Scott Rasmussen, "Just 21% Favor GM Bailout Plan, 67% Oppose," Rasmussen Reports, May 31, 2009; available at: http://www.rasmussenreports.com/public_content/business/auto_industry/may_2009/just_21_favor_gm_bailout_plan_67_oppose.

35. Scott Rasmussen, "Only 18% Say UAW, Government Will Do Good Job Running GM, Chrysler," Rasmussen Reports, May 4, 2009; available at: http://www.rasmussenreports.com/public_content/business/auto_industry/may_2009/only_18_say_uaw_government_will_do_good_job_running_gm_chrysler.

36. Scott Rasmussen, "57% Expect Government Will Give GM, Chrysler Unfair Advantages," Rasmussen Reports, May 8, 2009; available at: http://www.rasmussenreports.com/public_content/business/auto_industry/may_2009/57_expect_government_will_give_gm_chrysler_unfair_advantages.

37. Scott Rasmussen, "Just 12% Would Prefer A Car From A Bailed-Out Automaker," Rasmussen Reports, March 10, 2009; available at: http://www.rasmussenreports.com/public_content/business/auto_industry/march_2009/just_12_would_prefer_a_car_from_a_bailed_out_automaker.

38. "Editors, "Busy Not Running GM, And not choosing GM's Office Space, *Wall Street Journal*, June 3, 2009; available at: http://online.wsj.com/article/SB124389952143874411.html.

39. Sharon Terlep and Kevin Helliker, "Obama Auto Team Presses GM to Consider Getting Rid of GMC Brand," *Wall Street Journal*, April 17, 2009; available at: http://online.wsj.com/article/SB123989177238225323.html.

40. Omar Rana, "Obama Administration Halves Chrysler's Marketing Budget," EGM Car Tech, May 12, 2009; available at: http://www.egmcartech.com/2009/05/12/obama-administration-halves-chryslers-marketing-budget/.

41. Michelle Maling, "A Look at the Protected Chrysler Dealerships," MichelleMalkin.com, May 27, 2009; available at: http://michelle-malkin.com/2009/05/27/a-look-at-the-protected-chrysler-dealerships/.

42. Mark Tapscott, "Furor Grows Over Partisan Car Dealer Closings," *Washington Examiner*, May 27, 2009; available at: http://www.washingtonexaminer.com/opinion/blogs/beltway-confidential/Furor-grows-over-partisan-car-dealer-closings-46261447.html.

43. David Shepardson, "Auto Dealers Criticize Obama, White House sought closing of franchises now offered openings," *Detroit News*, April 3, 2010.

44. David Shepardson, "Obama Administration Predicts $30 Billion
     Loss on Auto Bailout," *Detroit News*, December 8, 2009; available
     at: http://detnews.com/article/20091208/AUTO01/912080414/
     Obama-administration-predicts-$30B-loss-on-auto-bailout.

45. Daniel Wagner, "GMAC Bailout Could Cost Taxpayers $6.3 Billion,
     Says Watchdog," Associated Press, March 11, 2010; available at:
     http://www.huffingtonpost.com/2010/03/11/gmac-bailout-could-
     cost-t_n_494564.html.

Chapter 11

1.   Martha R. Gore, "Obama Trying to Weaken FBI Whistleblower
     Protection?" Examiner.com, August 8, 2009; available at: http://
     www.examiner.com/examiner/x-2547-Watchdog-Politics-Exam-
     iner-y2009m8d8-Obama-trying-to-weaken-FBI-whistleblower-
     protection [accessed June 30, 2010].

2.   Byron York, "What's behind Obama's sudden attempt to fire the
     AmeriCorps inspector general?" *The Washington Examiner*, June
     11, 2009; available at: http://www.washingtonexaminer.com/
     opinion/blogs/beltway-confidential/Whats-behind-Obamas-sudden-
     firing-of-the-AmeriCorps-inspector-general-47877797.html
     [accessed June 30, 2010].

3.   Ibid.

4.   Ann Sanner and Pete Yost, "In Spat with Friend, Obama Removes
     AmeriCorps's IG," *The Washington Times*, June 12, 2009.

5.   Ibid.

6.   Byron York, "What's behind Obama's sudden attempt to fire the
     AmeriCorps inspector general?" *op. cit.*

7.   Jake Tapper, "White House Plays Hardball; Says Fired IG Walpin
     Was 'Confused, Disoriented" Engaged in 'Inappropriate Conduct,'"
     ABC News, Political Punch, June 16, 2009; available at: http://
     blogs.abcnews.com/politicalpunch/2009/06/white-house-plays-hard-
     ball-says-fired-ig-walpin-was-confused-disoriented-engaged-in-inap-
     propriate-co.html [accessed June 30, 2010].

8.   Byron York, "Fired AmeriCorps IG responds: White House charges
     are false," *Washington Examiner*, June 17, 2009; available at:
     http://www.washingtonexaminer.com/opinion/blogs/beltway-

confidential/Fired-AmeriCorps-IG-responds-White-House-charges-are-false-48257187.html [accessed June 30, 2010].

9. Ibid.

10. Ibid.

11. Quin Hillyer, "IG Witness Blows Up White House Excuse," *The Washington Times*, June 17, 2009; available at: http://www.washingtontimes.com/weblogs/watercooler/2009/jun/17/ig-witness-blows-white-house-excuse/ [accessed June 30, 2010].

12. Byron York, "White House refuses to answer Senate questions on AmeriCorps IG firing," *Washington Examiner*, June 17, 2009; available at: http://www.washingtonexaminer.com/opinion/blogs/beltway-confidential/NEW-White-House-refuses-to-answer-Senates-questions-on-AmeriCorps-IG-firing-48285832.html [accessed June 30, 2010].

13. Byron York, "AmeriCorps stonewalls questions of White House involvement in IG firing," *Washington Examiner*, July 9, 2009; available at: http://www.washingtonexaminer.com/opinion/blogs/beltway-confidential/AmeriCorps-stonewalls-questions-of-White-House-involvement-in-IG-firing-50354822.html [accessed June 30, 2010].

14. Ibid.

15. Byron York, "Americorps IG sues government over 'unlawful' firing," *Washington Examiner*, July 18, 2009; available at: http://www.washingtonexaminer.com/opinion/blogs/beltway-confidential/AmeriCorps-IG-sues-government-over-unlawful-firing-51094442.html [accessed June 30, 2010].

16. Byron York, "Probe finds new clues in Americorps IG scandal," *Washington Examiner*, July 31, 2009; available at: http://www.washingtonexaminer.com/politics/Probe-finds-new-clues-in-Ameri-Corps-IG-scandal—52109667.html [accessed June 30, 2010].

17. Jake Tapper, "President Obama Fires Controversial Inspector General," *ABC News Political Punch*, June 12, 2009; available at: http://blogs.abcnews.com/politicalpunch/2009/06/president-obama-fires-controversial-inspector-general-.html [accessed June 30, 2010].

18. Byron York, "Probe finds new clues in Americorps IG scandal," *op. cit.*

19. Byron York, "Walpin scandal update: Grassley blocks nomination, accuses administration of stonewalling," *Washington Examiner*, September 21, 2009; available at: http:// www.washingtonexaminer.com/opinion/blogs/beltway-confidential/ Walpin-scandal-update-Grassley-blocks-nomination-accuses-admin-istration-of-stonewalling-60063967.html [accessed June 30, 2010].

20. Sam Stanton, "U.S. Attorney Rules in Favor of Federal Official Obama Fired," *Sacramento Bee*, November 10, 2009; available at: http://www.mcclatchydc.com/2009/11/1078657/us-attorney-rules-in-favor-of-.html [accessed July 7, 2010].

21. Editors, "Editorial: Walpin-gate Opens Wider," *The Washington Times*, November 15, 2009; available at· http·//www.washington-times.com/news/2010/jun/16/walpin-gate-swings-wide-open/ [accessed June 30, 2010].

22. Byron York, "Inspector General: Rhee visited me to intervene for Johnson," *The Washington Examiner*, November 24, 2009; available at: http://www.washingtonexaminer.com/politics/Inspector-general_-Rhee-intervened-for-Johnson-8577747-71924762.html [accessed June 30, 2010].

23. Byron York, "Congressional Report: Rhee did 'damage control' after sex charges against fiance Kevin Johnson," *The Washington Examiner*, November 20, 2009; available at: http://www.washing-tonexaminer.com/politics/Exclusive-Congressional-Report-Rhee-did-damage-control-after-sex-charges-against-fiancee-Kevin-Johnson.ht ml [accessed June 30, 2010].

24. Ibid.

25. Byron York, "Grassley: 'Evidence points' to political motive in Americorps firing," *Washington Examiner*, November 20, 2009; available at: http://www.washingtonexaminer.com/opinion/blogs/ beltway-confidential/Grassley-Evidence-points-to-political-motive-in-AmeriCorps-firing-70638472.html [accessed June 30, 2010].

26. Byron York, "New documents: White House scrambled to justify AmeriCorps firing after the fact," *The Washington Examiner*, November 23, 2009; available at: http://www.washingtonexaminer. com/politics/New-documents-White-House-scrambled-to-justify-AmeriCorps-firing-after-the-fact-71483647.html [accessed June 30, 2010].

27. Ibid.

28. Byron York, "Did AmeriCorps official lie about possible First Lady link to IG firing?" *The Washington Examiner*, December 14, 2009; available at: http://www.washingtonexaminer.com/politics/Did-AmeriCorps-official-lie-about-possible-First-Lady-link-to-IG-firing-79209617.html [accessed June 30, 2010].

29. Byron York, "White House blocks testimony by former top aide to First Lady," *The Washington Examiner*, December 22, 2009; available at: http://www.washingtonexaminer.com/opinion/blogs/belt-way-confidential/White-House-blocks-testimony-by-former-top-aide-to-First-Lady—79891752.html [accessed June 30, 2010].

30. Byron York, "Walpin update: New charges of political motive in IG firing; prosecutor who aided Obama ally sought job from Obama," *Washington Examiner*, March 2, 2010; available at: http://www.washingtonexaminer.com/opinion/blogs/beltway-confidential/Walpin-update-New-charges-of-political-motive-in-IG-firing-prose-cutor-who-aided-Obama-ally-sought-job-from-Obama-85949732.html [accessed June 30, 2010].

31. Editorial, "Obama's Sacked Inspector General," *The Washington Times*, November 25, 2009; available at: http://www.washington-times.com/news/2009/nov/25/obamas-sacked-inspector-general/?page=2 [accessed June 30, 2010].

32. Tom Hamburger and Peter Wallsten, "Dispute Grows Over TARP Chief's Powers," *Los Angeles Times*, June 18, 2009; available at: http://articles.latimes.com/2009/jun/18/nation/na-tarp-inspector18 [accessed June 30, 2010].

33. Jake Tapper and Matt Jaffe, "Treasury Department Challenges Independence of TARP Inspector General," *ABC News*, Political Punch, June 18, 2009; available at: http://blogs.abcnews.com/politi-calpunch/2009/06/treasury-department-challenges-independence-of-tarp-inspector-general.html [accessed June 30, 2010].

34. Evan Perez and Deborah Solomon, "Treasury Retreats From Stand-off With TARP Watchdog," *The Wall Street Journal*, September 3, 2009; available at: http://online.wsj.com/article/SB125193355469281319.html [accessed June 30, 2010].

35. Editorial, "Inspectors need independence," *Washington Times*, August 23, 2009; available at: http://www.washingtontimes.com/

news/2009/aug/23/inspectors-need-independence/?feat=article_
related_stories [accessed June 30, 2010].

36. Byron York, "Walpin defeat means president can fire IGs at will,"
The Washington Examiner, June 19, 2010; available at: http://www.
washingtonexaminer.com/opinion/blogs/beltway-confidential/
walpin-defeat-means-president-can-fire-igs-at-will-96714994.html
[accessed June 30, 2010].

Chapter 12

1. Hibah Yousuf, "Economists: The stimulus didn't help," CNN-
Money.com, April 26, 2010; available at: http://money.cnn.com/
2010/04/26/news/economy/NABE_survey/ [accessed July 2, 2010].

2. Ricardo Alonso-Zaldivar, "Report Says Health Care Will Cover
More, Cost More," *The Daily Caller*, April 22, 2010; available at:
http://dailycaller.com/2010/04/22/report-health-overhaul-will-
increase-nations-tab/ [accessed July 2, 2010].

3. Steven Erlanger, Katrin Bennhold and David E. Sanger, "Debt Aid
Package for Europe Took Nudge from Washington," *The New York
Times*, May 10, 2010; available at: http://www.nytimes.com/2010/
05/11/business/global/11reconstruct.html [accessed July 2, 2010].

4. Howard Schneider and Scott Wilson, "President Obama Urges G-20
Nations to Spend; They Pledge to Halve Deficits," *The Washington
Post*, June 28, 2010; available at: http://www.washingtonpost.com/
wp-dyn/content/article/2010/06/27/AR2010062701754.html
[accessed July 2, 2010].

5. Elisabeth Meinecke, "Gingrich Calls Greece Bailout 'Absurd,'"
Human Events, May 23, 2010; video available at: http://www.
humanevents.com/article.php?id=37086 [accessed July 2, 2010].

6. David Goldman, "Stimulus is Now $75 Billion More Expensive,"
CNNMoney.com, January 26, 2010; available at: http://money.cnn.
com/2010/01/26/news/economy/stimulus_cbo/index.htm [accessed
July 2, 2010].

7. "What GOP Leaders Deem Wasteful in Senate Stimulus Bill,"
CNNPolitics.com, February 4, 2009; available at: http://www.cnn.
com/2009/POLITICS/02/02/gop.stimulus.worries/index.html
[accessed July 2, 2010].

8. Stephen W. Smith, "Biden Vows To 'Follow The Money,'" *CBS News*, Political Hotsheet, February 25, 2009; available at: http://www.cbsnews.com/8301-503544_162-4827236-503544.html [accessed July 2, 2010].

9. Barbara Hollingsworth, "Phantom zip codes also found in Virginia," *The Washington Examiner*, January 6, 2010; available at: http://www.washingtonexaminer.com/opinion/blogs/beltway-confidential/Phantom-zip-codes-also-found-in-Virginia-80795072.html [accessed July 2, 2010].

10. Barbara Hollingsworth, "Stimulus Watch: Now it's fake zip codes," *The Washington Examiner*, January 4, 2010; available at: http://www.washingtonexaminer.com/opinion/blogs/beltway-confidential/Now-its-fake-zip-codes-80627972.html [accessed July 2, 2010].

11. Jeremy Redmon and John Perry, "For-profit Colleges Reap Big Benefit from Stimulus," *Atlanta Journal-Constitution*, June 6, 2010; available at: http://www.ajc.com/news/for-profit-colleges-reap-541761.html [accessed July 2, 2010].

12. Veronique de Rugy, "Did the Stimulus Create Jobs?" Reason.com, December 11, 2009; available at: http://reason.com/archives/2009/12/11/did-the-stimulus-create-jobs [accessed July 2, 2010].

13. Carl Hulse, "Job Bill Passes in Senate With 11 Republican Votes," *The New York Times*, March 17, 2010; available at: http://www.nytimes.com/2010/03/18/us/politics/18cong.html [accessed July 2, 2010].

14. "Why Obama's Stimulus Failed," The Heritage Foundation's *Morning Bell*, June 7, 2010; available at: http://blog.heritage.org/2010/06/07/morning-bell-why-obamas-stimulus-failed/ [accessed July 2, 2010].

15. David M. Dickson, "CBO Report: Debt Will Rise to 90% of GDP," *The Washington Times*, March 26, 2010; available at: http://www.washingtontimes.com/news/2010/mar/26/cbos-2020-vision-debt-will-rise-to-90-of-gdp/ [accessed July 2, 2010].

16. Ibid.

17. Steve McCann, "America's Growing Vulnerability to Catastrophe," *American Thinker*, May 3, 2010; available at: http://www.americanthinker.com/2010/05/americas_growing_vulnerability_1.html [accessed July 2, 2010].

18. Brian Riedl, "Obama Budget Raises Taxes and Doubles the National Debt," The Heritage Foundation, March 9, 2010; available at: http://www.heritage.org/Research/Reports/2010/03/Obama-Budget-Raises-Taxes-and-Doubles-the-National-Debt [accessed July 2, 2010].

19. Conn Carroll, "Budget 2011: Past Deficits vs. Obama's Deficits in Pictures," The Heritage Foundation, February 5, 2010; available at: http://blog.heritage.org/2010/02/05/past-deficits-vs-obamas-deficits-in-pictures/ [accessed July 2, 2010].

20. Brian Riedl, "The Obama Budget: Spending, Taxes, and Doubling the National Debt," The Heritage Foundation, March 16, 2009; available at: http://www.heritage.org/Research/Reports/2009/03/The-Obama-Budget-Spending-Taxes-and-Doubling-the-National-Debt [accessed July 2, 2010].

21. Dick Morris, "Behind Obama's Phony Deficit Numbers," DickMorris.com, February 1, 2010; available at: http://www.dickmorris.com/blog/2010/02/01/behind-obamas-phony-deficit-numbers/ [accessed July 2, 2010].

22. Martin Crutsinger, "Federal Budget Deficit Hits April Record," Townhall.com, May 12, 2010; available at: http://townhall.com/news/business/2010/05/12/federal_budget_deficit_hits_april_record [accessed July 2, 2010].

23. Steve McCann, "America's Growing Vulnerability to Catastrophe," *op cit.*

24. Ibid.

25. "Obama Budget Projects $1.56T Deficit," CBSNews.com, February 1, 2010; available at: http://www.cbsnews.com/stories/2010/02/01/politics/main6162494.shtml [accessed July 2, 2010].

26. Ibid.

27. "Ryan to Geithner: Why Propose a Budget You Admit Is Not Credible, Not Sustainable?" State News Service, February 3, 2010.

28. Brian Riedl, "Obama's Faith-Based Economics," *The Foundry*, February 18, 2010; available at: http://blog.heritage.org/?p=26669 [accessed July 2, 2010].

29. Brian Riedl, "Obama Budget Raises Taxes and Doubles the National Debt," *op. cit.*

30. Ibid.

31. Curtis Dubay, "Small Businesses Face Steep Tax Hikes Unless Congress Acts Soon," The Heritage Foundation, May 6, 2010; available at: http://www.heritage.org/Research/Testimony/Small-Businesses-Face-Steep-Tax-Hikes-Unless-Congress-Acts-Soon [accessed July 2, 2010].

32. Justin Fishel, "Obama Announces $75 Billion Foreclosure Prevention Plan," FoxNews.com, February 18, 2009; available at: http://www.foxnews.com/politics/2009/02/18/obama-announces-billion-foreclosure-prevention-plan/ [accessed July 2, 2010].

33. Peter S. Goodman, "U.S. Loan Effort Is Seen as Adding to Housing Woes," *The New York Times*, January 1, 2010; available at: http://community.nytimes.com/comments/www.nytimes.com/2010/01/02/business/economy/02modify.html?src=tp [accessed July 2, 2010].

34. Ibid.

35. Alan Zibel, "Borrowers Exit Troubled Obama Mortgage Program," Townhall.com, June 21, 2010; available at: http://townhall.com/news/business/2010/06/21/borrowers_exit_troubled_obama_mortgage_program [accessed July 2, 2010].

36. Les Christie, "75% of modified home loans will redefault," CNNMoney.com, June 16, 2010; available at: http://money.cnn.com/2010/06/16/real_estate/failing_HAMP_mods/index.htm [accessed July 2, 2010].

37. Ben Lieberman, "The Waxman-Markey Global Warming Bill: Is the Economic Pain Justified by the Environmental Gain?" The Heritage Foundation, June 2, 2009; available at: http://www.heritage.org/Research/Testimony/The-Waxman-Markey-Global-Warming-Bill-Is-the-Economic-Pain-Justified-by-the-Environmental-Gain [accessed July 2, 2010].

38. Ben Lieberman, "A Clean Energy Economy Is A Weak Economy," The Heritage Foundation, April 16, 2010; available at: http://www.heritage.org/Research/Commentary/2010/04/In-Green-Spain-Unemployment-Nearly-Twice-Our-Woeful-10-Percent-Rate [accessed July 2, 2010].

39. "Cap and Trade Was Never About the Climate," The Foundry, March 6, 2009; available at: http://blog.heritage.org/2009/03/06/cap-and-trade-was-never-about-climate/ [accessed July 2, 2010].

40. Ben Lieberman, "The Waxman-Markey Global Warming Bill: Is the Economic Pain Justified by the Environmental Gain?" *op. cit.*

41. Chip Knappenberger, "The American Power Act: A Climate Dud," MasterResource Blog, May 12, 2010; available at: http://www.masterresource.org/2010/05/the-american-power-act-a-climate-dud/ [accessed July 2, 2010].

42. Patrick J. Michaels, "Kerry and Lieberman Unveil Their Climate Bill: Such a Deal!" *Cato @ Liberty*, May 12, 2010; available at: http://www.cato-at-liberty.org/2010/05/12/kerry-and-lieberman-unveil-their-climate-bill-such-a-deal/ [accessed July 2, 2010].

43. "Obamacare's True Costs Coming to Light," Heritage Foundation's *Morning Bell*, June 2, 2010; available at: http://blog.heritage.org/2010/06/02/morning-bell-obamacares-true-costs-coming-to-light/ [accessed July 2, 2010].

44. Julie Crawshaw, "Study: Obamacare Fails to Pay for High Risk Pools," MoneyNews.com, June 3, 2010; available at: http://www.moneynews.com/StreetTalk/Obamacare-Pay-High-Risk/2010/06/03/id/360969 [accessed July 2, 2010].

45. Connie Hair, "Medicare Report: Obamacare Bad for Seniors," *Human Events*, April 27, 2010; available at: http://www.human-events.com/article.php?id=36680 [accessed July 2, 2010].

46. Robert B. Bluey, "The Inconvenient Number Cruncher," *Politico*, April 30, 2010; available at: http://www.politico.com/news/stories/0410/36614.html [accessed July 2, 2010].

47. Paul Howard, "Obamacare's Hidden Costs – Democrats Have Unleashed a Tidal Wave of Unintended Consequences," *City Journal*, May 13, 2010; available at: http://www.city-journal.org/2010/eon0513ph.html [accessed July 2, 2010].

48. Editorial, "ObamaCare Mulligan," *The Wall Street Journal*, April 26, 2010; available at: http://online.wsj.com/article/SB10001424052748704133804575198322718759844.html [accessed July 2, 2010].

49. The Prowler, "What Lies Beneath," *The American Spectator*, April 26, 2010; available at: http://spectator.org/archives/2010/04/26/what-lies-beneath [accessed July 2, 2010].

50. Editorial, "One Million Votes Against Obamacare," *The Washington Times*, May 12, 2010; available at: http://www.washington-

times.com/news/2010/may/12/one-million-votes-against-obamacare/ [accessed July 2, 2010].

51. Ricardo Alonso-Zaldivar, "Small Business Lobby to Go to Court on Health Law," Townhall.com, May 14, 2010; available at: http://dailycaller.com/2010/05/13/small-business-lobby-joins-challenge-to-health-law/ [accessed July 2, 2010]. See also, "State Attorneys General Sue Over Health Bill," msnbc.com, March 23, 2010; available at: http://www.msnbc.msn.com/id/36001783/ns/politics-health_care_reform/ [accessed July 2, 2010].

52. Michael D. Tanner, "The Mythology of Health Care Reform," Cato Institute, March 3, 2006; available at: http://www.cato.org/pub_display.php?pub_id=5871 [accessed July 2, 2010].

53. Michael D. Tanner, "Who Are the Uninsured?" The Cato Institute, August 20, 2009; available at: http://www.cato.org/pub_display.php?pub_id=10449 [accessed July 2, 2010].

54. Sally C. Pipes, "Understanding all the facts about the uninsured," *The Washington Examiner*, October 25, 2009; available at: http://www.washingtonexaminer.com/opinion/columns/Sunday_Reflections/Understanding-all-the-facts-about-the-uninsured-8430034-65806797.html [accessed July 2, 2010].

55. Sally Pipes, *The Top Ten Myths of American Health Care: A Citizen's Guide* (San Francisco, CA: Pacific Research Institute, 2008), 39.

56. David Freddoso, "Taking the red pill, Mr. President," *The Washington Examiner*, July 23, 2009; available at: http://www.washingtonexaminer.com/opinion/blogs/beltway-confidential/Take-the-red-pill-Mr-President-51473502.html [accessed July 2, 2010].

57. Barack Obama, "Obama's 17-Minute, 12-second Answer on Taxes and Health Care," *USA Today*, April 4, 2010; available at: http://content.usatoday.com/communities/theoval/post/2010/04/obamas-17-minute-12-second-answer-on-taxes/1 [accessed July 2, 2010].

58. Scott Gottlieb, "What Doctors and Patients Have to Lose Under Obamacare," *The Wall Street Journal*, December 23, 2009; available at: http://online.wsj.com/article/SB10001424052748704254604574613992408387548.html [accessed July 2, 2010].

59. Ben Domenech, "Obama Nominee Donald Berwick's Radical Agenda," RedState.com, May 12. 2010; available at: http://www.

redstate.com/ben_domenech/2010/05/12/obama-nominee-donald-berwick%E2%80%99s-radical-agenda/ [accessed July 2, 2010].

60. Robert M. Goldberg, "The Fix Is In," *The American Spectator*, April 26, 2010; available at: http://spectator.org/archives/2010/04/26/the-fix-is-in [accessed July 2, 2010].

61. Joseph Ashby, "'Death Panel,' is Not in the Bill . . . it already exists," *The American Thinker*, August 15, 2009; available at: http://www.americanthinker.com/2009/08/death_panel_is_not_in_the_bill.html [accessed July 2, 2010].

62. Michael D. Tanner, "The Mythology of Health Care Reform," *op. cit.*

63. Matt Patterson, "Obamacare Would Drive Doctors Out of Business," The National Center for Policy Analysis, March 2010; available at: http://www.nationalcenter.org/NPA606.html [accessed July 2, 2010].

64. Betsy McCaughey, "Ruin Your Health With the Obama Stimulus Plan," Bloomberg, February 9, 2009; available at: http://www.bloomberg.com/apps/news?pid=newsarchive&sid=aLzfDxfbwhzs [accessed July 2, 2010].

65. Joseph Ashby, "'Death Panel' is Not in the Bill . . . It Already Exists," *op. cit.*

Chapter 13

1. "Obama: America a Superpower 'Whether We Like It or Not,'" FOX News, April 15, 2010; available at: http://www.foxnews.com/politics/2010/04/15/obama-america-superpower-like/ [accessed July 6, 2010].

2. "Brian Ross and Rehab El-Buri, "Obama's Pastor: God Damn America, U.S. to Blame for 9/11," *ABC News*, March 13, 2008; available at: http://abcnews.go.com/Blotter/DemocraticDebate/story?id=4443788&page=1 [accessed July 6, 2010].

3. Mark Finkelstein, "Obama's Spiritual Guide: 'God Damn America,'" NewsBusters.org, March 13, 2008; available at: http://newsbusters.org/blogs/mark-finkelstein/2008/03/13/could-mccain-be-candidate-pastor-obamas-god-damn-america-wright [accessed July 6, 2010].

4. Ronald Kessler, "Barack Obama's Racist Church," Newsmax.com, January 7, 2008; available at: http://www.newsmax.com/Ronald-Kessler/Obama-Church-Racism/2008/01/07/id/322582 [accessed July 6, 2010].

5. Ed Lasky, "Barack Obama and Israel, " *American Thinker*, January 16, 2008; available at: http://www.americanthinker.com/2008/01/barack_obama_and_israel.html [accessed July 6, 2010].

6. David Squires, "Rev. Jeremiah Wright Discusses President Obama and Jews," *Hampton Roads Daily Press*, June 10, 2009; available at: http://www.dailypress.com/news/dp-local_wright_0610jun10,0,7603283.story [accessed July 6, 2010].

7. Tim Graham, "ABC: Obama's Race Speech Doesn't Match Year of Wright Spin," Newsbusters.org, March 20, 2008; available at: http://newsbusters.org/blogs/tim-graham/2008/03/20/abc-obamas-race-speech-doesnt-match-year-wright-spin [accessed July 6, 2010].

8. Jodi Kantor, "Disinvitation by Obama is Criticized," *The New York Times*, March 6, 2007; available at: http://www.nytimes.com/2007/03/06/us/politics/06obama.html [accessed July 6, 2010].

9. Jake Tapper, "Just What Did Obama Know about Wright's Past Sermons?" *ABC News*, March 15, 2008; available at: http://blogs.abcnews.com/politicalpunch/2008/03/just-what-did-o.html [accessed July 6, 2010].

10. Michael D. Shear, "At West Point, Obama Talks Up Security Strategy," *Washington Post*, May 23, 2010; available at: http://www.washingtonpost.com/wp-dyn/content/article/2010/05/22/AR2010052201586.html [accessed July 6, 2010].

11. "Obama Call for 'International Order' Raises Questions About U.S. Sovereignty," FOX News, May 24, 2010; available at: http://www.foxnews.com/politics/2010/05/24/obama-international-order-raises-questions-sovereignty/ [accessed July 6, 2010].

12. "On World Stage, Obama Uses Podium to Express Regret," FOX News, May 12, 2009; available at: http://www.foxnews.com/politics/2009/05/12/world-stage-obama-uses-podium-express-regret/ [accessed July 6, 2010].

13. Karl Rove, "The President's Apology Tour," *The Wall Street Journal*, April 23, 2009; available at: http://online.wsj.com/article/SB124044156269345357.html [accessed July 6, 2010].

14. Jake Tapper, "US Cites AZ Immigration Law During Human Rights Talks with China, Conservatives Call It An Apology," *ABC News*, May 17, 2010; available at: http://blogs.abcnews.com/politicalpunch/2010/05/arizona-immigration-law-human-rights-china-conservatives-apology.html [accessed July 6, 2010].

15. 2009 Report on Mexico, Amnesty International, http://www.amnesty.org/en/region/mexico/report-2009 [accessed July 6, 2010].

16. Jared E. Peterson, "Is This Just a Nightmare, or Did It Really Happen?" *American Thinker*, May 24, 2010; available at: http://www.americanthinker.com/2010/05/is_this_just_a_nightmare_or_di.html [accessed July 6, 2010].

17. "NIE Report: Iran Halted Nuclear Weapons Program Years Ago," *ABC News*, December 3, 2007; available at: http://blogs.abcnews.com/politicalradar/2007/12/nie-report-iran.html [accessed July 6, 2010].

18. David E. Sanger, "Iran Deal Would Slow Making of Nuclear Bombs," *The New York Times*, October 21, 2009; available at: http://www.nytimes.com/2009/10/22/world/middleeast/22nuke.html?_r=1&adxnnl=1&adxnnlx=1278424844-ovMChEMk+/Y2Zpau77V3vw [accessed July 6, 2010].

19. Editors, "Diplomatic Rubes," *Investors Business Daily*, October 30, 2009.

20. Gregg Easterbrook, "What Will Iran Do with Nuclear Weapons?" Reuters, April 22, 2010; available at: http://blogs.reuters.com/gregg-easterbrook/2010/04/22/what-will-iran-do-with-nuclear-weapons-probably-nothing/ [accessed July 6, 2010].

21. "Clinton Warns Iran, N. Korea About Nuclear Ambitions," *CBC News*, July 22, 2009; available at: http://www.cbc.ca/world/story/2009/07/22/clinton-iran-north-korea.html [accessed July 6, 2010].

22. Ross Calvin, "Obama Says He Wants Progress with Iran by Year's End," Reuters, May 18, 2009; available at: http://www.reuters.com/article/idUSTRE54H4QX20090518 [accessed July 6, 2010].

23. Hossein Jaseb, "Iran's Ahmadinejad Dismisses West's Year-end Deadline," Reuters, December 22, 2009; available at: http://www.reuters.com/article/idUSTRE5BL0J420091222 [accessed July 6, 2010].

24. Jonathan Tobin, "Obama's Iran Deadline Gets Thrown Down the Memory Hole," *Commentary Magazine,* Contentions Blog, January 8, 2010; available at: http://www.commentarymagazine.com/blogs/index.php/tobin/213746 [accessed July 6, 2010].

25. "Iran Accepts Clinton Non-deadline on Nuke Talks," *China Daily*, January 5, 2010; available at: http://www.chinadaily.com.cn/world/2010-01/05/content_9269641.htm [accessed July 6, 2010].

26. Massimo Calabresi , "To Obama's Piles of Woes, Add a Failing Iran Policy," *Time.com*, January 25 2010; available at: http://www.time.com/time/world/article10,8599,1956075,00.htm [accessed July 7, 2010].

27. Charles Krauthammer, "Iran's Revolution, Obama's Shame: The President has hung the democratic movement out to dry," *New York Daily News*, December 25, 2009; available at: http://www.nydailynews.com/opinions/2009/12/25/2009-12-25_irans_revolution_obamas_shame.html [accessed July 6, 2010].

28. "Iran's 'New Deal' on its Nuclear Stockpile: A Real Turkey," The Heritage Foundation, *The Foundry*, May 17, 2010; available at: http://blog.heritage.org/2010/05/17/iran%E2%80%99s-new-deal-on-its-nuclear-stockpile-a-real-turkey/ [accessed July 6, 2010].

29. Editorial, "Obama's Diplomatic Flop," *The Washington Times*, June 10, 2010; available at: http://www.washingtontimes.com/news/2010/jun/10/obamas-diplomatic-flop/ [accessed July 6, 2010].

30. Fouad Ajami, "The Arabs Have Stopped Applauding Obama," *The Wall Street Journal*, November 29, 2009; available at: http://online.wsj.com/article/SB10001424052748703499404574558300500152682.html [accessed July 6, 2010].

31. Miret el Naggar and Margaret Talev, "Muslim Praise for Obama Dries Up a Year After Cairo Speech," *McClatchy Newspapers*, June 3, 2010; available at: http://www.mcclatchydc.com/2010/06/03/95317/muslim-praise-for-obama-dries.html [accessed July 6, 2010].

32. Fouad Ajami, "The Arabs Have Stopped Applauding Obama,"*op. cit.*

33. Ben Feller, Associated Press, "Obama Defends Venezuela Position At America's Summit," *Huffington Post*, April 19, 2009; available at: http://www.huffingtonpost.com/2009/04/19/obama-defends-venezuela-p_n_188730.html [accessed July 6, 2010].

34. Jake Tapper, "Chavez Gifts Obama With Book That Assails U.S. for Exploiting Latin America," *ABC News*, Political Punch, April 18, 2009; available at: http://blogs.abcnews.com/politicalpunch/2009/04/chavez-gifts-ob.html [accessed July 6, 2010].

35. "Obama Endures Ortega Diatribe," FOX News, April 18, 2009; available at: http://www.foxnews.com/politics/2009/04/18/obama-endures-ortega-diatribe/ [accessed July 6, 2010].

36. Helen Murphy and Joshua Goodman, "Obama Gets History Lesson from Latin American Leaders," Bloomberg, April 18, 2009; available at: http://www.bloomberg.com/apps/news?pid=newsarchive&sid=aun_fNO0161g [accessed July 6, 2010].

37. "Chavez Predicts Failure in Copenhagen Summit and Criticizes Obama," Reuters, December 18, 2009.

38. "Biden Questions Vote but Sticks to Policy on Iran," *New York Times*, June 14, 2009; available at: http://www.nytimes.com/2009/06/15/world/middleeast/15diplo.html [accessed July 6, 2010].

39. Mark Memmott, "McCain: Obama Needs To Condemn 'Sham, Corrupt Election' In Iran," NPR.org, June 16, 2009; available at: http://www.npr.org/blogs/thetwo-way/2009/06/mccain_us_needs_to_condemn_sha.html [accessed July 6, 2010].

40. Nile Gardiner, "The Iranian Election: Barack Obama's Cowardly Silence," *The Telegraph*, June 15, 2009; available at: http://blogs.telegraph.co.uk/news/nilegardiner/10063438/the_iranian_election_barack_obamaas_cowardly_silence/ [accessed July 6, 2010].

41. Thomas Erdbrink and William Branigin, "Iran's Khamenei rejects U.S. outreach," *The Washington Post*, November 4, 2009; available at: http://www.washingtonpost.com/wp-dyn/content/article/2009/11/03/AR2009110301397.html [accessed July 6, 2010].

42. "Honduras Votes Against Manuel Zelaya Reinstatemen," *Times Online*, December 3, 2009; available at: http://www.timesonline.co.uk/tol/news/world/us_and_americas/article6942029.ece [accessed July 6, 2010].

43. "Honduras ex-leader Manuel Zelaya Begins Exile," BBC , January 28, 2010; available at: http://news.bbc.co.uk/2/hi/8484181.stm [accessed July 6, 2010].

44. David Saltonstall, "London aghast at President Obama over gifts given to Prime Minister Brown," *New York Daily News*, March 7,

2009; available at: http://www.nydailynews.com/news/politics/2009/03/06/2009-03-06_london_aghast_at_president_obama_over_gi.html [accessed July 6, 2010].

45. Tim Shipman, "Barack Obama 'too tired' to Give Proper Welcome to Gordon Brown," *The Sunday Telegraph*, March 7, 2009; available at: http://www.telegraph.co.uk/news/worldnews/northamerica/usa/barackobama/4953523/Barack-Obama-too-tired-to-give-proper-welcome-to-Gordon-Brown.html [accessed July 6, 2010].

46. Patrick Wintour, "Barack Obama Snubs Gordon Brown Over Private Talks," *The Guardian*, September 24, 2009; available at: http://www.guardian.co.uk/politics/2009/sep/23/barack-obama-gordon-brown-talks [accessed July 6, 2010].

47. Nile Gardiner, "Does Obama Have it in for Britain?" *Daily Mail*, December 9, 2009; available at: http://www.dailymail.co.uk/debate/article-1234291/NILE-GARDINER-Does-Obama-Britain.html [accessed July 6, 2010].

48. Jennifer Carlile, "Brits Blame Obama as BP-linked Pensions Plummet," MSNBC, June 10, 2010; available at: http://worldblog.msnbc.msn.com/_news/2010/06/10/4490597-brits-blame-obama-as-bp-linked-pensions-plummet [accessed July 6, 2010].

49. Alex Singleton, "On Foreign Relations," *The London Daily Telegraph*, April 11, 2010.

50. Charles Bremner, "Barack and Michelle Obama Decline Dinner with the Sarkozys," *Times Online*, June 5, 2009; available at: http://www.timesonline.co.uk/tol/news/world/europe/article6434141.ece [accessed July 6, 2010].

51. Bruce Crumley, "Sarkozy's Comments On Leaders Draw Shock, Denial," *Time*, April 18, 2009; available at: http://time.com/time/world/article/o,1892375,00.html.

52. Charles Bremner, "Barack and Michelle Obama Decline Dinner with the Sarkozys," *op. cit.*

53. D.K. Jamaal, "Ouch! French President Sarkozy slams 'naïve' Obama for living in 'virtual world' on Iran," *San Francisco Examiner*, September 26, 2009; available at: http://www.examiner.com/x-19823-PostPartisan-Examiner~y2009m9d26-OUCH-French-Pres-Sarkozy-slams-naive-Obama-for-living-in-virtual-world-on-Iran [accesed July 6, 2010].

54. Ibid.

55. Jake Tapper, "Sources Say Sarkozy Finds Obama's Iran Policy 'Arrogant,' Utterly Immature,'" ABC News Political Punch, October 28, 2008; available at: http://blogs.abcnews.com/politicalpunch/2008/10/sources-say-sar.html [accessed July 6, 2010].

56. "Avertible Catastrophe," *Financial Post*, June 26, 2010; available at: http://www.financialpost.com/Avertible + catastrophe/3203808/story.html [accessed July 6, 2010].

57. Swapan Dasgupta, "Arrogant Obama Alienates Friends," *The New Delhi Daily Pioneer*, April 11, 2010; available at: http://www.daily-pioneer.com/248392/Arrogant-Obama-alienates-friends.html [accessed July 6, 2010].

Chapter 14

1. See the dossier on Khalidi at http://www.discoverthenetworks.org/individualProfile.asp?indid=1347 [accessed July 6, 2010].

2. P. J. Gladnick, "LA Times Publishes Excuses for Not Releasing Khalid Video," Newsbusters.org, October 31, 2008; available at: http://newsbusters.org/blogs/p-j-gladnick/2008/10/31/la-times-publishes-excuses-not-releasing-khalidi-video [accessed July 6, 2010].

3. Peter Wallsten, "Allies of Palestinians See a Friend in Obama," *Los Angeles Times*, April 10, 2008; available at: http://articles.latimes.com/2008/apr/10/nation/na-obamamideast10 [accessed July 6, 2010].

4. Aaron Klein, "Obama Church Published Hamas Terror Manifesto," *WorldNetDaily*, March 20, 2008; available at: http://www.wnd.com/?pageId=59456 [accessed July 6, 2010].

5. Steve Gilbert, "Obama Church Did Pro-Hezbollah Article," Sweetness & Light Blog, May 11, 2008; available at: http://sweetness-light.com/archive/obamas-church-published-pro-hezbollah-articles [accessed July 6, 2010].

6. Ed Laski, "Barack Obama and Israel," *American Thinker*, January 16, 2008.

7. Noel Sheppard, "Will Media Report Anti-Semitic Article at Obama's Website?" *NewsBusters*, June 8, 2008; available at: http://

newsbusters.org/blogs/noel-sheppard/2008/06/08/will-media-report-anti-semitic-article-obamas-website [accessed July 6, 2010].

8. See: Organizing for America, http://my.barackobama.com/page/community/search?q=jewish + lobby [accessed July 6, 2010].

9. Jeff Dunetz, "National Security Adviser Jones: Jews Are Greedy Merchants," RedState.com, April 26, 2010; available at: http://www.redstate.com/jeffdunetz/2010/04/26/national-security-adviser-jones-jews-are-greedy-merchants/ [accessed July 6, 2010].

10. "Obama Authorizes $20 Million in Aid to Gaza Palestinians," Voice of America, January 30, 2009; available at: http://www1.voanews.com/english/news/a-13-2009-01-30-voa17-68810337.html [accessed July 6, 2010].

11. Aaron Klein, "Obama 'Guarantees' West Bank Withdrawal," WorldNetDaily.com, February 2, 2009; available at: http://www.wnd.com/index.php/news/index.php/index.php?fa=PAGE.printable&pageId=87860 [accessed July 6, 2010].

12. Tzvi Ben Gedalyahu, "US Ducks Bush Support for Jewish Cities in Yesha," *Israel International News*, June 3, 2009; available at: http://www.israelnationalnews.com/News/News.aspx/131687 [accessed July 6, 2010].

13. "U.S. to pledge $900 million for Gaza rebuild," MSNBC.com, February 23, 2009; available at: http://world-news.newsvine.com/_news/2009/02/23/2468615-us-to-pledge-900-million-for-gaza-rebuild [accessed July 6, 2010].

14. James Phillips, "The Gaza Aid Package: Time to Rethink U.S. Foreign Assistance to the Palestinians," The Heritage Foundation, March 9, 2009.

15. Marcia Kramer, "Jewish Leaders Blast Clinton Over Israel Criticism," WCBSTV.com, February 27, 2009; available at: http://wcbstv.com/national/hillary.clinton.israel.2.945238.html [accessed July 6, 2010].

16. "United States rejoins U.N. rights council," *USA Today*, March 4, 2009; available at: http://www.usatoday.com/news/world/2009-03-04-rights-council_N.htm [accessed July 6, 2010].

17. Jason Koutsoukis, "Obama's Stance Worries Israelis," *The Age*, April 18, 2009; available at: http://www.theage.com.au/world/oba-

mas-stance-worries-israelis-20090417-aa90.html [accessed July 6, 2010].

18. Karin Laub, "Obama Envoy: Two-State Solution is Only Solution," Associated Press, April 17, 2009.

19. Aaron Klein, "Obama will 'Quickly" Give Palestinians State," *WorldNetDaily*, April 17, 2009; available at: http://www.wnd.com/index.php?fa=PAGE.printable&pageId=95231 [accessed July 6, 2010].

20. Akiva Eldar, "U.S.: Palestinians need not recognize Israel as Jewish state before talks," Haaretz.com, April 19, 2009; available at: http://www.haaretz.com/print-edition/news/u-s-palestinians-need-not-recognize-israel-as-jewish-state-before-talks-1.274334 [accessed July 6, 2010].

21. Tzvi Ben Gedalyahu, "U.S.: Syria and Israel Must Talk; Syrian FM Praises Ahmadinejad," *Arutz Sheva*, April 25, 2009; available at: http://www.israelnationalnews.com/News/News.aspx/131026 [accessed July 6, 2010].

22. "White House Links Iran Nukes to Palestinian State," *Israel Today*, May 4. 2009; available at: http://www.israeltoday.co.il/default.aspx?tabid=178&nid=18709 [accessed July 6, 2010].

23. Eli Lake, "Exclusive: Secret U.S. – Israel Nuclear Accord in Jeopardy," *The Washington Times*, May 6, 2009; available at: http://www.washingtontimes.com/news/2009/may/06/us-weighs-forcing-israel-to-disclose-nukes/ [accessed July 6, 2010].

24. Louis Charbonneau, "U.S. and other big powers back Mideast nuclear arms ban," Reuters, May 5, 2010; available at: http://www.reuters.com/article/idUSTRE6443YG20100505 [accessed July 6, 2010].

25. Caroline Glick, "Obama's Green Light to Attack Iran," *The Jerusalem Post*, May 8, 2009; available at: http://www.jpost.com/Home/Article.aspx?id=141612 [accessed July 6, 2010].

26. Joel C. Rosenberg, "Netanyahu Stood His Ground with Obama," *Worldview Times*, March 29, 2010; available at: http://www.worldviewweekend.com/worldview-times/article.php?articleid=5972 [accessed July 6, 2010].

27. "Netanyahu Says All Jerusalem to Remain Israeli," MSNBC.com, May 21, 2009; available at: http://www.msnbc.msn.com/id/ 30871494/ [accessed July 6, 2010].

28. Aluf Benn and Natasha Mozgovaya, "Obama Warns Netanyahu: Don't Surprise Me with Iran Strike," Haaretz.com, May 14, 2009; available at: http://www.haaretz.com/print-edition/news/obama-warns-netanyahu-don-t-surprise-me-with-iran-strike-1.275993 [accessed July 6, 2010].

29. Mark Landler and Isabel Kershner, "Israeli Settlement Growth Must Stop, Clinton Says," *The New York Times*, May 27, 2009; available at: http://www.nytimes.com/2009/05/28/world/middleeast/ 28mideast.html [accessed July 6, 2010].

30. "Obama Draws Line on Israeli Settlements," Breitbart, May 27, 2009; available at: http://www.breitbart.com/article.php?id=CNG. a1d6d72707e6c8c00552b56fb85c5f61.101&show_article=1& catnum=3 [accessed July 6, 2010].

31. Aaron Klein, "Official: Obama Admin Sees Jerusalem Divided," *WorldNetDaily*, May 24, 2009; available at: http://www.wnd.com/ ?pageId=99106 [accessed July 6, 2010]. See also: Natasha Mozgovaya, Barak Ravid, and Nadav Shragai, "U.S. Congressmen Doubt Netanyahu Can Advance Peace Process," Haaretz.com, May 25, 2009; available at: http://www.haaretz.com/print-edition/news/u-s-congressmen-doubt-netanyahu-can-advance-peace-process-1.266812 [accessed July 6, 2010].

32. Aaron Klein, "Obama Promises Arabs Jerusalem will be theirs," *WorldNetDaily*, May 30, 2009; available at: http://www.wnd.com/ ?pageId=99664 [accessed July 6, 2010].

33. Avi Yellin, "Is the US Eroding Israel's Qualitative Edge?" *Israel National News*, March 24, 2010; available at: http://www.israelnationalnews.com/News/news.aspx/136660 [accessed July 6, 2010].

34. Kathryn Jean Lopez, "Caroline Glick on Netanyahu & the World," *National Review Online*, June 15, 2009; available at: http://corner.nationalreview.com/post/?q=YTgyNzVjMzQ5NGM0NzE2ZDQ 2Zjg0OTYxYWQyMzU5NWU= [accessed July 6, 2010].

35. Patrick Goodenough, "'Jerusalem Is Not a Settlement,' Netanyahu Reminds Obama Administration," CNSNews.com, July 20, 2009;

available at: http://www.cnsnews.com/news/article/51247 [accessed July 6, 2010].

36. Janine Zacharia, "U.S. Condemns Israel's Plans to Build Housing in East Jerusalem," *The Washington Post*, March 10, 2010; available at: http://www.washingtonpost.com/wp-dyn/content/article/2010/03/09/AR2010030900497.html [accessed July 6, 2010].

37. Leo Rennert, "Biden Trip Reveals Ominous Side of Obama's Treatment of Israel," *American Thinker*, March 12, 2010; available at: http://www.americanthinker.com/2010/03/biden_trip_reveals_ominous_sid.html [accessed July 6, 2010].

38. Editorial, "Diplomacy 102," *The New York Times*, March 10, 2010; available at: http://www.nytimes.com/2010/03/11/opinion/11thu1.html [accessed July 6, 2010].

39. "Ties Between Israel and US 'Worst in 35 Years,'" BBC News, March 15, 2010; available at: http://news.bbc.co.uk/2/hi/8567706.stm [accessed July 6, 2010].

40. Caroline Glick, "Republicans, Democrats and Israel," CarolineGlick.com, April 30, 2010; available at: http://www.carolineglick.com/e/2010/04/republicans-democrats-and-isra.php [accessed July 6, 2010].

41. Editorial, "The Settlement Rift," *The Washington Post*, June 7 2009; available at: http://www.washingtonpost.com/wp-dyn/content/article/2009/06/06/AR2009060601796.html [accessed July 6, 2010].

42. Charles Krauthammer, "The Settlements Myth," *The Washington Post*, June 5, 2009; available at: http://www.washingtonpost.com/wp-dyn/content/article/2009/06/04/AR2009060403811.html [accessed July 6, 2010].

43. "AJC Urges U.S. Administration to Halt Public Denunciations of Israeli Government," Breitbart, March 15. 2010; available at: http://www.breitbart.com/article.php?id=xprnw.20100315.DC71033&show_article=1 [accessed July 6, 2010].

44. Ed Koch, "A Dangerous Silence," *Jewish World Review*, April 13, 2010; available at: http://www.jewishworldreview.com/0410/koch041310.php3?printer_friendly [accessed July 6, 2010].

45. Ed Koch, "Obama's Treatment of Israel is Shocking," *Real Clear Politics*, March 29, 2010; available at: http://www.realclearpolitics.

com/articles/2010/03/29/never_again_will_we_be_silent_104961.
html [accessed July 6, 2010].

46. Ben Smith, "Schumer: Obama's 'counter-productive' Israel policy
'has to stop,'" *Politico*, April 22, 2010; available at: http://www.
politico.com/blogs/bensmith/0410/Schumer_Obamas_Counterpro-
ductive_Israel_policy_has_to_stop.html [accessed July 6, 2010].

47. Gil Ronen, "Poll: Obama Has Lost Almost Half of his US Jewish
Support," *Arutz Sheva*, May 9, 2010; available at: http://www.
israelnationalnews.com/News/news.aspx/137449 [accessed July 6,
2010].

48. Caroline Glick, "Making Israel's Case," CarolineGlick.com, May
14, 2010; available at: http://www.carolineglick.com/e/2010/05/
making-israels-case.php [accessed July 6, 2010].

Chapter 15

1. Ralph Peters, "The smell of our fear," *New York Post* May 5, 2010;
available at: http://www.nypost.com/p/news/opinion/opedcolum-
nists/the_smell_of_our_fear_mYzCYnFsrWpPfJv2p8lcyN [accessed
July 6, 2010].

2. Victor Davis Hanson, "Yes, Words Do Matter!" *National Review
Online*, May 5, 2010; available at: http://corner.nationalreview.com/
post/?q=ZDc3NzgyODhiZmVjNTM0NDMyOWM4YmU1ODIwM
DdiNzg= [accessed July 6, 2010].

3. "Obama Nominee for Deputy Attorney General Says 9/11 Attacks
Not Acts of War, Likens Them to Domestic Crimes of Murder,
Rape," CSNnews.com, June 14, 2010; available at: http://www.
cnsnews.com/news/article/67704 [accessed July 6, 2010].

4. Mark Silverberg, "Paper Tiger," Ariel Center of Policy Research,
October 7, 2005; available at: http://www.jfednepa.org/
mark%20silverberg/papertiger.html [accessed July 6, 2010].

5. J. J. Green, "Bin Laden Had 'No Clue' about Sept. 11 Retaliation,"
WTOP.com, April 27, 2010; available at: http://www.wtop.com/
?nid=778&sid=1943289 [accessed July 6, 2010].

6. "Obama Signs Order to Close Guantanamo Bay Facility," CNN
Politics, January 22, 2010; available at: http://www.cnn.com/2009/
POLITICS/01/22/guantanamo.order/index.html [accessed July 6,
2010].

7. Scott Wilson and Al Kamen, "'Global War on Terror' Is Given New Name," *The Washington Post*, March 25, 2009; available at: http://www.washingtonpost.com/wp-dyn/content/article/2009/03/24/AR2009032402818.html [accessed July 6, 2010].

8. Del Quentin Wilber and Peter Finn, "U.S. Retires 'Enemy Combatant,' Keeps Broad Right to Detain," *The Washington Post*, March 14, 2009; available at: http://www.washingtonpost.com/wp-dyn/content/article/2009/03/13/AR2009031302371.html [accessed July 6, 2010].

9. Sean Hannity, "Terrorism' No Longer Exists for Secretary Napolitano?" FOX News, March 18, 2009; available at: http://www.foxnews.com/story/0,2933,509655,00.html [accessed July 6, 2010].

10. Editorial, "Stop Mirandizing," *The Washington Times*, June 12, 2009; available at: http://www.washingtontimes.com/news/2009/jun/12/stop-mirandizing-terrorists/ [accessed July 6, 2010].

11. Terrence P. Jeffrey, "CIA Confirms: Waterboarding 9/11 Mastermind Led to Info that Aborted 9/11-Style Attack on Los Angeles," CNSNews.com, April 21, 2009; available at: http://www.cnsnews.com/news/article/46949 [accessed July 6, 2010].

12. John Crewdsom, "Spilling Al Qaeda's Secrets," *Chicago Tribune*, December 28, 2005; available at: http://articles.chicagotribune.com/2005-12-28/news/0512280233_1_ksm-al-qaeda-waterboarding [accessed July 6, 2010].

13. Terrence P. Jeffrey, "CIA Confirms: Waterboarding 9/11 Mastermind Led to Info that Aborted 9/11-Style Attack on Los Angeles," *op. cit.*

14. Michael Hayden and Michael B. Mukasey, "The President Ties His Own Hands on Terror," *The Wall Street Journal*, April 17, 2009; available at: http://online.wsj.com/article/SB123993446103128041.html [accessed July 6, 2010].

15. "CIA Off the Hook for Past Waterboarding," CBSNews.com, April 16, 2009; available at: http://www.cbsnews.com/stories/2009/04/16/politics/100days/main4950212.shtml [accessed July 6, 2010].

16. "Obama: Holder Will Decide Whether To Prosecute Torture Authors, Support Bipartisan Truth Commission," Think Progress, April 21, 2009; available at: http://thinkprogress.org/2009/04/21/obama-holder-prosecutions/ [accessed July 6, 2010].

17. Steven Thomma and Marisa Taylor, "In Reversal, Obama Opens Door to Prosecuting Top Bush Aides" *McClatchy*, April 21, 2009; available at: http://www.mcclatchydc.com/2009/04/21/66596/in-reversal-obama-opens-door-to.html [accessed July 6, 2010].

18. Carrie Johnson, "Prosecutor to Probe CIA Interrogations," *The Washington Post*, August 25, 2009.

19. "Inside Story of Leon Panetta's Tirade over CIA Probe," FOXNews.com, August 27, 2009; available at: http://www.foxnews.com/politics/2009/08/24/special-prosecutor-probe-cia-interrogations/ [accessed July 6, 2010].

20. "Ex-CIA Chiefs Decry Holder Interrogator Probe in Letter to Obama," FOX News, September 18, 2009; available at: http://www.foxnews.com/politics/2009/09/18/ex-cia-chiefs-decry-holder-interrogator-probe-letter-obama/ [accessed July 6, 2010].

21. Bill Burck and Dana Perino, "Holder's Office of Professional Irresponsibility," *National Review Online*, March 5, 2010; available at: http://article.nationalreview.com/427021/holders-office-of-professional-irresponsibility/bill-burck-and-dana-perino [accessed July 6, 2010].

22. Andrew C. McCarthy, "Eric Holder's Hidden Agenda," *National Review Online*, August 28, 2009; available at: http://article.nationalreview.com/404522/eric-holders-hidden-agenda/andrew-c-mccarthy [accessed July 6, 2010].

23. Bill Burck and Dana Perino, "Holder's Office of Professional Irresponsibility," *op. cit.*

24. "Holder Blames Congress for Forcing Hand on Military Commissions for 9/11 Detainees," FoxNews.com, April 4, 2011; available at http://www.foxnews.com/politics/2011/04/04/khalid-sheikh-mohammad-military-commission-trial/.

25. Shailagh Murray, "Senate Demands Plan for Detainees," *The Washington Post*, May 20, 2009; available at: http://www.washingtonpost.com/wp-dyn/content/article/2009/05/19/AR2009051903615.html [accessed July 6, 2010].

26. "Illinois Prison Eyed for Gitmo Detainees," MSNBC.com, November 15, 2009; available at: http://www.msnbc.msn.com/id/33938067/ [accessed July 6, 2010].

27. "U.S. to Move Some Guantanamo Prisoners to Illinois," Reuters, December 15, 2009; available at: http://www.reuters.com/article/idUSTRE5BE0MV20091215 [accessed July 6, 2010].

28. Bill Edelblute, "61 freed Gitmo prisoners fight for Taliban, reveal Rep. Kirk and NATO Major General," *St. Louis Examiner*, January 10, 2010; available at: http://www.examiner.com/x-32288-Spokane-Elections-2010-Examiner~y2010m1d10-Illinois-Republican-claims-all-freed-Gitmo-prisoners-are-fighting-for-Taliban [accessed July 6, 2010].

29. Tom Coghlan, "Freed Guantanamo Inmates Are Heading for Yemen to Join al-Qaeda Fight," *Times Online*, January 5, 2010; available at: http://www.timesonline.co.uk/tol/news/world/middle_east/article6975971.ece [accessed July 6, 2010].

30. "'Scores' of Guantanamo Inmates Back on Battlefield," Breitbart, January 10, 2010.

31. Steven R. Hurst, Associate Press, "Holder: Miranda May Need Changes for Terrorists," *Seattle Times*, May 9, 2010; available at: http://seattletimes.nwsource.com/html/politics/2011822566_apus-timessquaremiranda.html?syndication=rss [accessed July 6, 2010].

32. Editorial, "Terrorism Rises on American Soil," *The Washington Times*, May 4, 2010; available at: http://www.washingtontimes.com/news/2010/may/04/terrorism-rises-on-american-soil/ [accessed July 6, 2010].

33. "TTP Leader Hakimullah Mehsud Declares: 'From Now On, the Main Targets of Our Fidaeen [Suicide Bombers] Are American Cities," The Middle East Media Research Center, May 2, 2010; available at: http://www.memri.org/report/en/0/0/0/0/0/0/4131.htm [accessed July 6, 2010].

34. Daniel Pipes, "Maj. Hasan's Islamist Life," *Front Page Magazine*, November 20, 2009; available at: http://frontpagemag.com/2009/11/20/major-hasan%E2%80%99s-islamist-life-%E2%80%93-by-daniel-pipes/ [accessed July 6, 2010].

35. "Eric Holder Refuses to Say 'Radical Islam,'" YouTube, May 13, 2010; video available at: http://www.youtube.com/watch?v=HOQt_mP6Pgg [accessed July 6, 2010].

36. Pete Hoekstra, "Hoekstra Statement on the White House Report on the Terrorist Attack on a Detroit-Bound Aircraft," Hoekstra.house.

gov, January 7, 2010; available at: http://hoekstra.house.gov/News/
DocumentSingle.aspx?DocumentID=165615 [accessed July 6,
2010].

37. Pete Hoekstra, "Hoekstra Opening Statement on the Flight 253 Terrorist Attack," Hoekstra Press Release, January 13, 2010; available
at: http://hoekstra.house.gov/News/DocumentSingle.
aspx?DocumentID=166582 [accessed July 6, 2010].

38. Phil Stewart, "Fort Hood Shooting Was Terrorism," U.S. Says,"
Reuters, January 15, 2010; available at: http://www.reuters.com/
article/idUSTRE60E5TA20100115 [accessed July 6, 2010].

39. Mark Thompson, "The Fort Hood Report: Why No Mention of
Islam?" *Time*, January 20, 2010; available at: http://www.time.com/
time/nation/article/0,8599,1954960,00.html [accessed July 6, 2010].

40. Byron York, "Holder Senate testimony postponed; delay raises questions," *The Washington Examiner*, March 23, 2010; available at:
http://www.washingtonexaminer.com/opinion/blogs/beltway-
confidential/Holder-Senate-testimony-postponed-delay-raises-
questions-88895867.html [accessed July 6, 2010].

41. Robert Spencer, "Great News: 6000 More Somalis Coming to the
U.S. in 2010," Jihad Watch, January 26, 2010; available at: http://
www.jihadwatch.org/2010/01/great-news-6000-more-somalis-com-
ing-to-the-us-in-2010.html [accessed July 6, 2010].

42. Editorial, "Obama Won't Connect the Terror Dots," *The Washington Times*, February 1, 2010; available at: http://www.washington-
times.com/news/2010/feb/01/obama-wont-connect-terror-dots/
[accessed July 6, 2010].

43. Walid Phares, "Major Hasan and the Ideological Blinders," *American Thinker*, January 23, 2010; available at: http://www.american-
thinker.com/2010/01/major_hasan_and_the_ideologica.html
[accessed July 6, 2010].

44. Jim Kouri, "Fort Hood Cover Up Denied by Secretary Gates," *St.
Louis Examiner*, April 18, 2010; available at: http://ww.examiner.
com/x-2684-Law-Enforcement-Examiner~y2010m4d18-Fort-Hood-
cover-up-denied-by-Secretary-Gates [accessed July 6, 2010].

45. Barack Obama, "Obama-Caucus4Priorities," YouTube, October 27,
2007; available at: http://www.youtube.com/watch?v=
7o84PE871BE [accessed July 6, 2010].

46. David E. Sanger and Peter Baker, "Obama Limits When U.S. Would Use Nuclear Arms," *The New York Times,* April 5, 2010; available at: http://www.nytimes.com/2010/04/06/world/06arms.html [accessed July 6, 2010].

47. "U.S.-Russia Nuclear Treaty Runs Into Resistance on Capitol Hill," FOXNews.com, April 11, 2010; available at: http://www.foxnews.com/politics/2010/04/11/nuclear-treaty-runs-resistance-capitol-hill/ [accessed July 6, 2010].

48. Robert Maginnis, "Obama Walks The Atomic Plank," *Human Events*, April 8, 2010; available at: http://www.humanevents.com/article.php?id=36405 [accessed July 6, 2010].

49. "Morning Bell: the New START Threat to Missile Defense," *The Foundry*, May 18, 2010; available at: http://blog.heritage.org/2010/05/18/morning-bell-the-new-start-threat-to-missile-defense/ [accessed July 6, 2010].

50. "START Places No Limit on US Missile Defense: Clinton, Gates," AFP, May 18, 2010; available at: http://www.google.com/hosted-news/afp/article/ALeqM5gNP_Wfc_wblNu6m18FXsIUm7q6Qw [accessed July 6, 2010].

51. Editors, "Honest Ahmadinejad," *Wall Street Journal*, May 3, 2010; available at: http://online.wsj.com/article/SB10001424052748704342604575222351143435766.html [accessed July 6, 2010].

INDEX

If you enjoyed *Crimes Against Liberty*, look for these other great titles by David Limbaugh...

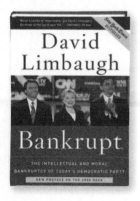

Bankrupt: The Intellectual and Moral Bankruptcy of Today's Democratic Party

The Democratic Party has sold itself to left-wing extremists, losing its mind and soul, claims Limbaugh in his *New York Times* bestseller, *Bankrupt*. Charting how liberals have embraced a politics of ideological hate and nihilism, Limbaugh offers a sobering and shocking portrait of a Democratic Party too morally and intellectually bankrupt to serve our country.

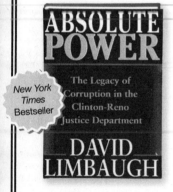

New York Times Bestseller

Absolute Power: The Legacy of Corruption in the Clinton-Reno Justice Department

In his *New York Times* bestseller, *Absolute Power*, Limbaugh offers a comprehensive indictment of the Clinton-Reno Justice Department, detailing how federal law was politicized, and precedents were set for a legal war against the traditional civil liberties of the United States.

A dispassionate exposition on corruption at the highest level, *Absolute Power* is a case-by-case analysis of the now-defunct Clinton Justice Department—and a testament to what must never be allowed to happen again.

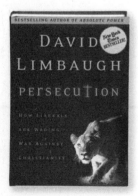

Persecution: How Liberals Are Waging War Against Christianity

In this *New York Times* bestseller, Limbaugh exposes the liberal hypocrisy of promoting political correctness while discriminating against Christianity. Using court cases, case studies, and true stories, *Persecution* reveals the widespread assault on the religious liberties of Christians in America today and urges Christians to fight back to restore their First Amendment right to religious freedom.

Available at Regnery.com

Since 1947
REGNERY PUBLISHING, INC.
An Eagle Publishing Company • Washington, DC